FILE MANAGER

Mastering Windows 3.0

Mastering Windows™ 3.0

Robert Cowart

SYBEX®

San Francisco • Paris • Düsseldorf • Soest

Acquisitions Editor: Dianne King
Editor: Christian T.S. Crumlish
Technical Editor: Daniel Tauber
Series Designer: Julie Bilski
Chapter Art and Layout: Eleanor Ramos
Technical Art: Delia Brown
Proofreader: Patsy Owens
Indexer: Nancy Anderman Guenther
Cover Designer: Thomas Ingalls + Associates
Cover Photographer: David Bishop

Library of Congress Card Number: 90-70565
ISBN: 0-89588-458-5

Manufactured in the United States of America
10 9 8 7 6 5 4 3

To my mother, who doesn't do windows.

ACKNOWLEDGMENTS

I sincerely want to thank all the people who helped me during the process of creating this book.

The assistance I received from the SYBEX editorial and production teams was indispensable. They were professional, courteous, efficient—and humorous.

Special thanks go to Dr. R. S. Langer, Dianne King, and Bret Rohmer for signing me up for both the writing and production of the book; to managing editor Barbara Gordon for her patience and calm demeanor; to my editor, Christian Crumlish who did terrific editing and coordination right down to the last minute; to technical editor Dan Tauber for reviewing the entire book and helping with endpapers; to Patsy Owens, the tireless proofer and schedule coordinator who had to remember more things than everybody put together; to "Chaslie" Cowens, Dan Brodnitz, and especially Bob Myren, for Ventura pinch-hitting and late-night camaraderie; to Delia Brown for sharing her office with me and creating the illustrations; to Tami Baron for the loan of her Jack & Jill tee-shirt characters; to Eleanor Ramos, the book designer and paste-up coordinator who had to handle tons of last-minute work; and to all the other folks in the production department who helped out at the last minute, including Ingrid, Lisa, Lucie, Charlotte, Helen, and Suzanne.

Not to be overlooked at SYBEX are those who have worked enthusiastically behind the scenes to sell and distribute these books both domestically and abroad. Particular thanks in this regard go to Alan Oakes, John McCarthy, Cindy Johnson, Michelle Quintana, Kathy Jones, and the many sales representatives in the field.

Next there're my own assistants who helped so much with the word processing and typesetting—Lisa who worked up till a week before delivering baby Erin, and Claudia, Valerie, and Diana. I couldn't have done it without you all.

Also mucho gratitude to my good buddy Steve Cummings for his assitance with the writing of Chapter 15; and to Steve Rosenthal, Eric Braun, and Brian Knittel for their technical assistance.

Last but certainly not least, thanks to all my friends for not assuming that I had passed on to the Great Void when I neglected to return their telephone calls for a month—especially to Kathy for seeing to it that I took out time to eat and rest, and to Diane for her support and patience during my disappearance.

CONTENTS AT A GLANCE

TABLE OF CONTENTS

INTRODUCTION

This book is designed to help you get the most out of the Windows 3.0 with the least amount of effort. I've written this book with both the novice and the experienced PC user in mind. The intention was to produce a volume that would prove both accessible and highly instructive to all Windows users—new or veteran.

From the outset, this book does not require that you have a working knowledge of Windows but only a modicum of familiarity with DOS. So, if you are new to Windows, a bit "PC-literate," and ready to learn, this book is a good choice. I think you will find it easy to read and not over your head. There are lots of everyday examples to explain the concepts, and there's even a little humor thrown in to cut the computer boredom.

If you're a "power user," already familiar with earlier versions of Windows and the intricacies of DOS, the explanations and procedures, along with the Fast Tracks that start each chapter, will quickly bring you up to speed with Windows 3.0. The detailed "Advanced Topics" section will be of use if you want to supercharge your Windows hardware and software setup or fine-tune your PIFs to take advantage of Windows 3.0's advanced memory-management and multitasking features. You will also find the appendices on troubleshooting non-Windows programs and networking valuable.

And, of course, for all Windows users, the inside front and back covers of the book provide information that you'll want to refer to regularly.

WHY THIS BOOK?

Though there are manuals supplied with Windows, they have to include every detail about Windows—probably more than you care to know or want to wade through. Also, the explanations in the manuals are sometimes vague. So, I've done the legwork for you in advance. I've boiled down the manuals, experimented for months on various machines, and then written a book explaining Windows in normal everyday English.

In researching this book, I've tried to focus on not just the "how to's" but also on the whys and wherefores. Too many computer books tell you exactly how to perform a sample task without explaining how to apply it to your own work. In this book, step-by-step sections explain how to perform specific procedures, but in addition, the descriptive sections explain general considerations about what you've learned. So, as you read along and follow the examples, you should not only become adept at using Windows, you'll also learn the most efficient ways to accomplish your own work.

WHAT IS MICROSOFT WINDOWS?

Microsoft Windows (or simply Windows) is a software program that makes your PC (or equivalent, including AT's and clones) a lot easier to use. If you've used a Mac (Apple Macintosh) before and wondered why IBM PC's couldn't work just as simply, well, they can—with Windows. In a nutshell, Windows is a program that makes your PC work much the way a Mac does.

What separates the Mac from a PC is the simplicity of its user interface. *User interface* is a computer buzzword that refers to the way you give your computer commands—the way you interact with it. Usually the interface between you and the computer consists of the screen and the keyboard. You interact with the computer by responding to what's on the screen, typing commands on the keyboard, and so forth. With a typical PC, you type in cryptic commands from the keyboard to do your work. These commands can be confusing and difficult to remember, and they often differ from program to program. For example, the command for saving a file in Lotus 1-2-3 is different from that in Microsoft Word or dBASE.

Normally, you type these commands at the DOS prompt. (DOS stands for Disk Operating System—and is the software that makes your computer run). DOS often isn't very intelligent at interpreting your commands, and as a user interface it's

downright terrible. Who wants to learn lots of computer gobbledegook just to write a letter, copy a file, or format a disk?
Thus, many people have been deterred from using IBM PC's,
opting for the Mac or trying to get by with a knowledge of the
barest rudiments of DOS. I know plenty of folks in both clubs.
A classic example is a good friend of mine who recently bought
an expensive PC and explained to me that she wasn't going to
buy DOS because she didn't need it, and heard it was just a pain
anyway. She didn't understand that DOS is a necessary evil.

Windows changes much of this. What was missing from the
PC was a program that makes it easy to use. Windows is just such
a program. If you want to, you can forget about DOS altogether,
and only use Windows. Or, you can use Windows only for certain
tasks and still have access to the DOS prompt for certain nitty-
gritty computing. With Windows, you can run programs, enter
and move data around, and perform DOS-related tasks simply
by using the mouse to point at objects on the screen. (For
anyone who doesn't know, a mouse is a little electronic gadget,
that you move around on the top of your desk.) Of course, you
also use the keyboard to type in letters and numbers.

So, with Windows, instead of typing in commands such as

```
copy c:\*.* a:
```

to copy files from drive C to drive A, you'll just use the mouse to
point at the names of the files you want to copy, and click on a
few command names. Windows interprets your actions and tells
DOS and your computer what to do.

In addition to making DOS housekeeping tasks such as copying
files, formatting disks, and so forth, easier, Windows makes running your favorite applications easier too. (An application is a
software package that you use for a specific task, such as word-
processing. WordPerfect is an example of an application. In this
book, I'll use the words *program* and *application* interchangeably.)

Windows owes its name to the fact that it runs each program
inside of a separate "window." A window is a box or frame on the
screen. You can have numerous windows on the screen at a time,

each containing its own program. You can then easily switch between programs without having to close one down and open the next. With certain limitations, Windows will then let you copy material from one program to another, making it easy to "cut and paste" material from, say, a spreadsheet into a letter or from a report to a charting program.

As more and more application programs are written to run with Windows, it'll be easier for you to learn how to use those programs. This is because all application programs that run with Windows use similar commands and procedures. With time, IBM-PC programs will be as easy to master as those for the Mac are today.

In addition to expediting the way you use your existing programs, Windows comes with a few of its own. Some of them are very handy, and we will discuss them in this book. There's a word-processing program called Write, a drawing program called Paintbrush, a communications program called Terminal for connecting to outside information services over phone lines, small utility programs that are helpful for keeping track of appointments and notes, a couple of games to help you escape from your work, and a few others.

THE ORIGINS OF WINDOWS

Years of research went into developing the prototype of today's popular graphical user interfaces. It was shown in the early 1980's that the graphical user interface, in conjuction with a hand-held pointing device (now called the mouse), was much easier to operate and understand than the older-style keyboard-command approach to controlling a computer. A little-known fact is that this research was conducted by the Xerox Corporation and first resulted in the Xerox Star computer before IBM PCs or Macintoshes existed. It wasn't until later that the technology was adapted by Apple Computer for its Macintosh prototype—the Lisa. (In fact, lawsuits over who developed what are raging as of this writing.)

For several years now there have been graphical user interfaces for IBM PC's. Windows (from Microsoft) and GEM (from Digital Research) have been the two primary contenders. Another similar interface, DesqView is fairly popular, but its appearance on the screen is not as sophisticated as Windows since it doesn't take advantage of higher-resolution graphics. Recently Windows took the lead, particularly since IBM officially endorsed it in 1989, and since so many software companies have written programs designed for it. So now, with this new version of Windows (Version 3.0), we have the latest incarnation of a type of computer interface that has, in effect, been in the making for close to a decade, and promises to become a well-ensconced standard. I believe that the time you spend learning to use Windows won't be wasted, nor the benefits short-lived since Windows (or something very similar, such as OS/2's Presentation Manager) is likely to be around for some time.

WHAT YOU NEED IN ORDER TO USE THIS BOOK

There are a few things about your level of knowledge and your computer setup that this book assumes.

WHAT YOU SHOULD KNOW

If you are new to computers, you should at least have some understanding of DOS, the PC's Disk Operating System. Though Windows takes much of the effort out of using DOS, it's still a good idea for you to understand how DOS works so that you'll know what Windows is doing for you. Though I'll be covering techniques for performing typical DOS tasks from Windows, such as copying files, formatting disks, and moving between directories, I'm assuming that you already understand why you'd want to do these things. Of particular importance is an understanding of disk files, disk directories, and the differences between data files and program files. You may want to take some time out to bone up on these topics if your knowledge is shaky in these areas.

WHAT YOU SHOULD HAVE

In order for this book to make sense, and for Windows to work, it is assumed you have the following:

- An IBM or compatible PC-XT, AT, 80386, or 80486 computer with at least 640K of RAM.

- A hard disk with 6 to 8 megabytes of free space on it.

- A monitor that is supported by Windows. The Setup program (explained in Appendix A), when run, shows you a list of the supported monitors.

- A printer, obviously, if you want to use Windows to print out your work on paper. Some of the exercises in this book will cover printing. Though not necessary for most of the book, it will be to your advantage if you have a printer.

- A mouse. Though you can operate Windows without a mouse (from the keybaord), it's quite a bit more cumbersome to do so. The mouse makes almost all Windows operations so much easier that you really should get a hold of one. In order to leave more room in the book for useful information about Windows, most instructions will assume you have a mouse.

HOW THIS BOOK IS ORGANIZED

There are essentially three parts to this book. The first part, consisting of eight chapters, introduces Windows and then covers all the essentials of Windows usage. After reading and following along on your computer, you'll know how to control the

Windows graphical environment, run programs, copy data between programs, and manage your files. You should read these chapters if you've never used Windows before.

Part II of the book covers the supplied programs—the Windows "accessories." There you'll learn all the ins and outs of Write, Terminal, Paintrush, Notepad, Cardfile, Recorder, Calendar, and Calculator. Though not the most sophisticated programs in their respective classes, these programs are well-thought-out, handy, and thrown in for free with Windows. Like me, you'll probably end up using them more than you might think at first, which is why I've included a sizeable section covering them.

Part III gets into the finer aspects of Windows operations. There you'll learn how to fine-tune your non-Windows applications to run best within Windows, and how to supercharge your Windows set up so that it runs as fast as possible.

There are then three appendices. Appendix A tells how to install Windows on your computer if you haven't already done so. Appendix B has lots of troubleshooting information, in case you run into difficulty. Appendix C covers special procedures that you might need to know when running Windows on a local area network.

In addition, each chapter has what's called a Fast Track. The Fast Track for each chapter consists of two pages summarizing the main explanations and procedures discussed in the chapter. The page references for each topic are listed there too, so that you can quickly turn to the right page for more information. I've written the Fast Tracks so that you could conceivably get by reading only them. This is a great way to get "up and running" with Windows quickly. In some cases, though, there wasn't room for all the procedures in two pages of Fast Tracks, so they aren't always a complete indicator of what's in the chapter. The table of contents is a better source for that information. After you've read a chapter, though, or if you are already familiar with a procedure, the Fast Tracks can be a convenient, concise reminder.

CONVENTIONS USED IN THIS BOOK

There are a few conventions used throughout this book that you should know about before beginning. Though a majority of the book is written in standard paragraphs, there are many procedures that are presented as number steps. For example:

    4. Now press ↵ twice to put in a blank line.

Obviously, this is an instruction that you would follow in order to complete the procedure. Usually the steps are very specific, and you'll have to follow them exactly for Windows (or the program I'm describing) to do what you want. Occasionally the procedures are general recommendations of steps you should take, and not necessarily text you have to type in or specific commands to execute as you read. When they are more general like this, I'll tell you.

Notice the ↵ symbol in the example above. This is used throughout the book to indicate when you should press the Enter key on your keyboard. Many keyboards also have this symbol on their Enter keys, which is why we use it here.

When a procedure only has one step in it, we'll use a different symbol to indicate the step like so:

    ❐ This is a single-step instruction.

Finally, there are things you type in from the keyboard, and messages you receive from Windows that appear on your screen. When you have to type something in, the instruction may be shown on a line by itself, like this:

    win /r ↵

or it might be included right in a paragraph like this: Now type **win /r ↵**.

More often than not, responses from Windows will be shown in figures so that you can see just what the screens look like, rather than reading a long description of it. Sometimes, though, when Windows' response is only a line or two, I'll skip the picture and just write it in like this:

Cannot read from drive A

Last, but not least, there are many side comments in this book, called margin notes. They appear in a different color, and are positioned in the left margin of the page, next to the material to which they refer. There are four kinds of margin notes: Note, Tip, Speed Tip, and Caution. They look like this:

NOTE This is a note. Notes are used for information that is pertinant to the procedure or topic being discussed.

TIP This is a tip. Tips are used to indicate practical hints that might make your work easier.

SPEED TIP Speed tips are like tips, but they always contain information that will help speed up your work.

CAUTION A caution box is used to alert you to something very important. Generally, cautions are used to inform you about the potential problems you might encounter if you use a procedure incorrectly or without careful forethought.

BEFORE YOU BEGIN

Before you can begin working with Windows, make sure you have installed the program on your computer's hard disk. A large portion of what appear to be software problems is often the result of incorrect installation. If your copy of Windows is already installed and operating correctly, you have no need to worry about this, and you can move ahead to Chapter 1. However, if you haven't installed Windows, please do so by turning to Appendix A, which covers the Windows Setup program.

PART
ONE

1

The Essentials

Part I of this book consists of eight chapters. In these chapters, you will learn the rudiments of Windows 3.0. This is an essential section to read, even if you've used earlier versions of Windows, since numerous aspects of Windows 3.0 are new.

The first chapter explains what Windows is, and generally how it works. Chapters 2 and 3 explain how you run and manage your programs from within Windows, using the Program Manager. Chapter 4 covers the File Manager—the part of Windows that you use to work with and manage disk files. Chapter 5 explains how to customize various aspects of Windows with the Control Panel. Chapters 6 and 7 discuss installing and using your printer. Finally, Chapter 8 covers techniques for copying information between programs with the Clipboard.

CHAPTER ONE

1

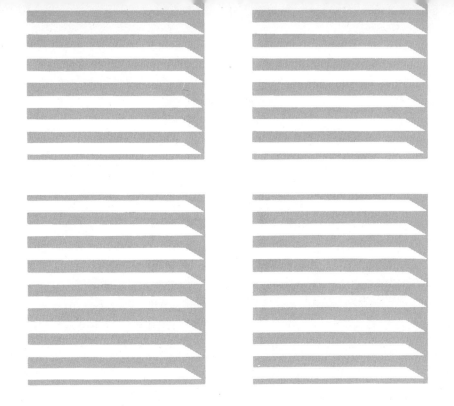

What Is Windows?

Fast Track

To start Windows,   7

make sure you've installed Windows properly (see Appendix A). Boot up your computer as usual. Type **WIN** ↵ .

About windows: 8

A window is used to contain each group, program, or document you're working with. All the work you do in Windows is (not suprisingly) done in windows. You can have multiple windows on the screen at once. You can easily switch between them. A window can use the whole screen (called *maximized* size) or be sized down to fill just a portion of the screen (called *restored* size). Windows can overlap, or be adjusted in a "tiled" fashion so you can see them all at once.

To minimize a window   15

first, activate the window. Then position the mouse pointer on the Minimize Box (the down arrow in the upper-left corner of the window) and click. The window reduces to the size of an icon. The window's name is shown below the icon so you know what it is. (This is also called iconizing the window.)

To restore a Window from an icon,   15

double click on the icon (the faster approach) or click once, and when the *Control* menu appears above the icon, press ↵, type **R**, or click on the word *Restore*. The window returns to its previous size.

To maximize a window,   15

> activate the window, and then click on the Maximize box (the up arrow in the upper-right corner of the window). The window expands to fill the entire screen or the entire program window it's in if it's a document. The Maximize box changes to a Restore box with both up and down arrows. Click on this box to once again restore the window to its previous size.

To adjust a window's size manually,   16

> position the cursor on any edge or corner of the window that you want to resize. The cursor shape will change to a two-headed pointer. Keeping the mouse button depressed, drag the window edge or corner to the desired position, and then release the mouse button.

To get help,   30

> open the Help menu and a window appears. From the Help screen, select the item you want to read and the topic appears. Maximize the window for easier reading. When the cursor changes to a hand, clicking looks up a cross-reference. Clicking on Backup takes you back to the previous topic.

To exit Windows,   36

> activate the Program Manager window. Double click the Control box. You will be asked to confirm exiting and possibly to close any open applications. Alternatively, single click the Control box and select Exit from the menu.

CHAPTER 1

BEFORE BEGINNING TO LEARN ABOUT THE BASICS OF Windows, make sure you've read the Introduction to this book and, if necessary, installed Windows correctly on your computer. You use the Setup program for installation, as explained in Appendix A.

In this chapter you'll learn the basics of how Windows works. If you've never used Windows before, you should read this chapter thoroughly while experimenting with Windows on your computer. This is because it covers all the basic concepts and skills you'll need to understand and use Windows. You should feel free to experiment, if you do it with some caution. Specifically, when we get to the section on dialog boxes, you can experiment by changing any settings you like. Just make sure to cancel the dialog box when you are done by clicking on the Cancel button.

If you're already familiar with Windows, you might still want to skim this chapter, particularly if you've only used Windows version 2, to pick up the material that relates to the newer Windows 3.

If at any time during your reading of this chapter, you have to quit Windows to do other work or to turn off your computer, just jump to the end of the chapter and read the section "Getting Out of, or Exiting, Windows." Also, if at any time you are really stuck, try reading the section near the end of this chapter that covers Windows' built-in Help facility. If all else fails, you can reboot your computer and start up Windows again. Though this isn't a great idea, and you may lose part of any documents you're working on, it won't hurt the Windows program or your computer.

STARTING WINDOWS

To start Windows, follow these steps:

1. Boot up your computer the usual way. The DOS prompt appears (usually the C prompt, though your computer may show a different drive name such as D:).

2. At the DOS prompt, type **WIN**⏎.

The Windows sign-on screen appears for a few moments and then disappears. After a few more moments, during which parts of the program are being retrieved from the hard disk, the Windows starting screen appears (Figure 1.1).

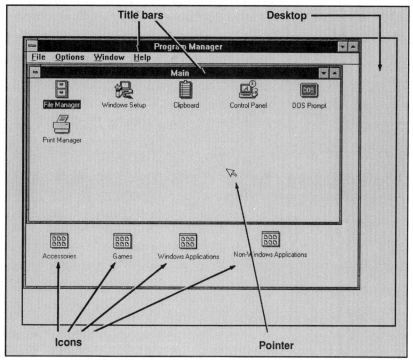

Figure 1.1: The initial Windows screen. This "starting screen" belongs to the windows application Program Manager, the part of Windows that organizes your programs for you.

PARTS OF THE WINDOWS SCREEN

Now let's take a quick look at the three basic parts of the Windows startup screen: the desktop, windows, and icons. Once you understand these three essential building blocks, we'll look closer at them, examining the finer details of each.

THE DESKTOP

The Desktop is your overall work area while in Windows. It's called the desktop because Windows uses your whole screen in a way that's analogous to the way you'd use the surface of a desk. As you work in Windows, you move items around on the desktop, retrieve and put away items (as if in a drawer), and perform your other day-to-day tasks. You do all of this using graphical representations of your work projects. The analogy of the desktop falls a bit short sometimes, but it's useful for understanding how the program helps you to organize your activities. Because of this graphical representation, working with your programs is often faster and easier than it would be with DOS.

THE WINDOWS

When you want to do some work, you open up a program or document with the mouse or keyboard, and a window opens on the desktop. This is similar to pulling a file folder or notebook off the shelf, placing it on the desk, and opening it up. In Windows, you do this for each task you want to work on.

Windows always starts up by displaying the Program Manager window. As explained in Chapter 2, the Program Manager is the part of Windows that organizes and runs programs that you do your work with. It is actually a program itself, and thus appears in a program window.

Just as with a desktop, you can have a number of projects scattered about, all of which can be in progress. You can then easily switch between your projects, be they letters, writing, spreadsheets, games, or what ever. This is unlike normal PC computing under DOS where you have to "put away" one project before opening the next.

Of course, if you happen to be a neatnik, you can opt to have only one document or program open at a time, and keep the desktop clutter-free, so to speak. But there are advantages to the messy-desk approach. For example, you can view two documents (such as a spreadsheet and a report you are writing about it), simultaneously. You could place each document side by side in separate frames that you size to fit on the screen, as you see in Figure 1.2. Another advantage is that it allows you to copy material from one document to another more easily, by *cutting* and *pasting* between them.

Another feature designed into Windows is that it can be instructed to remember certain aspects of your work setup each time you quit. For example, you may use a certain group of programs regularly.

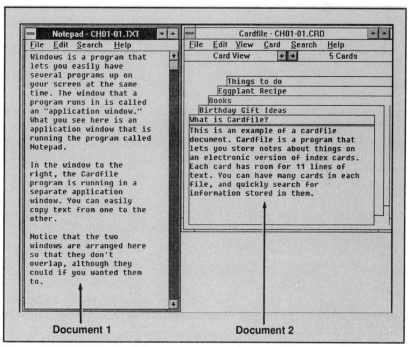

Figure 1.2: Windows lets you see several documents simultaneously

NOTE The number of icons in your Program Manager window is determined by whether you told Windows to install your Windows and non-Windows application programs for use with Windows when you ran the Setup program. You will have at least three icons—Main, Accessories, and Games—within the Program Manager window. (You may only see two icons at the present time, since the Main icon has been opened into a window that you are quite likely looking at.) If you chose to install Windows applications and non-Windows applications during Setup, you will see icons for them. As you modify your desktop to include your own applications, you'll be adding more icons.

You can set up Windows to start with those programs available with just a click of the mouse. Programs you use less frequently will be stored away, within easy reach, but not cluttering your desktop.

ICONS

Icons are the third basic element of the Windows screen. At the bottom of the Program Manager window in Figure 1.1, you see several small symbols with names under them. These are called icons. Windows uses icons to represent documents and programs when they are not currently opened up in a window. They may be sitting on the desktop waiting to be worked with, or they may be programs that are actually running, but have temporarily been shrunk down to get them out of the way for a moment. When a program or document is *minimized* (also called *iconized*) in this way, it's as if the program is in suspended animation. The program or document is still available, but you can't use it.

A special class of icons, called a *group icon* is used to represent a collection of programs that you decide to group together for convenience. As you will see in Chapter 2, the Program Manager uses group icons to help you organize your programs.

TYPES OF WINDOWS

Now let's look a little more closely at the various parts of the desktop. There are two possible types of windows that you'll encounter while working: *application* windows and *document* windows.

APPLICATION WINDOWS

Application windows are those that contain a program that you are running and working with, such as Word, Excel, PC Paintbrush, WordPerfect, and so on. Most of the work that you do will be in application windows. Figure 1.3 shows a typical application window.

DOCUMENT WINDOWS

However, some programs—those designed specifically to work with Windows (such programs are often called *Windows applications*)—will let you work on more than one document at a time. For example, Microsoft Word for Windows allows you to have multiple Word documents open at once, in separate document windows. Instead of running Word several times in separate application windows, you just run it once in an application window, and open several document windows *within* the application window. Figure 1.4 shows the File Manager application with two document windows open inside it.

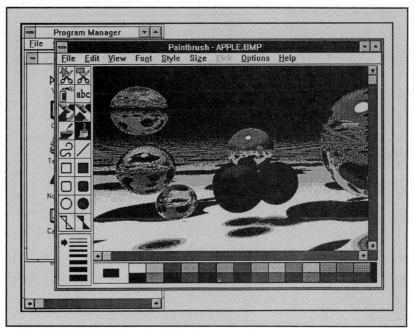

Figure 1.3: An application window

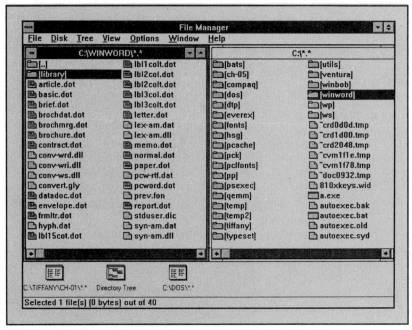

Figure 1.4: Two document windows within an application window

ANATOMY OF A WINDOW

Now let's consider the parts of a typical window. The first time you start Windows, the desktop comes up in the arrangement shown in Figure 1.1 (please refer to it or look at your screen) Notice that there are two windows open already—the Program Manager window and the Main window.

THE TITLE BAR

The name of each program or document appears at the top of its respective window, in what's called the title bar. In this case, the title bars read Program Manager and Main. But if you were running another program, its name would be shown there instead.

In an application window, the name of the application is often followed by the name of the file being worked on. For example, in Figure 1.5, the Notepad application is running in a window. The title reads Notepad, followed by the file being edited, PHONE.TXT.

In addition to displaying the name of the application and document, the title bar serves another function. It also indicates which window is *active*. Though you can have lots of windows on the screen at once, there is only one active window at any given time. (The active window is the one you're working on.) When a window is active, the title bar changes color (On monochrome monitors, the intensity of the title bar will change.) You activate a window by clicking anywhere within its border.

NOTE Clicking or *clicking on* means positioning the mouse pointer on the item in question and then clicking the left button once. *Double clicking* or *double clicking on* means clicking twice in quick succession.

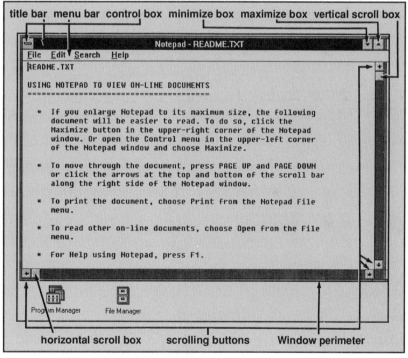

Figure 1.5: Parts of a typical window

MINIMIZE AND MAXIMIZE BOXES

There are several small squares, called *boxes*, at the ends of the title bar. On the far right side of the title bar are a pair of boxes with small arrows (triangles) in them. The box with the arrow facing up is called the *Maximize box*. The other one is called the *Minimize box*. After a window has been maximized, the Maximize box changes to a *Restore box*. Restore boxes have both up and down arrows. (Sometimes the Minimize icon also disappears.)

These boxes are little control buttons with which you quickly change the size of a window.

There are essentially three sizes that a window can have:

Minimized   The window becomes an icon at the bottom of the desktop, where it's ready to be easily opened again but takes up a minimum of screen space.

Normal   The window is open and takes up a portion of the desktop, the amount of which is determined by how you manually size the window, as explained in the next section. This is also called the *restored* size.

Maximized   The window takes up the whole desktop. When you maximize a document window, it expands to take up the entire application window. This may or may not be the entire screen depending on whether or not the applicaton has been maximized.

Here are the basic mouse techniques to quickly change the size of a window. Try these techniques on the Main window (or any other window that might be on your screen) to get the idea of it:

To Minimize a Window

1. First, you have to activate the window, so click anywhere within its perimeter.

2. Position the mouse pointer (the arrow that moves around on the screen when you move the mouse) on the Minimize Box (the down arrow) in the upper-left corner of the window and click. The window reduces to the size of an icon. The window's name is shown below the icon so you know what it is.

To Restore a Window from an Icon

There are two ways to restore a window to its previous size once it's an icon.

❏ Double click on the icon, *or*

❏ Click once on the icon. Then a menu appears above the icon, as you see in Figure 1.6. (A menu is a list of options you can choose from.) Press ↵, type **R**, or click on the word *Restore.* The window returns to its previous size.

To Maximize a Window

To maximize a window so that it takes up the whole screen, do the following:

1. Activate the window by clicking within its perimeter.

2. Click on the Maximize box. The window expands to fill the entire screen, or the entire program window, if a document is being maximized. The Restore box replaces the Maximize box. Clicking on this box will once again restore the window to its previous size.

To Manually Adjust the Size of a Window

You can manually adjust the size and position of a window to fit wherever you want.

SPEED TIP The easiest way to resize a window is to drag its lower-left corner. Once it's sized, you can then move a window around the screen by dragging it from its title bar. (Click on the title bar and hold the button down, and then move the mouse.)

1. Carefully position the cursor on any edge or corner of the window that you want to resize. When you are in the right position, the cursor shape changes to a two-headed pointer, as you can see in Figure 1.7. Click and hold (this means press the mouse button and hold it down). The

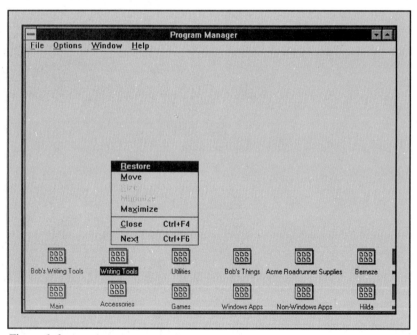

Figure 1.6: When you click once on an icon, a menu appears

color or intensity of the window's edge will change to indicate that you are resizing the window. *Drag* the window edge or corner to the desired position, and then release the mouse button. (Dragging simply means keeping the mouse button depressed while moving the mouse.)

THE CONTROL BOX

The box at the left side of the title bar is called the *Control Box.* (It's supposed to look like a little file cabinet drawer with a handle on it, because it has to do with controlling files.) It has two functions. First, it can open a menu, called the Control menu. This is the same menu you get when you single click on an icon, as you see in Figure 1.8. This menu only comes up when you single click.

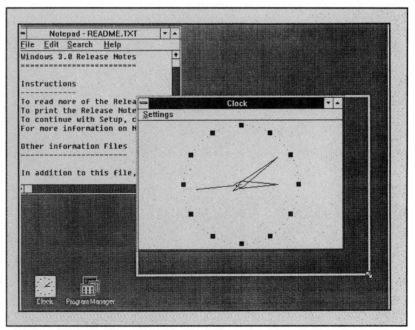

Figure 1.7: Changing a window's size by dragging its edge

Most of the commands on this menu let you control the size of the window from the keyboard, so if you're using a mouse, you don't have to be concerned with them. (Menus are covered in detail later in this chapter.)

Second, the Control Box will *close* the window (terminate the program or close the document) when you double click on it.

SCROLL BARS, SCROLL BUTTONS, AND SCROLL BOXES

On the bottom and right edges of many windows, you'll find *scroll bars, scroll buttons,* and *scroll boxes.* These are used to "pan across" the information in a window, up, down, left, and right. This is necessary when there is too much information (text or

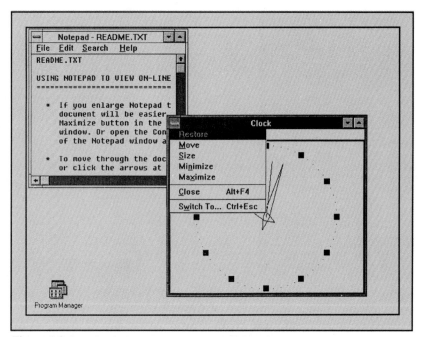

Figure 1.8: Single clicking on the Control Box brings up the Control menu. Double clicking quits the program or document, eliminating the window.

> *NOTE* When you double click the Control Box of a group window (such as the main window) it iconizes the window.

graphics) to fit into the window at one time. For example, you might be writing a letter that is two pages long. Using the scroll bars lets you move around, or scroll, within your document to see the section you're interested in, since two full pages of text won't display in a window at one time. Scrolling lets you look at a large amount of data through what amounts to a small window—your screen. Figure 1.9 illustrates this concept. Many Windows operations, such as listing files on your disks, reading Help screens, or displaying lots of icons within a window require the use of scroll bars and boxes.

Scroll bars have a little box in them called the *scroll box* or *elevator.* Just as an elevator can take you from one floor of a building to the next, the scroll bar takes you from one section of a

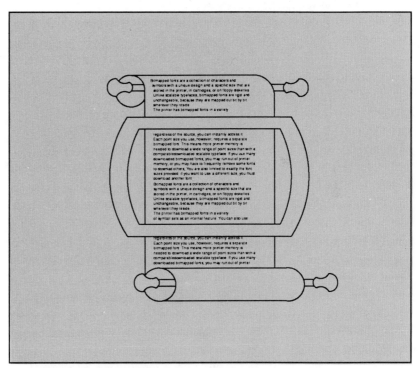

Figure 1.9: Scrolling lets you work with more information than will fit on your screen at one time

window or document to the next. The elevator moves within the scroll bar to indicate which portion of the window you are viewing at any given time. By moving the elevator with your mouse, you cause the document to scroll.

Try these exercises to see how scroll bars and boxes work:

1. With the Main window open (in normal, not maximized size), size the window so that it shows only three icons— File Manager, Control Panel, and Print Manager (see Figure 1.10). A vertical scroll bar appears on the right edge of the window. This indicates that there are more icons in the window than are visible, since the window is now so small. What has happened is that one icon is now out of view.

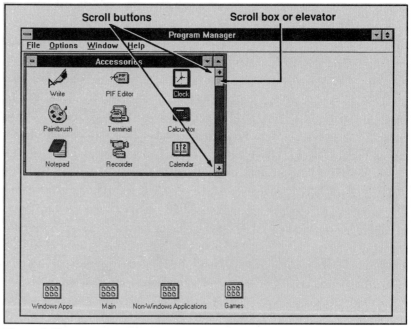

Figure 1.10: A scroll bar appears to indicate that there is more in the Main window than is currently visible

2. Drag the elevator up and down by positioning the pointer on the elevator, holding the mouse button down, and moving the mouse toward or away from you. Notice that as you do this, the little elevator moves along with the pointer. When you release the mouse button, the window's contents are repositioned. If you pull the elevator to the bottom of the scroll bar, the hidden icon appears in the window.

3. Now try another approach to scrolling. Click on the scroll buttons (the little arrows at the top and bottom of the scroll bar). With each click, the elevator moves a bit in the direction of the button you're clicking on. If you click and hold, the elevator continues to move, rather than just jumping once.

4. One more approach is to click within the scroll bar above or below the elevator. Each click scrolls the window up or down a bit.

This example used only a short window with relatively little information in it. In this case, maximizing the window or resizing it just a bit would eliminate the need for scrolling, and is probably a better solution. However, with large documents or windows containing many icons, scrolling becomes a necessity, as you'll see when you learn how to use Windows' built-in Help System.

ALL ABOUT MENUS

The last major item you need to know about when using Windows is called the menu bar. The menu bar is a row of words that appears just below the title bar. (It appears only on application windows. Document windows do not have menu bars.)

If you click on one of the words in the menu bar (called menu *names*), a menu opens up, displaying a series of options that you can choose from. It is through menus that you tell all Windows applications what actions you want carried out.

Try this as an example:

1. With the Program Manager window open and active, click on the word *File* in the menu bar. A menu opens, as you see in Figure 1.11, listing eight options. You can see why its called a menu. It's a bit like a restaurant menu listing things you can order.

2. Click on the other names in the menu bar (Options, Window, or Help) or press the → key to see the other menus and their choices.

Each menu name, when clicked on, will open up its own menu, with choices somewhat relevant to the menu's name. The names on the menu vary from application to application, but there are always several that are the same, such as File, Edit, and

SPEED TIP You could also have pressed Alt-F to open the File menu. If there is an underlined letter in any menu's name, holding down Alt and pressing that letter opens the menu. If more than one menu has the same under-lined letter, additional presses of the same key will advance to the next menu.

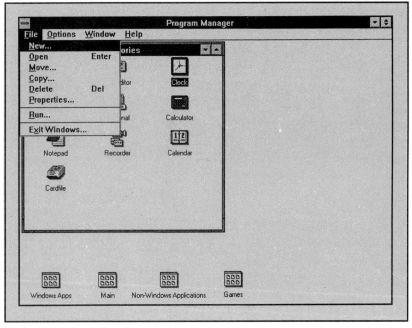

Figure 1.11: Opening a menu by clicking on its name in the menu bar

Help. It may take a while for you to become familiar with the commands and which menus they're located on, but it will become more automatic with time. In any case, it's easy enough to look around through the menus to find the one you want.

SELECTING MENU COMMANDS

Once a menu is open, you can select any of the commands in the menu that aren't dimmed. (The dimmed command names are ones that are not available at the time.) You can select a menu command in several ways:

☐ By typing the underlined letter in the command name

☐ By clicking on the command name

☐ By highlighting the command name using the ↑ and ↓ keys and then pressing ↵

NOTE At this point, don't experiment with any of the commands. That is, don't select any of them just yet. We'll begin using the commands in a bit.

Cancelling a Menu

You can cancel a menu (that is, make the menu disappear without selecting any commands) by simply pressing the Esc key, or by clicking in the work area of the active window.

SPECIAL INDICATORS IN MENUS

Windows and Windows applications menus often have special symbols that tell you more about the menu commands. For example, examine the menus in Figure 1.12.

Notice that many of these comnmands have additional words or symbols next to the command name. For example the New command (for creating a new file) has ellipses (three dots) after it. Other commands may have check marks, triangles, or key-combinations listed beside them. Here are the meanings of these words or symbols.

A Grayed (Dimmed) Command Name

When a command is shown as grayed, or dimmed, it means that this choice is not currently available to you. A command can be dimmed for a number of reasons. For example, a command for changing the typestyle of text will be grayed if no text has been selected. Other times, commands will be grayed because you are in the wrong program mode. For example, if a window is already maximized, the Maximize command on the Control menu will be dimmed, since this choice doesn't make sense.

Ellipses (...)

Ellipses next to a command means that you will be asked for additional information before Windows or the Windows application will execute the command. When you select the command, a *dialog box* will appear on the screen, asking you to fill in

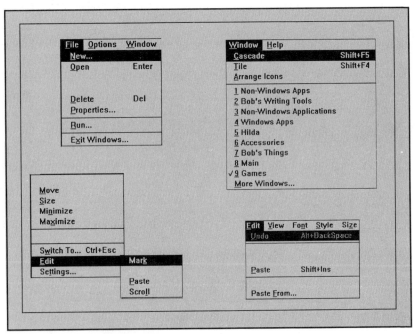

Figure 1.12: Typical menus

the needed information. We will discuss dialog boxes in the next section of this chapter.)

A Checkmark (✓)

A checkmark preceding a command means the command is a toggle that is activated (turned on). A *toggle* is a command that is alternately turned off and on each time you select it. It's like a toggle switch, or those old car high-beam switches on the floor that you step on to change between high beams and low beams. Each time you select one of these commands, they switch from active to inactive. If there is no checkmark, then the command or setting is inactive. This is typically used to indicate things like whether selected text is underlined or not, which font is selected, what mode you are in within a program, and so on.

A Triangle (▶)

A triangle to the right of a menu command means that the command has additional sub-choices for you to make. This is called a *cascading menu* (because the next menu starts to the right of the previous one and runs down from there, a bit like a waterfall of menus). You make selections from a cascaded menu the same way you would from normal menus. Figure 1.12 shows an example of a cascaded menu.

A Key Combination

Some menu commands list keystrokes that can be used instead of opening the menu and choosing that command. For example, in the Program Manager's File menu (shown in Figure 1.11), you'll notice that the Open command could be executed by pressing the Enter key, and the Delete command could be executed by pressing the Del key. These alternative time-saving keystrokes are called *shortcut keys*. (Don't worry if you don't understand these commands yet. They will be explained later.)

ALL ABOUT DIALOG BOXES

A dialog box will always appear when you select a command with elipses (...) after it. Dialog boxes pop up on your screen when Windows or the Windows application program you're using needs more information before continuing. Some dialog boxes ask you to enter information (such as file names), while others simply require you to check off options or make choices from a list. The list may be in the form of additional sub-dialog boxes or submenus. In any case, after you enter the requested information, you click OK and then Windows or the application program continues on its merry way, executing the command.

Though most dialog boxes ask you for information, other boxes are only informative, alerting you to a problem with your system or an error you've made. Such a box might also request confirmation on a command that could have dire consequences or explain why the command you've chosen can't be executed. These alert boxes often have a big letter *i* (for *information*) in them, or an exclamation mark (!) if it's more important. Generally, these boxes only ask you to read them and then click OK (or cancel them, if you decide not to proceed). Some boxes only have an OK button.

Let's look at some typical dialog boxes and how they work.

MOVING BETWEEN SECTIONS OF A DIALOG BOX

As you can see in Figure 1.13, dialog boxes often have several sections to them. You can move between the sections in three ways.

- ❐ The easiest way is by clicking on the section you want to alter.

- ❐ If you are using the keyboard, you can use the Tab key to move between sections.

- ❐ You can also use the Alt key with the underlined letter of the box section you want to jump to or activate. Even when you are using a mouse, the Alt-key combinations are sometimes the fastest way to jump between sections or choose an option within a box.

ENTERING INFORMATION IN A DIALOG BOX

Now let's consider how you enter information into dialog boxes. There are six basic types of sections in dialog boxes. Text Box, Check Box, Option Button, List Box, Drop-Down List Box, and Command Button. Figure 1.13 illustrates these areas.

Once you've jumped to the correct section, you'll need to know how to make choices from it. Here is a list explaining how to use the sections.

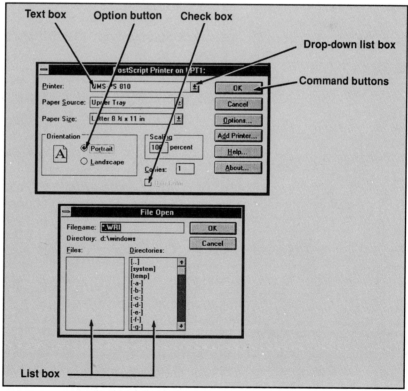

Figure 1.13: Typical dialog boxes

Text Boxes

In this sort of section, you are asked to type in text from the keyboard. Sometimes there will be text already typed in for you. If you want to keep it as is, you can just jump to another section of the box. To alter the text, simply type in new text. If the existing text is already highlighted, then the first key you press will delete the existing words. If it is not highlighted, you can backspace over it to erase it. You can also edit existing text. Clicking once on highlighted text will *deselect* it, and cause the *text cursor* (a vertical blinking bar) to appear when you put the pointer inside the text area. You can then move the text cursor around using the arrow keys or the mouse, and insert text (by typing), or delete text (by pressing the Del key). Text is inserted at the position of the text cursor. Text areas are most often used for specifying file names when you are saving or loading documents and applications, or text to search for in a word-processing document.

Check Boxes

Check boxes are the square boxes with X's inside of them. They are used to indicate nonexclusive options. For example you might want some text to appear as bold *and* underlined. Or, as another example, consider the Communications dialog box in the Windows Terminal program. In this box, you can have both the Parity Check and the Carrier Detect set on or off. These are toggle settings (as explained previously) that you activate or inactivate by clicking on the box.

Option Buttons

Unlike Check Boxes which are nonexclusive, Option Buttons are exclusive settings. You can tell the Option buttons, because they are round rather than square, and only one can be set on at a time. For example, using the same Communications dialog box referred to above, you may select 5, 6, 7, or 8 data bits in the Data Bits section of the dialog box. Clicking on the desired button turns it on (the circle will be filled), and turns any previous selection off. From the keyboard, you first jump to the section, then use the arrow keys to select the option.

Command Buttons

Command buttons are like option buttons except that they are used to execute a command immediately. They are also rectangular rather than boxes or circles. The most common command buttons are the OK and Cancel buttons found on almost every dialog box. Once you've filled in a dialog box to your liking, you click on the OK button, and Windows or the application executes the settings you've selected. If you change your mind and don't want the new commands on the dialog box executed, then click on the Cancel button. There is always a command button that has a thicker border. This is the button that will be executed if you press ⏎. Likewise, pressing the Esc key always has the same effect as clicking on the cancel button. Some command buttons are followed by ellipses (...). These commands will open additional dialog boxes for adjusting more settings. Finally, some command buttons include two > symbols in them. Choosing this type of button causes the particular section of the dialog box to expand so that you can make more selections.

List Boxes

SPEED TIP You can quickly jump to an option in a list box by typing the first letter of its name. If there are two choices with the same first letter and you want the second one, press the letter again, or press the down arrow key.

List boxes are like menus. They show you a list of options or items you can choose. For example, when choosing fonts to display or print text in, Windows Write shows you a list box. You make a selection from a list box the same way you do from a menu. Just click on it. From the keyboard, highlight the desired option with the arrow keys, and then press ⏎ to choose it. Some list boxes are too small to show all the possible selections. In this case, there will be a scroll bar on the right side of the box. Use the scroll bar to see all the selections. Some list boxes let you make more than one selection, but most only allow one. To make more than one selection from the keyboard, press the spacebar to select or deselect any item.

Drop-Down List Boxes

Drop-down list boxes are indicated by a small arrow in a box to the right of the option. The current setting is displayed to the left of the little arrow. Clicking on the arrow opens a list that works just like a normal list box, and has scroll bars if there are a lot of options. Drop-down list boxes are used when a dialog box is too crowded to accomodate regular list boxes.

GETTING HELP WHEN YOU NEED IT

So far, you've gotten a fairly detailed overview of the Windows interface. However, we haven't used any programs other than the Program Manager yet, so some of this information is still academic, unless you have experimented on your own with dialog boxes and windows. Perhaps you have tried running some other programs such as Notepad or Filecard, which would provide additional opportunity for experimentation. (Running programs is covered in the next chapter.) In any case, there will be times when you don't remember or understand how to use an operation or command. Luckily, you don't always have to drag out a a book or manual to get some quick help. The people at Microsoft have done a very good job of developing a built-in Help facility for Windows. Once you learn how to use it, it'll answer many of your questions. Windows applications from other software companies should have a help system that works the same way as described below.

TO GET HELP

To get help on what you're doing, open the Help menu (it's always the menu farthest to the right). The menu lists several choices, the number of which depends on the program you're using. You're probably using the Program Manager at this point, so there will be six choices, plus a choice called About Program Manager.

To get help, you just select the choice on the Help menu that seems most appropriate to you. For example, if you have a question about which keys to use from the keyboard, select Keyboard. If you are confused about the meaning of a word, select Glossary. Selecting Index brings up a general index for Windows and for the Program Manager. (Pressing F1 instead of opening the Help menu immediately opens the Help index.)

Once you make the appropriate choice, the Help window comes up. It looks like what you see in Figure 1.14 (though the content may differ).

Next, follow these steps:

1. The first thing to do is to Maximize the window so that you can read the Help information more easily. Remember, you do this by clicking on the up arrow to the right of the title bar.

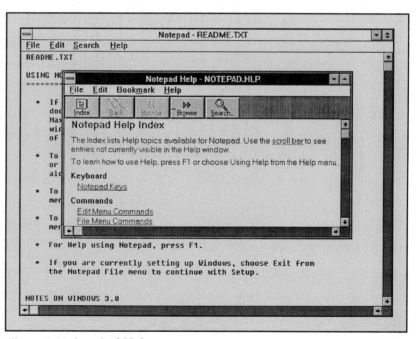

Figure 1.14: A typical Help screen

2. Once the Help screen is visible, try opening the Help menu. One of the selections is called Using Help. Choose it.

3. The title bar reads WINHELP.HLP. This is the file that is being displayed for you. It's help about how to get help. The first line reads "If you are new to Windows Help, choose Help Basics." Position the pointer on the words Help Basics. Notice that the cursor changes to the shape of a pointing finger, as shown in Figure 1.15.

Any underlined word (that is, any word with a solid underline) is a cross reference. Clicking on a cross reference

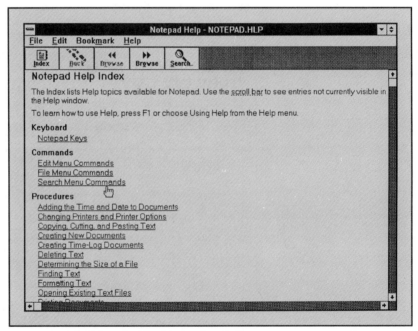

Figure 1.15: Solid underlined items in a help screen are cross references. Read the cross reference by clicking on the word.

causes Help to jump to the section in the on-line manual (the documentation that is on your hard disk) that is relevant to the word or procedure you're interested in.

4. Some words are underlined with a dotted line. These are terms for which there is a definition that you can see. Just position the pointer on the term. Once again, the cursor changes to a pointing hand. Then press and hold the mouse button down. The definition will appear in a box, as you can see in Figure 1.16. It will disappear when you release the button.

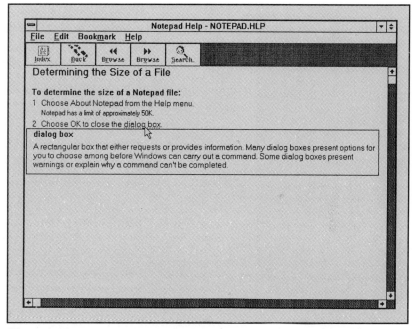

Figure 1.16: Dotted underlined words are terms. See the definition of the term by clicking on the word and holding the button down.

The Help screen has five large command buttons along its top row. Here's what they do when you click on them:

BUTTON	EFFECT
Index	This jumps you immediately to the help index for the application you are using. The index is a good jumping off place for getting help, and a good place to return to after reading help on one item if you want to see more on another, unrelated item.
Back	This pops you back to the place where you were before you took the last detour via a cross reference. If you've taken several detours, then each click on this button backs you up one step. When you're back where you started, the button becomes grayed, and you can't go any further.
Browse >>	This lets you look through a series of topics related to the current topic. It advances to the next in the series.
Browse <<	This moves you backwards through the series of related topics. When you get to the first screen on that topic, the button is grayed.
Search	This button lets you look for a specific word or topic. There is a list of *key words* for each topic in the Help system. This command shows you those words in a list box. You can select the word you want to read about, or you can type in the word you want to try looking up and press ↵ (or click on the Search button). Assuming the word is found, the associated topic appears in the bottom half of the dialog box. You then have to click on Go To to read the

help text. If the word you type isn't found there, Help jumps to the key word spelled most similarly.

KEEPING A SPECIFIC HELP SCREEN AT HAND

There are several ways to keep a specific help screen easily available. First, you can shrink the Help window down to a size where you can still read it, but it doesn't take up the whole screen. Make it a small wide band at the bottom of the screen, for example, and resize your other windows to accomodate it. An easier solution is to iconize it (click on the down arrow in the title bar). It will become an icon at the bottom of the screen. When you need to read the help topic again, just double click on the icon. This is particularly helpful for quickly recalling lists of keys commands or other information that is difficult to remember.

WHEN HELP DOESN'T HELP

In some cases, Help just won't tell you what you're interested in first time around. Try spending some time wandering through the help screens. There is a lot of information in the Help files supplied with Windows and the Windows accessories. Sometimes the Search command won't find what you need to know, but the information is in the Help system in another context.

MODIFYING THE HELP SCREENS

You can add your own notes to a Help topic. This is useful for reminding yourself of things you've figured out about an application program or where to find information on some topic that eluded you last time you looked. Each topic can have one *annotation.* An annotation is like a small piece of paper that you can "paper clip" to the topic.

1. Get to the Help screen where you want to leave the note. It might be on the index, or it might be on a very specific topic.

2. Open the Edit menu of the Help window and choose Annotate.

3. Type your notes into the dialog box that appears. You can edit the notes with the backspace key, the delete key, and the arrow keys. When you are done, click on OK or press ↵. A paper clip now shows up at the upper-left corner of the first line of the help topic you're reading.

4. You can read the annotation on any help screen (if there is a paper clip there) by selecting the Annotate command again.

5. You can delete an annotation by opening the annotation dialog box again and clicking on Delete.

GETTING OUT OF, OR EXITING, WINDOWS

When you're finished with a Windows session, you should get back to the DOS prompt before turning off your computer. This ensures that Windows saves your work on disk correctly, and that no data is lost. Even if you are running an application in Windows, and you close that application, you'll want to exit Windows too before turning off your computer. When Windows is running another application, that application is running "on top of " the Program Manager. Thus, to exit Windows, you're actually exiting the Program Manager, which is also a Windows program. Here are the steps for correctly exiting Windows:

1. Close any applications that you have running in Windows. If you forget to do this, the Program Manager will remind you.

2. Choose Exit Windows from the File menu of the Program Manager window. (Figure 1.17)

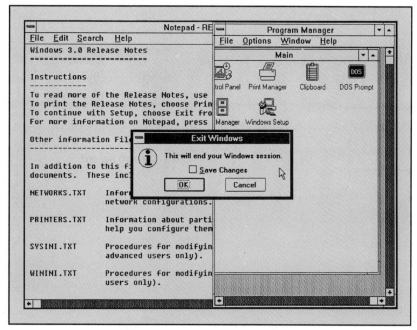

Figure 1.17: To exit Windows, select Exit from the File menu and click on OK.

3. Set the Save Changes check box on if you want the Program Manager to remember which group windows were open and how they were arranged when you quit.

4. Click on OK, and you'll be returned to the DOS prompt.

CHAPTER
TWO

Using the Program Manager

FastTrack

the program you want to run, double click it. If you don't
know where the program icon is, use the Run command.

To switch between applications that are running,   57

click on any part of the window you want to switch to, or press Ctrl-
Esc to move in a round-robin fashion through all open applications, including ones that are currently minimized (the
application's icon will be highlighted to indicate it's selected.
Double click on it to restore it if you wish).

Except for 386 Enhanced mode, switching means that only the
active window is actually alive and running. Others are temporarily suspended. Open as many applications as you want and switch
between them at will. (The number of application and document
windows allowed depends on the amount of RAM in your
machine. Windows will warn you if you're running out of space.)

To switch between applications using the Task List,   60

Click on any application window's Control box (all programs
running in a window have a Control box) or single click on
an iconized application. Choose Switch To from the menu.
The Task List appears. Double click the application you want
to jump to, or highlight it and click on Switch To. (You can
also open the Task List by double clicking the desktop or
pressing Ctrl-Esc.)

To quickly organize your screen,   62

Use the Task List's other commands. End Task closes the
highlighted application. Cascade and Tile neatly organize the
open windows in two different fashions. Arrange Icons lines
up the icons on the screen.

CHAPTER 2

BEFORE CONTINUING IN THIS CHAPTER, MAKE SURE you are familiar with the use of dialog boxes, menus, and the various elements of typical windows. See Chapter 1 if you are in doubt about any of these.

This chapter explains the essentials of using the Windows Program Manager. It covers the basics of how to run your programs from within Windows.

WHAT IS THE PROGRAM MANAGER?

The Program Manager is the heart of Windows. It's the part of Windows that is always running, either as a window, or as an icon, while you are using Windows. With the Program Manager's commands, you run your own programs, switch between them, and copy material between windows.

The Program Manager is, in effect, a conductor that directs the flow of data and keeps track of where you are and what you're doing while using Windows (Figure 2.1). It lets you run programs, remembers which window contains which program, remembers which window is active, and, along with Windows, works to control the computer's hardware (such as the printer, screen, hard disk and RAM) to let you switch between tasks by simply clicking on a window.

THE PROGRAM MANAGER AS ORGANIZER

In addition, the Program Manager helps you organize your programs. A feature in the Program Manager lets you assign icons

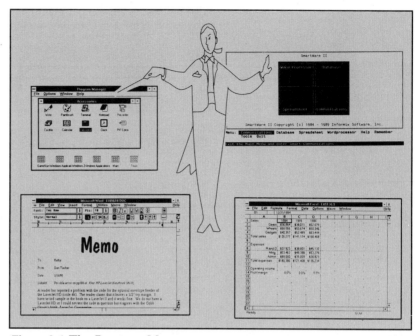

Figure 2.1: The Program Manager manages your system resources and applications whenever you are in Windows.

to your programs. You can then use these icons to select which programs you want to run. Instead of typing in the name of the program you want to run, you just click on the program's icon.

Once you've got your icons created, the Program Manager also lets you organize your program icons into *groups,* each with its own window, for easier access. For example, you might want to have all your accounting programs in one group, and all your writing programs (word processor, spell-checker, etc.) in another group.

You already have at least two program groups in your Windows setup. The Main and Accessories icons are group icons—they each contain a number of programs. If you open one of these by double clicking on it (or clicking once and selecting Restore), a window will open, displaying the programs that are in the group. In Figure 2.2, I've opened the Accessories group icon. All the icons in the resulting window represent the accessory progams supplied with Windows.

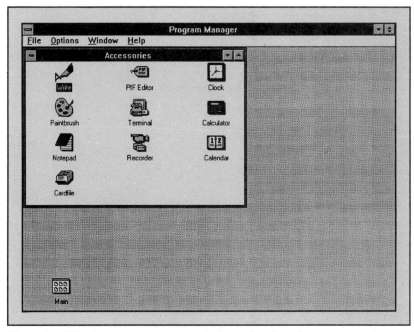

Figure 2.2: The Accessories group window, showing the programs it contains. Each icon is a program.

If you told Windows to install your existing Windows programs (if you had any on your hard disk) and your non-Windows applications, you'll have two other group icons—Windows Applications and Non-Windows Applications—that you can open and examine.

Later, in Chapter 3, we'll cover the techniques for creating new program icons and new groups to contain those icons, but first, we'll cover techniques for running programs that already have icons.

RUNNING PROGRAMS FROM WINDOWS

Though the purpose of the Program Manager is to let you forget about many of the details of what's happening in your computer, it's in your interest to understand the basic concepts of the Program Manager so that you can control it. Without this knowledge, you can get lost trying to do simple things that you may already know how to do perfectly well in DOS.

The most obvious of these things is the simple task of running programs. One of the primary advantages of Windows over DOS is that it lets you run more than one program at a time. In addition, this often allows you to copy material from one program to another more easily. However, not all programs will utilize the Windows graphical interface to the same degree. Some programs will only run in what's called *full-screen* mode, wherein they take over the whole screen. In this case, the Windows desktop disappears while the program is running, and it appears as it would if you were running the program from DOS. Windows applications, however, will appear in a normal window, complete with menus, and so forth.

IMPORTANT HARDWARE AND MODE CONSIDERATIONS FOR RUNNING APPLICATIONS

There are several important points to know concerning your system and how Windows will run applications for you. One consideration is that the number of programs that will run simultaneously depends on the amount of memory in your computer (that's RAM, not hard-disk space). Since programs and documents vary in size, it's not possible to calculate an exact number of programs that can run in a given amount of RAM. In general, however, the more memory you have the better. Windows will warn you if you are running out of memory.

Second, whether a program will run in a window or has to run full-screen depends on your computer's innards and the *mode* in which you are running Windows. As you may know, there are three different types of CPU (Central Processing Unit) chips that are used as the heart of IBM-type personal computers. Listed in decreasing order of their speed and power, these chips, sometimes called *microprocessors*, are the 80386, 80286, and the 8086. Rather than referring to particular brands and models of computers, PC's are often classed by their CPU. Thus, in popular computer lingo, there are the 386, 286, and 8086 machines.

There are also three modes that Windows can run in: Real, Standard, and 386 Enhanced. Most non-Windows applications will run in a window if you have a 386 computer and are running Windows in 386 Enhanced mode. (The modes are explained below.) If you have a 286 or 8086 computer, non-Windows applications must run full-screen.

With any of the three types of machines and modes, Windows can actually handle your Windows programs with *multitasking* — that is, in such a way that they *appear* to be running simultaneously, thanks to a little computer chicanery. In reality, each program runs for a short period of time in turn, one after the other. So, the processing is not actually simultaneous. But the switching between programs happens so quickly that it appears to be simultaneous. As a result, your computer could be sorting a database and calculating a spreadsheet while you are writing a letter or working on some other task.

In Standard and Real modes, multitasking will take place with Windows programs only. When a non-Windows program is active, other programs are temporarily suspended from operation. In 386 Enhanced mode, however, multitasking will include non–Windows applications.

If you are in doubt about which mode you're running Windows in, select the About Program Manager command from the Program Manager's Help menu. A dialog box will display the mode and the amount of RAM still available for use. Windows installs itself appropriately for your system when you run the setup program. However, you can change the mode by adding a parameter to the WIN command when you start Windows, as follows:

COMMAND	*EFFECT*
WIN /R ↵	Starts Windows in *Real* mode. Real mode is most compatible with earlier versions of Windows programs. It is also the only mode that an XT class (8086) machine or any computer with less than 1 megabyte of

memory can run in.

WIN /S ↵   Starts Windows in *Standard* mode. Standard mode is the normal operating mode for Windows. It requires an 80286 or 80386 machine and at least 1 megabyte of memory. More memory will speed things up and allow more programs to run simultaneously.

WIN /386 ↵   Starts Windows in *386 Enhanced* mode. 386 Enhanced mode requires a 80386 machine with 2 megabytes or more of memory. It lets you run non-Windows applications within a window, rather than full-screen. It also supports multitasking.

WIN ↵   Starts Windows in the default mode, based on Window's assesment of the type of computer and amount of memory you have.

FOUR WAYS TO RUN YOUR PROGRAMS

There are several ways to run programs from Windows, some easier than others. Here are the four basic techniques.

❐ Double click on a program icon. (As an alternative, you can highlight the icon and press ↵.)

❐ Choose the Run command from the File menu of the Program Manager or File Manager, and enter the name of the program. (The File Manager is explained in the next chapter.)

❐ Double click on a program file (or a PIF file) from a directory window in the File Manager. (PIF files are detailed in Chapter 14.)

❐ Double click on the DOS Prompt icon in the Program Manager's Main window. Then run the program from DOS. (This only applies to non-Windows programs.

Windows programs must be run using one of the other techniques.)

Regardless of the technique you use to run application programs, the following will be true. If the program is a Windows application, it will appear in a window. If it is not a Windows application, it will run full-screen unless Windows is running in 386 mode. If it's running full-screen, you will be returned to Windows when you exit the program. Very importantly, though, you will still be able to switch between Windows and your DOS program easily, without having to quit either one. This is explained later in this chapter, in the section "Switching Between Applications."

Now let's look closer at the procedures for each of these techniques.

RUNNING PROGRAMS FROM ICONS

The technique you choose for runnning a program depends on how frequently you use that program. For programs you use a lot, I suggest you make up icons for them, put them in groups, and run them by double clicking on them. For programs you use less frequently, use the other procedures listed in the next several sections.

Here's an example of how you run a program from an icon:

1. Open the Program Manager, or activate its window (if it isn't active already).

2. Expand the Accessories group icon to a window by double clicking on it. There are 10 programs in the Accesories group.

3. Double click on the Calculator icon. This tells Windows to run the program, and the Calculator accessory will appear on the screen in its own window, as you see in Figure 2.3.

4. While the Calculator is open, try experimenting with it. Try changing the calculator to a scientific format by choosing the Scientific command from the View menu.

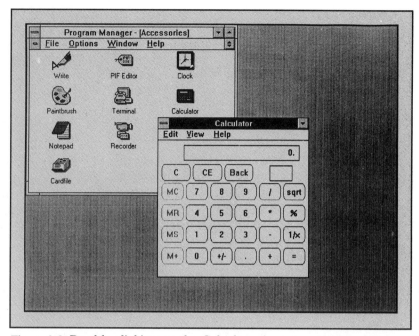

Figure 2.3: Double clicking on the Calculator icon opens the program in a window

You can move the calculator around the screen by dragging its title bar. Notice that if you click within the Program Manager window, a portion of the calculator will be covered by it. Clicking on the Calculator window again causes the calculator to "come to the front" of the stack of windows.

5. Click on the Minimize box (in the calculator's upper-right corner) to reduce the program to an icon on the desktop.

6. If you don't see the icon on the desktop, it is because the Program Manager's window is covering it. Click on the Program Manager's restore box (the double-arrowed box in the upper right corner). Then resize the window so you can see the bottom portion of the desktop. Your screen should look something like that in Figure 2.4.

✈ *SPEED TIP* If you know you have a program running but can't seem to find its window or icon, it's probably covered up by another window. Windows puts icons of running programs on the desktop, not in the Program Manager's window, so don't get confused. Look on the desktop by moving windows around or iconizing them. Don't click on the program's icon in the Program Manager window or other group window a second time. That will run the program again, and you'll have two sessions of the same program running, which will tie up memory. An easy way to find a program is by pressing Ctrl-Esc and selecting it from the Task List (see "Switching Between Applications" later in this chapter).

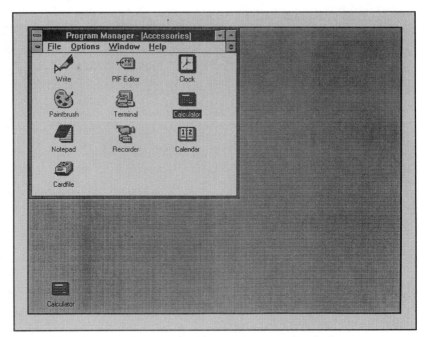

Figure 2.4: The Calculator reduced to an icon on the desktop

Since the calculator is now on the desktop, it is quickly available for your use—more quickly than if you were to run the program again by double clicking on the Calculator in the Accessories window.

7. Double click on the calculator icon at the bottom of the screen, and it appears more quickly than it did the first time.

8. Now we'll exit, or *close*, the Calculator program. Click on the Control box (in the upper-left corner of the Calculator's window). The Control menu appears, as you see in Figure 2.5. Choose Close from the menu, and the program will be closed. (You could also have double clicked on the Control box to close the program.)

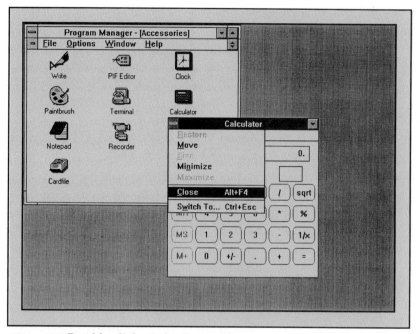

Figure 2.5: Double click on the Control box or choose Close from the Control menu to exit a program.

You've just run the Calculator program, reduced it to an icon, restored it to a window, and then closed it. While it was an icon, it was technically still running, though you couldn't see it or work with it. (See "Running Programs Simultaneously in 386 mode," later in this chapter, for more details on this.) The advantage of iconizing the program was that it was made easily available to you, even if the Program Manager had been closed and other windows were open on the screen.

Try running the other accessory programs supplied with Windows. The clock is a particularly easy one, since all it does is display a clock on your screen. Notepad, Calendar, Write, and Cardfile are also fairly easy to figure out. (These are covered in more detail in Chapter 13.) Try opening several windows, one for each program, and then switching between them by clicking on their respective windows. Switching between programs is discussed further later in this chapter.

RUNNING PROGRAMS
WITH THE RUN COMMAND

Both the Program Manager and the File Manager (the File Manager is covered in Chapter 4) have a Run command in their File menus. This command lets you run a program by typing its name just as you would from the DOS prompt. The only difference is that you type it into a dialog box instead of at the DOS prompt. You may also specify *parameters* that you normally give to your program when you call it up from DOS. A parameter is a word or letter you enter before or after the name of the program. For example, the line

    WS MYLETTER

would run WordStar and open the file MYLETTER.

Here's an example of running a DOS program using the Run command. Suppose you wanted to run a program such as WordStar from Windows and you didn't want to go about making up an icon for it.

1. Open the File menu on the Program Manager's window.

2. Choose Run. A dialog box appears, prompting you to enter a DOS command, as you see in Figure 2.6

3. Type in WS.COM (or another program name) and click on OK (or press ↵). Precede the program name with the drive and directory if they are not in your computer's normal search path. Type the exact name, including extension, if there is one. If you want the program to immediately be minimized to an icon, click on the Run Minimized check box.

If you don't specify the program's directory in the command, the program you want to run has to be in the current directory (the Windows directory) or a directory on the search path in your autoexec.bat. Otherwise, Windows will not find the program, and will display a dialog box like the one shown in Figure 2.7. Either change your path command or enter the path name before the program name.

RUNNING A PROGRAM BY DOUBLE CLICKING ON ITS FILE NAME

You can also run programs with the File Manager, which is covered thoroughly in Chapter 4. The File Manager lets you see a directory of files, just as the DIR command in DOS does. However, one of the differences is that you can just double click on a file's name to run it. The file, of course, must be a program,

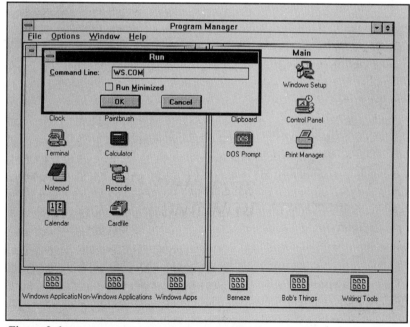

Figure 2.6: Running a program from the File menu's Run command. Enter the name of a program in the dialog box and press ↵.

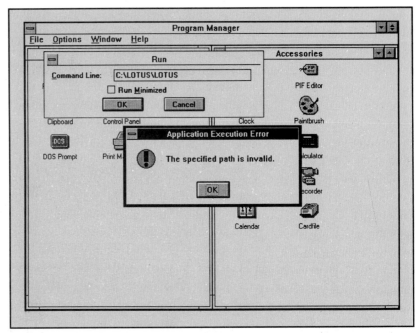

Figure 2.7: If the program you are trying to run can't be found, Windows will show a message similar to this. It doesn't mean the program isn't on your disk, only that Windows can't find it.

with an extension of *.bat, .com, .exe* or *.pif* in order to run. Running programs from the File Manager in this way is useful when you're not sure where the program you want is located. You can just point and shoot. Here are the steps for running an application in this way.

1. Run the File Manager and open the directory containing the desired program.

2. Double click on the program's file name, as shown in Figure 2.8. It must be an application or a document that has a program associated with it (associations are covered in Chapter 4).

3. When you are through running the program, exit it as usual. If you were running full-screen, you will be returned

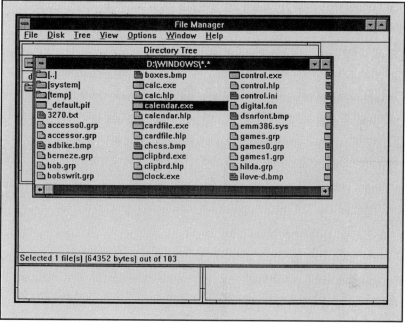

Figure 2.8: Running a program from within the File Manager

CAUTION Certain DOS programs should not be run from the Windows DOS prompt. Technically speaking, any program that modifies the file allocation table (FAT) should be run from outside of Windows. That is, you should quit Windows and return to DOS to use them. If you don't, you could end up losing your work, and causing your files to become jumbled. Most notably, this applies to the CHKDSK command when used with the /F option to recover lost fragments of files. (CHKDSK by itself can be used without trouble.) Also, programs that undelete erased files or those that defragment or optimize the hard disk, such as the Norton Utilities, should be run outside of Windows.

to Windows. If you were running in a window, the window will be closed.

RUNNING PROGRAMS FROM THE DOS PROMPT

If you like, you can run programs from the DOS prompt. This is handy for running programs you very rarely use, or if you want to be able to type in a series of commands at the DOS prompt without having to type each one into the Run dialog box. The Program Manager has a DOS Prompt icon in the Main group window for this purpose, so you don't have to leave Windows to do this.

1. Double click on the DOS Prompt icon in the Program Manager's main group.

2. The DOS prompt appears. Type in DOS commands as you normally would, just as if Windows weren't running. Run your programs and so forth.

3. When you are finished using the DOS prompt, type EXIT ↵, and you will be returned to Windows. You don't have to exit DOS to return to Windows, however. See the section below, on switching between applications.

RUNNING ADDITIONAL SESSIONS OF THE SAME PROGRAM

As you know, Windows is designed to let you run several programs at one time, and switch between them. However, there's no reason why the programs you run have to be different ones. One application of this capability is to have several copies of the same program running simultaneously.

For example, if your word-processing program doesn't let you edit more than one document at a time, you could run it twice and use Windows to switch between them. Then you could use the Windows Clipboard to cut and copy text between programs (the Clipboard is covered in Chapter 8).

Each running copy of the program is called a *session*. You can have as many sessions of a program as you want, limited only by your computer's memory.

As an example of running multiple sessions, try this experiment:

NOTE Notice that the second hands on the clocks don't move at exactly the same time. This illustrates the fact that computers can only do one thing at time. The microprocessor in your computer calculates the time for one clock, then moves on to the next one, in sequence.

1. Open the Accessories group in the Program Manager.

2. Double click on the clock icon. This runs the clock program.

3. Position the clock window so that the clock icon is visible.

4. Double click on the clock icon again. This runs the clock again. (The first clock may disappear, but that's because it's on the desktop, behind the Program Manager's window.) Double click several more times, so that you have about five clocks running.

5. Minimize the Program Manager window so that you can see the desktop. You should have about five or six clocks sitting there in a jumble. Arrange them by dragging them by their title bars, and set them up to look interesting, perhaps like the way I did it in Figure 2.9.

6. Now close all except one of the clock windows. (Remember, you do this by double clicking on the Control box of each window, or by single clicking and selecting Close.)

SWITCHING BETWEEN APPLICATIONS

Often you'll have a number of applications open at one time. They'll either be in windows or reduced to icons on the desktop. They could also be full-screen applications that are in a sense "invisible" when you are back in Windows. Similarly,

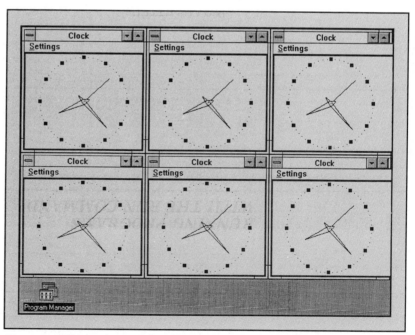

Figure 2.9: Six sessions of the Clock program running simultaneously

when you are running a full-screen application, Windows temporarily disappears, along with any windows or icons. At other times you may have a lot of windows stacked on top of each other, making some of the applications difficult to see, especially if they're all maximized.

Things can get pretty confusing with so much going on! Remember that you can only really be working on one window at a time—the active window. (The active window is identified by its title bar being a unique color or intensity.) So, the question is, how can you easily activate the window you want? As with most Windows operations, there are a number of ways to do this:

❐ When you can see the window of the application you want to switch to, the easiest thing is just to click on it. If you can't see the other window, or you have full-screen programs running, use one of the other choices.

❐ Use the Task List dialog box by clicking on the Control Box of any application window or the icon of any currently running program. Then choose the Switch To command. (Faster ways to open the Task List are to double click anywhere on the Desktop or press Ctrl-Esc.) Once the Task List is open, select the application you want to switch to by double clicking it or by highlighting it and clicking on Switch To.

❐ From any application, including the DOS prompt, press Alt-Esc. Each press will move you to another of the open applications in a round-robin fashion. The Program Manager is considered one of the open applications.

TIP You can use the Cascade or Tile command buttons in the Task List dialog box to rearrange all the open windows. Then you can click on the one you want to activate.

Here are the details for each of these approaches.

CLICKING ON THE APPLICATION WINDOW YOU WANT

If you can easily see the application window you want to activate, simply click anywhere within its perimeter. This will activate the window, and it will "jump" to the front of whatever was lying on top of it. The window(s) in front will be overwritten by the newly activated window, appearing to move behind it. The active window's menu bar color or intensity will change to indicate its newly activated status. (Incidentally, the colors Windows uses can be altered with the Control Panel program, which is covered in Chapter 5.)

If you like using this approach, adjust your application windows so that just a little edge of each one is visible at all times. All you need is to leave a corner or edge. Then you just click on the small exposed section. Figure 2.10 shows an example of several applications windows arranged such that their title bars are easily visible.

Another solution to desktop clutter is to always keep all but one of your running programs iconized. When you open your programs, immediately iconize (minimize) them. Then when

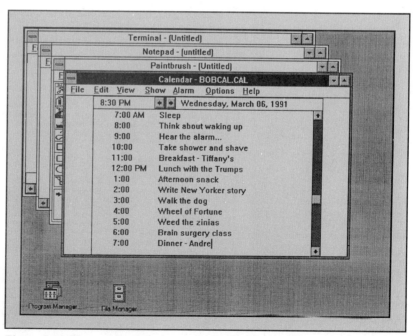

Figure 2.10: You can arrange your application windows so that you can easily click on their title bars

you want to switch to an application, double click on its icon. When you want to switch to another application, iconize the current one first. Then double click on the one you want to open up next. This will leave the desktop uncluttered, and allow you to see all your icons easily.

Some people like to adjust all their application windows to allow the line of icons at the bottom of the desktop to show, as you see in Figure 2.11. Then they can easily pull up the Calculator, Calendar, or whatever programs are iconized.

USING THE TASK LIST TO SWITCH BETWEEN APPLICATIONS

The Task List dialog box makes switching between applications very easy, because Windows will show you a list of the current applications. Here's how to use the Task List dialog box:

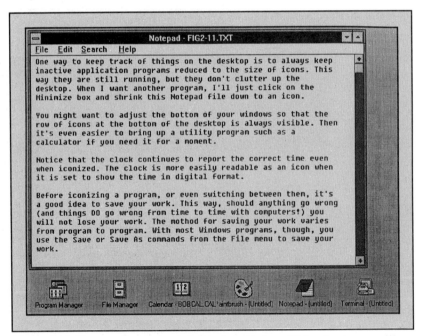

Figure 2.11: If you adjust your applications to be a little shorter, you'll always be able to see a row of icons on the desktop

1. From any Control menu, select Switch To.

2. The Task List dialog box appears on your screen. It'll look something like the one in Figure 2.12, listing your currently running programs. The active application will appear first in the list, with its name highlighted.

3. Select the name of the program you want to switch to. (Double click on it, or single click on it and then click on the Switch To command button.) The task (application window) you selected will be activated. If the application is a full-screen one, Windows will disappear and the program's screen will reappear. If the application can run in a window and is currently running as an icon, it will be restored.

NOTE You can get to a Control menu in two ways: You can either click on the Control box in the upper-left corner of any application window, or you can click once on the icon of any running program.

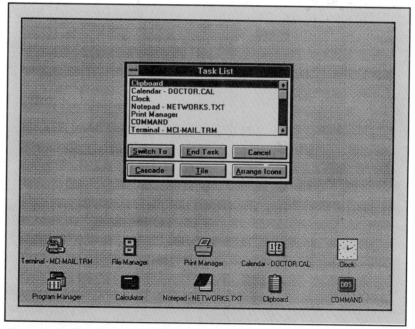

Figure 2.12: The Task List dialog box lets you choose which program to jump to. You can also close applications from here.

Notice that the Task List dialog box has four other command buttons: End Task, Cascade, Tile, and Arrange Icons. These are all useful to helping you switch between and organize your various application windows. Here's what each does:

COMMAND	EFFECT
End Task	Closes the application you highlight.
Cascade	Causes all the open Windows to be sized and staggered in such a way that the title bar and edge or corner of every window is visible, like that in Figure 2.13. DOS sessions or full-screen applications will be shown as icons at the bottom of the screen.
Tile	Causes all the open windows to be sized and lined up like tiles on a bathroom wall.

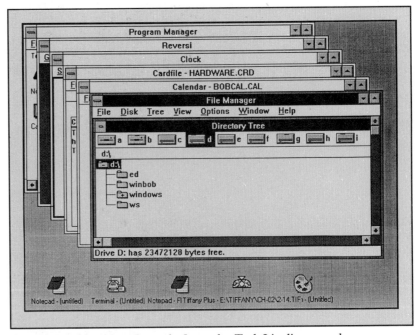

Figure 2.13: Choosing Cascade from the Task List lines up the open application windows like this for your convenience

TIP When running in 386 Enhanced mode, you can toggle a non-Windows application between full-screen and windowed display by pressing Alt-↵.

NOTE When you switch from a full-screen application back to Windows, the full screen application is represented as an icon on the desktop. Even pressing Alt-Esc at this point does not switch back to the application. It only highlights the icon. You have to double click the icon or open its Control menu and choose Restore in order to reactivate it.

See Figure 2.14. Again, DOS sessions or full-screen applications will be shown as icons at the bottom of the screen.

Arrange Icons Lines up all the icons on your desktop. You could drag them around with the mouse, but this command does it faster.

USING ALT-ESC TO SWITCH BETWEEN APPLICATIONS

Finally, you can use Alt-Esc to switch between applications. Each time you press these keys, Windows will jump to the next application. This works even while in full-screen applications. In fact, it is the only way to switch out of a full-screen application while it is running. This is the fastest way to switch between

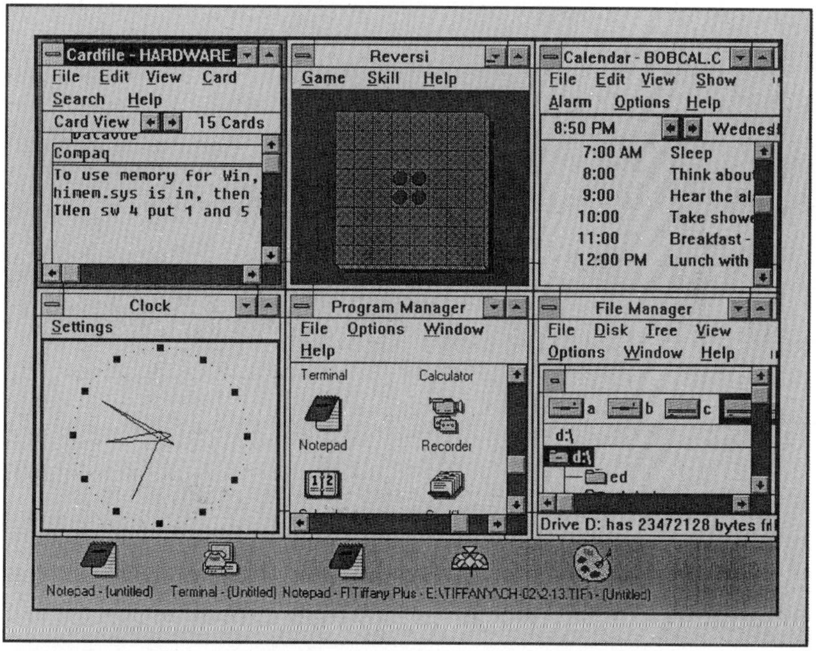

Figure 2.14: Choosing Tile from the Task List lines up the open application windows like this

SPEED TIP When in a non-Windows full-screened application, pressing Alt-Tab lets you quickly choose which application to jump to. Each press of the Tab key then displays another application name. Release the Alt key when the desired application name appears at the top of your screen.

while it is running. This is the fastest way to switch between applications if you only have several running and you want to shuttle back and forth between them quickly. Pressing Ctrl-Esc while in a full-screen application in Standard or Real mode will momentarily cause your screen to display *Switching....* Then the next application's window or screen will appear. In 386 Enhanced mode you will not see this notice.

CHAPTER THREE

3

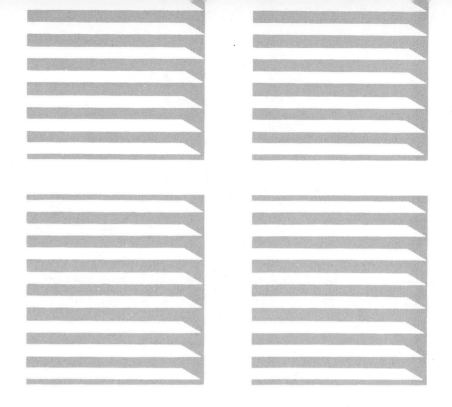

Creating and Using Groups

Fast Track

CHAPTER **3**

CHAPTER 2 INTRODUCED YOU TO THE PROGRAM Manager and explained the essentials of running programs within Windows. This chapter tells you how you use the Program Manager to set up icons for Windows and non-Windows programs and how to create new groups to hold those icons.

Recall that the Program Manager arranges applications (such as the ones supplied with Windows) into groups. Though you can run applications directly from the Program Manager or File Manager with the Run command, it's more convenient to open the group they're stored in and then double click on the icon of the application you want to run. Furthermore, when you quit Windows, if you elect to save your changes from the Exit dialog box, Windows will start your next session with the group windows, group icons, and program icons in the same arrangement you left them in last. Recall also that there are two types of icons: group icons and program icons.

- Group icons all look the same, (they have six miniature icons on them) and they only show up within the Program Manager's windows. (You can't drag them outside the window.) When you double click a group icon, a *group window* opens, displaying program icons assigned to that group.

- Program icons simply represent your programs. Double click on one to run the program it represents.

So the relevant questions are how do you create an icon for each of your applications, and how do you then assign them to groups?

SIZING CONSTRAINTS OF GROUP WINDOWS

Before we get into the details of creating program and group icons, there's one thing you should know, if it isn't already clear to you from using Windows programs. Document windows are limited by the size of the application window they are running in.

The Program Manager is an application, and group windows are considered document windows within the Program Manager. Therefore, just as with other types of windows, group windows can be resized and moved and even iconized, but their maximum size cannot exceed the size of the Program Manager's window. You'll have to maximize the Program Manager's window if you need to enlarge a group window significantly.

When you resize a group window, some of the icons may not show up. This is because they may be beyond the periphery of the window. If you choose the Arrange Icons command from the Window menu, they will reappear. If you want Windows to automatically rearrange your icons whenever you resize a group window, then choose the Auto Arrange option on the Options menu of the Program Manager.

NOTE The *parent* window is the window running the program you're working with. For example, if you're running Microsoft Word for Windows, the parent window is called Word. When you open documents to work with, such as a letter, a report, etc., each document is opened in a *child* window.

INSTALLING WINDOWS APPLICATIONS

Windows applications come in two basic flavors—those designed for Windows 3.0, and those designed for previous versions of Windows. When you use either the Setup program or the New command to install an application, Windows checks to see if it's a Windows application and places the new icon in an appropriate location. It uses an icon built into the application. If you're adding the program via Setup, Windows will put the new program icon into the Windows Applications group. It's then your choice either to leave it there or move it into another group. If you're installing the program with the New command, it goes into the active group window if there is one. If there isn't one (that is, if all windows are minimized), then it goes into the Windows Applications group, just as non-Windows applications are automatically dumped into the non-Windows group unless you have another group open and active.

RUNNING WINDOWS APPLICATIONS

Windows applications can only be run from Windows. If you try to run a Windows application from DOS by typing its name followed by ↵ you will see this message:

This program requires Microsoft Windows

NOTE This message varies somewhat from application to application. Some Windows applications (for example Excel and Word for Windows) are smart enough to start Windows automatically in order to run. So you can start Excel by typing **excel** ↵ at the DOS prompt. This brings up Windows, and then runs Excel.

When you run a Windows application from within Windows, the application is first checked for its status. If you are running in Real mode, Windows doesn't care if the program was designed for Windows 3.0 or earlier versions. However, if you are running in Standard or 386 Enhanced modes, and the program was not designed for Windows 3.0, you will see the following message:

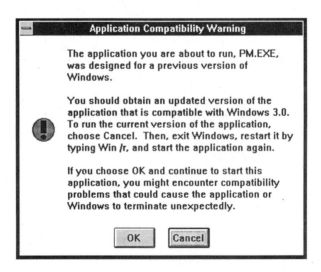

Microsoft recommends that you choose Cancel and then get an updated version of the program, one designed for Windows 3.0. However, if you exit Windows and run it again in Real mode, chances are good that the program will run reasonably well, since Real mode is designed to be compatible with older Windows applications. You run Windows in Real mode by typing

```
win /r ↵
```

You should be aware, though, that in Real mode, Windows doesn't use your computer system's resources very wisely. For example, it doesn't use extended memory at all (it does use expanded memory). If you are used to running in Standard or 386 Enhanced modes with lots of programs running, running in Real mode will cramp your style.

When running older programs, even in Real mode, you may have some odd problems such as fonts, bitmap pictures, or colors that are not displayed correctly. In addition, your program might become what the Microsoft Windows manual calls "unstable," which means it's likely to bomb. As the warning suggests, it's best to get an updated version of your program.

LETTING WINDOWS CREATE PROGRAM ICONS

As mentioned in Chapter 1, it's possible that the Windows Setup program has already created two groups for your applications—Windows Applications and Non-Windows Applications. If you opted not to have Windows set up your programs when you ran the Setup program, then you won't have these icons in the Program Manager window yet.

Generally speaking, Setup is only successful at figuring out a few of today's most popular PC programs and installing them automatically. It installs these programs when you first run Setup to put Windows on your computer. (If you didn't run Setup, you can follow instructions in this section to do so.) Anyway, you may have many programs that didn't show up as icons, leaving you wondering what happened to them. (Setup does a better job of installing Windows applications.) So for all the other non-Windows programs, you'll have to install them outside of Setup, as described later in this chapter, and in Chapter 14.

If you didn't have Setup install programs for you, or if you've added programs to your hard disk subsequent to installing Windows and want them to be added to your Windows or Non-Windows program groups, you can run Setup to install them at any time. (If you've already done this during setup and have no new programs on your hard disk, skip to the next section.)

NOTE Windows figures out which hard disks are on line and looks through them. However, you might want to select Path Only to search only through your computer's path as set by the autoexec.bat file or through a specific hard disk if you have more than one.

1. Open the Main group by double clicking it.

2. Run the Windows Setup program by double clicking on it. A dialog box will appear, showing the current parameters of your Windows setup.

3. Open the Options menu and choose Set Up Applications.

4. Windows will ask which drives to search for applications. Choose drives from the drop down menu. The default choice of All Drives is satisfactory for most computers.

5. Click on OK, and the Setup program will do its best to find applications to set up for you. When Setup is finished looking for programs, they'll be displayed in a dialog box like the one you see in Figure 3.1.

6. Click on the name of each program you want added to either the Windows or Non-Windows groups. (Don't worry about which group each goes to. Windows will handle that.) Then click on Add. The names will be added to the list in the right-hand box.

7. Click on OK, and Windows will create the two groups for you, if necessary. The windows will be displayed and icons added as you watch.

8. Exit the Setup program via the Options menu. Then you can open either of the groups to examine what's been added and run the programs, if you want to.

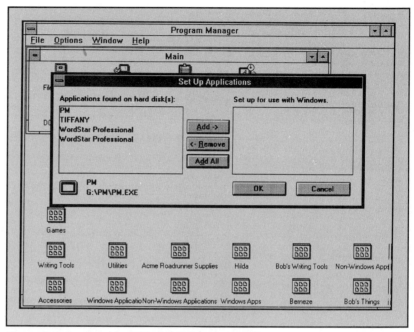

Figure 3.1: Letting the Windows Setup program prepare the icons for your applications

CREATING YOUR OWN GROUPS

Suppose you want to create your own icons and groups, though. Here's how to do it. First I'll demonstrate how to create a group icon, then a program icon.

CREATING A NEW GROUP

Creating a new group is simple. As an example, here are the steps used to make up a group called Writing Tools. This is actually a group I have on my computer, and it contains the programs I use most frequently for writing projects.

1. Open the Program Manager window.
2. Open the File menu and select New.

3. From the dialog box that appears, choose Program Group, as shown in Figure 3.2, and click on OK.

4. Another dialog box will appear. This is the Program Group Properties dialog box. It has two text sections—Description and Group File. Figure 3.3 shows an example with typical Description and Group File names.

- Description is the name that will appear under the group's icon and in the title bar of the group's window. Keep this line short so that your icon names don't overrun each other when they're side by side on the desktop.

- Group File is the name of the file that Windows puts on your hard disk to hold information about the group. This file is invisible to you. Windows creates

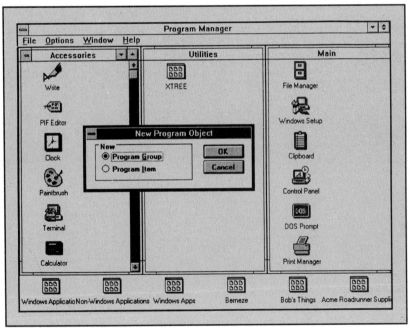

Figure 3.2: To create a new program group, choose File, New, and then choose Program Group

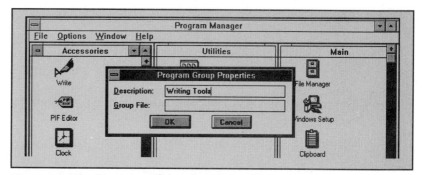

Figure 3.3: The Program Group Properties dialog box. You only have to fill in the Description part. This is the name that will appear under the icon and in the group window's title bar.

the name for you, so you're not required to fill this line in, though you may if you want to. If you do, the name you supply will be used. Leave the extension blank, since .grp (for "group") is automatically added by the Program Manager.

5. Fill in the Description line with the words Writing Tools (or a different name, if you wish).

6. Click on OK, and a new, empty group window appears. Notice that its title bar reads Writing Tools (or whatever you named it).

If you decide later that you want to change the name of the group, select the Properties command from the Program Manager's File menu, and type the new name into the description line. Don't change the group file name.

Deleting groups is covered later in this chapter.

ADDING APPLICATIONS TO A GROUP

Once you have a group created, the next step is to add programs (and/or documents) to it. This can be done in a variety of ways.

- Program icons can be moved into the new group from an existing group by dragging the icons from one group window to another. You can also use the Program Manager's Move command from the File menu to achieve the same result. (One other approach is to drag a file from a File Manager window. This will be covered in Chapter 4.)

- Program icons can be created with the New command while the new group window is active. Windows will then automatically add the new program icon to the group.

- Program icons can be copied into the new group from existing groups using the Copy command on the File menu. This creates a duplicate icon in the new group.

These techniques can be used with existing groups too, incidentally. So if you already have a group set up, it's easy to modify its contents to accomodate changes in your work patterns, or to update it when you buy a new program or want to delete an old one. Note, however, that it's a good idea to leave the supplied groups (Main and Accessories) as they are, since Windows expects to find its supplied programs in a particular arrangement. Add your own groups for your programs.

Here are some examples of the procedures to follow for adding programs to groups.

DRAGGING A PROGRAM ICON INTO A NEW WINDOW

This example moves the Solitaire icon (in the Games group) into the Writing Tools group you created above.

1. Open the Games group window.

2. Open the Writing Tools group window (if it is not already open).

3. Choose the Tile command from the Window menu. You should be able to see both windows easily.

4. Drag the Solitaire icon from the Games window to the Writing Tools window. Remember, to drag means to click on the icon and keep the button held down while moving the mouse. The pointer disappears while you are dragging, as you can see in Figure 3.4. (Make sure not to double click on the icon or the program will run.)

5. Writing Tools now contains the Solitaire program. This will remain the case even if you close and then reopen the two groups.

6. Now move the Solitaire program back to its original position.

CREATING A NEW PROGRAM ICON FROM SCRATCH

This example creates a new icon from scratch. In this case, it's for the WordStar word-processing program, (though you can apply this technique to other programs just as easily). You tell Windows the name of the icon and the name of the program it is to represent. Windows then creates the new icon and places it in the active window.

1. Activate the Writing Tools window.

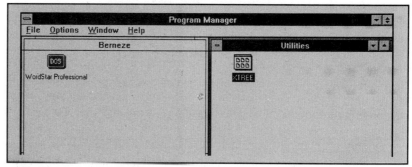

Figure 3.4: Moving a program icon from one group to another by dragging with the mouse

2. Select New from the Program Manager's File menu. A dialog box appears, as shown in Figure 3.5. Choose Program Item and click OK.

3. The Program Item Properties dialog box appears. There are two lines that you have to fill in:

   • Description is the name you want under the icon and in the title bar when the program is running. If you don't type anything into this area, Windows will try to come up with something reasonable. But it makes more sense to name the icon something that will help you remember what it's for. Also, keep the description relatively short, or your icons' names will run over each other.

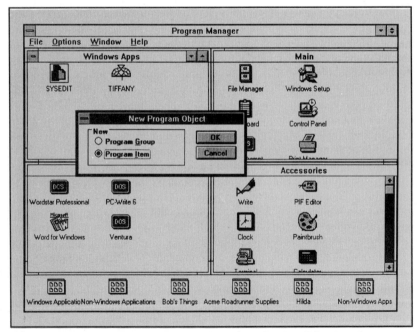

Figure 3.5: Creating a new program icon by selecting Program Item from this box

want the program
to start up with a dif-
ferent default direc-
tory, it can be done.
For example, say you
wanted to start Word-
Perfect (which is in the
\WP5 directory), but
you want it to come up
with \letters as the cur-
rent directory. Make
sure the path for the
program itself is in the
autoexec.bat search
path. Then, include the
desired default direc-
tory in the the command
line. For the above ex-
ample, this would be
c:\letters\wp.exe. Win-
dows will switch to the
c:\letters directory first
and then run wp.exe,
using the search path
to find it. (The startup
directory can also be
set by the program's
PIF file. This is ex-
plained in Chapter 14.)

- Command Line is the command that the icon is
going to give to DOS when you double click it. So, in
this line, you type the name of the program you want
the icon to run (Figure 3.6). You must also include
the extension of the program's file name. (The extension is the last three letters after the period, such
as *.exe, .com,* or *.bat.*) You should also include the
file's path name if the drive and directory that it is
stored in is not included in your computer's search
path as stipulated in your autoexec.bat file. For example, if the program is wp.exe and that file is
stored in \wp5, then the command line \wp5\wp.exe
should be used unless \wp5 is included in your path.

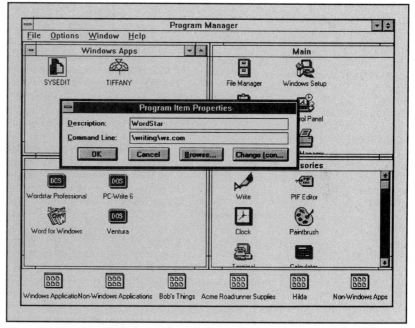

Figure 3.6: Telling Windows the name for the new icon, and the DOS
command line the icon represents (note that you include the entire
path name and extension of the file)

NOTE   Clicking
on the double
dots between brackets
[..] backs you up one
level in the directory
tree. If you are looking
for a *.com* file rather
than an *.exe* file, change
the Filename section to
read *.com That will
limit the display to only
the files with a *.com* extension. If you want to
browse through files
with any name, type in
.. This is similar to
specifying a DIR listing
in DOS using wildcards.

4. If you don't know the name of the file, you can use the
Browse command button in the dialog box to help you
find it. This lets you look through directories for the file
name you want, and then you select it from the list.
(Note the default file specification of *.exe. You will
have to change this to look for files ending with *.bat,
.com*, or *.pif.*)

For example, take a look at Figure 3.7. There you see the
Browse dialog box. The right-hand box shows directories and drives, while the left side shows file names.
Double click on the name of the directory you want to
look through and the files in that directory will appear
in the Files box. Then highlight the name of the program you want and click OK. The name and its path pop
into the Command Line area.

5. Once the Command Line is filled in, the final step is to
choose which icon you want. This is purely a subjective

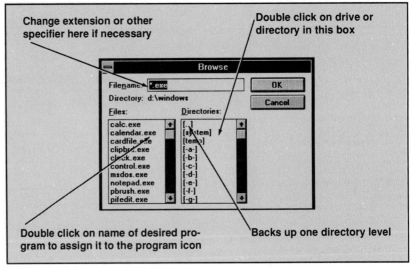

Figure 3.7: The Browse box lets you scan through directories for the
program file you want to assign to an icon. Double click on drive and
directory names to see files. Then double click on the correct file.

matter, and doesn't influence the workings of your program. Click on the Change Icon button in the Program Item Properties dialog box to do this. You'll see the dialog box shown in Figure 3.8. Click on View Next to see the choices. Click OK when you are happy with the icon. The DOS icon is appropriate for most DOS programs. If Windows says there is only one choice, try changing the File Name line in the Select Icon dialog box to read PROGMAN.EXE and click on View Next. This gives you more choices. Most Windows applications will have their own icons that will automatically be chosen when you add the program.

6. Finally, click OK in the Program Item Properties box, and Windows will add a new icon to your group window.

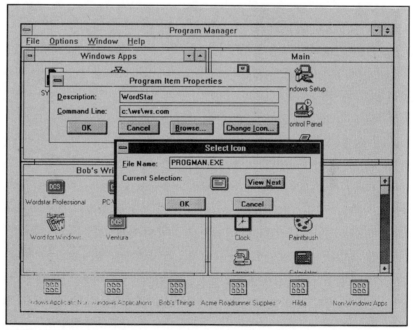

Figure 3.8: Windows chooses an icon for each application you add, but you can choose your own from a list. Each click of the View Next button shows another icon.

COPYING AN ICON FROM ANOTHER WINDOW

As a last example, suppose you wanted the same program to be included in more than one group. This would be useful in a number of different situations. For example, perhaps several people use the same computer and some of the same programs. An easy way to organize each person's programs is to set up a group for each. You can name each group after the person's name: Bob, Hilda, Berneze, and so on. Then, for each icon you want duplicated, you just create it once and copy it into the respective group windows. Here are the steps.

1. First, create the groups you want to copy the icon to.

2. Open the group window containing the icon you want to copy, and select the icon by clicking on it once.

3. Open the File menu and choose Copy. The Copy Program Item dialog box appears. It has a drop-down list from which you choose the destination group for the icon. Open the list by clicking on the down arrow. Groups are listed in alphabetical order. Your screen should look something like Figure 3.9. (Notice that I've tiled the new groups so I can see them all.)

4. Choose the desired destination group from the list, and click OK. A copy of the icon is then added to the new group.

5. Repeat the process to copy the icon to other groups. I've copied the WordStar Professional icon to each of my co-workers' groups, as you can see in Figure 3.10.

Copying an icon from one group to another in the Program Manager does not copy the program itself, as does the DOS *COPY* command. In the above example there is still only one copy of *ws.exe* on the hard disk, not four. The copy command just changes the group (grp) file for each group to include the new icon. Thus, you can make many copies of an icon without worrying about cluttering up your hard disk, or using up lots of hard disk space.

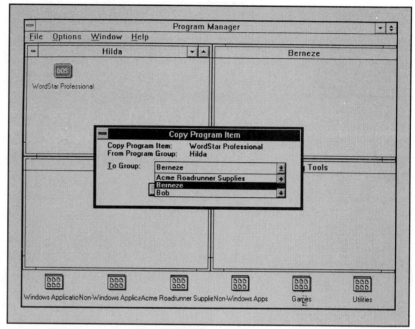

Figure 3.9: When copying program icons to another group, you choose the destination group from this dialog box

MODIFYING THE PROPERTIES OF DUPLICATE ICONS

Once an icon is copied, it can be altered to suit specific needs, should you want to. This applies regardless of whether you've copied the icon to a different group or within the original group. Copying to the same group lets you make up slightly different versions of the icon for different purposes.

For example, each of your co-workers may want to start up WordStar with a different default directory or have it automatically open a particular document when run.

These types of alterations are done by tailoring the *properties* of the icon via the Properties command on the Program

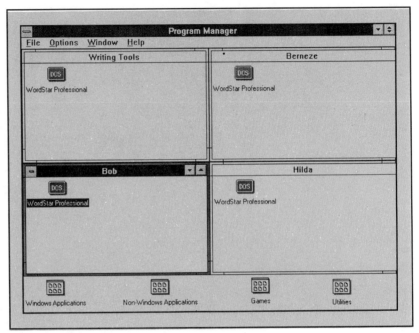

Figure 3.10: The result of copying a program icon to several program groups

Manager's File menu, as follows:

1. Select the icon to be altered.

2. Open the File menu and select the Properties command. The Program Item Properties dialog box appears. (This is the same box you use to create a new program icon, so you may recognize it.)

3. Alter the icon's command line and/or name to your needs, and click OK. Figure 3.11 shows a command line altered to start Wordstar with the current directory set to \hilda\letters. Note that for this to work, *ws.exe* would have to be in a directory listed in the autoexec.bat search path. Note also that the name of the icon has been changed to read Hilda's Wordstar Pro.

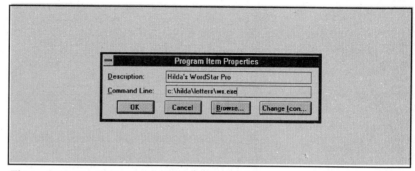

Figure 3.11: Modifying an existing icon's name and command line via the Properties command on the Program Manager's File menu

CREATING ICONS FOR INDIVIDUAL DOCUMENTS

You can also create icons for individual documents. Clicking on such an icon opens the document using the program indicated in the command line. Adding a document file's name after the program name would open that file.

For example, an icon could be set up to run WS and open the file called proposal. This is just like typing

    ws proposal ↵

at the DOS prompt. The command line would read *ws.exe proposal*. If the document is in another directory, add the path name in the command line, such as

    ws.exe \business\proposal

You could also change the icon's name to *Proposal* to remind you what happens when you click on it.

If there are a number of documents you use regularly, just use the Copy command to create as many icons for the same program as you need. Then modify them accordingly, with each

NOTE There is another technique for choosing a document file from a list and having Windows open both the associated program and document in one fell swoop. It's called setting up *associations* and is covered in Chapter 4, since it's done from the File Manager.

one set to open a different document. Figure 3.12 shows such a group of icons. They all run Excel, but each one opens a different document.

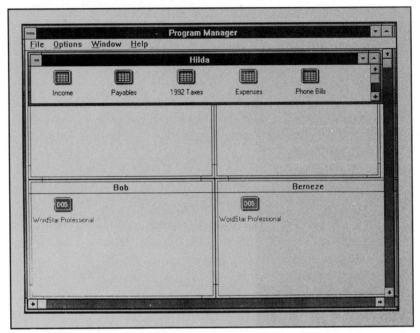

Figure 3.12: You can make up icons that run the same program but open different documents. These are all Excel documents set to open various spreadsheets. The Command Line for each icon opens a different document.

RUNNING PROGRAMS FROM A FLOPPY DISK

You can create icons that are set up to run programs from a floppy disk rather than from the hard disk. This isn't something you're likely to do regularly, but it can be done. Here's how.

1. Simply specify the drive name in the command line, such as:

    a:\xtree.exe

2. Insert the proper disk in drive A when setting up the properties of the icon or Windows will give you a warning message saying the path is invalid. (If this happens, just click on OK, and the the icon will be created anyway.)

3. Windows will present another dialog box entitled Removable Path Specified alerting you to the fact that the file you're making an icon for might not be available at a later time. Click on OK.

4. Run the program as usual. If you have the wrong disk in the floppy disk drive, Windows will alert you to this fact with the relatively obscure message seen in Figure 3.13. Replace the disk and try again.

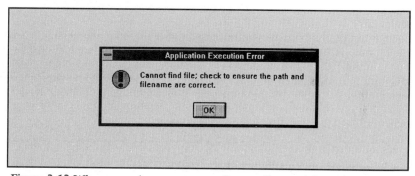

Figure 3.13: When running a program from a floppy drive using a program icon, you'll see this message if you have the wrong disk in the drive

DELETING PROGRAM ICONS

Occasionally you'll need to delete programs from your groups. Perhaps you'll stop using a program often enough to

NOTE Deleting the program icon doesn't delete the program itself from your hard disk, so don't worry about doing something catastrophic by deleting an icon. You can always recreate the icon. If you do want to delete the program file from your hard disk, you'll have to use the DOS *ERASE* command or the Windows File Manager, as described in Chapter 4.

warrant having an icon for it, and would be willing to run it via the Run command. Or perhaps you'll switch to a new spreadsheet program and want to delete the old one and its icon from your system and replace it with a new one. Whatever the reason, deleting a program icon is occassionally necessary. Here are the steps for doing so:

1. Open the group window with the icon you want to eliminate.

2. Highlight the icon.

3. Select Delete from the File menu (or press Del). A dialog box (Figure 3.14) asks you if you're sure you want to delete the icon. Click on Yes, and the icon will be deleted from the group window.

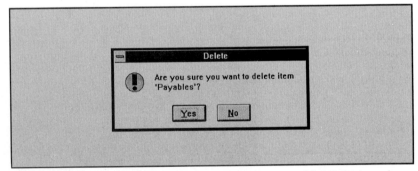

Figure 3.14: To delete a program icon from a group, highlight it and select Delete from the File menu. The dialog box you see here will appear, asking you to confirm the deletion.

DELETING GROUPS

Just as you may need to delete program icons, you can delete group icons and windows. When you delete a group, all the program items in the group are erased too. This doesn't delete the programs or documents, however. It only erases the grp file.

1. Select the group icon (it must be iconized, not open as a window).

2. Select Delete from the File menu. You'll see the dialog box displayed in Figure 3.15. Click Yes to delete the group.

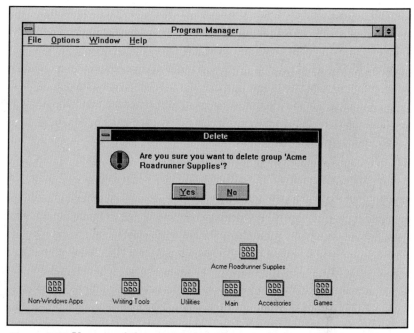

Figure 3.15: You can delete an entire group, including all its icons, by selecting its icon and choosing Delete from the file menu

CUSTOMIZING OTHER PROGRAM ICON PARAMETERS

There are numerous parameters that will affect how a non-Windows program runs from Windows beyond those discussed in this chapter. For example, you may want to stipulate how the program should use the screen and keyboard, how much RAM it requires, how much of the computer's processing power is used on each program (386 machines only), and so forth.

Normally, Windows sets these parameters according to built-in defaults designed to work with most programs. So, in most cases all that is required in the program icon creation process is to fill in the program name and command line, as you've already learned how to do in this chapter. Occasionally you will want to exercise more control over the way Windows runs a program. To do this, you have to create what's called a *PIF file* (for Program Information File), or use a PIF file supplied with the program. PIF files and the use of the PIF Editor is covered in Chapter 14. If you've installed a program from the Program Manager and it doesn't run properly, you can probably cure the malady by creating a PIF file for it.

CHAPTER
FOUR

4

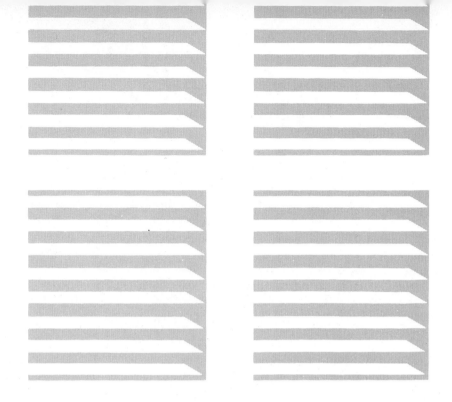

Using the File Manager

Fast Track

CHAPTER 4

ONE OF THE MOST CONFUSING ASPECTS OF DOS
(or any computer operating system for that matter) is the job of
managing your files. Most application programs nowadays consist of numerous files. Add to this the plethora of files you are
likely to collect and create, and your hard-disk directory can
easily become impossibly cluttered. With the advent of afford-
able high-capacity hard disks (80 or 110 megabyte disks are not
uncommon these days), hard-disk housekeeping becomes even
more of a necessity.

If you've used DOS to any degree, you know it can be quite a
hassle to keep your files organized and up to date, not to mention the often overlooked chore of making backup copies of important documents and programs. File-management tasks via
the DOS interface requires exacting attention to syntax and
spelling, both of which are sometimes difficult or tedious to
remember. One of the more grueling jobs in DOS—copying
files between directories—is enough to challenge even the
multilingual or the highly computer-literate. Even if you remember the proper syntax for a complex DOS file-management
command, make one misspelling and your carefully construc-
ted command bombs, with DOS issuing a dispassionate and
hieroglyphic reply such as

```
Bad command or file name
```

or

```
Not ready error reading drive A
Abort, Retry, Fail?
```

Who but those of us with the lowest self-esteem would choose anything other than to Retry? It's enough to intimidate even seasoned computerites.

Then there's the job of purging your disks of unnecessary or obsolete files. Typing in the name of each file name you want to squish is simply a pain, and one false move with the ERASE or DEL commands can wreak havoc on your files. For example

```
erase *.wk? ↵
```

would erase all the 1-2-3 worksheets in the current directory in about the same amount of time it takes to realize you've locked your keys in the car. And just like your car, DOS doesn't bother to ask "Yo. Do you really want to do this?"

With Windows 3, DOS file management is much simplified by the File Manager. Your hard disk's directories can be displayed in separate windows, from which you employ the "point and shoot" approach to copy, move, or delete any file or files you choose. You just select the desired files and drag them to their new directories or drives. You can even run programs or open document files by double clicking on their names. You can elect to see only certain files, sort them in various orders, search the entire disk for a certain file, even format floppy disks. You can also create and delete directories.

A REVIEW OF DOS DIRECTORIES

This book assumes you understand the basics of DOS direc-tories, and have used DOS commands to perform directory-related file housekeeping. However, if you're a little rusty on the topic, the File Manager won't make much sense to you. So here's a thumbnail sketch of directory workings.

DOS stores all files in directories on your disk. A directory is simply a collection of files. Directories let you keep files that are somehow related nested together, just to help cut down on con-fusion. Typically you'll keep related work files, such as letters, in one directory, spreadsheets in another, and so forth. With occasional limitations imposed by specific programs, you can organize your files any way the spirit strikes you.

Directories are organized in a system analagous to a "tree," as illustrated in Figure 4.1. In fact, the organization of directories is call the *directory tree*. The directories are organized in a hierarchical manner, from the *root* (the highest level) to various branches off the root, and branches off those branches.

It is possible that you've never used directories before, since, theoretically you can put all your files in the default directory (the root). If you've never created a new directory, it's possible that all your files are stored in the root directory. However, it's wise to divide things up according to the way you work, by creating appropriate directories and assigning your files to them according to some sensible scheme.

The root directory is always indicated by a single backslash (\). All other directories have names that you assign. For example,

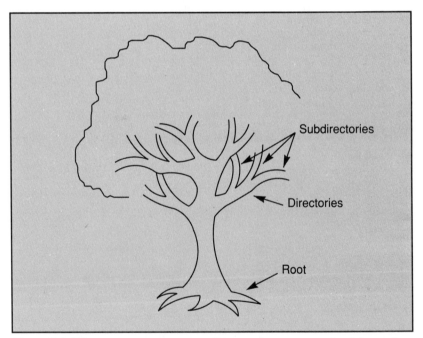

Figure 4.1: Directory-tree structure. Directories are organized from the root outward.

the Windows Setup program created a directory branch called Windows. Subordinate to Windows, it created another branch called *system*. The official name of the system directory is c:\windows\system. This is called the directory's *path name*. The name describes the path you'd take to get to the directory, just as if you were climbing the tree—from the root up to the particular branch. Notice that the \ (indicating the root) precedes the directory name, and that branches in the path name are also separated by a backslash.

In working with directories, the main thing to keep in mind is the "you can't get there from here" rule. To switch between branches there are times when you have to work your way back down to the root, directory by directory. For example, if you were working in the \windows\system directory and wanted to save a file in the \letters\personal directory, you'd have to back up to the root level first, and then move into the letters directory, and then into the personal directory. While working with Windows applications and some dialog boxes in windows, you'll need to remember this.

You may have noticed that some dialog boxes have a listing of files in them that you can choose from. These boxes always show the various drives, and available directories. If you're currently in a subdirectory (i.e., anything other than the root directory (\) you'll also see the symbol [..]. This is the "back-up" symbol. Clicking on this backs you up one level toward the root. If you are down several levels in the directory tree, you will have to double click on the back-up symbol several times to get back to the root.

STARTING THE FILE MANAGER

Now for some experimentation with the File Manager: to run File Manager, open the Main group and double click on the filing cabinet icon. This will bring up the File Manager's initial screen, as shown in Figure 4.2. (If you have used the File Manager before, the window's size may be different, since the File Manager has an option that saves its setup, just as the Program Manager does,

NOTE The figures in this chapter show directories and file names with lowercase letters. The default setting in Windows is to display these in uppercase. You can change the setting from the View menu to make file names easier to read.

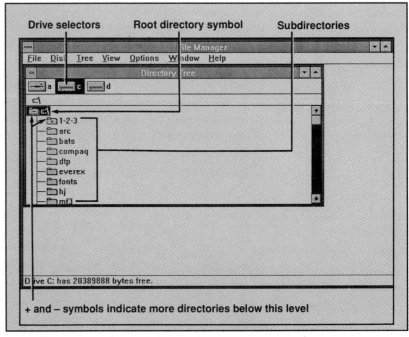

Figure 4.2: The File Manager screen

when you exit Windows. Also, the actual directory and file names you see will reflect your particular hard disk's contents, rather than mine, which is what you see in this chapter's figures.

What you see is the main File Manager window and a child window within it, showing the directories on your hard disk. Whenever you request to view a directory or disk drive's contents, they'll be displayed in a child window. You can open as many child windows as you want, each showing different directories. Then you can copy and move files between them, delete files, or run programs. Here are the techniques for each procedure.

Notice that the child window is called *Directory Tree.* This is always the first window you see when running the File Manager. It displays the names of all directories on the current drive. The current drive is indicated by the highlighted drive icon in the first line of the directory tree window. Notice that I have a D drive, which also appears in Figure 4.2 as a drive icon. Your screen may show only drives A and C. If you have a second floppy drive, it will be drive B. If you have a RAM drive or network drives, these will have distinct icons, too.

The second line in the Directory Tree window indicates in longhand form (DOS format) which directory is selected. Try moving the directory highlight down through the tree. (Use the arrow keys on the keyboard, or single click with the mouse.) Notice that the directory line changes as you do so.

Then, below that, you see a graphical representation of your directory's layout. Each little file folder icon symbolizes one directory and the straight lines connecting them indicate how they're related. The name of each directory appears after the icon. If you have more directories than can be seen at one time, the window will have a scroll bar which you can use. Better yet, try maximizing the window to see as much as possible all at once. It makes working with a directory tree much simpler. Remember that the maximum size of a child window is determined by the size of the parent window. If you want the Directory Tree window to use the whole screen, maximize the File Manager window.

The last line of the window tells you how much room is left on your drive.

SWITCHING DRIVES

SPEED TIP You can also change drives by pressing Ctrl and the drive letter. Thus, Ctrl-A would switch to drive A, Ctrl-B to drive B, etc.

To switch drives, you simply click on the appropriate drive icon. If you choose a floppy drive icon (ones with a single line in the middle, instead of two lines), you'll have to insert a floppy disk in the selected drive or you'll get an error message.

Once you change drives, the File Manager examines the new drive, and displays its directories in the Directory Tree window. Typically your floppies will have only one directory (the root) so you'll see only one file folder. A hard disk may have many directories. A plus sign (+) in a file folder indicates that there are additional subdirectories below it.

WORKING WITH DIRECTORIES

Once you have the correct drive selected, you can work with the various directories and files it contains. Before getting into working with files, let's first consider how the File Manager displays and manipulates your drive's directories.

Activate the Directory Tree window again by clicking on it (adjust the size and position of your windows so that the Windows directory tree is showing).

EXPANDING AND COLLAPSING DIRECTORY LEVELS

You may have noticed that some file folders in the Directory Tree window have a plus sign (+) in them. Others have a minus sign (–). The plus indicates that there are additional subdirectories attached to the directory, and that these are not currently showing. A minus indicates that all the immediate subdirectories are currently showing.

There are several ways to alter the display to either show or hide these directories. The first step when using any directory is to select it. Only one directory can be selected at a time. You select a directory by clicking on it, typing its first letter, or moving the highlight to it with the arrow keys. When selected, the directory icon and name become boxed in a dotted rectangle.

- Click once on any directory that has either a plus or minus sign in its file folder. The directory will alternately *branch* or *collapse* with each click. (Be careful not to double click, or a directory window showing files will open instead.)

- Select the directory you want with the arrow keys or by pressing its first letter on the keyboard. Then open the Tree menu. Select Expand One Level. This shows the next directory level. Choose Expand Branch to see all the directories subordinant to the selected one (if there are more than one).

- The easiest way to see the entire subdirectory scheme of your disk is to select Tree ⇨ Expand All. This displays all the branches. Figure 4.3 illustrates the effect.

- The easiest way to collapse all the branches is to click on the topmost folder (the root). To reopen just the first level, click once again on the root icon or select Tree ⇨ Expand One Level.

CREATING A NEW DIRECTORY

Creating new directories is easy, and because of the graphical nature of the directory tree, it's much easier to visualize what you're doing than when creating directories from the DOS command line. Once you've created a new directory, you can employ the file commands explained in the next section to copy or move files into it.

1. From the directory window, select the directory *under which* you want to create a subdirectory. If you select the root, then the directory will be directly off it.

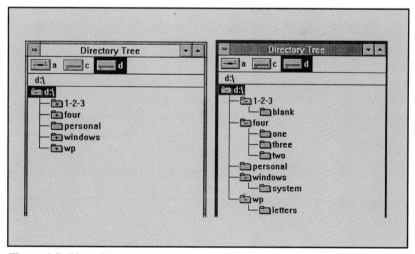

Figure 4.3: The effect of the Tree menu's Expand All command. The window on the left shows the tree before it was expanded.

2. Choose File ⇨ Create New Directory. A dialog box will appear.

3. Type in the name of the new directory.

You can see below the effect of selecting the *wp* directory and adding a subdirectory called *letters*.

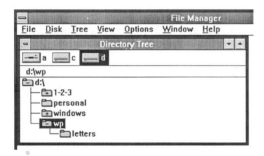

DELETING A DIRECTORY

The File Manager includes a very convenient but potentially catastrophic command that will delete an entire directory and all its files in one fell swoop. Once deleted, files cannot be easily recovered. Many times they can't be recovered at all. (DOS doesn't let you wipe out a directory directly—you have to erase all the files manually first.)

Luckily, the default settings for this command are such that you are asked to confirm the operation before the files are all irreversibly erased. Obviously you should be very careful when using this command. Make sure you really want to trash all the files in the directory first.

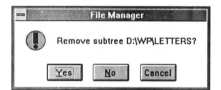

1. In the Directory Tree window select the directory you want to delete.

2. Select File ⇨ Delete. A dialog box will appear with the name of the directory in it. You can have a different directory if you want, but normally you'd just leave it as is.

3. Click OK and the following confirmation box appears:

4. Do you really want to delete the directory and all its files? If so, click on Yes.

SPEED TIP To quickly erase an entire floppy disk, select the drive, and then select the root. Turn off the confirmations. Press Del. All directories and files will be erased. Make sure to set the confirmations back on to prevent accidental erasures on other drives.

File Manager

Remove subtree D:\WP\LETTERS?

Yes   No   Cancel

TIP If you do accidentally erase files, there is some hope of recovering them with a file-recovery program such as the Norton Utilities.

You can turn off the confirmation message if you want to, via the Confirmation dialog box (covered in more detail in the "Working with Files" sections below.) But be cautious. This eliminates the one safety feature that prevents accidental file erasure. On the other hand, it lets you erase a whole branch, or the entire disk for that matter, in short order. Just set all the confirmations off, select the directory to delete (even as high as the root) and press Del or choose File ⇨ Delete. All the files in the directory as well as all subordinate directories and their files will be deleted.

WORKING WITH FILES

Once the correct drive and directory are selected, you'll likely want to open a directory to get at its files. Only then can you copy, move, run, or delete the files.

OPENING A DIRECTORY WINDOW

Opening a directory means showing the directory's files in a window. There are only two types of windows in the File Manager—the Directory Tree windows and directory windows. As you already know, Tree windows display the directory structure. Directory windows (the second type of window) list files. You do all your work with files by selecting them in a directory window and then choosing commands from the menus.

To open a directory window:

> *SPEED TIP* You can jump quickly to a directory name by typing its first letter on the keyboard. If there is more than one directory with the same first letter, each press of the key will advance to the next choice.

1. Double click on the directory you want to open. As an example, try opening the *windows* directory. (Make sure you're on the right drive first, probably C.)

2. The File Manager now opens up a second child window, showing the contents of the directory (Figure 4.4). Notice the complete path name of the directory in the new window's title bar. Try enlarging the window to see more of the files.

Notice that each file has an icon. File Manager chooses these icons based on each file's extension.

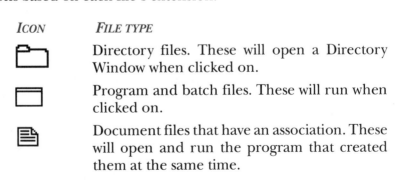

ICON	FILE TYPE
	Directory files. These will open a Directory Window when clicked on.
	Program and batch files. These will run when clicked on.
	Document files that have an association. These will open and run the program that created them at the same time.

All other files. Clicking on these will do nothing except get you an error message.

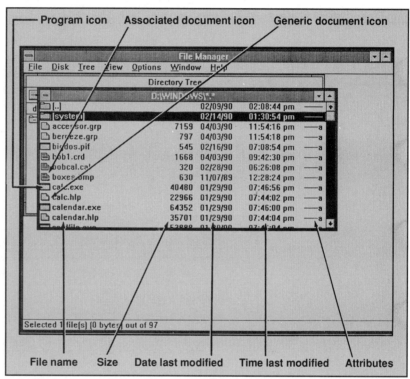

Figure 4.4: The Windows directory appears after you double click its file folder

MODIFYING A DIRECTORY LISTING TO SHOW SPECIFIC INFORMATION

Normally, opening a directory window shows all the files in the directory with as little information about each as possible. You just see the file name and an icon. Suppose you want to see all the detail information about the files, similar to a DOS *DIR* listing. If you want to see the files' names and sizes, or some other combination, there's quite a bit of flexibility available, via the View menu's commands: open the menu and choose the appropriate command to modify the listing to your needs.

COMMAND	EFFECT
Name	Lists only the name and icon of each file. Use this setting to see the greatest number of files in the window. As you can see in Figure 4.5, Windows packs in three times as many files this way than when all the information is displayed. This is the default setting.
File Details	Lists all the data.
Other	Lets you set various options from the dialog box shown in Figure 4.6. The choices are

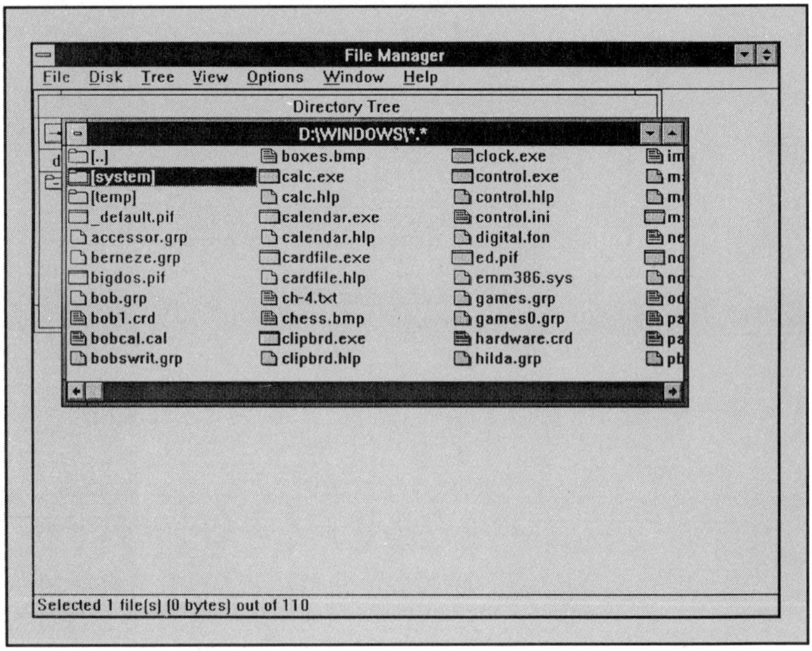

Figure 4.5: Choosing View ⇨ Name packs the maximum number of files on the screen

self-explanatory. Setting each one on (clicking until there is an X in the box) causes the described information to be shown. File flags are attributes—Read Only, System, Hidden, and Archive. (These are covered below, in "Changing a File's Attributes.") Once you have settings you like, clicking on Set System Default will save the setup, and the File Manager will use it to display directories until you change it.

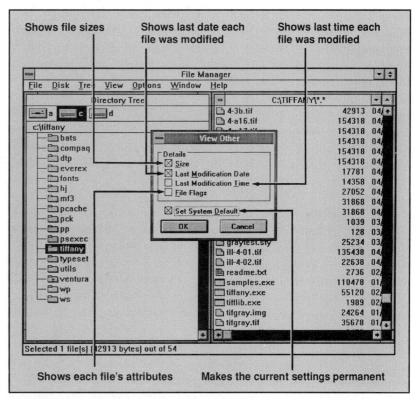

Figure 4.6: The Windows directory appears after you double click its file folder

SORTING THE DIRECTORY LISTING

Normally the files in a directory window are alphabetically sorted according to their names. Using the View menu, you can elect sorting based on other information. You can sort the listing by Type, meaning alphabetically by file extension (the last three letters after the period in the file's name). Choosing View ⇨ Sort By opens the menu you see in Figure 4.7. This gives you all the sorting options, including Name and Type which have the same effect as choosing them directly from the menu. However, in addition, this menu box lets you sort by two additional options: Size, which lists files by their size, from largest to smallest, and Last Modification Date, which lists oldest files first, most recently altered files last.

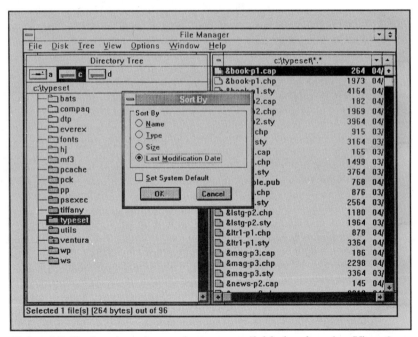

Figure 4.7: Optional sorting options are available by choosing View ⇨ Sort By

You can make your settings permanent by checking the Set System Default box.

SHOWING ONLY SPECIFIC FILES

You can choose to see only specific files in a directory window, temporarily hiding the rest. This is similar to specifying wild-cards or a file name when using the DOS *DIR* command. For example, at the DOS prompt you might type the following command to see all the executable program files:

```
dir *.exe ↵
```

Or, as another example, you might type

```
dir 198?.wks ↵
```

to see all files with *198* as the first three of four characters and *.wks* as the extension. Or you might type

```
dir accounts.wks ↵
```

to look for a file with this exact name.

With Windows, these same DOS rules for listing files apply. The only difference is that you use a dialog box instead of entering the command at the DOS prompt. Also, as a convenience, the dialog box has the most common options included as check boxes. This means you won't have to enter the most common extensions. To limit a directory listing, follow these steps:

1. Choose View ⇨ Include. The dialog box shown in Figure 4.8 appears.

2. Normally all four File Type boxes are checked, meaning that all files (except hidden and system files) are shown. (Hidden files are files that you or an application chooses to make invisible to normal directory listings. System files are files added to your disk by DOS and used to boot up and run your computer.) Leave an X

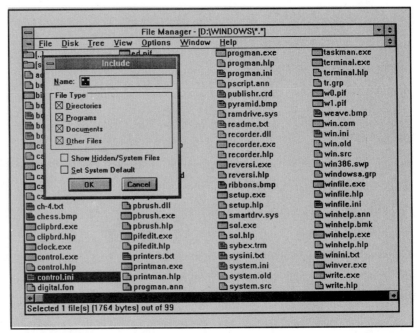

Figure 4.8: Choosing View ⇨ Include presents this dialog box. Choose which files to include in directory windows by checking boxes or typing in wildcards.

next to only the type of files you want to see, and click OK. (Refer to the earlier section "Opening a Directory" for a description of each type of file.)

Entering Your Own Criteria

Sometimes you'll want to limit a directory listing to a very specific subset of files. It's likely that the choices in the dialog box are too general for this. So, you just type in the DOS *filter* as you would if you were using the DIR command from the DOS prompt. The file manager will only display files with names that meet the filter criteria.

1. Type the file name or wildcard filter into the Name portion of the dialog box.

NOTE You can use the ? and * wildcards. (The ? represents any single characters. The * represents any number of characters.) For example, to see all files with the extension bat you would type ***.bat** into the Name area. To see all files with three letters in their first name and ws as an extension, you would type **???.ws** into the Name area. To see files that have no extension, type ***.** into the Name area. See your DOS manual for more about using wildcards.

NOTE If when viewing a directory listing you notice that a multitude of files have suddenly disappeared, don't panic. You probably limited the listing via the Include command. Look at the directory window's title bar. It should read *.*. If it doesn't, select the Include command again, make sure the Name line reads *.*, and include the four file types. All files should be displayed again.

2. Set the four File Type check boxes on, unless you want to eliminate some groups of files from the listing.

3. Check the Set System Default box *on* if you want the settings to apply to any future directory windows you open, rather than just the current one.

4. Click OK. The listing will be updated, and the window's title bar will reflect the current DOS filter.

Figure 4.9 shows the listing of just the help files (files with the extension *.hlp*). This was obtained by entering ***.hlp** into the Name area of the Include dialog box. Notice that the Directory Tree is also showing in this screen. I used the Window ⇨ Tile command to evenly divide the screen between the two windows. Tiling is useful when you begin to copy files between directories.

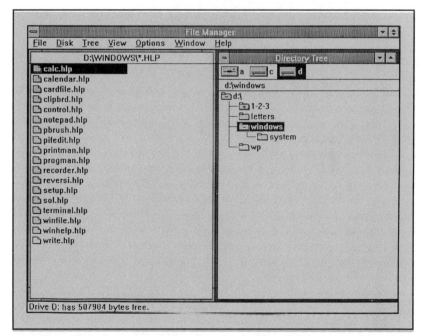

Figure 4.9: This directory window shows only files with the extension *.hlp* because ***.hlp** was typed into the Name section of the View ⇨ Include dialog box

VIEWING MORE THAN ONE DIRECTORY AT A TIME

Normally, every time you open another directory, each newly opened directory will be displayed in its own window. The new window overlays the previously active one. However, this can lead to clutter on the screen.

There is a command that controls this, though. It's the *Replace on Open* command, found on the View menu, and it's a toggle that's off by default. When it's turned on, the contents of the directory window are replaced when you open a new directory from the Directory Tree window. The directory window's contents are replaced with the new directory's file names. This is a convenience, eliminating unnecessary windows that would be left around when you're examining various directories.

When turned off, it allows any number of directories to be displayed, each in its own window.

Though your screen stays neater when Replace on Open is on, there are advantages to using the default (off) setting. With multiple windows open, you can rearrange, close, iconize, or maximize the directories just as you would any other window. Tiling and cascading are particularly useful for this. You can also switch drives without losing a directory listing. Figure 4.10 shows a number of directories open in separate windows.

1. Open the View menu. Set the Replace on Open command to *off* if it isn't already (no checkmark).

2. Click on the Directory Tree window to activate it.

3. Open as many directories as you wish by clicking on the desired directory icon. Each new directory will be given its own window. The title bar indicates the directory and whether a filter is in use.

4. Use the Tile or Cascade commands to organize the windows for easier use. If you expect to need quick access to the directories later, adjust the windows to a usable size, then iconize them. The next time you double click them, they'll pop up in the size and location you left them.

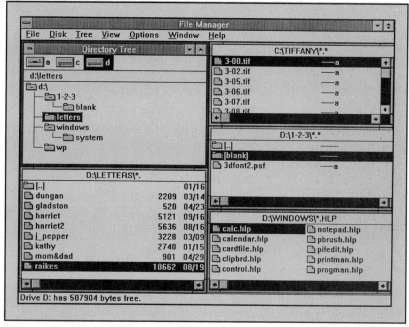

Figure 4.10: You can have multiple directory listings all on the screen at once. Turn off the Replace on Open setting to prevent erasure of the directory window's contents when you open a new directory.

REFRESHING THE DIRECTORY

Sometimes other programs will affect the contents of a directory window that's open. For example, you might switch to a program window and edit a file that's also displayed in the directory window, changing its size. Normally Windows will take care of this type of situation, updating the information in any directory window after it senses that another program has altered a file. However, there are times when this doesn't happen reliably. Particularly, when you are connected to a network, Windows may have trouble detecting that a directory's contents have changed. This will also be an issue if you change floppy disks and want to see the directory of the new disk. If you suspect that a directory may have been changed in some way that isn't reflected in the directory window, just press F5 or choose the Window ⇨ Refresh command.

SEARCHING FOR A SPECIFIC FILE

Looking for a specific file when you can't remember where it is on your hard disk can be a real headache. If you have a lot of directories, opening each one and examining the files can take a ridiculous amount of time. Even in DOS, the DIR command is no help, since you have to keep switching directories and retyping the command. Some utility programs such as Norton's File Find are real time savers if you're using DOS. But what about within Windows? Well, the Microsoft people were thoughtful enough to build such a utility into the File Manager—only it's better because the files it finds are plopped into a window that you can keep on the screen or iconized for later access. Here's how to use it:

1. Select File ⇨ Search.

2. A dialog box appears, similar to the one in Figure 4.11. Type in the name of the file you're looking for. Use wildcards if you want. If you want to search the whole disk, check the Search Entire Disk box. Otherwise only the current directory and all it's subordinant directories will be searched. (By *current* I mean the one highlighted in the Directory Tree or the one in the active window.)

3. Click OK. Windows will look all over the current disk (floppy or hard) and report its search results in a new directory window called Search Results. If no files are found, a message to that effect will appear on the screen.

The next time you conduct a search, the Search window's contents will be erased and then replaced with the new search results.

SELECTING FILES IN A DIRECTORY WINDOW

Before you can work with the files in a directory, you have to select one or more of them. As with other objects in Windows, you select files by highlighting them. Here are various methods of selecting (and deselecting) files:

To Select One File

❐ Click once on the file. Notice that the status line (the last line in the File Manager window) indicates that one file is selected.

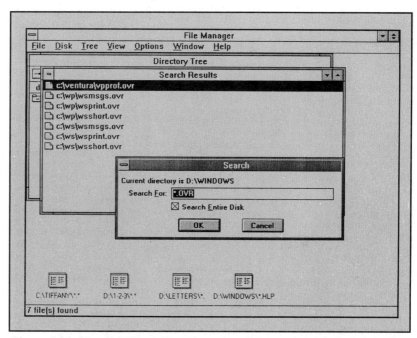

Figure 4.11: Use the File ⇨ Search command to search the entire disk for a specific file or group of files. Here you see the results of a search for all files with the extension *.ovr.*

To Select More Than One File

1. Click on the first file to select.

2. Press the Ctrl key and hold it down.

3. Click on each additional file you want to select.

To Select a Group of Consecutive Files

1. Click on the first file in the series.

2. Press the Shift key and hold it down.

3. Move to the bottom of the group you want to select and click again. All the files between the first and last click will be selected.

To Select Several Groups of Consecutive Files

1. Select the first group as described above.

2. To select the second group, hold down the Ctrl key and click on the first file in the second group.

3. Press the Shift and Ctrl keys simultaneously and click on the last file in the second group. Repeat steps 2 and 3 for each additional group.

Figure 4.12 shows three groups of files selected in this way.

To Select All the Files in a Directory

❒ Choose File ⇨ Select All.

SPEED TIP Don't overlook the possibility of selecting a series of files with the help of the Search command. If all the files have names that are similar, use this to create a search window. Then select all the files in the resulting window. Another trick is to use the Sort commands in the View menu to help organize files for easier selecting.

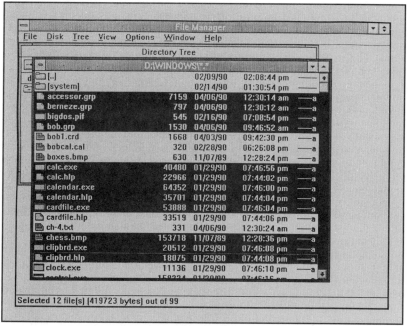

Figure 4.12: You can select several nonconsecutive groups of files

To Deselect File(s)

❐ To deselect *all* the files currently selected, either click on a single file (release the Shift key first), or choose File ⇨ Deselect All.

❐ To deselect a single file from a group of selected files, hold down the Ctrl key and click on the file again.

Once highlighted, a file or group of files can be operated on via the commands in the File menu. Open the File menu and you will see the commands shown in Figure 4.13. Here's what each one does (a few are not explained here because they are discussed elsewhere):

COMMAND	EFFECT
Open	Opens a document file, such as a letter, report, or worksheet, by running the program associated with it, and then opening the document itself. You can also open a document by double clicking it. Except for the supplied Windows programs, this requires setting up an association first (as discussed later in this chapter). If the file is a program, this runs the program. The file must be a program file (with a *.bat, .exe, .com,* or *.pif* extension). You can also run a program by double clicking on it.
Run	Presents a dialog box into which you can type a program name (with a *.bat, .exe, .com,* or *.pif* extension). This is like typing a program name from the DOS prompt.
Print	Prints text files. Use it only with ASCII files, such as those created by Notepad.
Associate	Tells Windows what application a document was created with. The program will then be run when you open the document. This command will be discussed later in the chapter.
Move	Moves file(s) to another directory or drive.
Copy	Copies file(s) to another directory or drive.
Delete	Deletes selected file(s).
Rename	Renames selected file(s).
Change Attributes	Sets the DOS file flags for selected file(s). Flags are explained below, in the section titled "Changing File Attributes."

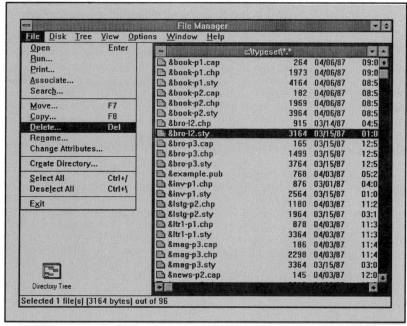

Figure 4.13: To work with a file, select it by clicking on it. Then open the File menu. Notice the status line, which indicates number of files selected and total size of the selected file(s).

CREATING ASSOCIATIONS

An association is simply a way of telling Windows what program to run for each type of file extension. For example, if you click on a file that has a *.crd* extension, Windows will run the Cardfile program *(cardfile.exe)* and open the file you clicked on. There is already an association made up for *.crd* files and stored in the Windows program, which is why this works. But you can make up your own associations.

For example, say you use lots of 1-2-3 files. Many 1-2-3 files have the extension *.wks.* You can set up an association that tells Windows "when I click on a *.wks* file, run Lotus 1-2-3 and open the file I clicked on."

Obviously the trick to using associations is to have a consistent system for your file's extensions. Not all programs require specific extensions, so you may have to impose your own rules. For example, I never use extensions on my word-processing files—I just keep them in separate directories, one for each program. To use an association, I'd have to start adding some unique extension to my file names. I could use *.ws* for my WordStar files, *.pcw* for my PC-Write files, and so on.

These are most important associations that are already set up:

FILE EXTENSION	*ASSOCIATED PROGRAM*
.crd	Cardfile
.cal	Calendar
.hlp	Help
.trm	Terminal
.txt	Notepad
.ini	Notepad (these files are used by Windows)
.wrt	Write
.bmp	Paint

All associated files are assigned a special icon (called a document icon) in the directory windows so that you can see which documents can be opened just by double clicking them. The icon is a lined page with a bent corner.

Making the Association

To actually set up an association you just perform the following steps once. It will then affect all programs with the same extension.

1. Open a directory that contains a file you want to make an association for.

2. Single click on any document that has the extension in question. If you double click, you'll get an error message saying that there isn't an association for that type of file.

3. Choose File ⇨ Associate. A dialog box will appear (Figure 4.14). Enter the exact name and path of the program that you want to run when you double click this type of file. (If your path command contains the directory the program is in, you can omit the directory.)

In Figure 4.14, I've created an association between .*chp* files and Ventura Publisher Professional. Since Ventura uses a batch file in the root directory to start up with, I've used the name of the batch file.

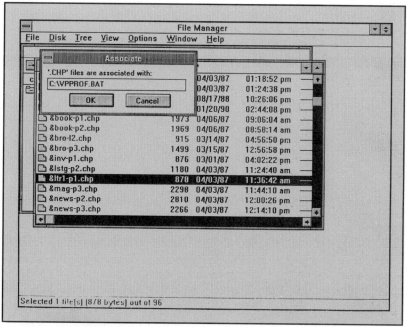

Figure 4.14: Creating an association. This setup links all .*chp* files with Ventura Publisher. After this, when any .*chp* file is double clicked, Windows will run vpprof.bat and tell Ventura to open the selected document.

OPENING DOCUMENTS FROM THE FILE MANAGER

Once documents are associated with applications, you can open them easily from the File Manager.

❐ Double click the file name or icon in a directory window. Windows will run the application and open the document in a window. If the program can't run in a window and requires full-screen mode, the File Manager will disappear until you exit the program.

If a document doesn't have an association, you can still tell Windows to open it. However it's a little tricky. Here are the steps:

1. Open the directory containing the document.

2. Open the directory containing the application program (if they're not both in the same directory)

3. If you have two windows open, adjust them so both their contents can be seen.

4. Drag the document's icon into the application's icon and release the mouse. Along the way, the document's icon might turn into a circle with a line through it, but when you line it up on the application file, it will return to the correct shape.

A dialog box will ask you to confirm the action (Figure 4.15). In this instance I dragged the document *d-hidy.ed* into *ed.exe* (PC-Write).

RUNNING PROGRAMS FROM THE FILE MANAGER

As mentioned earlier, you can run programs directly from the File Manager. You do not have to return to the Program Manager to bring up a DOS prompt or create a program icon.

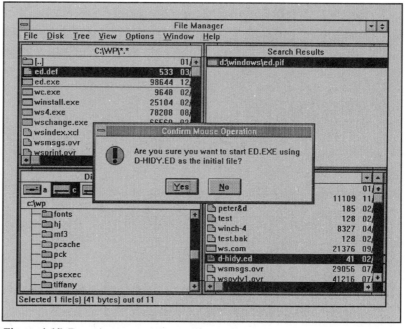

Figure 4.15: Running a program and opening a document at the same time. To do so, drag the document icon into the applications icon.

This is most useful for occasionally running a program that you don't use often. Here are two ways to run programs:

❐ Double click on the program name. It should be an *.exe,* *.com,* or *.bat* extension.

❐ Choose File ⇨ Run. Type the name of the program into the dialog box. Include the path name if it's not part of your system's path command. (Always include the extension.)

PRINTING FROM THE FILE MANAGER

You can print certain files from the File Manager, as long as they are simple ASCII files (files with no control codes in them). The File ⇨ Print command sends the selected file to the printer port, using Windows' Print Manager. There are a few advantages to this approach, but generally it's better to print from your application program so that you get all the page formatting you expect.

If however, you just want to print simple files, such as files created by SideKick, PC-Write, or the Notepad, you can. One advantage of printing from the File Manager is that it lets you send text to a PostScript printer. Since some applications don't support PostScript printers, this is a nifty way of typing out plain ASCII files you've created with them. Also, because the Print Manager does the printing, the files will be *spooled*, which is a process wherein printing is done behind the scenes, letting you get back to work. (The Print Manager and spooler are covered in detail in Chapters 6 and 7.)

To print this way:

1. Select the file you want to print.

2. Choose File ⇨ Print. A dialog box appears with the file's name typed in, as you can see in Figure 4.16. Change it if you want to, and then click on OK .

MOVING FILES BETWEEN DIRECTORIES AND DRIVES

Sometimes you'll want to move a file or group of files from one directory to another. Once again, this is a process that is normally a real pain from the DOS prompt, requiring you to copy the files to the new directory, and then erase the old ones.

The File Manager makes this potentially tedious task a breeze. You select the files to be moved, and then drag them as a group to the new destination. (Keep in mind that moving is not copying. After the operation, there is still only one copy of the files you've moved—they're just in a new location.)

The new destination can be an open window, an iconized window, a folder in the Directory Tree window, a disk drive icon in the Directory Tree window, or a group icon or window in the Program Manager. You've got a lot of choices. The rule of

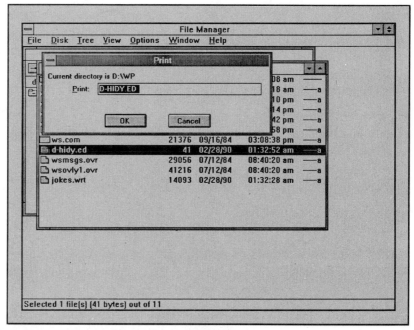

Figure 4.16: Printing a file from the File Manager

thumb is—if you want to move it, try selecting it and dragging it to the new location. If Windows can't do it, you'll be told, but the chances are good that you can drag a file or a directory to almost any icon or window.

Here are the general steps for moving files around.

1. Open the directory containing the file(s) you want to move.

2. Adjust your display so that an icon, folder, or window of the destination is visible. Tiling the windows can make this easier.

3. Select the file(s) you want to move.

4. If you are moving files to a directory on a different disk drive, hold down the Alt key. (You can skip this step if you are moving files to a different directory on the *same* drive.)

5. Click on one of the selected files and drag them into the destination icon, folder, or window. As you do so, the mouse pointer will change to a document icon. (If you're moving more than one file, the icon will look like three little folders.)

6. Release the mouse button (and then the Alt key, if you're moving to another drive). You'll see a dialog box asking you to confirm that you want to move the files, as shown in Figure 4.17.

7. Click Yes to complete the move.

MOVING DIRECTORIES

In addition to enabling you to move files easily, the File Manager lets you move complete directories. When you move

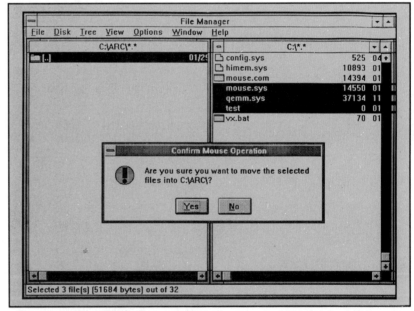

Figure 4.17: To move files, select them and drag their icons to their new destination. Hold the Alt key down if you're moving them between drives.

a directory, all the files in the directory are moved automatically.

You can select the directory to be moved either from the directory tree or from a directory window. First-level directories are listed in the root window (double click on the root icon of the tree to open the root window).

When you move a directory to another directory, Windows adds it *below* the destination directory. When you move a directory to a new drive, Windows adds it below the current active directory.

More often than not, people want to move directories around on the same drive, a bit like rearranging their furniture. This is extremely easy with the File Manager. After using this feature, you'll wonder how you ever did without it.

1. Open the directory tree for the drive containing the directories you want to rearrange.

2. Select the directory you want to move and drag it to its new location. As you slide the mouse over its possible targets, a line forms around the target, indicating where the directory will land if you release the mouse button. If you are moving the directory between drives, hold the Alt key down while dragging.

3. When you release the mouse button (and, if necessary, the Alt key), the directory will be added as a subdirectory one level below the destination directory (and any subdirectories will be arrayed below it as before).

Moving Multiple Directories Simultaneously

You can move the contents of more than one directory at a time, but you have to do this from a directory window, not from the Directory Tree window. For example, suppose you wanted to move directories \one, \two, and \three to be subdirectories under a directory called \four. You could do this by dragging one directory at a time as explained above. But it's faster to do it in one fell swoop. Open the root directory, and select the directories [one], [two], and [three]. Drag them as a group from the root window into [four]. Figure 4.18 shows one way of doing this and the resulting dialog box. Figure 4.19 shows the change to the directory tree. Notice that directories \one, \two, and \three were added under \four as subdirectories. When moving directories, the File Manager asks if you want to delete the original directory. If you want to keep the original (thus copying instead of moving the directory) click on No. If you really want to *move* the directory and its contents, click on Yes.

Entering the Destination from the Keyboard

Sometimes just typing in the name of the destination is easier than dragging the files and directory icons around, especially if you're fast at the keyboard. With this technique, the destination

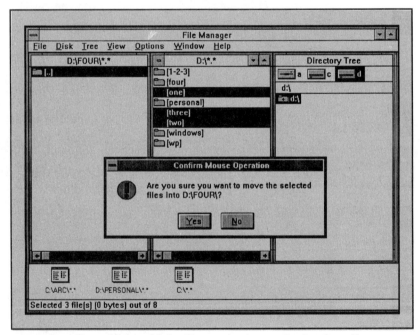

Figure 4.18: Dragging multiple directories into a destination directory. The source directories will become subdirectories of the destination directory.

does not have to be visible. Just select the source files or directories and choose File ⇨ Move. Type the name of the destination into the dialog box that appears. Figure 4.20 shows an example of this. Notice that if multiple files are selected, the From box lists them all, end to end, with a space separating the names. You can type in more names this way, or leave the From line alone. You *do* have to type in the destination drive and directory. When moving a directory, remember that it will be added *below* the destination directory.

MOVING FILES AND DIRECTORIES TO ANOTHER DISK DRIVE

Moving files and directories to another disk drive can be done two ways. The first way uses the approaches described above. That is, you open windows for the source and destination, then

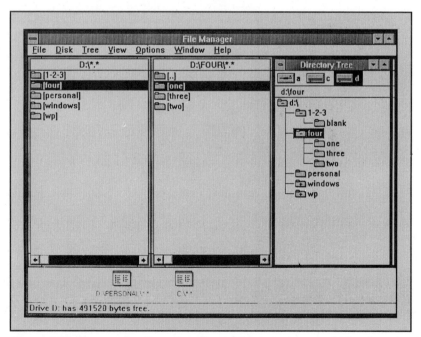

Figure 4.19: The result of moving directories *one*, *two*, and *three* into directory *four*. Notice the altered directory tree.

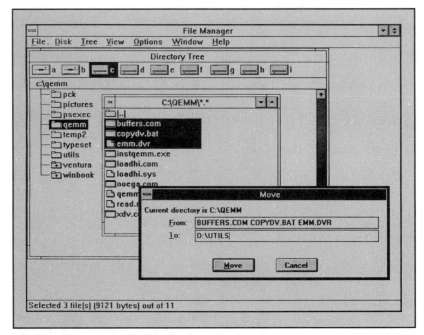

Figure 4.20: You can use the File ⇨ Move command to move files. This is sometimes easier than setting up the screen to accomdate the dragging technique of file moving. Simply select the files, choose File ⇨ Move, and type in the destination directory.

drag the directories or files from the one to the other. The trick to remember is that only one tree window can be open at a time, so you have to use two directory windows to copy between drives with this technique. Of course you can also use the Move command and type in the destination drive and directory, which is sometimes the easiest thing to do.

However, there's one more trick you should know. You can drag selected files or directories to another drive using the drive icons at the top of the tree window. The File Manager will use the current directory of the target drive as the final destination.

To do this,

1. Open an appropriate tree or directory window for the source files or directories.

2. Select the files or directories.

3. Hold down the Alt key, since you're moving them to another drive.

4. Drag them into the destination drive icon at the top of the directory tree window. The icon you're dragging may temporarily become a circle with a line through it, but it will revert when you align it with the drive icon. If you're moving the dierctories or files to drive A, make sure you have a formatted floppy disk in the drive, or you will get an error messsage.

5. A dialog box will ask if you want to move the items. Click Yes. If the dialog box asks about copying (not moving), you forgot to hold down the Alt key. Cancel and try again.

6. After you move a directory, the File Manager asks if you want to delete the original. When moving files, you are not asked this (they are just deleted).

NOTE When you move a whole directory by clicking on its name in a directory window, the File Manager *doesn't* tell you the collective size of the files you're about to copy! This can be a real bummer. But if you open the directory in a window and select all the files with the File ⇨ Select All command, the status line will then report the size.

When you move files to a floppy, there may not be enough room on the floppy for all the source files. File Manager shows you how many bytes you've got selected down at the bottom of its window. When you click on the directory window for the floppy, the status bar tells you how much room is left on it. So, if you open one window for the floppy and one for the hard disk directory you're copying from, you can switch back and forth between the two to make sure you aren't going to run out of space during the copying process. Figure 4.21 shows one possible setup.

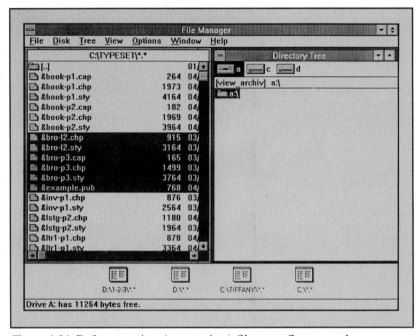

Figure 4.21: Before moving (or copying) files to a floppy, make sure you have enough room. Check the status line for the available space on the floppy and then the total size of the files selected.

COPYING FILES

Copying differs from moving in that copying duplicates the items you're working with. Copying is most often used for transferring files to other computers via floppy disk. It's also often used as a safety procedure. If you copy a file or directory, then you have a backup in case of some catastrophe like spilling your Monday morning cappuccino on the floppy containing your tax return spreadsheet or the Ph.D. dissertation you just spent five years researching. The other thing it protects you against is the ominous "hard-disk crash." That's when your hard disk unexplicably croaks, taking everything with it.

Though there are programs specifically designed to back up your entire hard disk in an efficient manner, the copy command is useful for making backups of individual files.

NOTE Just as with moving, you can stipulate the source and destinations of items by selecting the File ⇨ Copy command. If you select the source items using the mouse, they'll be inserted into the From line. Then you just type in the To information.

SPEED TIP You can copy program files or document files from a File Manager window to a Program Manager window or group icon. To do this, arrange your screen so the destination icon or window in the Program Manager is showing. Then drag the selected directory or files from File Manager into it. You will only be allowed to copy applications or documents (that have associated applications) this way.

You copy files and directories virtually the same way you move them (see the previous section), with a couple exceptions.

1. Arrange the screen so that source and destination windows, icons, files, or drives are visible.

2. Select the item(s) to be copied.

3. Press the Ctrl key (instead of the Alt key, as you do when moving).

4. Drag the items to their destination drive, icon, window or directory.

5. Answer dialog boxes appropriately. Check the dialog box to make sure it says Copy, not Move. Make sure you see the correct destinations, too. If not, type in the changes or try again.

After a copy, the originals are left intact, so you don't have to worry about losing anything if you make a mistake. The only thing to worry about is copying a file on top of a file with the same name. The File Manager will ask you if you want to overwrite the old file with the new one, unless you have turned off this confirmation message (see the next section, "Changing the Confirmation Settings").

CHANGING THE CONFIRMATION SETTINGS

The File Manager has some safeguards against accidental erasure of files and directories. Usually, it's a good idea to leave these settings as they are. Once you have more experience with the ways of the File Manager, though, you might want to change them so they don't nag you every time you want to overwrite an old file, or delete a directory that has a bunch of subdirectories under it.

1. Choose Options ⇨ Confirmation

2. The dialog box shown in Figure 4.22 appears. The settings have the following meanings:

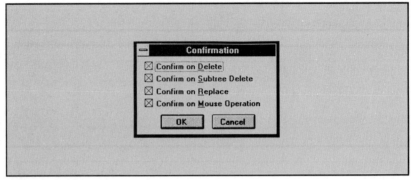

Figure 4.22: Setting the Confirmation options. Be cautious about changing these. Confirmation helps to prevent accidental erasures.

BUTTON	IF THE CHECK BOX IS SET ON
Confirm on Delete	Asks for okay to delete files.
Confirm on Subtree Delete	Asks for okay to delete directories.
Confirm on Replace	Asks for okay to overwrite an existing file.
Confirm on Mouse Operation	Asks for okay any time you attempt to copy, delete, or move files or directories with the mouse.

DELETING FILES

Deleting files means erasing them! It's difficult to recover them after they're deleted. Delete a file or files by following these steps:

1. Select the file(s).

2. Choose File ⇨ Delete. A dialog box appears.

3. Check the information in the box. If it's correct, click OK. If not, cancel it or change the information by typing in

another file name. You can add a drive letter and path, just as with the *DEL* command in DOS.

RENAMING FILES AND DIRECTORIES

Renaming files is done in a manner similar to deleting. It simply changes the name of the file or directory selected. This command can also be used with directories.

1. Select the item to be renamed. If it's a file, you must select it in a directory window.

2. Choose File ➪ Rename. A dialog box appears.

3. Type in the new name and click on Rename.

CHANGING FILE ATTRIBUTES

Changing file attributes is easier with Windows than with DOS, by far. You simply select the files, open a dialog box and set the check boxes appropriately. The most common setting change for files is to set them to Read Only. Once this is set, nobody can accidentally erase or overwrite them.

Here's how to set the various attributes:

1. Select the file(s) whose attributes you want to alter.

2. Choose File ➪ Change Attributes.

3. The following dialog box appears.

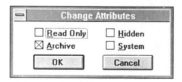

Check the boxes appropriately. Here are the meanings of the choices:

Setting	*If Set On*
Read Only	Won't allow users to make changes to the file.
Archive	Indicates the file has been modified. This is used by backup programs such as the DOS *BACKUP* command.
Hidden	Will hide the file from directory listings in DOS and directory windows in File Manager (unless you choose View ➪ Include ➪ Show Hidden).
System	Tells Windows and DOS that this is an operating system file. It will normally be hidden.

WORKING WITH DISKS

NOTE Working with network drives is discussed in Appendix C.

The file manager has a few features that apply specifically to managing your disks, particularly floppy disks. These commands make the process of formatting disks and copying disks a bit simpler. There's also a command for changing the *volume label* of a disk, the optional name that each floppy or hard disk can be assigned, typically for archival purposes.

FORMATTING DISKS
AND MAKING SYSTEM DISKS

CAUTION Formatting erases all data from the disk! There isn't even the slightest hope of recovery!

What with the myriad disk capacities and sizes around these days, formatting a floppy disk can turn out to be quite an exercise in futility. The DOS manual is usually not much help either. There are enough options to the format command to choke a rhino. Well, you might become a real fan of Windows just for this command. Here's how to format a disk now:

1. Put the disk to be formatted in the floppy drive and close the door (or push the button, etc.).

2. Choose Disk ⇨ Format Diskette.

3. If you have more than one floppy drive, a dialog box appears letting you choose drive A or B. (If you have only one, the program assumes you are fomatting drive A.) Click OK.

4. The dialog box you see below now appears. Click on Format.

5. Now you are asked to choose the capacity of the format from the dialog box below:

Select the correct capacity. If High Capacity is not checked off, then the disk will be formatted as 360K for a 5¼-inch disk or 720K for a 3½-inch disk. Select Make System Disk if you want the disk you're formatting to be able to boot up a computer from the A drive. The necessary hidden system files will be copied to it during the formatting process.

6. Click OK and the formatting begins. You will be apprised of the progress.

COPYING DISKS

You can make copies of disks two ways. If the disks are the same capacities, you can use the Disk ⇨ Copy Diskette command. If they are not, you can't. Then you have to use the File ⇨ Copy command as explained earlier. Just select all the files with wildcards (*.*) in the From section of the Copy dialog box.

If the two diskettes have the same capacities, use the Copy Diskette command (it's faster). However, be aware that this command, like the DOS *DISKCOPY* command erases everything on the destination disk before creating an exact copy of the source disk.

1. Put the source disk in one drive and the destination disk in the other. If you only have one drive, insert the source disk in it.

2. Click on the drive icon for the source disk.

3. Choose Disk ⇨ Copy Diskette.

4. If you have two drives, you'll have to choose the destination drive from the dialog box.

5. Follow the instructions on the screen. If you only have one drive, you'll have to swap the disks a few times.

CHANGING A DISK'S LABEL

All floppy and hard disks can have a *volume label*. This is not the paper label on the outside, but a name encoded into the directory on the disk. It shows up when you type DIR at the DOS prompt and on the top line of the Directory Tree window when you switch to that drive in File Manager. The label really serves no functional purpose other than to identify the disk for archiving purposes. Newly formatted disks have no label. However, you can add one or change the label should you need or want to. Here's how.

1. Insert the disk in the drive.

2. Choose Disk ➪ Label Disk.

3. Type the label into the dialog box (up to 11 characters) and click on OK.

CHAPTER FIVE

5

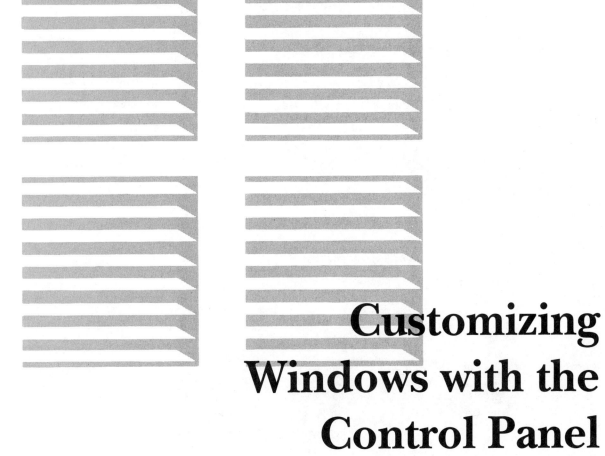

Customizing Windows with the Control Panel

Fast Track

CHAPTER 5

NOTE Two of the Control Panel options, *Printer* and *386 Enhanced* are not covered in this chapter. Refer to Chapter 6 for information about setting up printers and to Chapter 14 for details regarding multitasking operations while running in 386 mode.

THOUGH YOU MAY, UP TO THIS TIME, HAVE BEEN using Windows pretty much as it comes from Microsoft, there are numerous alterations you can make to customize Windows to your liking. These things include screen colors, mouse speed, keyboard repeat rate, and so forth. Most of these adjustments are not necessities as much as they are niceties that make using Windows just a little easier. These adjustments are made via the Control Panel. Once set, the changes are stored in the Windows initialization file (win.ini) and loaded when you run Windows again.

RUNNING THE CONTROL PANEL

You open the Control Panel by switching to the Program Manager, opening the Main group, and double clicking on the Control Panel icon. The Control Panel window then opens, as shown in Figure 5.1.

There will be between 10 to 12 items to choose from, depending on whether or not you are running Windows in 386 Enhanced mode and/or using a network. You will see the 386 Enhanced icon only if you are running in that mode and the network icon only if you are currently hooked up to and running on a network.

ICON	USED FOR
Color	Setting the colors (or gray levels) of various parts of Windows' screens, title bars, scroll bars, and so forth.

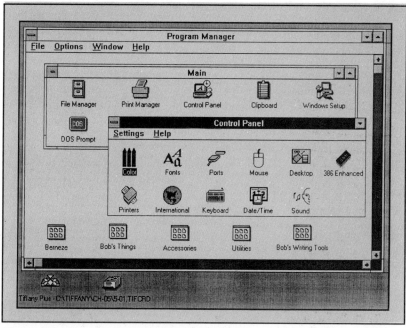

Figure 5.1: The control panel window. Each item opens a window from which you can make adjustments.

Fonts	Adding and deleting typefaces for your screen display and printer output.
Ports	Setting up the serial port on your computer for use with various communications programs and serial printers.
Mouse	Setting the speed of the mouse pointer's motion relative to your hand motion, and for setting how fast a double click has to be to have an effect. You can also reverse the functions of the right and left buttons.
Desktop	Setting the background pattern or picture for your desktop (it doesn't have to be just a plain color). Also used to set the blinking rate of the cursor.

Network	Varies with the network type. Possibly lets you log on and off the network.
Printers	Selecting which printer to print to, which port to use, and which paper orientation and size will be used when you print. Also used to install printer "drivers." (Printers and printer drivers are covered in Chapter 6.)
International	Setting how Windows displays things that vary from country to country, such as times, dates, numbers, and currency.
Keyboard	Setting the rate at which keys repeat when you hold them down.
Date/Time	Setting the current date and time.
Sound	Turning off and on the computer's beep.
386 Enhanced	Setting specifics about time and resource contention between programs running simultaneously in 386 mode.

SETTING THE SCREEN COLORS

The Color icon lets you change the way Windows assigns color to various parts of the screen. If you're using a monochrome monitor (no color), altering the colors may still have some effect (the amount will depend on how you installed Windows with Setup), so it's not just for systems with color screens.

Windows sets itself up using a default color scheme that's fine for most screens, and if you're happy with it, you might not even want to futz around. However, the color settings options for Windows are very flexible and easy to modify. The Microsoft people really give you a lot of bang for your buck here, so why not experiment? You can modify the color setting of just about any part of a Windows screen. For those of you who are very particular, this can be done manually, choosing colors from a palette. Once created, they can be saved on disk for later use.

For more expedient color reassignments, there's a supplied number of "canned" color schemes that you can easily choose.

Upon opening the Color window, you see the dialog box shown in Figure 5.2.

The various parts of the windows graphical environment that you can alter are shown (and named) in the bottom portion of the dialog box. As you select color schemes, these samples change so that you can see what the effect will be without having to go back into Windows proper.

LOADING AN EXISTING COLOR SCHEME

Before playing with the custom color palette, first try loading the supplied ones. You may find one you like.

1. Open the drop-down color scheme list (drop-down lists are opened by clicking on the arrow at the far right of the current selection—probably Windows Default).

2. Choose a selection whose name suits your fancy. The

NOTE In some cases the screen driver that you chose when installing Windows has some effect on the display of colors, too. You may want to experiment with these by running Setup again (it's an icon in the Main group) and choosing a variation on your display type from the drop-down list. Specifically, if you're using a monochrome VGA display that can render colors as "shades of gray," selecting the normal VGA option (which is color) and then experimenting with the colors schemes can give you a more pleasing display. Your setup will have the new 3-D look (it's not apparent when you install the monochrome driver). In fact, the figures for this book were taken from just such a setup, with some fine tuning for the scroll and title bars.

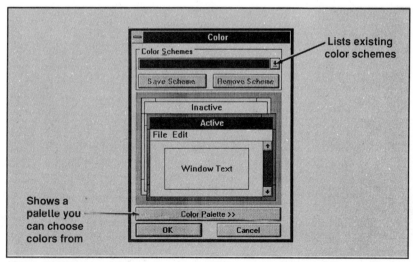

Figure 5.2: The dialog box for setting the colors. Choose existing color schemes or click on Define Colors to set up your own.

colors in the dialog box change, showing the scheme.
Try them out. Some are garish, others more subtle. Adjusting your monitor may make a difference, too.

3. Click OK, and the settings are applied to all Windows
   activities.

CHOOSING YOUR OWN COLORS

If you don't like the colors schemes supplied, you can make
up your own. It's most efficient to start with one that's close to
what you want, and then modify it. Once you like the settings,
you save it under a new name. Then it's there any time you want
it. Here are the steps:

1. Click on the Color Palette button. This expands the dialog box, as shown in Figure 5.3. You now have 48 colors
   to choose from, and another drop-down list.

2. From the drop-down list, choose the element of the
   screen that you want to alter.

3. Click on one of the 48 colors (or intensity levels, if you
   have a monochrome monitor) to assign it to the chosen
   element.

4. Once the color scheme suits your fancy, you can save it.
   (It will stay in force for future Windows sessions even if
   you don't save it, but you'll lose the settings next time
   you change colors or select another scheme.) Click on
   Save Scheme.

5. Type in a name for the color scheme and click OK.

If you want to remove a scheme (such as one you never use),
select it from the drop-down list, and then click on the Remove
Scheme button.

NOTE You have
to use solid colors
for the following ele-
ments: Window Frame,
Window Text, Window
Background, Menu Bar,
Menu Text, and Title
Bar Text. If you use a
nonsolid color (a color
with a dot pattern),
Windows adjusts it to
become a similarly
tinted solid color.

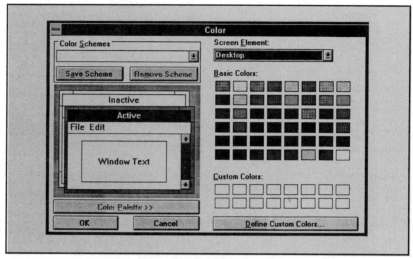

Figure 5.3: The expanded Colors dialog box. Choose an element and then assign a color by clicking on it.

MAKING UP YOUR OWN COLORS

If you don't like the colors that are available, you can create your own. There are 16 slots at the bottom of the color palette for storing colors you set using another fancy dialog box called the *color refiner.*

1. Click on Define Custom Colors in the expanded Color dialog box. The Custom Color Selector appears (Figure 5.4).

2. There are two cursors that you work with here. One is the luminosity bar, and the other is the color refiner cursor. To make a long story short, you simply drag these around one at a time until the color in the box at the lower left is the shade you want. As you do, the numbers in the boxes below the color refiner will change. You can also type in the numbers or click on the arrows next to the numbers if you want, but it's easier to use the cursors. When you like the color, click on Add Color, and

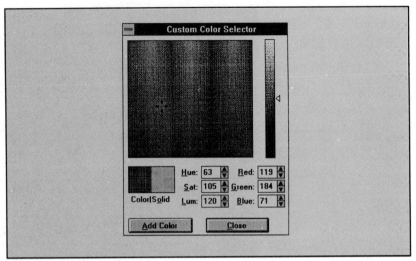

Figure 5.4:   The custom color selector lets you create new custom colors

the new color is added to the palette.

- *Luminosity* is the amount of brightness in the color.

- *Hue* is the actual shade or color. All colors are composed of red, green and blue.

- *Saturation* is the degree of purity of the color. Saturation is decreased by adding gray to the color, and increased by subtracting it.

3. You can switch between a solid color and a color made up of various dots of several colors. The solid colors will look less grainy on your screen, but give you fewer choices. The Color/Solid box shows the difference between the two. If you click on this box before adding the color to the palette, the solid color closest to the actual color you chose will be added instead of the grainier composite color.

4. Once a color is added to the palette, you can modify it. Just click on it, move the cursors around and then click Add Color again.

5. Click on Close to close the color refiner box. Then continue to assign colors with the palette.

6. When you are content with the color assignments, click OK. If you decide after toying around that you don't want to implement the color changes, just click Cancel.

ADDING AND REMOVING FONTS

NOTE Actually, Webster's defines a font as "a complete assortment of printing types of one size and style." So, in that sense, each point size in each style (normal, bold, underline, italic) constitutes a different font. However, largely due to coloquial desktop publishing nomenclature, *font* has come to mean a typeface, such as Times or Helvetica in any size or style.

Fonts are the various type styles that you can use when composing a document, viewing it on the screen, or printing it on paper. If you have played with the Write program supplied with Windows, you may have tried typing in some text and changing the font via the Character menu. If you have, then you've seen several fonts display on your screen. Just as an example, three of the most popular type styles in today's printing are Courier, Times, and Helvetica.

This is Times
This is Courier
This is Helvetica

Fonts are specified by size as well as by name. The size of a font is measured in points. A point is $1/72$ of an inch.

This is 12 point Times

This is 18 point Avant Garde
This is 20 point Zapf Chancery

Windows comes supplied with a reasonable stock of fonts, some of which are installed on your hard disk and integrated into your Windows program during the setup procedure. The number and types of fonts installed depends on the type of screen and printer you have. When you told the Setup program what type of printer you had, a printer driver was installed. The printer driver takes care of installing all the Windows-supplied fonts that your printer can use.

However, some application programs, such as word processors, may have additional fonts supplied with them—fonts not supplied with Windows—that you may want to use. In addition to fonts that are supplied with application programs, you can also purchase font packages separately.

Regardless of where you get your fonts, the question is this: How do you tell Windows you've got them? In other words, how do you install them into your Windows setup? Sometimes, fonts come with their own installation programs, which automatically handle this detail when you copy the application program onto your hard disk. In this case, just follow the instructions in the supplied manual. In cases where there is, no such installation program, you can use the Control Panel's utility for installing (and removing) fonts.

NOTE Screen fonts for Windows 2 are usable with Windows 3.

There are two types of fonts to be considered—*screen fonts* and *printer fonts*. Screen fonts control how the letters look on your screen, while printer fonts handle your printout. Your printer may have fonts in it that Windows doesn't have screen fonts for. In most cases, though, Windows will handle day-to-day printing jobs just fine, and substitute another similar screen font with the correct size for displaying your work on the screen. Even though it might not look exactly like the final printout, the line length and page breaks on your screen will be right.

ADDING FONTS

To add a font, follow these steps.

1. Make sure the new font you want to install is on your hard disk.

2. Open the Fonts window by double clicking on its icon in the Control Panel window. The dialog box is shown in Figure 5.5. All the installed fonts are displayed in the Installed Fonts section.

3. Click on any font name and you'll see an example of it displayed in the lower portion of the box. The words (All res) means the font is a *vector* font, and can be displayed in any size. Otherwise, the screen sizes supplied will be listed. (This is not a necessary step, it's just useful to see what font types are installed in your system.)

4. Click on Add. A file box (a dialog box that lets you choose a directory and file name) appears now, as shown in Figure 5.6. Choose the new font file that you want to add.

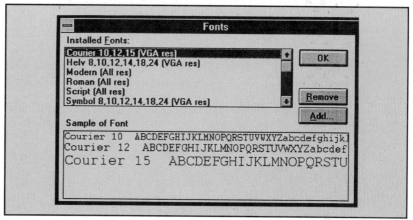

Figure 5.5: Checking the installed fonts

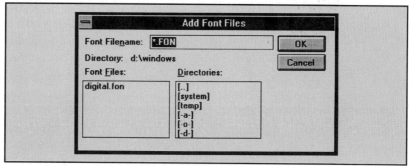

Figure 5.6: Choosing a font file to install

5. Click on OK. The font is then added to the list.

REMOVING FONTS

Removing fonts is similar to adding fonts, except you use the Remove button. Deleting fonts increases the available memory in your computer, letting you run more programs simultaneously. If you are having memory limitation problems, you could gain some room by eliminating fonts you never use. However, don't remove the Helvetica font, since it's used in all the Windows dialog boxes.

To remove a font, follow these steps:

1. Open the Fonts window by clicking on its icon in the Control Panel window. The dialog box in Figure 5.5 comes up. All the installed fonts are displayed in the Installed Fonts section.

2. Select the name of the font file you want to remove.

3. Click on Remove.

4. Click on OK. The font is removed.

SETTING THE SERIAL PORTS

If you've ever used the DOS *MODE* command to set up the communications parameters of your computer's serial COM ports, you know that it's a hassle to remember the exact syntax and arguments (arguments are the numbers and letters you type in after the command) required for a specific setup. Since most programs that use the serial ports (such as communications program, mouse drivers, or slow-speed networks) take care of setting the COM ports, it's rare that you need to deal with these directly anyway. As a case in point, the Terminal program supplied with Windows has its own dialog box for making the appropriate settings for baud rate, parity, stop and start bits, etc.

But there is the occasional exception, such as when you're using a serial printer connected to a COM port, and you need to initialize the port's settings.

In any case, should the need arise, the Control Panel lets you easily set the COM port parameters, and it sure beats using the MODE command to do it, since you just choose the settings from a dialog box. Here's how:

1. Double click the Ports icon in the Control Panel window. A dialog box appears (Figure 5.7).

2. You can set up the parameters of any of the four possible COM ports. (LPT ports cannot be altered because they are not serial ports and do not have settings.) Click on the icon corresponding to the port you want to alter. A second dialog box pops up, as shown in Figure 5.8.

3. Now make the settings applicable to the job you're doing. The settings should match the settings of the equipment you are connecting to the port. If you're in doubt about them, consult the manual supplied with the external equipment. You may also want to refer to a book specializing in the use of asynchronous serial communications interfaces, such as *The RS-232 Solution, Second Edition,* by Joe Campbell (SYBEX).

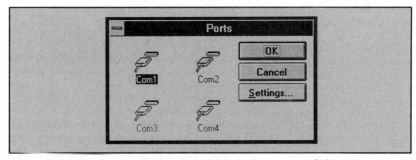

Figure 5.7: Setting the COM ports. Choose the port and then click on Settings.

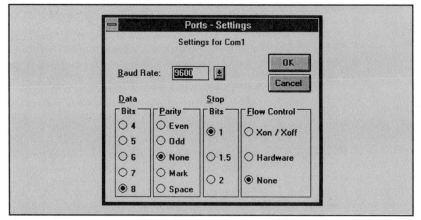

Figure 5.8: Choosing the settings for a COM port

ADJUSTING THE MOUSE

You can adjust three aspects of your mouse's operation:

- Tracking speed
- Double-click speed
- Left-right button reversal

Tracking speed is the speed at which the mouse pointer moves relative to the movement of the mouse. Believe it or not, mouse motion is actually measured in "Mickeys"! (Somebody out there has a sense of humor.) A Mickey equals ¹⁄₁₀₀th of an inch of mouse movement. The tracking-speed setting lets you adjust the relationship of Mickeys to *pixels*. Pixels are the dots on your screen. If you want to be very exact in your cursor movement, you'll want to slow the tracking speed, requiring more Mickeys per pixel. However, this requires more hand motion for the same corresponding cursor motion. If your desk is crammed and your coordination is very good, then you can increase the speed (fewer Mickeys per pixel). If you use the mouse with other programs (such as Ventura Publisher or AutoCAD), you might want to adjust the Windows mouse speed to match that

TIP Incidentally, if you think the mouse runs too slowly in your non-Windows applications, there is a fix. MouseWare is a memory-resident program that lets you adjust the tracking speed for non-Windows programs. It's available from Metroplex Digital Corporation, P.O. Box 815729 Dallas, TX 75381-5729. Phone (214) 231-8944. Also, if you're using a Logitech mouse, a program called Click that is supplied with the Logitech mouse lets you easily control the mouse tracking. See the Logitech manual for details.

of your other programs so you won't need to mentally adjust when you use such non-Windows programs.

Double-click speed determines how fast you have to double click to make a double-click operation work (that is, to run a program from its icon, to close a window by double clicking its Control box, or to select a word by double clicking on it while in Write). If the double-click speed is too fast, it's difficult to make things happen. If it's too slow, you end up running programs or opening and closing windows unexpectedly. However, I find the slowest speed to work well for me.

Left-right button reversal simply switches the function of your mouse's buttons. For lefties, being able to switch the mouse buttons may be a boon. If you use other programs outside of Windows that don't allow this, then it might just add to the confusion. If you only use the mouse in Windows programs and you're left handed, then it's worth a try.

Here are the steps for changing Mouse options:

1. Double click on the Mouse icon in the Control Panel window. The dialog box you see in Figure 5.9 appears.

2. Drag the sliders within their scroll bars to adjust the mouse parameters.

3. Notice that the tracking speed changes instantly. Move the cursor around to test out the new speed. Double

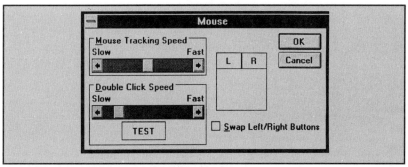

Figure 5.9: Setting the Mouse options

click on the Test button to try out the new double-click
speed. The color in the box will change if the double
click registered.

4. Click on the Swap Left/Right Buttons check box if you
   want to switch them.

5. Click OK when you've choosen settings you are happy
   with.

FINE-TUNING THE DESKTOP

There are several alterations that you can make to the Windows Desktop. You can change the

- Background patterns
- Background wallpaper
- Sizing grid
- Border width of all windows
- Icon spacing
- Cursor blink rate

The patterns and wallpaper settings simply let you decorate
the desktop with something a little more festive. *Patterns* are
repetitious designs, such as the woven look of fabric. *Wallpaper*
uses larger pictures that were created by artists with a drawing
program. You can create your own patterns and wallpaper or
use the ones supplied. Wallpapering can be done with a single
copy of the picture placed in the center of the screen or by
tiling, which gives you four identical pictures covering the whole
screen. Some of the supplied wallpaper images cannot be used
if you are running in Real mode. This is because the larger bit-
mapped images take up too much RAM. If an image can't be used,
the Control Panel will inform you when you try to select it.

The *sizing grid* is an invisible grid that causes the borders of
windows to "snap" into place more easily. It makes aligning

windows easier. It also affects the alignment of icons. The grid's setting is called *granularity*. If the setting is zero, the grid is off. The range is 0 to 49. Each increment of 1 corresponds to 8 pixels on the screen. I find a setting of 1 or 2 to be sufficient.

The *border width* settings let you make the borders of windows wider for visibility purposes, I suppose. When windows are tiled, thicker borders may help you to distinguish between them visually. The borders of windows in this book have been set to 4. The range is 0 to 49.

Icon spacing determines the distance between icons, both on the desktop and in group windows. Increasing the spacing prevents icon names from overwriting each other, but sometimes makes icons harder to find since they will be spaced out across more of the desktop and are thus more likely to be obscured by a window. I use a spacing of 106.

Cursor blink rate determines how fast the vertical bar (called the insertion point or text cursor) blinks. On some screens, it's easier to see if the speed is altered. The text cursor appears whenever you are editing text (in the text portion of a dialog box, in a Cardfile document, in a Notepad document, etc.).

To make any of these adjustments:

NOTE Because of memory limitations, some complex wallpaper images can't be used in Real mode.

1. Double click on the Desktop icon in the Control Panel window. The dialog box shown in Figure 5.10 appears.

2. Open the drop-down lists for wallpaper or patterns, and select the pattern or wallpaper you want. You'll have to try each one to see the effect because they don't go into effect until you leave the dialog box. You can only have wallpaper *or* a pattern showing at one time. You can't have both.

3. If you choose wallpaper, click on Tile or Center.

4. Set the cursor blink rate by sliding the box in the scroll bar or clicking on the arrows at either end of it. You can see the effect as soon as you move the mouse cursor off the slider button.

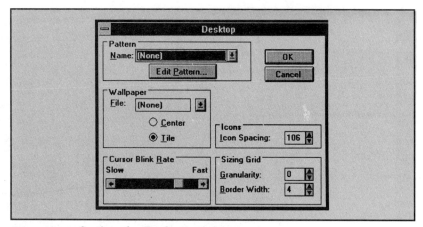

Figure 5.10: Setting the Desktop options

5. Adjust the border width and grid spacing (granularity) by clicking on the up and down arrows or by clicking on their assigned values and typing in the desired new value.

6. Click OK.

Unfortunately, this is one of those boxes that you'll have to open, reset and OK a million times to see all the patterns and wallpaper choices, and to see the effect of changing the border size and the granularity. Anyway, with some experimentation, you'll find the settings you like.

Figure 5.11 shows some of the patterns and wallpaper selections supplied with Windows.

CHANGING A PATTERN

If the supplied patterns don't suit you, make up your own with the built-in bit-map editor.

1. Click on Edit Pattern in the Desktop dialog box. A new dialog box appears (Figure 5.12).

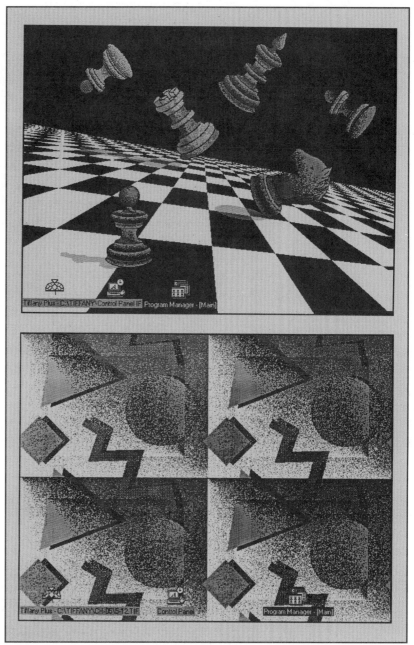

Figure 5.11: Some of the supplied patterns and wallpapers

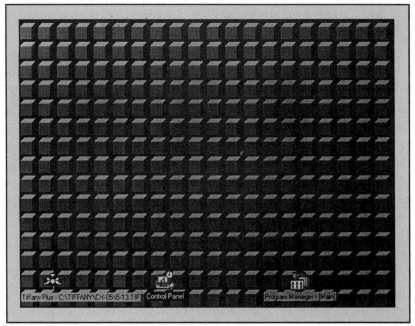

Figure 5.11: Some of the supplied patterns and wallpapers (continued)

2. In the Name section of the box, type in a name for the new pattern.

3. Create the pattern by clicking in the large box. What you are doing is defining the smallest element of the repeated pattern. It is blown up in scale to make editing it easier. Each click reverses the color of one pixel. The effect when the pattern is applied across a larger area and in normal size is shown in the *Sample* section.

4. When you like the pattern, click on Add, and the pattern is added to the list. You can then select it later from the Desktop dialog box.

If you later want to remove a pattern, select the pattern while in the editor, and click on Remove.

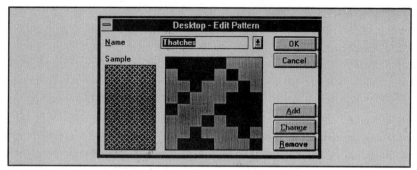

Figure 5.12: You can edit a desktop background pattern with this box

LOADING A NEW SLICE OF WALLPAPER

The images used in wallpaper are actually BMP files. These are bit-mapped files created by programs such as Paintbrush. Other programs create bit-mapped BMP files too, though, so the sky's the limit as far as what you can use as wallpaper. For example, you could use a scanned color photograph of your favorite movie star, a pastoral setting, some computer art, a scanned Mastisse painting, or a photo of your pet lemur. Figure 5.13 shows an example of a custom piece of wallpaper.

You can also edit the supplied BMP files with Paintbrush if you want. And since Paintbrush will read PCX files and convert them to BMP files, you can also use virtually any PCX file as wallpaper. Just load it into Paintbrush and save it as a BMP file by choosing File, Save As, Options.

Here's how to load a new BMP file and display it as wallpaper.

1. Create the image with whatever program you want, so long as it creates a BMP bit-mapped file.

2. Copy the file into the Windows directory. Only then will it appear in the list of wallpaper options.

3. Choose it from the Desktop dialog box.

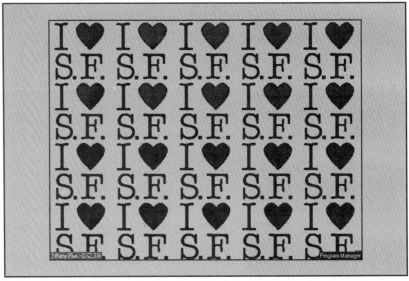

Figure 5.13: A custom piece of wallpaper created with Micrografx
Designer

NETWORK OPTIONS

> **NOTE** Appendix
> C discusses connec-
> ting to and disconnect-
> ing from network
> drives.

If you see a network icon in the Control Panel dialog box, this
means you are connected to a network, and the network
software is running. Beyond that, it is difficult for us to predict
here just what you will see when you click the icon. The dialog
box that you see (if any) when you click this icon will depend on
the type and brand of network attached. It's likely that you will
have some choices such as logging on and off the network,
selecting printers, passwords, and so forth.

INTERNATIONAL SETTINGS

The international settings customize your Windows for use in
other countries. If you're using Windows in English in the U.S.,
don't bother making any changes unless you want to rearrange
the keyboard to act like a Dvorak keyboard. (The Dvorak keyboard layout rearranges the keys for faster typing, but you have

to relearn the key locations.) The settings made from this box pertain exclusively to Windows and Windows applications. Other programs won't take advantage of them. Even some Windows applications won't. You should do some experimenting with the settings to see if they make any difference, or read the application's manual for information about how to set the formats for it.

Choosing International from the Control Panel displays the dialog box you see in Figure 5.14

The international settings and their explanations are shown below:

OPTION	PURPOSE
Country	Selects which country you're in. All other settings change in accordance with the accepted practices in that country. Only bother changing the other options if necessary
Language	Selects the language Windows will use

NOTE You may have to insert one of the Windows floppy disks when making changes if Windows needs some files.

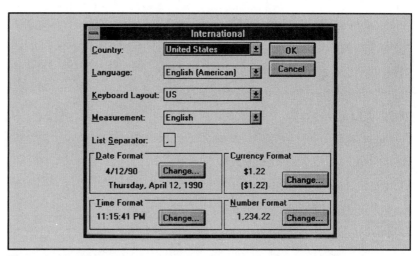

Figure 5.14: The International dialog box. Changes you make here affect only the applications that use the internal Windows settings for such functions.

	as a default. Some applications use this information when processing your data or text.
Keyboard Layout	There are many types of keyboard layouts, with variations for each country and language. Choose the one that applies to yours.
Measurement	Metric or English.
List Separator	In the sentence "Well, it's one, two, three, what are we fighting for..." the list separator is a comma. In other languages, items listed in a sentence are separated by other punctuation marks.
Date Format	You can choose from a myriad of date forms such as 3/6/53, 03/06/53, 3/6/1953, 06-03-1953, March 6, 1953, and others. Useful for programs that pop the date into text at the touch of a key, or that translate dates from one format to another.
Time Format	Similar to the date format options, allow 12 or 24 hour time indication, AM or PM indicators, choice of separators, and leading zeros.
Currency Format	Choose the currency indicator and location and number of decimal digits.
Number Format	Numbers can be displayed with or without decimals, with or without commas, using different decimal separators, and with or without leading zeroes.

To change the settings:

1. Open the International dialog box.

2. Choose Country, Language, Keyboard Layout and Measurement from the drop-down lists.

3. Set date, time, currency and number formats via additional dialog boxes that appear when you click on the Change button in their respective sections. Examples of the current settings are shown in each section, so you don't need to change them unless they look wrong.

CHANGING THE KEY REPEAT RATE

There's only one thing to change via the Keyboard icon—the key repeat rate. Most keys repeat when you hold them down. This setting lets you change the speed.

1. Double click on the Keyboard icon in the Control Panel dialog box. The box in Figure 5.15 appears.

2. Drag the slider to change the key repeat speed.

3. Test the key repeat speed by clicking in the Test Typematic area and holding down a letter key. If it's too slow or fast, adjust and try again.

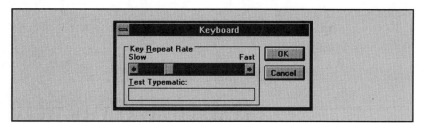

Figure 5.15: Changing the key repeat rate

SETTING THE DATE AND TIME

The Date/Time icon lets you adjust the system's date and time. These are used for date- and time-stamping the files you create and modify. All programs use these settings, regardless of

NOTE   You can
also adjust the
time and date using the
TIME and *DATE* com-
mands from DOS.

whether they are Windows or non-Windows programs.

1. Double click on the Date/Time icon.The dialog box in Figure 5.16 appears.

2. Adjust the time and date by typing in the corrections or clicking on the arrows.

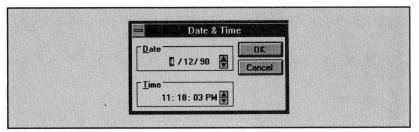

Figure 5.16: Changing the system Date and Time

TURNING THE WARNING BEEP ON OR OFF

The Sound icon allows the simplest of all the desktop alterations. All it does is turn off or on the beep you hear when Windows or a Windows application wants to warn you about something.

1. Double click on the Sound icon.The dialog box in Figure 5.17 appears.

2. Turn the warning beep on or off by clicking on the check box.

Figure 5.17: You can turn off the warning beep from this box if it bothers you

CHAPTER SIX

6

Installing a Printer

Fast Track

The default printer is used by programs that don't give the option of changing printers at print time.

To set the timeout parameters, 191

from the Configure dialog box, type in the time, in seconds.

To choose a network printer, 193

log onto the network, and make sure it's running. A printer or some printers should be available as a network printer. From the Printers dialog box choose Network. Choose the port, the printer path, and password (if necessary). Click on Connect.

To remove a printer and driver from your setup, 194

from the Printers dialog box, highlight name of the printer you want to remove. Click on Configure. From the Configure dialog box click on Remove. The driver is removed from the disk, assuming no other printer is using it. Font files are not removed.

If your printer isn't listed in the driver list, 195

check the compatibility list for a driver that will work with your printer. If there isn't one, contact Microsoft to see if there is a new driver available. If there isn't, contact the printer manufacturer for a Windows 3 driver. Drivers for version 2 should work in Real mode and may work in Standard and 386 Enhanced modes, though you may see a warning message on your screen about possible problems.

CHAPTER *6*

WHEN YOU INSTALLED WINDOWS USING THE SETUP program, you may have elected to install a printer. If you did, Windows ran the Control Panel and executed the printer installation program that is triggered when you click on the Printers icon in that window. Thus, you may be somewhat familiar with the procedure.

If your printer is already installed and seems to be working fine, then you can skip over this chapter. However, if you need to install a new printer, modify your current installation, or add an additional printer to your setup, then read on.

In this chapter I'll cover:

- How to install a new printer
- How to install a printer if it's not listed
- How to select the printer port
- How to configure your printer setup
- How to set the default printer
- How to select a printer when more than one is installed
- How to set specific printing options
- How to print over a network
- How to remove a printer from your setup

ABOUT PRINTER INSTALLATION

The first thing to know when installing printers is that there's a file in your Windows directory that contains various and sundry information pertaining to printers. It's called *printers.txt.* You should read this file because it's full of helpful hints not included in the manuals. It's the latest scoop about printing with Windows, and it's so recent that I can't even include it reliably in this book—it changes too often, particularly as Microsoft adds new printers to their list. You may have already read it if you elected to read on-line documentation during setup, though it may have made no sense at that time. In any case, the easiest way to read it is to get into the File Manager, open the *windows* directory and double click on *printers.txt.* Since it's a *.txt* file, and text files are associated with the Notepad application, it will load into a Notepad window. There are instructions at the beginning of the file explaining how to use it. There's lots of technical gobbledegook in the file, too, which you can forget about if you don't understand it or if it doesn't apply to your particular printer or printing jobs.

Okay, now let's consider the overall game plan for installing a printer. Here are the steps you have to complete:

- Install the printer driver file onto your hard disk.
- Select the printer's port.
- Select the type of printer.
- Select various printer settings, such as page orientation and type of paper feed.
- Select the default printer.

Each step is covered in a separate section of this chapter. You'll have to work through all the steps, in order, to perform a complete installation.

If you only want to modify one of the settings for your *currently* installed printer, look for the section that explains that topic and skip to it. You may, however, have to work your way up to the dialog box that contains the pertinent setting. Figure 6.1 shows all the dialog boxes associated with printer setup, and the paths taken to arrive there. (The dialog boxes shown are for a Post-Script printer. The boxes for your printer may look a bit different.)

INSTALLING THE PRINTER DRIVER

A printer driver is a file whose job is to translate the data you want to print so that your printer knows how to print it. Windows needs special printer drivers to work with your printer and many printer drivers are included with Windows. In cases where a driver for your printer isn't included with Windows, the printer's manufacturer may have one. Later in this chapter I'll describe what to do if your printer isn't listed and how to install a manufacturer-supplied printer driver.

A good printer driver will take advantage of all your printer's capabilities, such as its built-in fonts and graphics features. A poor printer driver may succeed in printing only stodgy-looking text, even from a top-of-the-line laser or ink-jet printer, or a highly capable 24-pin dot-matrix job.

Install the printer driver by following these steps:

1. Open the Control Panel and double click on Printers.

2. Click on Add Printers once the dialog box appears. The dialog box expands to look like that shown in Figure 6.2. (If no printers were previously installed, you don't have to click Add Printers. The box expands automatically.)

NOTE If your printer isn't included in the list, don't despair. There may still be hope. Consult the last section in this chapter, "What to Do If Your Printer Isn't on the Installation List."

3. Select your printer from the list. Make sure to select the exact printer model, not just the correct brand name. Consult your printer's manual if you're in doubt about the model.

4. Click on Install. You will most likely be instructed to insert one of your Windows disks into the A drive so that

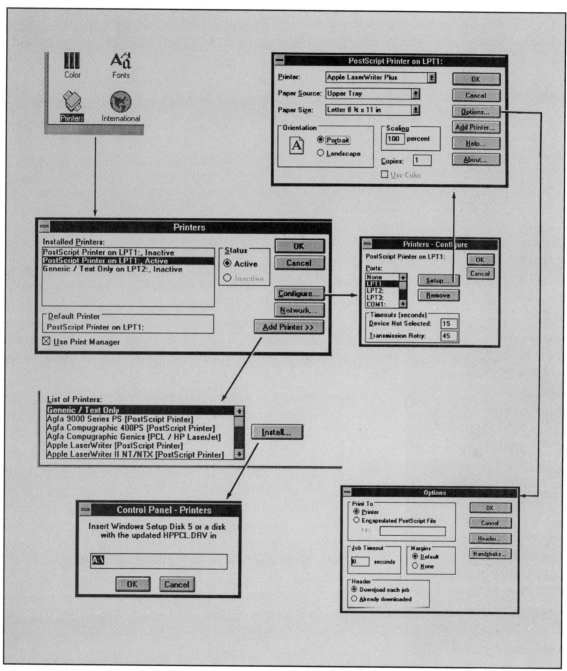

Figure 6.1: The complete road map of printer-related dialog boxes

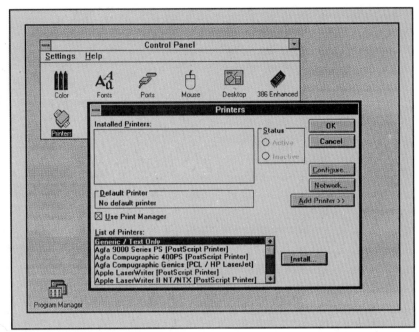

Figure 6.2: The main printer dialog box. From here you can install or remove a printer, or modify any printer setup.

Windows can copy the appropriate printer driver from it onto your hard disk.

5. If the printer driver with the correct name is already on the hard disk, then another dialog box will appear. You will have the option of reinstalling the driver, or using the old one. If you know the current driver to be older than the driver on your floppy disk, choose New from this box. Otherwise choose Current.

6. You'll next have to insert a disk containing the printer driver. The dialog box will tell you which disk to insert. You might also have to insert other disks for the font files. Just follow the instructions on screen.

7. If you want to install additional printers, you can do so at this point or later. Just repeat the above steps. The first printer you install will automatically be set to the

active state, and assigned to the LPT1 printer port, as indicated in the Installed Printers list. Additional printers will be set to the inactive state, and will not be assigned a port. In either case, you should follow the rest of the installation procedures before trying to print, or it's likely that the printer won't work.

ASSIGNING THE PRINTER TO A PORT

Once you've finished the above steps by installing the driver for your printer, the next task you have to complete is the assignment of a printer port. In other words, you have to tell Windows where your printer is physically hooked up to your computer.

1. The Printers dialog box should still be on your screen. If it isn't, select Printers from the Control Panel again.

2. Select the printer you want to set the port for. That is, just highlight it by single clicking it.

3. Click on the Configure button. This brings up the Configure dialog box, as shown in Figure 6.3.

4. At this point you're only going to select the port number for your printer, even though there are other settings that can be made from this box. Click on the port you want to use:

PORT	NOTES
LPT1:	The most common setting is LPT1, since most
LPT2:	PC-type printers hook up to the LPT1 parallel
LPT3:	port.
COM1:	If you know your printer to be of the *serial*
COM2:	variety, then chances are it's connected to the
COM3:	COM1 port. If COM1 is tied for use with
COM4:	some other device, such as a modem, then use
	COM2. (Make sure your printer is actually connected to the a serial port assigned to COM2.

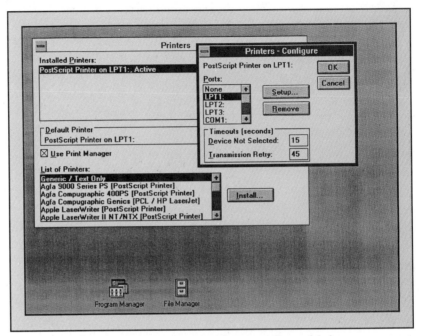

Figure 6.3: You set the printer port assignment from this box

Refer to your computer's manuals or ask someone who knows.)

EPT: If you're using an IBM Personal Pageprinter with it's own card, use this setting.

FILE: This is for printing to a disk file instead of to the printer. Later the file can be sent directly to the printer, or sent to someone on floppy disk or over a modem. Printing to files is covered in more detail in Chapter 7, "Using The Print Manager."

5. Click on OK, and the port is set. You're returned to the Printers dialog box. The name of the port now appears to the right of the printer's name.

ASSIGNING THE PRINTER TO THE DRIVER

As odd as it sounds, even though you've installed the printer driver and told Windows which port your printer is connected to, you now have tell Windows which printer is going to use the printer driver you installed. This may seem a little strange considering that you've already told Windows what type of printer you have, but that's just the way it works. Each printer driver can be used with more than one type of printer, so you have to tell your driver which printer you're using. As the old saying goes, ours is not to reason why....

1. In the Printers dialog box click on Configure. The Configure dialog box pops up again (see Figure 6.3).

2. Click on Setup. Now a new dialog box, the one shown in Figure 6.4, appears.

3. Open the first drop-down list (Printer) and choose the name of your exact printer (or one that the manufacturer of your printer claims yours is operationally identical to).

CHOOSING VARIOUS PRINT OPTIONS

NOTE The way you configure your printer while in Windows only affects printing from Windows applications. Non-Windows programs don't use these settings or the drivers, even if you run the program from within Windows. See Chapter 7 for more details about printing with Windows and non–Windows applications.

Next you have to make a series of choices that will affect what your print outs look like, such as font selection and paper orientation. These options are made from the dialog box that's already open, shown in Figure 6.4. Every printer driver comes with typical common defaults already set, so you don't necessarily have to change all the settings. However, you should at least examine them to see what they are, what options you might want to change at a later time, and how they're currently set.

Incidentally, you'll be able to make changes to any of these settings from the File menu of most Windows programs later on, when you're ready to print from that program. But making the

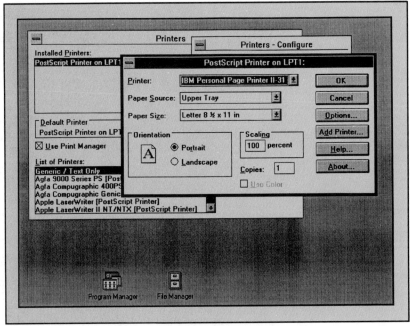

Figure 6.4: Configuring a particular printer for use by Windows requires checking and possibly altering numerous settings. The first step is to select the exact printer from a list of printers that work with the driver you selected earlier.

settings now determines the default settings that will be assumed until such a time.

The options that you have will depend on the type of printer driver you installed. Some options may be unavailable for your printer. In any case, here are all the possible options, with an explanation of each.

OPTION	DESCRIPTION
Paper Source (or Feed)	Some printers have more than one tray (for paper of different lengths). You can choose which tray or bin to use, whether the paper will be fed manually or by a *tractor*. Tractor-feed paper has holes along the edges and sprockets feed it into the printer.

Paper Size (or Format)	Normally, it's assumed you're using 8½ by 11 inch paper. Change this if necessary. There are seven sizes available.
Memory	How much memory (RAM) your printer has. This setting applies primarily to laser printers. If you don't know the amount, just leave this setting as is.
Orientation	Page orientation. Normal orientation is Portrait, which, like a portrait of, say, the Mona Lisa, is taller than it is wide. Landscape, like a landscape painting, is the opposite.
Cartridges	This section lists the possible font cartridges available for your printer (at least the ones known about at the time the driver was made). It also shows you how many cartridges can be physically plugged into your printer at one time. If two cartridges can be plugged in, select two names by holding down the Shift key while clicking on the names. This information is then used in the font dialog boxes in various Windows programs so that you can change the font of selected text.
Graphics Resolution	Some printers can render graphics in more than one resolution. The higher the resolution, the longer the printing takes, so you can save on time with your drafts by choosing a lower resolution. For finished high-quality work, choose the highest resolution.
Copies	Controls the number of copies of each page you print. Normally you want just 1. But if you always print more than 1, change the setting.

Fonts   This button lets you choose additional
                     font cartridges or downloadable font files
                     (sometimes called *soft fonts*) for your
                     printer. Don't confuse these with fonts
                     supplied with Windows. This button
                     refers to fonts and cartridges that you
                     purchase from other manufacturers such
                     as Bitstream, Hewlett-Packard, Adobe,
                     and others, or your computer dealer.

Options   Some printers will have additional op-
                     tions available. What they are depends on
                     the printer.

❐ Make the changes you want and click OK. This will
   return you to the Printers dialog box to make the settings described in the next section.

MAKING A PRINTER ACTIVE

It's possible to assign more than one printer to a port. You
might want to do this when you have some type of control box
that allows several printers to be plugged into the computer's
printer port, letting you select a given one by turning a switch.
Or perhaps you take the time to unplug one and plug in
another.

In any case, although you can assign more than one printer
to the same port, Windows keeps track of this, and prevents
more than one printer from *actively* being connected to the port
at any one time. This doesn't mean it physically disconnects one
or flips a switch if you choose a different printer, it just means
that the dialog boxes in various Windows applications (including the Print Manager—the program that controls printing
from Windows applications) will reflect the settings of the active

printer only, and use its printer driver when printing.

Therefore, if you have more than one printer driver installed and assigned to the same port, it behooves you to make one active for that port.

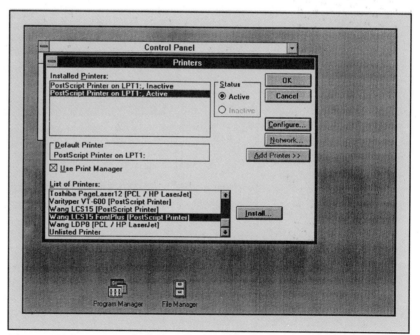

1. From the Printers dialog box, select the printer you want active.

2. Click on Active (if it isn't already on). If there was another printer that was active, its status changes to inactive, as shown next to its name. An example is shown in Figure 6.5. Notice that the two printers are assigned to the same port.

TIP If you have several printers assigned to different ports, then they will all have been activated when you installed the drivers, so you don't have to worry about a port conflict. If you only have one printer there's no competition for the port either, so once again, you don't have to do anything.

Figure 6.5: Choosing which printer is active. If more than one printer is assigned to the same port, only one can be active at a time.

SELECTING THE DEFAULT PRINTER

NOTE The
default printer has
to be an active printer
(as described above).

If you've installed more than one printer (regardless of port),
Windows needs to know which one is the *default* printer. The
default printer will be used by programs that don't give you a
choice of printers.

1. From the Printers dialog box, double click the name of
the printer to be set as the default printer.

2. Check to see that the dialog box section labeled Default
Printer reflects the new default printer, as you see in Figure 6.6

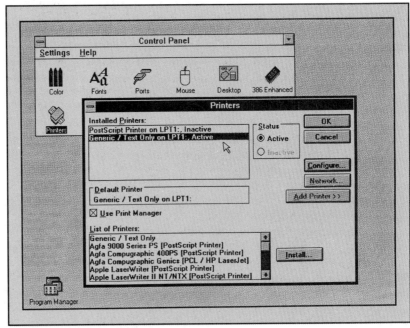

Figure 6.6: Double clicking on a printer's name in the Installed Printer
box selects it as the default printer

SETTING THE TIMEOUTS

Everybody who's used a computer for any length of time has experienced a print job bombing out in one way or another. When there's a problem with your printer, such as running out of paper, computer programs (and DOS) often aren't very nice about it. The result can be a printing job that gets unceremoniously terminated, or the appearance of a not very lucid description of the problem appearing on your screen, such as

```
DOS error writing device PRN
Abort, Retry, Fail?
```

Other times you're left sitting and waiting while your laser printer's data light happily flashes—particularly when printing graphics, which can seem to take an eternity. Quite reasonably, you assume that everything's fine. That is, until you realize that you've downed two cups of coffee waiting for your one-page report to print.

The culprit precipitating some of these printing migraines is called *timing out*. Printers, programs, and operating systems like DOS don't always agree on how long to wait in the case of an error before throwing in the towel. So, while you're busily adding paper to the tray, or changing a ribbon with the printer top open, or you've forgotten to put the printer "on line" to start with, something just decides to give up.

In all fairness, even without Windows, your computer usually tries a couple of times to send data to the printer before giving up. However, often it doesn't try long enough to handle typical problems such as loading paper or removing a paper jam. And it usually requires some user intervention such as typing a key on the keyboard to effect a retry. If you're not there to handle the problem, then the printing process is halted until you return.

Windows has an option that lets you decide, in advance, how long it should try before issuing an error message, should it appear there is some malady with your printer. Of course, the error message dialog box, just like the DOS Retry message, lets you retry the transmission from the point where it stopped, so as long as you're around to monitor the printing process, it's no big deal if your setting isn't perfect.

In any case, you control the time Windows waits by setting the time outs in the Configuration dialog box.

1. From the Printer dialog box, click on Configure.

2. On the Configure dialog box, there are two Timeout settings:

SETTING	MEANING
Device Not Selected	If your printer is "off line," how long should Windows wait before sending a message to that effect? Off-line is a state wherein the printer is temporarily disconnected from the computer and cannot receive data. Many printers automatically go off line when you remove a paper tray or they run out of paper. Some printers also have a panel switch that takes them off line. Make sure the printer is on-line before you start to print. This setting is normally 15 seconds, but you may want to increase it if, for example, the printer is quite a ways from the computer, and changing paper takes longer. Increasing this timeout would let you correct the problem and continue printing without having to tell Windows to retry (by clicking on Retry in the error dialog box).

Transmission Retry

Printers and computers communicate with each other about the progress of their data transmission. When the printer receives some data, it acknowledges this to the computer. The computer then sends the next portion of data. If for some reason, other than being off-line, the Windows Print Manager doesn't receive an acknowledgement from the printer (the reasons vary from printer to printer), the Transmission Retry setting comes into play. The default setting is 45 seconds, which is long enough for most purposes. If printing from your application regularly results in an error message about transmission problems, and retrying seems to work, increase the setting.

CHOOSING A NETWORK PRINTER

Assuming your Windows system is successfully hooked up to a local area network (LAN) that has a network printer on it, you should be able to print from that printer. However, you'll have to select the printer from a different dialog box, called Network Connections.

1. Make sure you've installed Windows correctly for use on the network. Please refer to the Windows manual and your network manual for more information.

2. You should have run the network software upon booting up and logged on in such a way that there is a network printer currently assigned and available to your system. Only then are you able to choose a specific network printer.

3. From the main Printers dialog box choose Network. A new dialog box appears. The contents of the dialog box will depend on the type of network you are using.

4. Open the Port drop-down list and choose the port you want to use. (Check your network operations manual if you don't know which logical port your printer is connected to.)

5. Type the name of the network printer in the Path box.

6. Type in the password if necessary.

7. Click on Connect. The printer is connected to Windows, and the printer name appears in the Network Printer Connections list. If there was already a printer connected to that port, you'll be alerted to the conflict, which you will have to correct before the connection is made.

8. When you want to disconnect a network printer from Windows, use the Disconnect button instead of the Connect button.

REMOVING A PRINTER

What if you get a new printer and decommision the current one? Well, then you have to remove the old printer from the list of available drivers and printers. Actually it's very easy to do this, and the process also removes the associated printer driver file unless another printer relies on it. This frees up disk space and reduces hard disk clutter. However, it doesn't remove all the fonts that might be associated with the driver. This could be a problem if disk space is tight, since fonts can take up considerable room. To remove fonts, use the Fonts command from the Control Panel, select the font and click on Remove. (This is described in more detail in Chapter 5.)

To remove a printer from the installed printers list:

1. Open the Printers dialog box by clicking on Printers in the Control Panel.

2. Highlight the name of the printer you want to remove.

3. Click on Configure. The Configure dialog box pops up.

4. Click on Remove. You are asked to confirm the removal.

5. Click OK. You will be returned to the main Printers dialog box. Then click OK to return to the Control Panel.

WHAT TO DO IF YOUR PRINTER ISN'T ON THE INSTALLATION LIST

If your printer isn't listed in the rather huge list of printers supplied with Windows, there is still hope. Many off-brand printers are designed to be compatible with one of the popular printer types, such as the Epson MX series, Hewlett-Packard LaserJets, or Apple LaserWriters.

The Windows manual comes with a hardware compatibility listing which you should check just to see if your printer is listed. If it is, then you can use the driver designed for the printer yours is compatible with.

If your printer is not listed there, it may still be compatible. Check the manual supplied with the printer and look for any indication of compatibility. It's usually listed up front, along with the description of the printer, or in the back if there is a technical description of operating modes. Setting the printer in a compatibility mode may require the adjustment of switches in the printer. Again, check the printer's manual for these.

Finally, if it looks like there's no mention of compatibility anywhere, you may have a printer manufactured by a company that simply wanted to build a better mouse trap. And they might have. (There's always room for improvements when it comes to printers!) It's possible that the manufacturer has a printer driver for Windows 3 that they will send you upon request. It's also possible that Microsoft has a new driver for your printer that wasn't available when your copy of the program was shipped. Contact Microsoft at (206) 882-8080 and ask for the Windows Driver Library Disk which will contain all the latest drivers. (They may ask for the serial number of your program or some other identification.)

You can always try using a Windows 2 driver with Windows 3. According to Microsoft, version 2 drivers will work with Windows 3 when running in Real mode. There may be problems running some version 2 drivers in Standard or 386 Enhanced modes, however.

Assuming you do obtain a printer driver, follow these instructions to install it.

1. Follow the instructions described in "Installing the Printer Driver." However, instead of selecting the name of the printer (which isn't in the list), scroll to the bottom of the list and pick Unlisted Printer.

2. Windows will ask you to insert the proper disk(s).

3. You may have to copy other files associated with the driver. They should be copied into the \windows\system directory unless otherwise directed by instructions supplied with the printer driver.

4. Follow the instructions described in "Assigning the Printer to a Port" to continue the installation.

CHAPTER SEVEN

Using the
Print Manager

Manager will stop sending data to the printer, and the current print job (the one with the printer icon to the left of its information line) will be temporarily suspended. (The printing may not stop immediately because your printer may have a buffer that holds data in preparation for printing. The printing will stop when the buffer is empty.)

To resume the printing process, 210

from the queue window, click on the large Resume button just below the word View in the upper-left corner. The Print Manager will continue sending data to the printer starting where it left off.

To move a file to another position in the queue, 211

click on the file you want to move and drag it to its new location.

To set the printing priority, 211

open the Print Manager's Options menu. Three commands on it adjust the priority of printing via the Print Manager. It is normally set to Medium Priority (meaning that printing receives equal CPU priority to other applications). If you notice that your other applications run too slowly while printing is going on in the background, set it to Low Priority. To speed up the printing while using other programs, use the High Priority setting. If no other applications are running, printing always runs as fast as possible.

To print from non-Windows applications, 220

because you cannot use the Print Manager, you print using the same procedures as from DOS.

CHAPTER 7

ONCE YOU HAVE YOUR PRINTERS SET UP, AS DESCRIBED in Appendix A and Chapter 6, Windows uses the Print Manager to print your documents. Just as the Program Manager and the File Manager help you organize programs and files, the Print Manager helps organize printing tasks within Windows. Thus, whenever you print from a Windows application, the Print Manager automatically takes control of the printing job, using the selected printer driver and setup options.

Unfortunately, the Print Manager does not work with non-Windows applications. A program has to be designed a certain way to function with the Print Manager. However, this doesn't mean you can't print from non-Windows applications while running Windows. You can, but unless you are running in 386 Enhanced mode, your computer will be tied up during the printing process, just as if you were printing with DOS, outside of Windows. That process is discussed in the section in this chapter entitled "Printing from Non-Windows Applications."

PRINT MANAGER BASICS

When you print from non-Windows programs in DOS, your computer and printer take over the show. You're reduced to taking a coffee-break, going for a jog around the block (probably not a bad idea), or pulling out a pencil and paper to continue your work. This is because most programs won't let you print a document and work on another one at the same time.

There are many programs available (called *spoolers*) that let you do this, however, and you may have tried one. They'll let you print from, say, WordStar, 1-2-3, or dBASE, and then go immediately back to work, while the program prints your files in the *background*. (Sometimes called *background processing*, this means that while you are working in the *foreground*, the computer appears to be working on another task behind the scenes.)

In fact a spooler program, print.com, is supplied with your copy of DOS. It lets you specify a list of files to be printed (such a list is called the print *queue*), and then prints them while you return to your work. However, it has numerous limitations and is awkward to use.

Though there are better spoolers available for use with DOS, these accessory programs are still only as elegant as their user interface. The DOS interface leaves a lot to be desired, and few DOS programs use identical printer protocols, so it's not uncommon that some programs print just fine, and others not so well. As you might suspect, since Windows requires consistency in the design of programs created for it, a task such as printing can be controlled in a more sophisticated manner than normally allowed under DOS.

The Print Manager is the program that provides that control. It handles all printing tasks within Windows. It's a well-designed spooler with the graphical interface and convenience typical of Windows applications. When printing with the Print Manager:

- You can start printing and immediately go back to work, even with another program.

- While one document is being printed, you can start other programs and print from them, too. Print Manager just adds subsequent documents to the queue.

- You automatically utilize all the capabilities of the printer driver and setup you installed. Your settings for such options as number of copies, paper tray, page orientation, and so forth are automatically used during the print job so you don't have to set them each time, though you can change the defaults if you like.

- You can easily see which jobs are currently being printed or are in the queue waiting to be printed. A window displays this information along with an indication of the current print job's progress.

- You add jobs to the print queue the same way you print them individually. The Print Manager handles the details.

- You can easily rearrange the order of the print queue or delete jobs from it.

- You can adjust how much of your computer's computing time goes to printing instead of to your work.

- You can temporarily pause or resume printing without causing printer problems.

- If you are connected to a network, you can print to a local printer or to a network printer.

You can also bypass the Print Manager and print directly to the printer port, to speed up printing on a network.

PRINTING FROM WINDOWS APPLICATIONS

As explained above, Windows applications automatically take advantage of Print Manager. If you print from Notepad, for example, it will automatically run the Print Manager, which then handles the print job. All of the printer settings you make from the Control Panel's Printer dialog boxes then go into effect, since the Print Manager uses the printer driver and printer setup you have already established.

The exact appearance of your printed documents may vary from program to program, though, depending on the degree to which your Windows application can take advantage of the printer-driver setup. Some programs, such as Write, let you change fonts, for example, while others, such as Notepad, don't.

NOTE There is one exception to this. When configuring a printer from the Control Panel, there is an option in the Printers dialog box that lets you turn off the Print Manager. When that check box is turned off, all print jobs will bypass the Print Manager and go directly to the printer. No spooling will occur, and your computer will be tied up until the print job is concluded. This can speed up printing on some networks.

Consult the program's manual to figure out what options are supported by your applications. You might have to experiment a bit by actually printing several times before you're satisfied with the results.

In general, the way Print Manager works is this: When you print from a Windows program, it actually prints to a disk file instead of directly to the printer. Print Manager then spools the file to the assigned printer(s), coordinating the flow of data and keeping you informed of the progress.

So, to print from any Windows application with the Print Manager, follow these steps:

1. Check to see that the printer and page settings are correct. Some applications provide a Printer Setup or other option on their File menu for this.

2. Select the Print command on the application's File menu and fill in whatever information is asked of you.

3. Click OK. The application writes the printer file to the hard disk, and tells Windows to start up the Print Manager (if it isn't already running.) The Print Manager icon appears at the bottom of the desktop and, depending on the appliction, you may see a little message box informing you that a document is being printed.

4. Click the Cancel button on this box (or follow other instructions depending on the program) if you want to abort the printing before it is added to the Print Manager queue. If you don't get to the Cancel button fast enough, don't worry. You can still stop the printing from the Print Manager window.

5. Just wait for the document to print, or go back to work. If there is an error, the Print Manager will alert you to it. When the document is finished printing, the Print Manager icon will disappear from the desktop (assuming the queue is empty), as Windows closes the program to free up memory.

So, printing a single document is easy. Once you have a number of documents printing though, there's more you might want to know about the status of your print jobs. Let's now consider the various Print Manager commands and options.

VIEWING THE QUEUE

Probably the thing you'll want to do most often from the Print Manager's window is check the status of the queue. This lets you see which job is currently printing, which printer it's printing to, and what percentage of the job is finished printing. You also see the names and sizes of other print jobs in the queue.

To experiment with viewing the queue, try printing something handy. An easy thing to open and print is a topic from the Help system. Follow these steps to give it a whirl:

1. Run the Print Manager by double clicking its icon. It's in the Program Manager's Main group. The opening screen comes up and looks like the one you see in Figure 7.1. (Maximize the window.)

2. Choose Help ⇨ Procedures. The Help window will open. Adjust it so that the top third of the Print Manager window is still showing.

3. Set up your printer with paper and make sure it's on line.

4. Choose File ⇨ Printer Setup and make sure the correct printer is selected.

5. Choose File ⇨ Print Topic. The Procedures topic of the Help file is printed to a disk file, and then the disk file is added to the print queue as shown in Figure 7.2. Printing should commence immediately.

6. Click on the Pause button in the Print Manager window. This will stop the printing and you can then add some

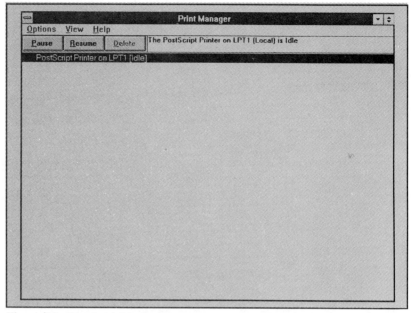

Figure 7.1: The initial Print Manager screen with no print jobs pending

more items to the queue before the first one finishes and vanishes from it. Notice that the message line indicates the printer is paused.

7. In the Help window, use the Browse button to view another topic, such as the commands or keys. Print each of them. They'll be added to the queue and there should then be three files waiting to print. Since the printer is paused, nothing will be printing. Your screen will look something like Figure 7.3

You may notice the following pieces of information in the print queue screen.

- The message box reports the name, port, and status of the printer.

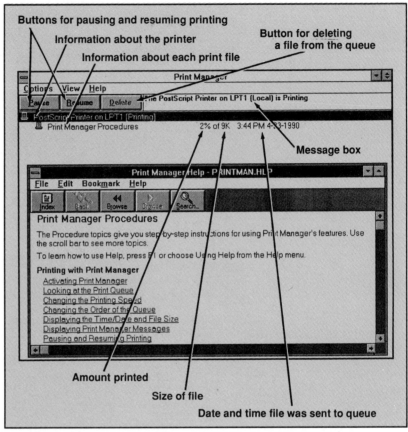

Figure 7.2: Printing a file from any Windows application automatically adds the file to the print queue

- The first line of the queue indicates the name of the printer, its status, and which port it's connected to. This is called the *queue information line.*

- Below that, each print job queued up for that printer occupies one line. These lines are called *file information lines.* The currently printing file shows a printer icon to its left. Subsequent jobs have numbers to their left, indicating their position in the queue. To the right of the numbers are the name of the originating application,

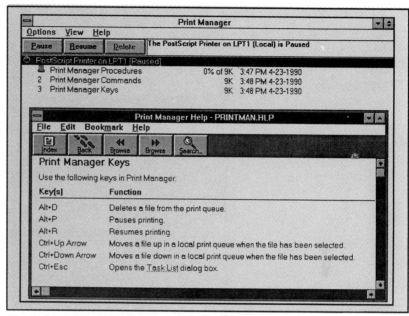

Figure 7.3: Printing additional documents adds them to the queue

the document being printed, the size of the file, and the time and date the file was put on the queue. If a file is printing, the percentage of the file that has been printed appears on its information line just to the left of the file size (e.g., *35% of 15K*).

• If files have been queued to other printers (including network printers), there will be additional printer information lines and file information lines.

DELETING A FILE FROM THE QUEUE

After sending a file to the queue, suppose you reconsider printing it. Perhaps you want to re-edit the file and print it later. If so, you can simply remove the file from the queue.

1. Select the file by clicking on it in the queue.

2. Click the large Delete button near the top of the Print Manager window.

3. A dialog box appears, asking for confirmation.

PAUSING THE PRINTING PROCESS

You can temporarily halt the printing process for Windows applications at any time. This may be useful in cases where you want to adjust the printer for some reason, or to quiet the printer (if it's a dot-matrix or impact type) so you can take a phone call, have a conversation, etc.

TO PAUSE THE PRINTING PROCESS

From the queue window, click on the large Pause button just below the word Options in the upper-left corner.

The Print Manager stops sending data to the printer, and the current print job (the one with the little printer to the left of its information line) is temporarily suspended. (The printing may not stop immediately because your printer may have a buffer that holds data in preparation for printing. The printing will stop when the buffer is empty.)

TO RESUME THE PRINTING PROCESS

From the queue window, click on the large Resume button just below the word View in the upper-left corner. The Print Manager will continue sending data to the printer, starting where it left off.

REARRANGING THE QUEUE ORDER

Once you have several items on the queue, you may want to rearrange the order in which they're slated for printing. Perhaps a print job's priority has increased because it's needed for an urgent meeting, or you have to get a letter in the mail, etc. Whatever the reason, it's easy to rearrange the print queue.

1. Click on the file you want to move and hold the mouse button down because you have to drag the file.

2. The cursor changes to a large arrow. Now drag the file to its new location. A dotted rectangle surrounds each file as you pass over it, indicating the position your file would jump to were you to release the mouse button.

3. Release the mouse button when you have the dotted rectangle in the correct spot. Your file is inserted in the queue, pushing the other files down one slot each.

SETTING THE PRINTING SPEED

You may recall that in the little experiment in Chapter 2 in which you ran several copies of the Clock program, the clocks' second hands did not all move at the same time. Each one moved separately, one after the other, but the effect was barely noticeable. This illustrates the fact that your computer can actually do only one thing at a time. It's only through computer wizardry that your machine appears to be working at two jobs simultaneously. Actually, it is splitting its *CPU time* between the tasks, focusing on each one in a round-robin fashion. (The CPU or Central Processing Unit is the chip that does the actual "computing" in your computer. CPU time is the amount of time the CPU spends on a given task, and splitting time between two or more tasks is called *time slicing.* In time slicing, CPU time is doled out by using a formula that *prioritizes* the tasks. Normally each task gets the same priority, and thus the same amount of CPU attention (a bit like dealing out cards in a poker game—the old "one for me, one for you" routine).

Obviously, there is only a finite amount of CPU time available. In a given period of time, say a second, the CPU can only do so much computing. Luckily, many programs do not come close to taxing the capabilities of the lightning-fast CPU. For example, with most word processors, the CPU is usually left twiddling its thumbs between the letters you type at the keyboard.

Naturally, running the Print Manager requires some CPU time, just like other programs, and it'll slow down whatever program you're working with. Whether the slowing is perceptible or not depends on what else you're doing in Windows. If you are doing work that requires considerable CPU attention, (such as spreadsheet calculations, database sorting, or desktop publishing) printing can slow down the response time of your computer—sometimes to the point of aggravation.

For this reason, the Print Manager lets you adjust the amount of CPU time it gets. It does this by letting you adjust the time-slicing formula. For example, you might double the amount of time you get for your applications, thus decreasing the amount the Print Manager gets (the old "one for you, two for me" routine). This translates to increasing the priority of your application and decreasing the priority of the Print Manager. The result will be increased speed for your application and decreased speed for printing. It is also possible to *increase* the priority of printing.

Three commands on the Print Manager's Options menu adjust the priority. If you notice that your other applications run too slowly while printing is going on, open the Options menu and choose one of the speed settings described below. The setting remains in effect until you change them again. They only affect printing through the Print Manager.

NOTE You can adjust the prioritizing of CPU time for other applications too. This is discussed in Chapter 14.

SETTING	RESULT
Low Priority	Reduces CPU time spent on printing.
Medium Prority	This is the default setting. Printing gets CPU priority equal to that of other applications.

High Priority   If you want to speed up the printing, you can try this command. If your other applications slow down too much, then go back to Medium.

SEEING PRINT MANAGER MESSAGES

Sometimes the Print Manager wants to alert you to a condition that may require your intervention in some way. Perhaps the printer runs out of paper, goes off line, or has paper jammed in it. Three commands on the Options menu let you determine how Print Manger's messages will be displayed in such instances.

SETTING	*RESULT*
Alert Always	If there is a problem, your computer will beep and Print Manager will pop up a dialog box regardless of what other programs or windows you are using.
Flash if Inactive	If the Print Manager is iconized or its window is open but not active, then the icon or the title bar in the window will flash and you'll hear a beep. When you restore or activate the window, the error message will then appear.
Ignore if Inactive	If the Print Manager is iconized or its window is open but not active, nothing happens. Printing just stops.

PRINTING WITH NETWORK PRINTERS

If you're connected to a network that is supported by Windows, you may have some additional options when printing and using the Print Manager. The options you have depend on the type of network you're connected to. With the most comprehensive network setup, you can:

- Print to a network printer instead of to the printer connected directly to your computer (the *local* printer).

- View the print queue of only the files *you* sent to the network printer.

- View the *entire* print queue for the network printer you are connected to.

- View the print queue for network printers that you're not connected to.

- Print directly to the network printer, without using the Print Manager, possibly increasing printing efficiency.

- Tell Print Manager not to poll (repeatedly request) the network's printer server for queue information, thus decreasing the demand on the network and increasing network efficiency.

PRINTING TO A NETWORK PRINTER

To print to a network printer, you must be logged onto the network and have selected the network printer for your output. This requires the use of the Network and Printers dialog boxes, reached through the Control Panel. These dialog boxes are discussed in Chapters 5 and 6, respectively.

When you print from an application, confirm that the network printer of your choice is selected from the Printer Setup dialog box. Then go ahead and print as usual. The Print Manager will automatically start up and handle the print job as described in "Printing from Windows Applications" at the beginning of this chapter. Then use the steps detailed in the next several sections below to view and control updates of the queue.

VIEWING THE QUEUE FOR NETWORK PRINTERS

Just as with a local printer, you'll probably want to check the network queue occasionally to see when your print jobs are coming up. This is particularly important on a busy network where there may be many people waiting for print jobs to be completed. You may not be able to speed things up, but at least you'll know if you should go out for lunch or not!

There are two basic categories of network printers—those you're connected to (via the Control Panel's Printer settings), and those you aren't. Print Manager lets you look at the queue for each type.

TO VIEW YOUR QUEUE ONLY FOR A NETWORK PRINTER YOU'RE CONNECTED TO

When you print to a network printer, the queue for your print files shows up just as it does when you print to a local printer. That is, the files are added to the queue in the order you printed them and displayed in that order. You may rearrange or delete them if you wish. However, you should be aware that the queue you see doesn't reflect all the print jobs slated for the printer. Other network users may have sent jobs to the printer too. If you don't care about that, just go back to work. If you want to see the entire queue for your printer or another network printer, read the two sections below.

TO VIEW THE ENTIRE QUEUE FOR A NETWORK PRINTER YOU'RE CONNECTED TO

If you want to see the entire queue, that is, your files and other users' files destined for printing on a particular printer, do the following:

1. Click on the network printer's information line in the Print Manger window. This should highlight it, as shown

in Figure 7.4. (If the network printer doesn't appear in the window, then you are not logged onto the network or not connected to the network printer. Check with your network manager, or your network manuals. Also refer to Chapters 5 and 6 and Appendix C regarding networks.

2. Choose View ⇨ Selected Net Queue. The queue for the network printer appears as a window. It will have scroll bars if there are more jobs in the queue than can be displayed at one time. An example is shown in Figure 7.5.

3. When you are finished examining the information, close the window by clicking on Close.

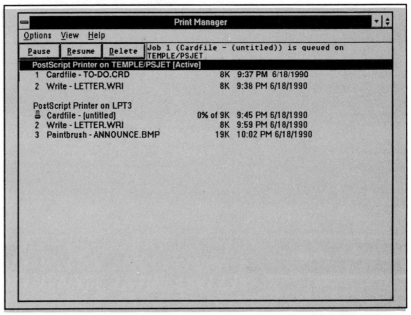

Figure 7.4: To see the queue for a network printer, first highlight it by clicking on it, as shown here

TO VIEW THE NETWORK QUEUE
FOR A PRINTER YOU'RE NOT CONNECTED TO

Sometimes you may want to see the queue for a network printer that isn't the one you're currently connected to. This can help you determine whether there is a printer on the network that has a shorter queue. You could conceivably switch to that printer before sending your print job down the line and save yourself some waiting. You would first have to connect yourself to the new printer via the Control Panel's Printer dialog boxes before printing.

1. Select View ⇨ Other Net Queue. A small text box appears at the bottom of the Print Manager window, asking you for the path name of the network printer's queue.

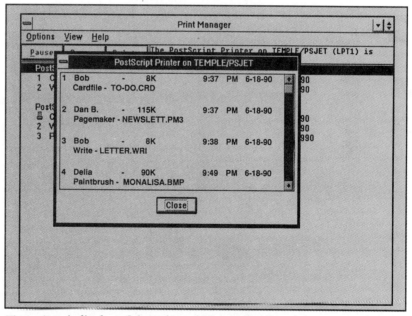

Figure 7.5: A display of the selected Network printer's queue appears when you choose the View ⇨ Selected Net Queue command

2. Type in the queue's name. This might be a rather complex name, similar to a DOS path name. You might need to refer to your network manager or the manuals supplied with your network to determine the exact path and printer name.

3. Click on View. The queue for the printer appears. An example of such a queue is shown in Figure 7.6.

4. You can view other queues by typing in another name and clicking on View again, if you want. Otherwise click Close when you are finished.

UPDATING THE QUEUE INFORMATION

If the window is left open, the queue will periodically be updated to reflect changes on the network, such as new print jobs added to the queue, or completed print jobs leaving the queue.

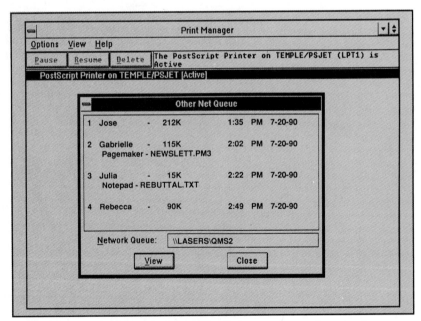

Figure 7.6: Use the View ⇨ Other Net Queue command to see the queue for a network printer you're not currently connected to

If you minimize the window to an icon, the queue will not be updated, but this doesn't matter, since you can't see it anyway.
However it does cut down on network data flow. Whenever you
restore the Print Manager window, the queue information will
be updated.

If you leave the window open and don't want to wait for the
periodic update, but want an update immediately, you can do
this:

❐ Choose View ⇨ Selected Net Queue.

This will update the queue information immediately.

If you want to leave the window open, and you don't want to
add to the network's traffic by having Print Manager request a
periodic update, you can do this:

1. Choose Options ⇨ Network. The Network Options
   dialog box appears, as shown below.

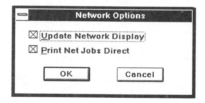

2. Turn off the Update Network Display check box.

From this point on, only updates pertaining to your print jobs
will be reflected in the queue. No other network queue information will be updated until you reset this box.

PRINTING THROUGH THE
PRINT MANAGER FOR NETWORK PRINTING

Normally, when you are connected to a network, Windows
prints directly to the network printer, not through the Print

Manager. This speeds up your printing by eliminating an additional software *layer* in the print processing. There are times when you might not want to bypass the Print Manager, however. In some odd cases, printing directly to the network may be slower than using Print Manager. This depends on your network, and the application you're printing from. So, you may want to experiment with a setting on the Network Options dialog box that lets you determine whether Print Manager is engaged or not during the process of printing. Regardless of this setting, you'll still be able to view the queue.

1. Choose Options ⇨ Network. The options dialog box appears.

2. Set the Print Net Jobs Direct box on or off as desired. When it's off (unchecked), printing passes through the Print Manager.

PRINTING FROM NON-WINDOWS APPLICATIONS

You cannot take advantage of the Print Manager when you are printing from non-Windows applications. This is because non-Windows applications are not designed to cooperate with the Print Manager, and haven't the slightest idea what's going on vis-a-vis Windows. Though you can run non-Windows applications from Windows, they are subject to certain limitations, one of which is not being able to use the Print Manager or the printer driver(s) you've installed. Therefore when you print from a non-Windows application, you are on your own. Consider these points:

• Make sure you have installed the application to run with your printer. Read the application's manual(s) to determine what printer drivers and/or procedures you need to follow to print correctly.

- Do not rely on Windows to handle any aspect of the printing process.

- Do not try to print from multiple non-Windows programs or from a mix of Windows and non-Windows programs at the same time on the same port. Unless you are running in Enhanced 386 mode, this will cause the output of the files to be mixed together like a computer cocktail! In 386 mode, you will be warned of the impending blending, but in Real or Standard mode, you won't. As rules of thumb, remember the following: Unless you're running in 386 mode, print a bunch of files only when they're all from Windows applications. When you want to print from a non-Windows program, do it when nothing else is in the Print Manager's queue, or, if necessary, when the queue is paused.

- If you really want to print a non-Windows application document with the Print Manager, it may be possible to have a compatible Windows application handle the printing. For example, the Notepad will read ASCII files. Write will read ASCII and Word files. Word for Windows and Ami will read numerous word processing and graphics file formats too. Excel will read 1-2-3 and dBASE files, and so on. Do a little research on file-format compatibility, and then use the appropriate Windows application to open and print the file from within Windows. This may also give you the ability to format the files with fonts and other refinements to look more pleasing, particularly in the case of programs such as dBASE that have little in the way of printer support. The Print Manager will then kick in and handle the details of queueing.

PRINTING TO A DISK FILE

Sometimes you may want to print to a *disk file* rather than to the printer. When you print to a disk file, the output from the application program that normally would go out the printer port on the back of your computer and over a wire to the printer goes instead into a file on a floppy or hard disk. You might think the file would then be just a copy of the file you were printing. Usually it isn't. This is because it contains all the special formatting codes that control your printer. Codes that change fonts, margins, page breaks, attributes such as underlines, bold and so on are all included in this type of file. Print files destined for PostScript printers include their PostScript *preamble*, too (unless you defeat the PostScript header downloading process via the Control Panel ⇨ Printers ⇨ Configure ⇨ Setup ⇨ Options dialog box).

In any case, printing to a file gives you several options not available when printing direct to the printer.

- You can send the file to another person either on floppy disk or over the phone lines with a modem and a communications program such as Terminal. That person can then print the file directly to a printer (if it is compatible) with Windows or the DOS *COPY* command. They don't need the application program that created the file, and they don't have to worry about any of the printing details such as formatting, setting up margins, etc. It's all in the file.

- You can print the file later. Maybe your printer isn't hooked up, or there's so much stuff on the queue that you don't want to wait, or you don't want to slow down your computer or the network by printing now. So, print to a file (which is significantly faster than printing on paper anyway). Later you can copy the file to the printer with the File Manager's Print command or the DOS *COPY* command. The Print command uses the Print Manager, so you can queue up as many files as you want, prepare the printer, and then print them without having to be around.

- Sometimes print files are used by applications for specific purposes. For example, you may want to print part of a database to a file that will later be pulled into a company report. Or you might want to print an encapsulated postscript graphics file to be imported into a desktop publishing document.

Regardless of the reason, the general game plan is this: You modify your printer driver to print to a file rather than to a port. Then, whenever you use that printer, it'll use all the usual settings for the driver, but will send the data to a file of your choice instead of to the printer port.

1. Choose Control Panel ⇨ Printers.

2. Select the printer that will eventually be used to print the file.

3. Click on Configure. The Configure dialog box appears.

4. Select FILE: from the Ports list box.

5. Make sure the Setup settings are correct by clicking on Setup and checking them.

6. Return to the Control Panel by clicking OK several times.

7. Print from the application. You'll be asked to specify a file name for the output. You'll have to type it in. To be safe, type in the complete path name for the file, including its drive letter (e.g., *c:\letters\wilma.prt*).

Be aware that until you reset your printer's configuation to its previous port assignment, you'll be printing to a file whenever you use this printer from any application. To reset the printer to its normal port, use the steps above but choose the proper port instead of FILE: from the Configure dialog box's Port list.

NOTE If you want to print the file as ASCII text only, with no special control codes, you should install the Generic/Text Only printer driver. Then select that as the destination printer.

NOTE If you want to print to an encapsulated PostScript file (EPS), install a PostScript driver, such as the Apple LaserWriter. Then set the Options dialog box for the printer to print to Encapsulated PostScript File, and type in the name of the file.

PRINTER PROBLEM SOLVING

The computer printing process is, by definition, fraught with maladies and pitfalls. The veracities of Murphy's law sometimes seem undeniably confirmed when you're struggling to achieve even the simplest of hard-copy renderings and your setup isn't correct.

I said that "by definition" printing is problematic because there are so many variables to contend with. In fact, things have much improved since the days when you had to make the cable and write the driver yourself. Printers probably work right about 90% of the time these days. But as you may recall, simply setting up the Windows printer driver alone required more dialog boxes than you could shake a stick at. Compound the possible errors made while setting the boxes with the zillions of available printers and computers, the varieties of cables to connect them (cables both correctly and incorrectly configured—especially the ones for serial printers), and the wide variety of applications programs (many of which don't explain printing in detail), and you have all the ingredients for major frustration.

On the other hand, if you're lucky, all goes well the first time because your computer is really IBM-compatible, your printer is really supported by a Windows driver (or a manufacturer–supplied one that is well-designed and tested), and the application program is well-designed. If this is the case, stop reading this now and skip to the next chapter.

Unfortunately, there isn't room here, or in any book, for all the tips and tricks you'd need to resolve every problem that can crop up in the software-computer-printer chain. So, I'll just outline the basic problem areas and their most likely remedies instead. Chances are good that you'll weed out the culprit and be printing correctly in short order.

GENERAL TIPS

Some of the solutions apply to problems other than those listed under the specific headings. If you don't see your particular problem listed here, still check the following points.

These are the most common causes of printer problems:

- Be sure you've installed the correct printer driver, port, and printer name. Refer to Chapter 6 and the on-line Help information.
- Check the cable between your printer and your computer.
- Check the switch settings and power to your printer.

IF NOTHING PRINTS

If nothing at all prints, there may be a fast fix, because it means something's *really* wrong. Here are some possibilities.

- Is the printer actually turned on and plugged in?
- Is the printer connected to the computer? Check to see that the cables are tight.
- Does the printer have paper?
- Is the printer on line? Check the switches. Try turning the printer off and then on again to reset it.
- Is there an error light or indicator that would alert you to a problem with the printer? If so, check the manual to see what it means, and try to correct the problem. It could be a paper jam, a ribbon that's dead, or a font cartridge that has to be plugged in.
- Is the correct printer selected from the application's Printer Setup, dialog box? If the application doesn't have a Setup dialog box, it assumes you want to use the default printer. Check to see that the default printer is the one you're trying to print to. (See Chapter 6 for information about setting the default printer via the Control Panel.)
- Is the printer driver set up to print to the correct port? Check the Configure dialog box. (Again, see Chapter 6 for details.)

- If the printer is connected to a serial port (COM1 through COM4), are the communications settings correct? They must be the same on both sides (printer/computer). Set them using the Ports icon on the Control Panel.

- Does the printer work with any application? Does it work outside of Windows? If it does, then the problem is with your Windows setup.

IF YOUR PRINTER PRINTS GARBAGE

Another common problem is printing *garbage*. This

!@^&*(ghAU"æYW© ÓëG)()*()*®%^#$!!

is garbage.

- Severe garbage invariably results when a serial printer's communications settings are configured incorrectly (though it could have other causes). Check the Port settings from the Control Panel and the switches on the printer. Baud rate, stop and start bits, and parity must all be set identically for the printer and computer. Try running at a slower baud rate.

- On a serial printer if everything prints okay for a while (a few lines or a couple of pages) and then goes bananas, the "handshaking" is not correct. The printer is telling the computer to stop sending data, in order to catch up (this is called handshaking), but the computer doesn't get the message and keeps sending. That's when the garbage starts. Check the handshaking setup for the printer's COM port via the Control Panel's Port icon. The setting is called Flow Control on that dialog box. The Xon/Xoff method is *Software* handshaking (as set from the Printer Handshake dialog box, described immediately below). The *Hardware* setting uses voltages on specific wires in your cable to control handshaking.

Make sure the settings in the flow control box match the setting in the Handshake dialog box. Check the Control Panel ⇨ Printers ⇨ Configure ⇨ Setup ⇨ Options ⇨ Handshake dialog box. (I think this is the longest chain of dialog boxes in Windows!) Your printer and Windows have to be using the same flow control (handshaking) method, so make sure the handshake method for the printer and for the port match. For additional help, click the Help button in the Configuration dialog box and read the section "Configuring the Printer Handshake."

- It's possible that your serial printer cable is wired incorrectly and isn't relaying the handshaking information to the right pin on the computer's serial port. Check that the cable is intended for use with an IBM PC and that your serial interface card is configured correctly (with the correct port and handshaking).

- Try another printer driver that's similar.

- Try another printer name that's similar (from the Options settings, as explained in Chapter 6.)

- Turn your printer off and on again. There may have been left over data in the buffer.

- Try another cable.

- Is the printer in the correct mode? It may be set to emulate another type of printer. For example, Apple Laserwriters and some other PostScript printers can be in HP mode, or Diablo mode. Check the manual.

- Try the Generic/Text Only printer driver.

- Try the printer's self-test if it has one. Maybe the printer is defective.

If the margins, page breaks, indents, tabs, or line spacing don't match what you see on the screen, one of the following may be wrong:

- Did you choose the correct printer before printing? One printer may act very differently than another, particularly when it comes to formatting. The letters may still print, but formatting codes will not be interpreted correctly.

- If the application didn't let you choose the printer, is the correct default printer selected? (See Chapter 6.)

- Is the printer in the correct mode? It may be emulating another type of printer. Check the manual.

- Check the switches on the printer. They may accidentally be set to override the printer driver, creating a specific page length, character width, or lines per inch. In general, settings should be as "generic" (plain) as possible. This allows the printer driver to control formatting. If in doubt, check the other points in this list, then come back to this point, and try changing some of the printer's internal formatting settings if it has them. The most common problem is a switch that causes an automatic line feed when a carriage return is received. This should be turned *off.*

- Check that you installed the correct printer driver for your printer. (See Chapter 6.)

- Check that you installed the correct printer name from the driver you installed. (See Chapter 6.)

- Check that the the printer is set up for the correct paper source.

IF DOWNLOADED FONTS OR
CARTRIDGE FONTS DON'T PRINT

If you try to use fonts that you've downloaded to a printer or fonts that are in a plug-in cartridge and they don't print, check the following:

- Did you install the fonts properly? There should be installation instructions supplied with the fonts.

- If the fonts were downloaded into the printer's RAM (sometimes called making the fonts *permanent*), they will be lost when the printer's power is turned off. You will have to download them again if the power was turned off at any time subsequent to the downloading.

- If you are using cartridge fonts, the cartridge may not be plugged in firmly. Turn off the printer's power and push the cartridge in all the way. Then power up again.

- Did you set the Options for your printer correctly, as covered in Chapter 6?

- Printers that accept downloaded fonts have a finite amount of RAM space for holding them. It is possible to completely fill the RAM font space, after which no more fonts can be accepted by the printer. Perhaps you downloaded more fonts than it can handle, so the last few fonts weren't actually installed. Some printers come with utility programs that will print out a list of the installed fonts. An example is PS Exec, supplied with some PostScript printers. Try running one of these to see if the fonts are really getting to the printer.

IF ONLY PART OF A GRAPHICS PAGE PRINTS

If only a portion of a page prints when you're printing graphics, consider the following:

Some laser or ink-jet printers have limited internal RAM that prevents them from printing a whole page of graphics in the highest resolution. Select a lower resolution and try printing again.

If your printer lets you add memory and it's likely that you've run into a memory limitation, install more memory. Typical laser printers have as much as 3 megabytes of memory. This much can handle extra fonts and full pages of graphics easily. If you do a lot of complex printing, it's worth the price.

Does the paper size selected in the printer's setup box match the paper you're using? Check and adjust it if necessary.

CHAPTER EIGHT

8

Copying Material with the Clipboard

Fast Track

About the Clipboard: 237

The Clipboard is a Windows utility that aids in the process of copying information between documents. When you *cut* or *copy* text and graphics, they are temporarily placed on the Clipboard. They can then be *pasted* into a new location, either in the same document or in other documents—even documents created by a different application.

To select text to be copied or cut from a Windows application, 238

you most frequently position the mouse cursor at the beginning of the text you want to copy, press the mouse button and drag across the text, and then release the button. (Selecting text or graphics varies from application to application. For graphics selection, refer to the application's manual.)

To cut or copy selected material from a Windows application, 243

choose Edit ⇨ Cut or Edit ⇨ Copy. Cutting erases the selected material from the document. Copy leaves it. In either case, the material is placed on the Clipboard, ready to be pasted.

To select text or graphics from a non-Windows application, 244

you must be running in 386 Enhanced mode and the program must be running in a window. Position the pointer over the beginning of the text or graphic, click and drag the mouse to extend the selection box, and then release the mouse button.

To copy selected material from a non-Windows application,   **296**

> open the Control menu for the application's window and choose Edit. From the cascading menu, choose Copy. This places the material on the Clipboard. If the application was running in text mode, this material will be treated as text by the Clipboard. If the application was running in graphics mode, it will be considered graphics. (This affects pasting.)

To paste Clipboard material into Windows applications,   **250**

> position the insertion point in the document into which you want to paste. Choose Edit ⇨ Paste from the destination application's menu bar. Some graphics programs don't have a specific insertion point. In this case, the graphic may be dropped elsewhere in the document, such as the upper-left corner.

To paste Clipboard material into a non-Windows application,   **252**

> if the application is in full-screen mode, position the cursor where you want the Clipboard material pasted. Press Alt-Esc to get back to Windows. Get to the desktop and click once on the destination application's icon to open the Control menu, and choose Paste. The application will reappear with the new material pasted in (you may have to move the cursor before the pasting occurs).
>
> If the application is in a window (386 mode only), activate the window and position the cursor where you want the Clipboard material pasted. Open the Control box and choose Edit. Then choose Paste from the cascading menu.

To view the Clipboard's contents,   **256**

> Run Clipboard from the Main group.

CHAPTER *8*

AS ALLUDED TO IN THE INTRODUCTION, ONE OF THE characteristics of a perfect operating system environment would be that of an almost seamless meshing of simultaneously running programs. Though this has never been realized completely by any computer system thus far, Windows bridges a few significant gaps, as you've seen. The ability to run several programs at once, switching between them at will, and even while printing in the background is a strong move in this direction.

Now let's consider another issue—that of copying data between the programs. Ideally, all computer programs would be able to read each other's documents or cut and paste information between them. Unfortunately, this is rarely the case. Many programs use proprietary file and data formats designed to work optimally with the particular program. These are often promoted by marketing departments of software companies in the hopes that they will eventually become the established standard. As a result, sharing data between programs is seldom easy, and often creates more headaches that it's worth. If you've ever tried to print a dBASE data file in, say, Ventura Publisher or copy a portion of a 1-2-3 file into a WordStar file, you know what I mean.

More and more conversion programs and utilities are becoming available or are supplied with programs these days to help in the process, however. For example, Word for Windows has conversion utilies for several text and graphics file formats. The database management program Paradox and desktop publishing program Ventura Publisher both offer a plethora of conversion options. Standards are now emerging to expedite the process of data transfer between programs, and with time more

NOTE Some so-phisticated Windows applications support an elaborate method of information sharing called Dynamic Data Exhange, or DDE. With DDE, the information in one document can be made to automatically update related data in another document. For example, a portion of a spreadsheet document, when altered, could update a related list of numbers in a linked word-processing document. If both programs fully supported DDE, alteration of the data within either document would update the other. This is bidirectional DDE. More often, programs support only unidirectional DDE. In business applications, DDE is useful for connecting spreadsheets, databases, and word processors. Scientific, engineering, or industrial-control programs may use DDE to exchange data between programs connected to electronic measuring devices, thermostats, switches, relays, counters, and so forth. If your application can use DDE, consult its manual for instructions on its use.

elegant and effortless solutions will become available. In the meantime, Windows can lend a hand.

Windows, though not capable of making significant conversions between file formats nor of any radical sleight-of-hand to miraculously render all programs compatible, does have one trick up its sleeve—the Clipboard.

The Clipboard is a built-in utility program that aids in the process of copying information between applications. Using the Clipboard, you can mark portions of text or graphics in one application window and drop it into the destination window of another. The Clipboard works with both text and graphics, and on both Windows and non-Windows programs, within certain limitations that mostly pertain to non-Windows applications.

Functionally, the Clipboard acts a bit like a real clipboard. It's a temporary storage area onto which you can clip a small amount of data that you can keep easily at hand. You copy or cut the information out of an active window. Then, when you want to use the information, a simple command pops it into a new location, either in the same window or in another one.

The Clipboard uses system resources (RAM and disk files) to temporarily hold the information. This information waits on the clipboard until you want to copy or move it to a new location, typically a document that is open in a window. The information stays on the Clipboard until you delete it, replace it, or exit Windows. So you can use the information in it more than once, dropping it into several documents if you want to, or into several places in the same document. You can also store and retrieve Clipboard information to and from disk for later use.

You use the *cut, copy,* and *paste* approach with the Clipboard. If you've worked with a Mac program such as MacWrite or are familiar with PC or Windows programs such as Word or Works, you're already familiar with these techniques. *Cutting* means removing the information from its source location and putting it onto the Clipboard. When you cut information, it is deleted from its source window. *Copying* information, as the name implies, leaves the original intact, simply placing a duplicate of it on the Clipboard. *Pasting* is the process of inserting whatever is on the Clipboard into the destination.

TECHNIQUES FOR SELECTING TEXT

Cutting and copying require a procedure that you may already have mastered through the use of Windows' dialog box text areas, or by experimenting with some Windows applications or programs on the Mac. The procedure is called *selecting* and is actually very easy to learn, but a bit less simple to explain. Before you can successfully cut or copy stuff to the Clipboard, you'll need to understand how it's done. If you already do know, then you can skip to the next section. Otherwise, read on.

The exact way you select material in Windows programs may vary slightly from program to program, but generally, the same techniques apply, particularly to text. There may be some shortcuts in specific programs, so you should read the manual or help screens supplied with the program. Graphics programs allow a wider variety of selection techniques, and some of those are discussed below in the section "Techniques for Selecting Graphics."

NOTE The Notepad is covered at length in Chapter 13.

To illustrate how you select text, let's work with a Notepad file supplied with windows. It's called printers.txt and the exercises below illustrate the steps you could take to select portions of text to be cut or copied onto the Clipboard. Since these procedures are used in lots of other Windows programs, you'll be able to apply what you learn here to more than just the Clipboard.

SELECTING BY DRAGGING

Before you can select anything, you obviously have to open the document it's in. So in this case, open the file called printers.txt, which Setup copied onto your hard disk during installation. This is one of the last-minute information files supplied with your copy of Windows. Depending on when you bought Windows, you may or may not have this exact file. If not, use another *.txt* file. Recall that you can open the file by starting

NOTE If you want to select more text than fits in the window, many applications will scroll up, down, left, or right when you pull the mouse cursor all the way to the edge of a window. Keep the mouse button depressed while doing this, and the selection will continue until you release the button.

the Notepad (found in the Accessories group) and choosing File ⇨ Open, or you can open the File Manager, display the directory the file is in, and double click the file. Since there's an association set up between *.txt* files and the Notepad, the Notepad will start with the document file opened. Then maximize the Notepad window so you can work with it more easily.

1. Now we're going to select some text. Assume you want to copy the second paragraph of text into another document. You'll have to select that paragraph. Start by positioning the insertion point just before the first letter of the second paragraph.

2. Click and hold the left mouse button down.

3. Drag the mouse toward you, (moving the pointer toward the bottom of the screen) while holding the button down. As you do so, the text is highlighted. You can move the mouse left, right, up, and down, to refine the selection, for as long as you keep the button depressed. You might notice that if you move the cursor toward the top of the screen, above the initial point of your selection, that the selection sort of reverses. That is, the starting point now appears to be the end point. This is because the first place you click when making a selection acts as an *anchor point*. It stays stationary. As long as the mouse button is depressed, all text between the anchor point and the cursor will be selected, regardless of whether the pointer is above or below. Release the mouse when all the text you wanted to select is highlighted.

Figure 8.1 shows some selected text in a Notepad document.

SELECTING BY SHIFT-CLICKING

There's another way to select text (some graphics programs work this way too). It's called *shift-clicking*. Try these steps:

1. "Deselect" any text you've selected by clicking anywhere

✈ *SPEED TIP* Some applications let you select text by clicking in the far left margin. One click will select the current line. You can extend the selection by dragging the mouse down the left margin. Some programs also have a Select All command on their Edit menu that selects everything in the file.

on the text. It doesn't matter where. This will *collapse* the selection.

2. Move the cursor to the beginning point of the section to be selected, and click.

3. Move the mouse to the end of the section you want to select. (Note that you can use the arrow keys and the scroll bars to move to a position in the text that is not visible.)

4. Press and hold down the Shift key, and then click the mouse (this is called *shift-clicking*). The text between your two clicks is now selected.

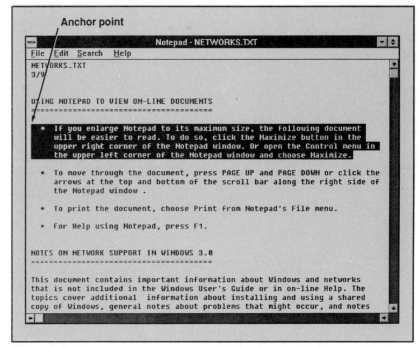

Figure 8.1: You can select text in most Windows applications by clicking in the upper-left corner of the text to be selected. Hold down the mouse button, and then drag the mouse down to the right. Release the mouse button, and the selection is made.

5. Close the Notepad for the time being. If asked whether you want to save any changes to the file you were experimenting with, say No.

In most text-based Windows applications, selected text will automatically be replaced by the first printing key (letter, number, symbol, or punctuation mark) you press on the keyboard. This makes the process of deleting unwanted text and inserting new text faster, but it also means you should be careful when selecting text. If you type a letter, the text may disappear and be replaced by the single letter. If this happens, some applications will let you recover the lost text by selecting Edit ⇨ Undo.

TECHNIQUES FOR SELECTING GRAPHICS

NOTE The Paintbrush program is covered at length in Chapter 12.

You select graphics approximately the same way as you do text. As an example, let's run the Paintbrush program supplied with Windows, load a picture, and select a portion of it.

1. Start the Paintbrush program by double clicking its icon.

2. When Paintbrush comes up, maximize the window.

3. Choose File ⇨ Open. Double click on chess.bmp in the File Open dialog box. The flying chess board appears in the window. (Incidentally, this is one of the desktop backgrounds you might recall from Chapter 5. It's really a *.bmp* file that you can edit in Paintbrush if you want.)

4. Once the picture loads in, click on the left of the two scissor boxes on the left side of the screen. These scissor boxes are the tools that Paintbrush uses for selecting portions of a picture. It is typical of graphics programs to have several types of *tools* for selecting items or areas.

5. Move the cursor out onto the picture and position it near the top of the flying pawn in the upper left section of the screen. Click and hold.

6. Now lasso the pawn by drawing a circle around it, and release the mouse button. A line forms around the pawn (or a portion of it, depending on how well you did). This is now the selected section of the picture. You can now, among other things, cut it, copy it, or move it by clicking in its middle and dragging. Figure 8.2 shows the effect of dragging it slightly.

7. Try the other selection tool—the scissor with the box. This one works more like text selecting. Start in the upper-left corner of the area to be selected and drag the mouse to the lower right. Then release the mouse button.

8. Close the Paintbrush application and document. Don't save the changes. If you do, it will mess up your flying chess board.

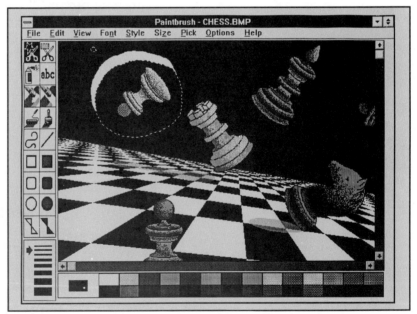

Figure 8.2: Selecting graphics is a bit different from selecting text. The techniques vary more between applications. Here a section of a Paintbrush picture has been selected and then dragged a bit.

CUTTING TO THE CLIPBOARD

You can *cut* to the Clipboard only from Windows applications. You can't cut from non-Windows applications, though you can copy from them (as explained later.)

When cutting from a Windows application, you first select the information you want to cut, and then use the application's Edit menu to cut the material. The information automatically goes into the Clipboard. Here are the typical steps:

1. Open the document you want to cut material from, if it isn't already open and on the screen.

2. Select the information to be cut. Exactly how you do this depends on the application. It's possible to cut a combination of text and graphics, as well as one or the other. Refer to the application's manual for specifics about it's particular selection capabilities and quirks.

3. Choose Cut from the application's Edit menu. The selected section of text or graphics vanishes. Actually it's still alive, only it's captured and living in Clipboard land.

4. Follow the steps in this chapter's section "Pasting Information from the Clipboard" to paste the stuff you've just cut into a new location.

COPYING TO THE CLIPBOARD

As explained earlier, the distinction between cutting and copying is that copying leaves the original information intact. Also, cutting is limited to Windows applications whereas copying is not, and copying gives you a wider variety of options as far as what you can copy. You can copy from both Windows and non-Windows applications. Here are the possible variations:

- Copy selected text or graphics from Windows applications.

- Copy selected text from non-Windows applications (386 mode only).

- Copy a bitmap image of the active window (386 mode only).

- Copy an image of the entire screen.

The technique you use depends on the type of application and whether the program is running full-screen or in a window. Each variation is described in a section below.

COPYING SELECTED TEXT OR GRAPHICS FROM WINDOWS APPLICATIONS

The method for Copying a selected area of text or graphics is similar to that used for cutting. Specifically:

1. Open the document you want to cut material from if it isn't already open and on the screen.

2. Select the information to be copied. Exactly how you do this depends on the application. It's possible to copy a combination of text and graphics, as well just as one or the other. Refer to the application's manual for specifics.

3. Choose Copy from the application's Edit menu. The selected section of text or graphics does not appear to change. However, a copy of it is now placed on the Clipboard.

4. Follow the steps in this chapter's section "Pasting Information from the Clipboard" to paste the copied information elsewhere.

COPYING SELECTED TEXT OR GRAPHICS FROM NON-WINDOWS APPLICATIONS

You can copy a selected area of graphics or text from non-Windows programs. However, you can only do this when you're running in 386 Enhanced mode and the non-Windows program is running in a window (not full-screen). If the program won't run in a window, you're out of luck. Some graphics programs, notably those that run in VGA graphics mode, can't be copied from for this reason.

Being able to copy text and graphics from a non-Windows application is a pretty nifty trick, and seems to work quite well. You can pull any text from a non-Windows application, including text that isn't actually in a document, such as program menus and instructions. When you copy text this way, Windows doesn't know the difference between your document and any other text or graphics on the screen. Whatever you copy is dumped on the clipboard as text or bit-mapped graphics, and can then be pasted into any Windows program that will accept text or graphics from the clipboard (e.g., Notepad, Write, Cardfile, Paintbrush, Terminal, Word, etc.).

Note that some non-Windows programs may appear to be in text mode (because they are displaying text) but are not. In this case, copying text may not work as expected. Microsoft Word, for example, can run in graphics mode in an attempt to better represent the final printed page. If you copy text from Word in this mode, however, you will be suprised to find that what's been copied to the Clipboard is a graphic—not text—and thus can't be successfully pasted into another text file. Switch Word back to text mode before copying, and you will succeed.

1. Make sure you're running in 386 mode. If you're in doubt about your mode, open or activate the Program Manager window, and choose Help ⇨ About Program Manager. The dialog box will report the current operating mode.

2. Open the non-Windows application you want to copy text from. It must be running in a window, not full-screen. If it's currently in full-screen, press Alt-Enter to move it into a window. (Some applications can't run in a window. Chapter 14 talks more about such quirks and considerations.)

3. In your application, open the document to be copied from, and scroll it so you can see the text to be copied. (You can only copy text that's actually on the screen.)

4. Select the text or graphics area to be copied by dragging the mouse as explained earlier in this chapter. Start in the upper-left corner of the desired text, and move down to the lower right. Then release the mouse. The selected text will be highlighted. An example is shown in Figure 8.3, where I've selected some text from a Wordstar document.

Notice that the moment you first click in the window, its menu bar changes. The word Select precedes the window name, indicating that you're in *select mode*. You can't use your application again until you finish the selection process or press Esc.

5. Now, open the Control menu for the application's window. There's a command called Edit, which, when selected will open up a cascading menu. Choose Copy

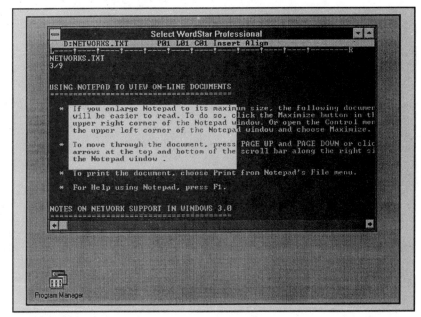

Figure 8.3: To select text from a non-Windows application in 386 mode, first put the document in a window, and then select the desired text with the mouse

from this cascading menu. This places the text on the Clipboard. Figure 8.4 illustrates the proper menu choice.

6. Follow the steps in this chapter's section "Pasting Information from the Clipboard" to paste the copied information elsewhere.

COPYING A BITMAP IMAGE OF THE ACTIVE WINDOW (386 MODE ONLY)

If you are running in 386 Enhanced mode, you can also copy the complete contents of the active window to the clipboard. The window may contain either a Windows or non-Windows application. The Clipboard translates the window's image into a *.bmp* (bitmap) file format that some graphics programs, such as Windows Paintbrush, can read and print. It's like taking a photograph of the window.

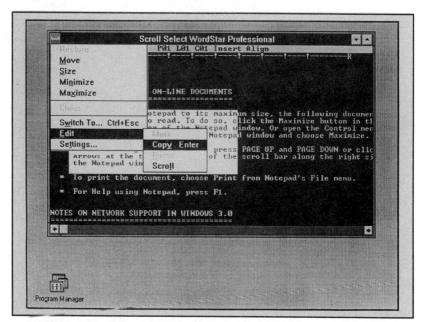

Figure 8.4: Once the text area is selected, open the Control menu and choose Edit ➪ Copy

Copying a window in this way can be useful if you're writing instruction manuals for Windows programs. You can pull the file into a program like Paint, modify it if necessary, and then save it on disk as a file. Then, when creating your manual, pull this picture into the word processing program or desktop publishing program in which the manual is being laid out. You may have to convert the *.bmp* file to another file format first if your layout program can't use *.bmp* files. Paintbrush will convert to PCX format, which is readable by many programs such as Ventura and PageMaker. Note that windows are graphic images, so even the text captured as part of a window is really graphics, not text.

Incidentally, the active window isn't always the window running the application you're using. The active window is sometimes an auxiliary window, such as a dialog box. So, you can capture individual dialog boxes for your instruction manuals, too. The color or shade of the title bar tells you which window is the active window.

Another point to consider if you are creating images for instruction manuals is this. There are several programs available for capturing screens and Windows that are more capable than the Windows Clipboard. The one used for this book is called Tiffany, and is very flexible in its capture modes and file formats, including gray-scaling capabilities. Other programs to consider are PixelPop, Hotshot, and Hijaak.

Here are the steps for copying the active window's image onto the clipboard:

1. Open the desired application in a window.

2. Adjust and size the window as needed.

3. Press Alt-PrintScreen. (Some keyboards label this key Prt Scr or something similar.) The image will be copied to the clipboard.

4. Follow the steps in this chapter's section "Pasting Information from the Clipboard" to paste the copied information elsewhere.

SPEED TIP   If you don't want to work with the window's image yet, you can save it to a disk file for later use. See the section "Saving the Clipboard's Contents to a File," later in this chapter.

NOTE   If Alt-Print-Screen doesn't seem to succeed in copying the image, try Shift-PrintScreen. Some older keyboards need this key combination instead.

COPYING A BITMAP IMAGE OF THE ENTIRE SCREEN

Suppose you want to capture an image of the entire screen, as opposed to a particular window. You don't even have to be running in 386 Enhanced mode to do this. Standard or Real mode will suffice.

NOTE If pressing PrintScreen doesn't seem to succeed in copying the image, try Shift-Print-Screen. Some older keyboards need this key combination instead.

1. Set up the screen you want the image of, adjusting and sizing windows as needed.
2. Press PrintScreen. (Some keyboards label this key Prt Scr or something similar.)
3. The image will be copied to the clipboard.
4. Follow the steps in this chapter's section "Pasting Information from the Clipboard" to paste the copied information elsewhere.

Note that when copying the screen image in Standard or Real mode, only text screens can be copied. Any program running in graphics mode (such as Word in graphics mode) will not be copied. In 386 Enhanced mode, graphics screens *can* be copied.

PASTING INFORMATION FROM THE CLIPBOARD

Once you've got something on the clipboard, you have two choices. You can paste it into a document you're working with (or that you open subsequently) or you can save it to a file. Saving to a file is described below in the section "Playing with the Clipboard's Contents." Here we'll consider the possibilities for pasting. Specifically, you have three major pasting choices:

- Pasting information into Windows applications
- Pasting into full-screen Non-Windows applications
- Pasting into windowed Non-Windows applications

Here's the scoop on each option.

PASTING INFORMATION INTO WINDOWS APPLICATIONS

Pasting into Windows applications is a simple procedure. Most Windows applications have a Paste command on their Edit menus. This is designed to work with the Clipboard for the express purpose of transferring information between documents or from place to place within a single document. The documents can even have been created by different applications.

To successfully paste information, all you have to do is set up the right conditions, and then issue the command.

NOTE Keep in mind that you don't even have to be copying between different applications. The techniques of copying or cutting and then pasting can be applied within the same application to move text or graphics around within a single application or between two document windows running in the same application window.

1. Copy or cut the desired text or graphics onto the Clipboard.

2. Open the program or window that will receive the information. It may already be open, in which case, activate the destination window or scroll to the appropriate spot in the current document for pasting.

3. If you're pasting text, move the text cursor to the position where you want the copied or cut text to be inserted, and click. If you're using other types of programs, figure out if the program has an "insertion point" tool or icon. Such a tool is used to tell the Clipboard where pasted material should begin. Check the application's manual if you don't know how the insertion point for it works. Some programs don't use insertion points.

4. Choose Edit ➪ Paste. The clipboard's contents will appear in the destination window.

If the material is text, it will flow into the text stream at the point of the cursor. If the material is graphics, the technique for pinpointing the destination within a document depends on the application. In Paintbrush, a selected section appears in the upper left corner of the screen. Other programs may require you to preselect the box, cell, or other starting location for the paste insertion. In most cases, the pasted material will automatically be selected after it is dropped in, so that you can manipulate it by moving, changing font, color, size, etc. If you decide the destination was wrong, make sure it's all still selected, and choose Edit ➪ Cut, press Delete, or choose Edit ➪ Undo (if the application has it). Then reposition and paste again.

Figures 8.5 and 8.6 show examples of text and graphics being pasted into documents. Figure 8.5 shows a section of text cut from the Cardfile into a Word for Windows document. Figure 8.6 shows a section of one of the supplied desktop background *.bmp* files pasted into another one of the *.bmp* files in Paintbrush.

Keep in mind that until you cut or copy again, or clear the Clipboard's contents (as explained below), the information is

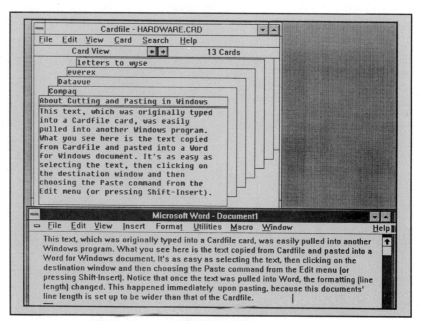

Figure 8.5: To paste text on the Clipboard into a Windows application, position the insertion point and click. Then choose Edit ➪ Paste. The text will appear at the insertion point.

still on it. You can paste as many times as you want. Figure 8.7 shows the effect of repeatedly pasting and moving slightly the same portion of a graphics file within the Paintbrush program.

PASTING INFORMATION INTO NON-WINDOWS APPLICATIONS

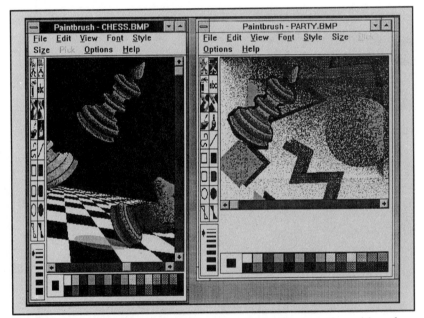

NOTE You are limited to pasting text into non-Windows applications. If you want to transfer graphics, you'll have to cut or copy the graphic into a program such as Paintbrush, PC Paintbrush, Corel Draw, or others, and then save the file in a format that's transferable.

Finally, let's consider pasting information into non-Windows applications. This is a bit trickier, and the results are not highly guaranteed, since non-Windows applications are not always that well behaved and they do not all operate by the same principles, in terms of how they will accept data.

Figure 8.6: To paste an image or graphic on the Clipboard, position the insertion point and click (if possible). Then choose Edit ⇨ Paste. The graphic appears at the insertion point, or is placed in the window at some predetermined location.

There are two main permutations of text pasting when using non-Windows applications:

- Pasting into full-screen non-Windows applications
- Pasting into windowed non-Windows applications (386 mode only)

Pasting into Full-Screen Non-Windows Applications

The following steps assume that you have some text on the Clipboard.

1. Start up the destination application in its full window.

2. Using whatever method applies to the application, position the cursor at the location where you want to insert the clipboard's material.

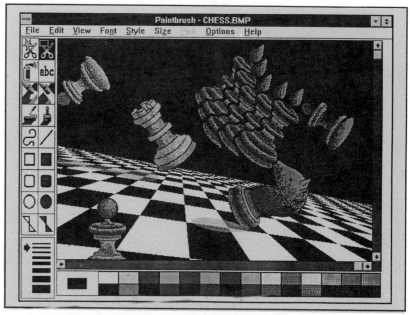

Figure 8.7: Since material stays on the Clipboard after a Paste command, you can paste again. Here you see several pastings of the same graphic.

3. Switch back to Windows by pressing Alt-Esc. As usual, you'll see the icon for the non-Windows application at the bottom of the desktop.

4. Click once on the program's icon. This opens the Control menu.

5. Choose Paste from the Control menu. (If you're running in 386 Enhanced mode, choose Edit, and then Paste from the cascading menu.) The text will be copied into your document.

What happens is this. The Clipboard's contents are transferred to the computer's keyboard buffer. The text is then inserted at the insertion point as though you were typing the text on the keyboard. For this procedure to work correctly, the program you are using must conform to certain DOS standards for accepting keyboard input and displaying it on the screen. Your application may not accept information in this way. There's no harm in trying, though, so give it a whirl. If things look really screwy when you try pasting, then quit your application without saving the changes. Your file will still be okay.

Pasting into Windowed Non-Windows Applications

Pasting into a non-Windows application that is running in a window is similar to the above procedure. You have to be running in 386 Enhanced mode, of course, since that's the only mode that allows running non-Windows applications in a window anway. Here are the steps, assuming you have some text on the clipboard.

1. Open the destination application in a window.

2. Make sure you're not in Select mode or Paste will be grayed. (Press Esc if you are.)

3. Move the application's cursor to the insertion point.

4. Open the application's Control menu by clicking on the window's Control box. Choose Edit ➪ Paste. The text is

inserted. The caveats described above apply less so with this approach since Window is orchestrating the display and keyboard operations for your program when it is running the application in a window. Figure 8.8 shows an example in which I inserted clipboard text from a help screen into a PC-Write file running in a window.

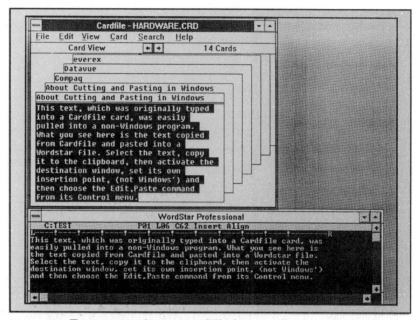

Figure 8.8: To paste text into a non-Windows application running in a window, position the cursor and select Edit ⇨Paste from the Control box.

PLAYING WITH THE CLIPBOARD'S CONTENTS

Sometimes you'll want to do more than simply cut, copy, and paste information between applications. The Clipboard program (it's actually a Windows program, just as File Manager and Print Manager are) has some other, free-standing capabilities of its own. These allow you to:

- View the Clipboard's contents
- Save the Clipboard's contents to a file
- Retrieve the contents of a Clipboard file
- Clear the Clipboard's contents

The purpose and particulars of each of these is described below.

VIEWING THE CLIPBOARD'S CONTENTS

Sometimes you'll forget what's on the Clipboard. Since every time you cut or copy in any application, the contents are replaced with the new material, it's easy to forget what's in the Clipboard's memory. Here's how to view the contents.

1. Run the Clipboard program by double clicking on its icon in the Program Manager's Main group.

2. The Clipboard's window comes up, displaying its current contents. Figure 8.9 shows a sample.

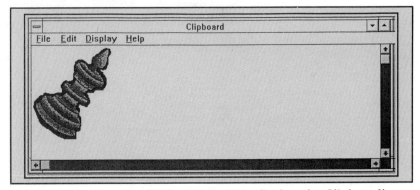

Figure 8.9: Opening the Clipboard program displays the Clipboard's contents

Changing the View Format

The contents may be displayed slightly differently from the way it looked when you copied it. For example, text line breaks may be in new positions. Don't worry about that. The material should still be intact, and will be okay when you paste it.

As you may know, graphics and text both have a considerable amount of potential formatting material associated with them, such as font size and type, and graphics setting for color, resolution, gray-scaling, and so forth. When you cut or copy material, the Clipboard does its best to capture all the relevant information. Then, when you paste, the destination program has to figure out what information it can use and what to ignore. The whole process is pretty iffy, considering all the possible variables. That is why viewing the contents of the Clipboard doesn't always reveal all of what's actually there in all its detail. However, the application you cut or copy from supposedly tells the Clipboard which formats the data can be viewed and accepted in. If there's more than one choice, you'll be allowed to change the view via the Display menu. By changing the display format, you may get a more accurate representation of the Clipboard's contents. The Auto setting returns the view to the original display format the material was shown with.

When you paste into another Windows program, incidentally, the destination program does its best to determine the optimal format for accepting the information in. This isn't determined by the Display menu's setting or current Clipboard window display.

For some fun, try leaving the Clipboard's window on the screen somewhere. Then open a few other programs, such as the Notepad and Paintbrush, and open a document for each. Size the windows so you can see all of them, including the Clipboard. Now go back and forth between the Notepad and Paintbrush, copying selected sections of text and pictures with the Edit menus. Notice how the contents of the Clipboard change each time you use the Copy command.

SAVING THE CLIPBOARD'S CONTENTS TO A FILE

Normally, when you exit Windows, or cut or copy anything new onto the clipboard, you'll lose the contents. Occasionally you may want to save the Clipboard contents to a file. This way you can resurrect it later (as explained in the next section), and paste it again after transferring other information or whenever you want. However, the Clipboard uses a proprietary file format that isn't readable by other popular programs. No doubt utility programs from other companies to convert Clipboard files to usable formats will eventually become available. Until that time, you'll have to use Clipboard as a middleman to drop text and graphics into your documents, rather than saving them as files and then reading them directly.

1. Open or switch to the Clipboard.

2. Choose File ⇨ Save as. The Save As dialog box will appear.

3. Type in a name for the saved file. As usual, you can change the path name and extension. However, you're best off leaving the extension as *.clp*, since Clipboard uses this as a default when you later want to reload the file.

4. Click on OK. The file will be saved, and can be loaded again as described below.

RETRIEVING THE CONTENTS OF A CLIPBOARD FILE

To reload the contents of clp file onto the Clipboard (and necessarily obliterate the current contents of the Clipboard), do the following:

1. Open or activate the Clipboard window.

2. Choose File ⇨ Open. The Open dialog box will appear.

3. Select the file you want to pull onto the clipboard. (Only *.clp* files can be opened.) Then click on OK.

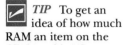 *TIP* To get an idea of how much RAM an item on the Clipboard is using, select the item, and then check the free memory amount from the Program Manager (Help ⇨ About Program Manager). Then clear the Clipboard and check again. The amount of RAM required to hold the item will equal the difference between the two numbers, assuming you didn't load or close any other programs or documents between these steps.

4. If there's something already on the Clipboard, you'll be asked if you want to erase it. Click on OK if you do.

5. Change the display format via the Display menu if you want to (assuming there are options available on the menu).

CLEARING THE CLIPBOARD

Keeping information on the Clipboard decreases the amount of memory available for other applications in Windows. If you're running Windows in Real mode or on a machine with limited memory, or if you need to have a sizable number of applications open at once, you should keep the Clipboard free of items that consume a significant amount of memory. Even if the item you clipped to it isn't large in appearance, the memory space required by Clipboard for the information may be considerable, especially since some items are stored in multiple formats. This means several copies of the information may coexist in RAM. If you're getting warning messages from Windows indicating that running another application isn't possible due to a RAM shortage, try clearing the Clipboard, as follows:

1. Open the Clipboard.

2. Choose Delete from the Edit menu, or press Del.

3. Choose OK. The Clipboard's contents will be deleted.

PART TWO

2

The Supplied Programs

Part II of this book consists of five chapters, all of which discuss the wealth of programs that are supplied with Windows—the Accessories. The first two chapters delve into the Write program quite thoroughly. Then Chapter 11 discusses the use of Terminal—the telecommunications program—for connecting to information services, bulletin board systems, and other computers. Chapter 12 details the use of Paintbrush, the newly updated and more powerful color drawing program supplied with Windows. Finally, Chapter 13 will show you how to use the remaining programs—Notepad, Calculator, Calendar, Recorder, and Cardfile. If you're looking for a discussion of the one additional accessory not covered here—the PIF Editor—that's explained in Chapter 14 (Part III).

CHAPTER NINE

9

Using Write
for Simple
Word Processing

Fast Track

To select a line or series of lines at a time,   280

> move the pointer into the left margin (the selection area) and click. The nearest line will be selected. To select more lines, drag the mouse up or down.

To select an entire sentence,   280

> place the insertion point anywhere within the sentence, hold down Ctrl, and click the mouse.

To select an entire paragraph,   280

> place cursor in the selection area next to the paragraph and double click.

To select an entire document,   280

> place the pointer in the left margin selection area. Hold down Ctrl and click.

To move a selected block,   284

> make the selection and choose Edit ⇨ Cut. Move the insertion point to the new location for the text. Choose Edit ⇨ Paste to drop the text into the new location.

CHAPTER 9

YOU WILL RECALL FROM THE INTRODUCTION THAT one of the applications supplied with Windows is Windows Write, or just Write. This is a simple but useful word processor. It boasts few significant frills compared to hefty programs like Word for Windows or Ami Professional, but will suffice to read and write letters, reports, or anything that doesn't require sophisticated formatting. Besides, the price it right, so you can't complain.

Though not a heavyweight at formatting text, Write can accept, display, and print graphics pasted to it from the Clipboard. Write lets you create word-processing documents of virtually any length, limited only by the capacity of your disk drive, and it has a fair number of features that make it useful as an everyday workhorse. In just a few months of using Windows 3.0, I've found myself wooed away from more sophisticated programs just by the convenience of Write.

This chapter includes a tutorial example that will give you the opportunity to learn by following specific steps. Through these steps, you will learn how to create, edit, and print a Write document, experimenting with all the major procedures involved in word processing with Write. In this example, you will create a simple one-page news story. First you will enter the text from the keyboard. Then you will edit the text, learning how to delete typos, move and copy sections of text, and alter the look, or format, of your document. Finally, if you have a printer, you will print out the story on paper. If you then want to learn more about Write, move on to Chapter 10, which explains more about paragraph and document formatting, setting Tabs, using

Search and Replace, changing the line spacing, and editing graphics in Write.

The example in this chapter uses sample text that you type in. If you don't want to type in the text, you can still follow along and learn the same skills. Just type in a few short paragraphs of your own and try the exercises by substituting your text for the references I make in the instructions.

CREATING YOUR FIRST DOCUMENT

Recall from the last chapter that every document you create in Windows, or any other program, for that matter, is stored by your computer in a file. The first step in creating your story will be to tell Windows that you want to begin a new file.

Follow these steps to open a new Write document:

1. Open the Accessories group and double click on the Write icon. Write will come up in a window. Notice that the file's name as indicated in the menu bar is *(Untitled)*.

2. Maximize the window. Your screen should now look like that shown in Figure 9.1.

There are several things to notice on your screen. As usual, up at the top you see the menu and title bars. The menu bar offers options for writing, editing, and formatting text. You experimented with some of these menus in Chapter 3, so they should be somewhat familiar.

Try pulling down each menu now, just to take a look at the various selections you have at your fingertips. The easiest way to do this is to open the File menu and then press → to see the next menu. You may even want to choose some of the menu choices that have dialog boxes associated with them (indicated by the ellipses after the name). You can always press Esc (or click on Cancel) to back out of a dialog box.

Referring to your screen or to Figure 9.1, notice that the title bar shows (Untitled) as the file name, since you haven't named the document yet.

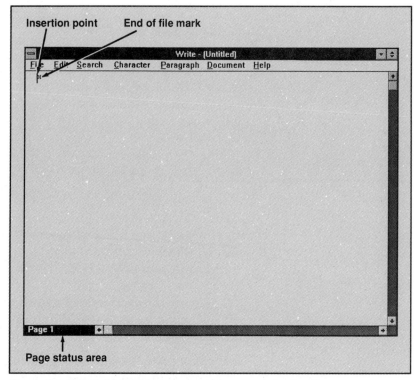

Figure 9.1: The initial Write screen with no text in the document

Finally, notice that the cursor sits blinking in the upper-left corner of your screen with another symbol to its right. This little boxy symbol indicates the end (bottom) of the document. Since you haven't typed in anything yet, the only thing between the top and bottom of the document is the insertion point. The mouse pointer is probably floating around on your screen somewhere. Move the mouse to see where it is.

ENTERING THE TEXT

Let's begin creating the story. It will contain five different elements: title, address, body, tabular list, and closing. Each of these elements will provide an opportunity to experiment with a different word-processing feature.

Type in the document by copying Figure 9.2. It has intentional errors in it that you can edit later.

Begin entering the text into your new file following the steps outlined here. If you make mistakes while you are typing, use the Backspace key (just above the ↵ key) to back up and fix them. If you don't see an error until you are long past it, don't worry. You'll learn how to fix such errors later.

1. Begin by typing in the title *NEWS FLASH* on the first line.

2. Next, press ↵ twice to move down a couple of lines to prepare for typing the address. Notice that pressing ↵ is necessary for adding new blank lines in a word processing document. Pressing the ↓ key will not move the cursor down a line at this point or create new lines. You will only hear an error beep from your computer if you try this.

3. Enter the first line of the address; then press ↵ to move down to the next line. Repeat this process for the last two lines of the address. So far this should remind you of using a typewriter.

4. Now press ↵ twice to put in a blank line.

5. Now begin entering the body of the story. Don't forget to leave in the spelling mistakes so that we can fix them later on. You shouldn't press ↵ at the end of each line because Write will automatically wrap to the next line for you. This is called *word wrapping*. All you have to do is keep typing.

6. When you reach the end of the first paragraph, move down by pressing ↵ twice and type the next one. Then type the third paragraph, if you want to, or skip to the list of findings. Now your letter should look something like that in Figure 9.3, though your line breaks and

NEWS FLASH

Society for Anachronistic Sciences
1000 Edsel Lane
Piltdown, PA 19042

The Society for Anachronistic Sciences announced its controversial findings today at a press conference held in the city of Pisa, Italy. As usual, Pisa was chosen as the sight for the conference because of its celebrated position in the annals of Western scientific history. The Society has made public its annual press conferences for well over 300 years and, as usual, nothing new was revealed. According to its members, this is a comforting fact and a social service in an age when everything else seem to change.

As noted by the Society's captivating keynote speaker Dr. Franz Anton Mesmer some 200 years ago at the Society's inauguration, Pizza was the obvious choice as the Society's eternal meeting ground. The incontrovertible need to debunk one of Eastern Europe's most emulated scientific quacks - Mr. Galileo - was reason enough to draw several hundred card-carrying members to make the initial pilgrimage way back when. The small but dedicated Society are hard-core believers in the superiority of subjective reason and personal observation and still scoff at what they consider the most rediculous of pseudo-scientific pranks - dropping a few balls off a precarious tower - a stunt which, for reasons they question, catapulted Galileo into the post-Aristotelean Science Project top 40.

At precisely twelve o'clock noon as measured on the ceremonial sun-dial, Dr. Peter Shickely, current Chair-in-Residence of the Society, annouced this century's findings. As Chair-in-Residence, he was behooved to recite the Society's creed, a phrase popularized by Geraldine "Flip" Wilson in the late 20th Century (and subsequently adopted by modern personal computer culture) -- "What you see is what you get." Below, in order of discovery, are the Society's nine findings for the current century.

Topic	Finding
1. Earth	A flat stone of enormous proportions
2. Sun	A bright light that orbits the Earth
3. Moon	A lesser bright light that is is swallowed by a malign force every month.
4. Stars	White dots in the sky.
5. Life	Spontaneously generated from unknown source, (e.g. frogs from mud).
6. Health	Good health results from a proper balance of humors within the body.
7. Airplanes	An illusion. Metal is heavier than air.
8. Science	If you can't see it, it didn't happen.
9. God	An intelligent life force pervading the known unverse except for certain parts of Northern New Jersey.

Though it was heartily disappointing to members of the Society that the awards could not be presented in person to the discoverers of the great truths, their descendants were on hand to posthumously accept. Among them were Sir Richard Aristotle from Devonshire, England, Jimmy "Bob" Aquinas from Bethpage, New York, and Martin Mesmer VIII from Salzburg, Austria.

Pierre Lapin
Paris Bureau

Figure 9.2: The story with intentional mistakes

typeface may be a bit different, depending on your selected printer, font size, and style.

USING THE TAB KEY

The next portion of the text is a simple table with two columns. Many letters, particularly business letters, will require setting up tables like this one, often with more columns. You use the Tab key to move from column to column, just as you would on a typewriter.

1. First, insert a blank line to separate the table from the previous paragraph. You will soon notice that when you reach the bottom of the screen, Write moves some text up and off the top of the screen in one big jump. You'll suddenly find the cursor (and the last line of the document) in the center of the screen instead of at the bottom. Write has simply scrolled the screen up to let

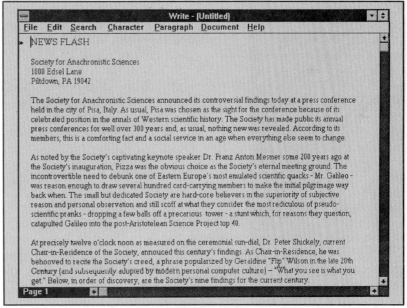

Figure 9.3: The first three paragraphs of the story typed in

you enter more text. (Many other word processors scroll the screen one line at a time when you're entering text.) Although a little disconcerting at first, this jumping to the middle of the screen is a thoughtful feature, since computer screens are usually better focused in the center than they are down at the bottom.

2. Type in the word

   Topic

   and press the Tab key four times. Each press advances the cursor to the next tab stop. Tab stops are initially set at half-inch intervals. (It's possible to set tab stops anywhere. Adjusting the tab stops is covered in Chapter 10.)

3. Now type

   Finding

4. Press ↵ again and begin entering the list. Type

   Earth

   and then press the Tab key twice (or until the cursor lines up with Notes).

6. Type

   A flat stone of enormous proportions

   and press ↵. This finishes the first line of the list.

7. Now repeat the process for the remaining five lines, using Figure 9.4 as a guide. Notice that each line will require a different number of tabs to line up the Notes column. If you press too many tabs, use the Backspace key to delete them.

ADDING THE ENDING

Now all that's left to type is the ending paragraph and then the closing.

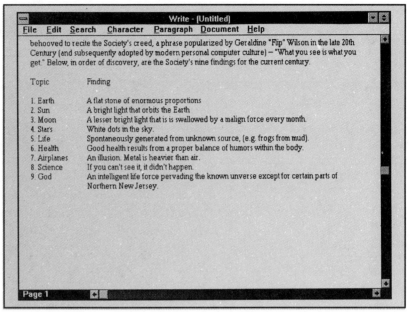

Figure 9.4: The items on each line are separated into columns by a tab or two

1. Press ↵ twice to create one blank line before the final paragraph.
2. Type in the rest of the letter, as shown in Figure 9.5.

EDITING YOUR TEXT

Now that you've typed in the basic content of the letter, you can begin editing it. If you made some mistakes of your own, that's okay. You'll soon see how how to fix errors.

Editing is simply the process of making changes, either major or minor, to your document. Everyone who uses a word processor inevitably develops their own style of editing. Some people like to print out a document and edit on paper, fix the errors, and then print again. Others find editing on the screen more efficient. You will no doubt decide for yourself later.

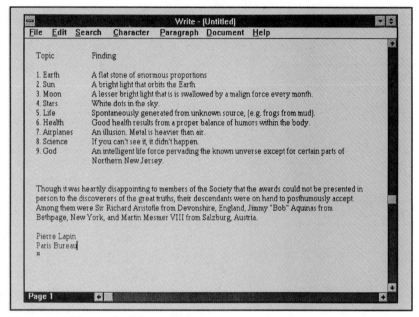

Figure 9.5: The end of the story

The first step in editing is learning to move around in the text. While actually entering the text, you seldom found it necessary to move the cursor around to any great extent. For the most part, it moved along by itself as you typed. But now, for editing purposes, you'll want to move up and down quite a bit in order to fix misspelled words and so forth.

MOVING AROUND WITHIN THE DOCUMENT

As you probably have surmised, the cursor marks the position where letters will appear when you begin typing. As you may recall from the previous chapter's discussion about pasting text from the Clipboard, this is called the *insertion point*. Editing your text involves moving the insertion point to the correct location and then using some commands to fix errors. This may require some scrolling. You should already be pretty familiar with scrolling. As with other Windows programs, you typically scroll using the scroll bars. You can also use the PgUp and PgDn keys to scroll your text a screen at a time. (Scrolling doesn't move the insertion point.)

Scrolling with the Keyboard

Practice scrolling by following these instructions:

1. Press the PgUp key (usually located on the 9 key in the numeric keypad). Make sure Num Lock is turned off; otherwise pressing that key will type the number 9 instead of scrolling the text. Pressing PgUp moves you up one screen toward the beginning of your document.

2. Now press PgDn. This has the opposite effect. Notice that your document takes up about two full screens. This amounts to about 40 lines of text, which is to say about ⅘ of a standard 8½" × 11" page if printed on a typical printer. (The actual size depends on your printer and the fonts supported. Your screen may look different.)

Since writing relies heavily on the keyboard, Write provides many keyboard combinations that can be used to move the insertion point. They are listed below. Note that the 5 key is used in combination with some arrow keys. This means the 5 key on the numeric keypad.

PRESS	TO JUMP TO THE
Ctrl-→	Next word
Ctrl-←	Previous word
5 →	Next sentence
5 ←	Previous sentence
Home	Beginning of the current line
End	End of the current line
5 ↓	Next paragraph

5 ↑	Previous paragraph
Ctrl-PgDn	Bottom of the window
Ctrl-PgUp	Top of the window
5 PgDn	Next Page
5 PgUp	Previous page
Ctrl-Home	Beginning of the document
Ctrl-End	End of the document

Scrolling with a Mouse

When you work with large documents, the scroll bar can be a guide to the relative position of the cursor within the document.

1. To move a screenful at a time, put the pointer somewhere in the scroll bar itself, either above or below the elevator, and click. Clicking above the elevator moves to the top; below moves to the bottom.

2. As discussed in Chapter 2, you can drag the elevator and pull it to any particular point on the scroll bar.

Consider the scroll bars to be a sort of measuring stick for your document, with the top of the bar representing the beginning of your document; and the bottom of the bar, the end. By dragging the elevator to the approximate relative position you want to scroll to, you can get close to your desired spot quickly. As explained in Chapter 3, the horizontal scroll bar works the same way as detailed for the vertical bar, but is only useful if your document is more than a page wide.

MOVING THE CURSOR

Once you've scrolled to the screen of text you want to edit, you then have to move the cursor to the exact location of the word or letter that you want to change. Then you can insert text, remove words, fix misspellings, or mark blocks of text for moving, copying, or deletion. Obviously the easiest way to do this is to just point and click. The insertion point will jump to the position where you clicked.

You can also use ↑, ↓, ←, and →, though, which may be easier at times. Here are some exercises to try.

1. Move to the second line of the story now and click just before the *t* in the word *sight*. This will position the insertion point just before that letter.

2. Now press → again and hold it down for a few seconds. Notice that once the key begins to repeat, the cursor moves faster. When it gets to the end of the first line, it wraps around to the second and third lines. Now press ← and hold it down. When the cursor gets to the beginning of the document, your computer starts to beep because the cursor can't go any farther.

3. Press → a few times until the cursor is on the first line of the address.

4. Now press ↓. Hold it down for a while and notice what happens when the cursor reaches the bottom of the screen. The screen scrolls up one line. The reverse happens when the cursor is at the top of the screen and you press the ↑ key.

5. Now press Ctrl-→. Each press of the arrow key moves ahead one word. Ctrl-← moves a word at a time in the other direction.

MAKING SOME CHANGES

Now that you know how to get around, you can begin to correct some of the typos in your letter. Let's start with the third line of the first main paragraph, where the word *site* is misspelled (as *sight*).

1. Position the cursor between the *i* and *g* in *sight*.

2. Press Del. This should remove the misplaced *g*. Notice also that the space where the *g* was closed up when you

> **NOTE** After positioning the cursor, don't forget to click. Otherwise, you'll end up making changes in the wrong place, since the text cursor doesn't jump to a new location until you click.

deleted the letter, pulling the letters to the right to close the gap. Repeat this to remove the *h*. Then add the *e*.

Many simple errors can be fixed using the Del or Backspace key. But suppose you wanted to delete an entire word, sentence, or paragraph. You could do this by moving to the beginning or end of the section you wanted to erase, and then holding down Del or Backspace until the key began repeating and waiting for all the words to disappear, letter by letter. But this is an unpredictable method. If you're not careful, you'll often erase more than you intended to. Instead, you can delete a whole block of text by first selecting it and then cutting it, as described in the last chapter. (As you may recall, this also puts it on the Clipboard.)

ABOUT MAKING SELECTIONS IN WRITE

Much of editing with a word processor centers around manipulating blocks of text. A *block* is a portion of your text, letters, words, or paragraphs. Many of the commands in Windows programs use this idea of manipulating blocks of information, sometimes text, sometimes other data, such as numbers.

CAUTION Be careful not to press keys other than the cursor-movement keys after you've made a selection. If you type *A*, for example, the whole selection will be replaced by the letter *A*. If this happens accidentally, choose Edit ⇨ Undo from the menu bar before doing anything else and your text will be returned to its previous state.

You must select a block before you can work with it. As long as an area of a document is selected, it will become the center of attention to Write and will usually be treated differently than the rest of the document. Some menu commands will affect the selection and nothing else. This remains the case until the block is "deselected" when you click elsewhere, or select another block.

Selecting Portions of Text

Once you've selected a section of text, you can manipulate it in any number of ways: you can cut or copy it, change its font size, alter the paragraph formatting, and so forth. Try these exercises to get the hang of selecting.

Selecting an Arbitrary Text Area with the Mouse

Selection is particularly intuitive and simple with the mouse. Mouse selection was also explained in Chapter 8 for copy and cutting to the Clipboard. Try this:

1. Deselect any possible selections by clicking somewhere in the text. It doesn't matter where.

2. Now move the pointer to the first letter in the second paragraph (you may have to scroll the window).

3. Hold the left mouse button down, and move the pointer down several lines. As you move the mouse, the selection extends. When you let up on the button, the selection is completed.

4. Click anywhere again to deselect the selection.

The *anchor point*, as I mentioned in the last chapter, is the point you first clicked. Dragging downward extends the selection downward from the anchor point. If you were to keep the mouse button down and drag *above* the anchor point, the selection would extend from the anchor point upward.

Selecting a Word at a Time

Often you'll want to quickly select a word, either to delete it, or to change some aspect of it, such as its font size. You can do this easily by double clicking. Let's say you want to change *Eastern* Europe in the second paragraph to *Western* Europe.

1. Double click on the word *Eastern* to select it.

2. Press Del to delete it. (Using Del doesn't put it on the Clipboard, incidentally. It just deletes it.)

3. Type **Western**.

Selecting a Line or Series of Lines

There's a shortcut for selecting an entire line or quickly selecting a series of entire lines.

1. Move the mouse pointer into the left margin. It changes into an arrow. This margin is called the *selection area.*

2. Position the pointer to the left of the first line of the second paragraph and click the mouse to select the entire line.

3. Starting from the same place, hold down the mouse button and drag the pointer down the left margin, selecting each line the pointer passes.

Selecting an Entire Sentence

Want to select an entire sentence? This is a great shortcut for writers, or anyone who considers sentences individually. If you don't like it and want to cut or move the whole thing, you can do so easily.

1. Press and hold down the Ctrl key.

2. Click anywhere on the first sentence in the second paragraph, highlighting it.

Selecting an Entire Paragraph

There's also a shortcut for selecting an entire paragraph.

1. Move the cursor into the selection area (left margin) next to the first paragraph.

2. Double click. The entire paragraph will be highlighted.

Dragging the pointer in the margin while still holding the mouse button down will select additional paragraphs.

Selecting an Entire Document

Sometimes you'll want to select the whole document. This can be useful for changing the font size or type of all the text, or changing other attributes, as discussed below. There's no menu choice for this, but it can be done with a key combination.

1. Move the cursor into the selection area.

2. Hold down Ctrl and click the mouse. The entire document will become highlighted.

Selecting with the Shift Key

There is another shortcut for selecting. You can use the Shift key in combination with the arrow keys or the mouse to select an arbitrary amount of text. Here's how:

1. First, deselect anything you already have selected.

2. Move the cursor to the first word in the second paragraph. Now press Shift- →. The selection advances one letter with each press (unless you hold the key down too long, in which case it moves by itself).

3. Now press Shift-↑ five times. Notice that as you move up past the anchor point, the selection reverses, moving upward in the text. Now text in the first paragraph is selected.

4. Now press Shift-Ctrl- →. The selection advances a word with each press.

5. Release the keys and click somewhere to deselect.

6. Click on the first word in the second paragraph.

7. Hold down the Shift key.

8. Click on a word in the middle of the paragraph. This changes the selection. It's now from the new anchor point to the point where you clicked.

MAKING THE CHANGES

Now that you've got the hang of selecting, let's get back to editing the story. For our first change, we want to select the word *Pizza* in order to delete it and then replace it with *Pisa*.

1. Select the word *Pizza* in the second line of the second paragraph.

2. Open the Edit menu and choose Delete, since we want to delete the currently selected word.

3. The menu disappears and you are returned to your text at just the right spot to type in *Pisa*. (You may have to add a space after the word, depending on how you selected *Pizza*.)

All of this may seem like a lot of work just to change a few letters, but for larger selections you will find it's worth the effort.

Let's try another approach. Here's a shortcut for replacing a word or selection with some other text. In this case we'll just change the last word in the third paragraph.

1. Double click on *century*.

2. With *century* highlighted, type in the word *year*. Notice that *century* is deleted. This saves the extra step of choosing Delete from the Edit menu.

Inserting Letters

Now let's move on to another kind of error—the word *unverse* in item number nine. This word is missing a letter, so the missing letter will have to be inserted into the middle of the word. Missing or dropped letters are probably the third most common form of typos, after misspellings and reversed letters. Here's how to insert the missing letter.

1. Position the insertion point to just after the *n*.

2. Type the letter *i*.

Notice that the word opened up to let the *i* in. Unlike on the typewritten page, lines on a computer screen are flexible, letting you insert the letter. In fact so flexible that you may have noticed Write rewraps all the lines of the paragraph almost instantly as you insert text.

Actually, you can insert any number of letters, words, or even paragraphs wherever you want within a document, and Write will accommodate the addition. This is called *inserting.* You may know that some word processors allow you to to deactivate inserting in favor of the old-style, typewriter-like *overwriting,* where newly typed letters overwrite the old ones instead of pushing them to the right. Write does not let you do this. The advantage is that you will never accidentally type over some text you want to keep. The disadvantage is that you will have to take action to delete unwanted text.

Your story should now look like Figure 9.6.

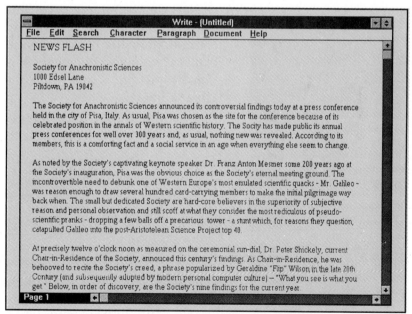

Figure 9.6: The top of the story with corrections made

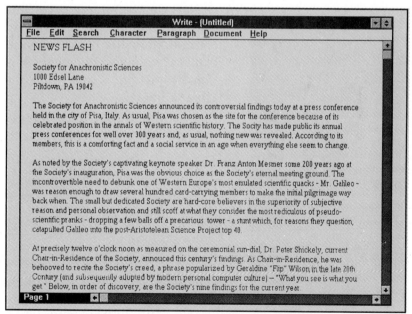 *TIP* You use this same technique for inserting letters in dialog text box text areas. By additionally using the Backspace and Del keys, you can easily edit such things as file and directory names this way.

MOVING SELECTED BLOCKS

The editing process often involves moving larger portions of text, such as sentences and paragraphs, within a document. Rather than inserting a block of text by retyping it, you can pick it up and move it from one place to another with the Cut, Copy, and Paste commands covered in the last chapter.

Here's an example of the Paste command that will reverse the order of the first two paragraphs in our letter.

1. Move to the top of the document.

2. Select the entire second paragraph with whatever technique you prefer.

   Since you want a blank line between the paragraphs after the move, one way to do this is to carefully select the blank line immediately below the paragraph, too. Just drag the mouse a little further down past the last line of the paragraph. If you double clicked in the margin to select the paragraph, press Shift to retain the paragraph selection and double click to the left of the blank line. You'll know the blank line is selected when a thin strip at the left margin becomes highlighted. This is the normally invisible "paragraph mark" associated with the blank line.

3. Open the Edit menu and choose Cut. Your text should now look like Figure 9.7.

4. Now move the insertion point to the place where you want to insert the paragraph, which happens to be just before the *T* of the word *The* in the first paragraph.

5. Choose Edit ⇨ Paste or press Shift-Insert. Now your text should look like Figure 9.8.

6. Now give yourself a little more practice by returning the second paragraph to its original position.

Sometimes after moving paragraphs around, you may have to do a little adjusting, such as inserting or deleting a line or some

TIP   Every paragraph has a paragraph mark. The paragraph attributes, such as alignment, tab settings, and margins are contained in the paragraph mark. Copying the mark copies these attributes. Copying the paragraph mark is an easy way of copying attributes from one place to another. Chapter 10 describes these attributes.

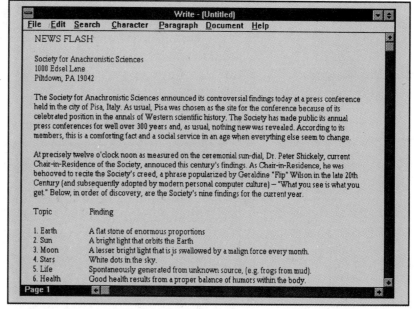

Figure 9.7: The story with a paragraph cut in preparation for pasting it above the first paragraph

spaces. But as you know, you can insert a line with ↵. If, after a move, you have extra blank lines, you can delete them by putting the insertion point on the first space of a blank line (the far left margin) and pressing the Backspace key. This "pulls" up all the text to the right of (and below) the cursor one line.

CENTERING A LINE

Now there is only one thing that remains to be done before actually printing out the letter: We still have to center the first four lines of the document. On a typewriter, centering is often a real headache because you have to count the number of letters in the line you want to center, divide by two, and then count outward from the center of the page to find your starting place. But since a computer is first and foremost a calculator, it performs

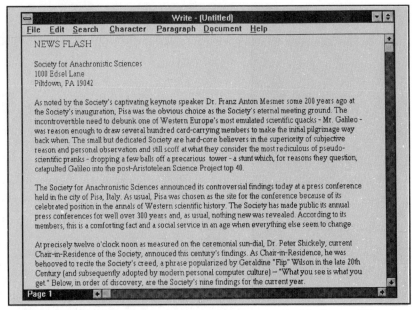

Figure 9.8: The first and second paragraphs reversed with Cut and Paste

this type of work extremely efficiently. Here's how you do it.

1. Put the cursor anywhere on the first line (the one that says *NEWS FLASH*).

2. Choose Paragraph ⇨ Centered. In a split second the line jumps to center stage.

3. Now select the three address lines.

4. Again choose Paragraph ⇨ Centered. All three lines jump to the center.

You can center any number of paragraphs by selecting any parts of them, even as little as one letter. Or, if you only want to alter the formatting of one paragraph, just put the insertion point anywhere in the paragraph and select Paragraph ⇨ Centered.

Now your screen should look identical to that shown in Figure 9.9.

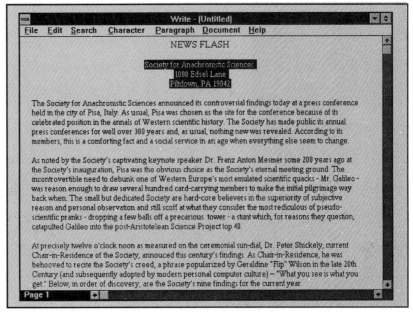

Figure 9.9: Four lines centered with the Paragraph ⇨ Centered command

SAVING YOUR WORK

Write stores parts of your documents in RAM while you work on it. Unfortunately, RAM is not a permanent storage area; thus your work will be lost when you turn off your computer unless you first save it on disk.

You save your documents with two commands on the File menu—Save and Save As. The first time you save a document, Windows applications such as Write will ask you for a name to give your document. After the initial save, Write assumes you want to use the current name, unless you indicate otherwise by using the Save As command.

In general, it's a good idea to save your work any time you can't afford to risk losing it, such as when you have done enough editing that reverting to the last version of your document would be bothersome. I try to save about every 15 minutes.

Before printing out the story, save it by using the following steps:

1. Choose File ⇨ Save. The Save As dialog box appears since this is the first time you've saved this file and Write needs to ask you for the name. Your screen should look like the one shown in Figure 9.10.

   You can type in a new name from the keyboard, but first you want to be sure that you are going to store the file on the correct disk drive, and that you have a formatted data disk (if you are using floppies) in the drive.

2. Notice that just below the file name, on the line that says Directory, you'll see the drive and directory setting.

   c:\windows

   This indicates where the file will be saved unless you

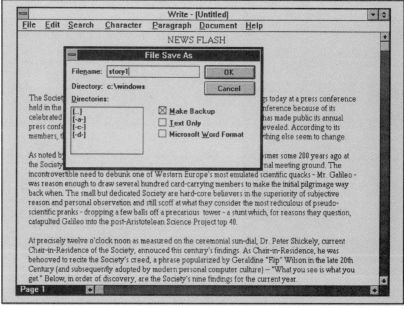

Figure 9.10: The File ⇨ Save As dialog box. After making sure the drive and directory are right, type in the file name.

type a different path name into the file name area or change the drive and directory setting by double clicking in the Directories section. Selecting drives and directories was covered in Chapter 3.

The check boxes will normally be set to make a backup copy (Write creates a file with the extension *.bkp* containing the previous version of the document), not to store the file as Text Only, and not to store the file in Microsoft Word format. You don't alter these settings unless you want to create a file that other word processors or other types of programs can read.

So, in short, to save the story:

1. Choose File ⇨ Save.

2. Adjust the Directory setting if necessary.

3. Type in the file name *story1*, and press ↵. Your disk drive light will come on, and the file will be saved.

PRINTING OUT THE LETTER

Assuming you have a printer connected, you can now try printing your letter in its final form. Refer to Chapter 7 for information about using the Print Manager to print documents. There is also additional information about printing from Write at the end of Chapter 10 in the section "Printing Your Document."

CHAPTER TEN

10

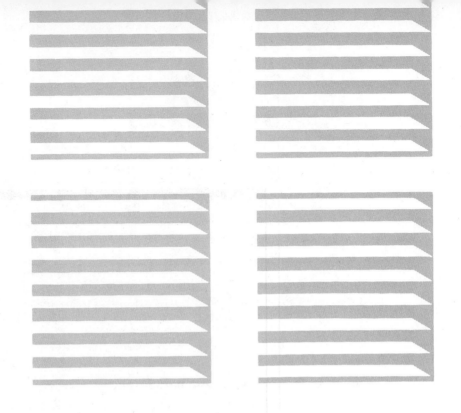

Polishing Your Write Documents

Fast Track

To format the whole document, 305

select the entire document by holding down Ctrl and clicking in the left margin. Then make the paragraph settings. This applies to character settings as well.

To format characters, 305

select the range of text to be affected. Then open the Character menu and choose the desired format. To change the font, choose the Font command and select the font from the dialog box.

To set tabs, 308

choose Document ⇨ Tabs. In the dialog box type in the desired tab locations. Or, click on one of the the tab icons in the ruler and then click in the area just below the ruler where you want the tab to be. You can drag the tab marker left and right to reposition it if you have to.

To search for a word, 314

choose Search ⇨ Find. A dialog box will appear. Type in the text you want to search for. Press ⏎ or click on Find Next. If you want to find complete words only or match upper- or lowercase, check those options in the dialog box.

To search and replace, 315

choose Search ⇨ Change. Type in the text to be found, and the replacement text in the indicated sections of the dialog box. Set the Whole Word or match Upper/Lowercase check boxes on if you need them. Click on the appropriate button in the box to begin the search.

CHAPTER 10

IN CHAPTER 9, YOU LEARNED THE BASICS OF WINDOWS Write. That chapter covered entering and editing text, moving blocks of text, and saving your text file on disk. Those skills are enough to enter and print a basic plain-jane document, but they don't give you much room for creativity. In this chapter, we'll extend your skills by discussing the various formatting features you can easily apply to your documents. Included in the discussion will be:

- How to format individual characters with font, style, and size alterations
- How to format paragraphs by changing line spacing, indents, and margins
- How to set the tab stops to aid you in making tables
- How to quickly search for and replace specific text
- How to include headers and footers
- How to paginate your document correctly
- How to incorporate and edit graphics
- How to copy text between two Write documents
- More about saving files
- More about printing files

OPENING AN EXISTING WRITE FILE

Before beginning, open the story1.wri document you created last chapter. If you rebelled and didn't want to type it all in, you can simply bring up Write and type in a paragraph or two of text. Then you'll have some text to experiment with. Assuming you did create a file last chapter or have one on disk that you want to use now, you can open it and load it into Write. Here are the steps for opening a file.

1. Choose File ⇨ Open.

2. Choose the file name from the File Open dialog box that appears. You can type in the full name of the file or double click on it.

3. Click on OK.

FORMATTING PARAGRAPHS

Paragraphs are the most essential divison of your text when it comes to formatting or controlling its looks. A paragraph is defined by Write as any text terminated by a carriage return (that is, the ↵ key). So even a single letter, line, or word will be treated as a paragraph if you press ↵ after it. Write handles each paragraph as a separate entity, each with its own formatting information. You may have noticed that the story file you created in Chapter 9 used a standard block paragraph format typical of many business letters. In that format, a paragraph's first line is not indented, and you have to separate paragraphs by pressing the ↵ key twice. Also notice that the right margin is ragged, rather than straight, or justified.

These and other qualities affecting the looks of your paragraphs can be altered while you are entering text or any time thereafter. As you change the formatting settings, you immediately see the effects. Bold letters will look bold, centered lines centered, italic letters look slanted, and so forth.

For most documents, you may find you are happy with the default format that Write is set up with. Write applies the standard default format for you, carrying it from one paragraph to the next as you type. If you decide you'd rather use a different format for a new document, you just alter some settings and begin typing away. Then everything you type into the new document will be formatted accordingly until you change the settings.

TURNING ON THE RULER

The ruler helps you keep track of where you are typing on the page, much like the guide on a typewriter. It also lets you alter the format of paragraphs by clicking on icons and symbols displayed within its boundaries. These alterations can be made from the Paragraph menu as well, but the ruler makes it easier. Figure 10.1 shows the ruler and its sections.

Normally the ruler is off (hidden), but you can turn it on if you wish to.

- Choose Document ⇨ Ruler On to show it.

- Choose Document ⇨ Ruler Off to hide it.

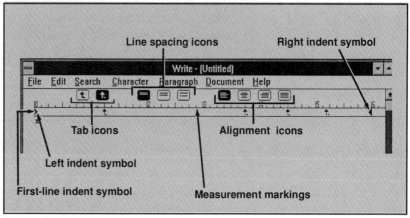

Figure 10.1: The ruler helps you align text, change line spacing and set tabs

Hiding the ruler lets you see extra lines of your text in the document window, but, as you'll see later, the ruler is useful to have around. (Figures in this chapter will be shown with the ruler on.)

The ruler has markings on it to help you gauge where your text will fall across the printed page, and to help you set up tab stops. Each inch is marked with a number and each tenth of an inch is marked by a small line. (You can change the ruler to show centimeters via the Document ⇨ Page Layout dialog box, though.)

Notice the ▶ and ◀ marks. These indicate the left and right indents (sometimes called margin settings). Also, though not easily visible, there is a small square dot within the ▶ mark on the left side of the ruler. This controls and indicates the setting of the first-line indent for each paragraph. The ruler can also show tab settings. The use of those settings will be explained later.

VIEWING AND ALTERING PARAGRAPH SETTINGS

Paragraph formatting falls into three categories with Write: *alignment*, *spacing*, and *indents*. The following sections explain and illustrate these catagories.

Unless otherwise noted, the examples here use inches as the basic unit of measure. If your dialog box indicates other units, such as centimeters, you can use the Document ⇨ Page Layout command to change to inches.

ALIGNMENT

Alignment refers to where the text in a paragraph sits within the margins. *Left* is the default, causing text to be flush (straight) against the left margin (and ragged right). *Center* centers every line of the paragraph. *Right* causes text to be flush against the right margin (and ragged left). *Justified* causes both the right and left margins to be flush by adding space between words and letters to fill out shorter lines.

Many printers can do what's called microspaced justification, a technique for spreading out the words and letters so that justified text looks more evenly spaced. Yours may be able to, but you should probably try printing out a justified document before deciding whether to use this format.

Figure 10.2 shows four paragraphs, each one with a different alignment type.

To display or modify the settings for a given paragraph, you put the cursor anywhere on it and then view or change the setting either from the ruler or from the Paragraph menu. Any time you position the insertion point in a paragraph, the ruler and menu will reflect that paragraph's current settings.

To modify the settings for several paragraphs, select an area

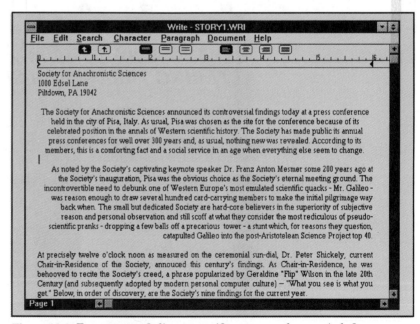

Figure 10.2: Four types of alignment (from top to bottom): left, centered, right, and justified

of text that includes portions of each paragraph you want to affect. Then use the Paragraph menu or ruler.

To View Paragraph Alignment

1. Move the insertion point to the paragraph in question.

2. If the ruler is on, look at it. The icons will indicate the alignment settings, as shown in Figure 10.3.

3. As an alternative, open the Paragraph menu. There will be a check mark next to the current paragraph's alignment setting. Figure 10.4 shows an example of a centered paragraph's menu.

To Alter the Paragraph Alignment

You can change the settings for a paragraph almost as easily as you can display them.

1. Move the insertion point to the paragraph or select several paragraphs (even a portion of each paragraph will suffice).

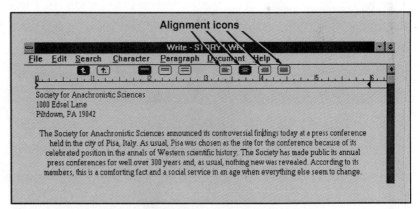

Figure 10.3: These icons in the ruler indicate and allow you to alter the alignment settings for a paragraph or selected paragraphs

2. Open the Paragraph menu and choose the alignment you want.

3. As an alternative, if the ruler is showing, click on one of its four alignment icons (this is faster).

LINE SPACING

Line spacing determines the amount of space between lines within the paragraph. Normally you'll want to use single or double spacing. However, you can also have 1½-spaced lines. (Text in font sizes of 24 points or over are not affected by line spacing.)

To Change the Line Spacing of a Paragraph or Paragraphs

1. Move the insertion point to the paragraph in question (or select several paragraphs). There need not be text on the line yet. (On a new line you must do this before you begin typing.)

2. If the ruler is on, look at it. The icons will indicate the line-spacing settings, as shown in Figure 10.5. Click on the icon representing the line spacing you want.

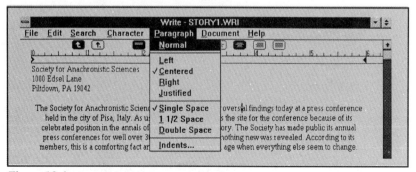

Figure 10.4: The Paragraph menu and the ruler always indicate the settings for the current paragraph (the one in which the insertion point is positioned)

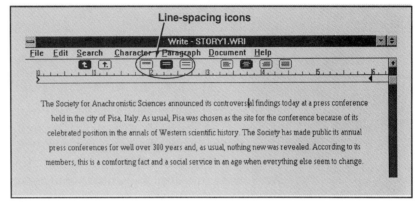

Figure 10.5: These icons in the ruler indicate and allow you to change the line-spacing settings for the current paragraph or selected paragraphs

3. As an alternative, open the Paragraph menu. There will be a check mark next to the current line-spacing setting. Change the setting by simply choosing another one.

INDENTS

The last kind of paragraph formatting is setting indents. Indents fall into three categories: *right indent, left indent* and *first-line indent*. Every paragraph has settings for each, and each paragraph's settings can be different. As with the other paragraph settings, these are carried from one paragraph to the next as you type, or you can change them after the fact. You set indents via the Paragraph menu's Indents command or by dragging the indent symbols on the ruler (see Figure 10.6).

The settings determine how far in from the left and right margins your text will appear. (They do not determine how far from the edge of the *page* the text will appear. That's established by the margins, set in the Page Layout dialog box from the Document menu, as will be discussed later in this chapter.) The first-line indent determines the starting position of the first line of each paragraph.

Setting the Left or Right Indent

You can change the left or right indent by two methods:

1. Place the insertion point in a paragraph or select several paragraphs whose settings you want to change.

2. Choose Paragraph ⇨ Indents. The Indents dialog box (shown below) will appear. Type in the desired indent and click on OK. If you type in just a number, it's assumed to be in inches. You can type **cm** after the number to indicate centimeters.

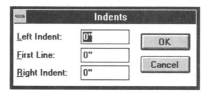

If the number you enter isn't acceptable, Write will tell you. This usually happens when you accidentally enter a value that is too large for the paper your printer driver is set up for.

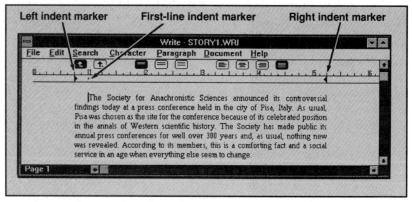

Figure 10.6: Dragging these symbols with the mouse changes the right, left, and first-line indents

You can also use the ruler to change the left or right indent:

1. Place the insertion point in the paragraph or select several paragraphs whose settings you want to change.

2. Turn on the ruler, if it's off, by choosing Document ⇨ Ruler On.

3. Drag the left indent marker in the ruler (▶) to a new position. By definition it will be under the zero. To get to the marker, you may first have to move the square dot sitting on top of it (that's the *first-line indent* symbol, which I'll explain next). Move the dot a bit, grab the triangle and drag it to the new position and then move the dot back.

Setting the First-Line Indent

On a typewriter if you want the first line indented, you have to type a tab or press the spacebar several times. It's easier to let Write do it for you with its first-line indent setting. This also lets you modify the look of a letter after the fact, since you can adjust the first line indents. You might write a letter in block form, then decide to change it to .5-inch indents.

The first-line indent setting will establish the relative indent for the first line of each new paragraph. Note that the setting is in addition to the left indent. So, if the left indent is 1 inch and the first line indent is .5-inch, the first line will start 1.5 inches from the left margin.

Incidentally, setting the first line indent to a negative number, such as −.5, will cause the first line to hang out that amount from the left indent. This is sometimes called a *hanging indent*, or an "outdent."

To change the first-line indent:

1. Place the insertion point in the paragraph or select several paragraphs whose settings you want to change.

2. Choose Paragraph ⇨ Indents. The Indents dialog box will appear. Type in the first-line indent and click on OK.

3. As an alternative, drag the first-line indent marker (the square dot) in the ruler to the new indent position.

In either case, Write will immediately reformat the paragraph in accordance with the new settings. Figure 10.7 shows examples of three different indent setups.

REVERTING TO THE NORMAL SETTINGS

One of the most popular formats for paragraphs is what's already set up as the default (normal) paragraph, single spaced, left aligned, with indents of zero. Simply open the paragraph menu and choose Normal for the current or selected paragraphs to revert to this setup.

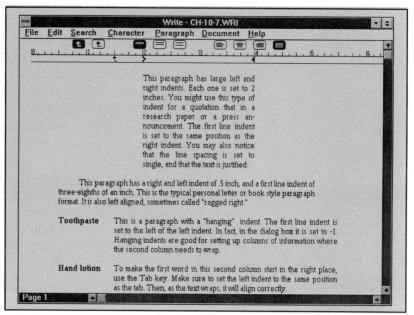

Figure 10.7: Three different indent setups. (The last two paragraphs use the same settings.)

REFORMATTING THE WHOLE DOCUMENT

You'll often want to reformat an entire document. That is, you'll print out the document, look at it and quickly realize it should have been 1½ spaced, or should have smaller (or larger) first-line indents, etc. Since each paragraph has its own settings, it can be a pain to alter each paragraph one at a time. But remember, settings are applied to all selected paragraphs, so you need only select the whole document first, and then change the settings.

FORMATTING CHARACTERS

Write includes commands for altering the look of the individual letters on the printed page. This is called *character formatting*. Commands for character formatting are on the Character menu. You can use character formatting to emphasize a section of text by making it bold, underlined, or italicized. Or you may want to change the size or even the type style (font) of the characters. On many printers, you can combine various character formats.

Just as with paragraph formatting, Write starts you off with a *normal* font, style, and line position (not super- or subscripted). (The normal font means the standard font for the default printer.)

The Fonts dialog box will show you what sizes and font names are available for your particular printer. Write measures character sizes in points. Typical point sizes are 9 to 14 for normal text. (This book is printed in 11.5-point type.) Typical newspaper headlines may appear in anything up to 60 points or so. Here are some examples of actual point sizes in Times Roman (Tms Rmn):

12 point

15 point

24 point

60point

Character formatting can be achieved in three ways:

- From the Character menu
- From the Fonts dialog box
- With shortcut Ctrl-key combinations

You can change the formatting of individual characters, selected blocks of text, or the whole document. Character formatting does not apply to paragraphs as a whole, unless they're actually selected.

FORMATTING EXISTING CHARACTERS

To change the formatting of characters you've already typed, follow these steps:

1. Select the text character(s) to be altered. You can select a single letter, a sentence, a paragraph, the whole document, etc.

2. Choose the new character format from the Character menu. You can use any of the Ctrl-key combinations listed on the menu as shortcuts. Note that some of these are cumulative. That is, you can have bold, underline and italic all on at once, for example. If you have several settings on and want to clear them all, choose Normal or simply press F5. Choosing Normal does not reset the typeface or size, only the five attributes in the first section of the Character menu.

3. If the font name you want isn't listed on the menu, use the Font command. A dialog box will appear, from

NOTE The three font names you most recently used are stored as options on the Character menu so you can easily select and switch between them. The type size for each choice is the default size for the font, usually 10 or 12 points.

which you can choose the font name and type size you want, as you see below:

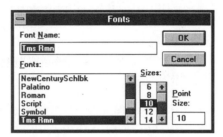

SPEED TIP You can change the font size quickly from the Character menu's Enlarge Font and Reduce Font commands. Each time you select one of these commands, the font size is bumped up or down by one setting. This achieves the same effect as opening the font box and clicking on the next smaller or large font size. When you reach the upper or lower size limit, nothing further happens.

4. Select the name of the font you want from the list. Then choose the size by clicking on it. You may have more options than are immediately visible, so scroll through the list if you don't see what you're looking for. You can type in the point size rather than choosing it from the list if you like. If your printer can scale fonts to any integer size, (as PostScript printers can) use this technique to select type sizes that don't appear on the list.

Formatting Characters As You Type

You can also change formats as you type. Subsequent characters will be entered with the new settings, which will remain in force until changed. This is particularly handy for italicizing or boldfacing words as you type.

1. Type in your text as usual

2. When you get to the point where you want to change the style, use the Character menu or the Ctrl-key combinations. Note that the menu choices and Ctrl-key combinations are toggles. For example, press Ctrl-B once to start typing bold characters. Press it again to revert to normal text.

WORKING WITH TABS

As with a typewriter, you can vary the tab settings to suit your needs. When you entered the table in the sample story in Chapter 9, you had to press the Tab key several times to get to the second column. But we could have eliminated the need for extra presses by setting the tabs exactly where we wanted them. For complex multicolumn tables, you'll probably want to set up your own custom tab stops in this way.

Default tabs are already set up across the page in half-inch increments. These tabs don't show up in the ruler. You can have as many as 12 of your own tabs, though, that will show up in the ruler, and they will apply to the entire document.

When you set a tab manually, Write automatically elimnates all default tab stops to the left of that one.

In addition to "normal" tabs, which are left aligned, you can also set decimal-aligned tabs. Left-aligned tabs line up on the left, beginning at the tab. Decimal tabs align text at the decimal point. This is useful for aligning columns of numbers with decimal points in them, as is the case with monetary figures.

Write does not include right-aligned tabs, but you can simulate them by setting a decimal tab as long as you don't use more that one period with text at that tab stop. Text you enter will right-align until a period is entered, at which point it begins aligning around the period. Figure 10.8 shows a table created with both normal and decimal tabs.

There are two ways to set and alter tabs—from the Tabs dialog box or from the ruler.

HOW TO SET TAB STOPS FROM A DIALOG BOX

Here's how to set tabs from a dialog box:

1. Select Document ⇨ Tabs. A dialog box will appear, as shown in Figure 10.9. There are 12 rectangular sections, one for each possible tab. You type in the position of each tab (e.g., 2.5 or 5.75) in a box. You don't have to fill all the boxes, only ones you want. They can be entered

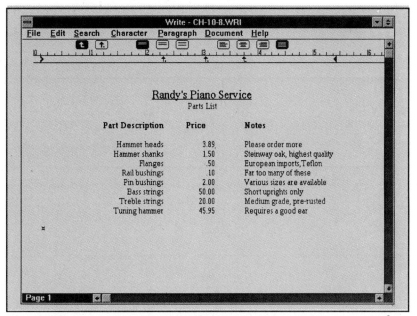

Figure 10.8: A three-column table showing left-, right-, and decimal-aligned tabs. Notice that the right-aligned tab column uses a decimal-tab setting.

in any order (for example, you could type 7.5 in the first box and 2.5 in the second). The next time you open the Tabs dialog box, they will be correctly ordered, from left to right.

2. Decide whether you want the tab stops to be left aligned or decimal. For a decimal stop, click on the Decimal check box below the tab location. For left alignment, leave it off.

3. Click on OK and the tabs will be set. The ruler will have new tab markers (little upward pointing arrows) in it to indicate the new tab positions and the text affected will adjust immediately.

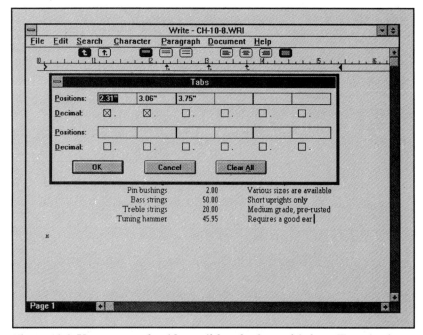

Figure 10.9: You can set the 12 possible tabs from this box. Type in the position in inches (or centimeters if your ruler has been set to centimeters from the Page Layout dialog box). There are three tabs set here: one at 2.31 inches, one at 3.06, and one at 3.75. The first two are decimal-aligned tabs.

HOW TO SET TAB STOPS FROM THE RULER

If you're good with the mouse, setting tabs is much easier and faster with the ruler. Here's how to do it:

1. Get the ruler on screen. Notice the two leftmost icons in the ruler. One has a bent stem. This is the left aligned tab icon. The other one is for decimal tabs.

2. Select the kind of tab you want by clicking on the tab icon in the ruler.

3. To position a tab, click on the correct spot just below the measurement indicator (in the narrow band where the indent markers reside). The tab marker will

be added at the spot where you clicked. You can drag the tab marker left and right to fine-tune it any time. The text affected will adjust immediately.

HOW TO REPOSITION EXISTING TAB STOPS

You can easily change existing tabs for a table or list to play with the look and size of your layout without ever having to retype columns or add or delete spaces between them. Just bring up the Tabs dialog box and make the changes. Or, from the ruler, just click on the tab markers you want to change and drag them one way or the other.

HOW TO CLEAR TAB STOPS YOU HAVE SET

You can clear any of your custom tab stops at any time, either from the ruler or from the dialog box. To clear a tab from the ruler:

1. Click the tab marker you want to delete and hold down the left mouse button.

2. Drag the marker down into the document as though you were pulling it off the ruler. It will disappear. Any text formerly aligned at that tab will move right to the next one.

To clear tabs from the dialog box:

1. Choose Document ⇨ Style.

2. Double click in any box that has a tab setting you want to axe. Then press Del. If you want to clear all the tabs, just click on Clear All.

3. Click on OK. Any text aligned at deleted tabs will move right to the next one.

—————————   **USING UNDO TO REVERSE MISTAKES** —————

The Undo command on Write's Edit menu helps accomodate our propensity for 20/20 hindsight. You may spend five minutes thinking about an editing or formatting change, make it, and then decide after all that you wish you hadn't.

Undo is a selection on the Edit menu. You'll most heartily appreciate it when you use it to salvage portions of text that you accidentally deleted. Undo can reverse the following:

- Block deletes made with the Delete command from the Edit menu or the Del key on the keyboard. Choosing Undo jumps back to the place in your text where the deletion occurred and replaces the deleted text.

- Individual or multiple letters that you erased using the Del or Backspace keys. Undo remembers the last place you deleted letters, jumps back to that location, and re-types the letters in their original places. Unfortunately, it will return only the last letter or series of letters erased. That is, once you move the cursor to another location using any of the cursor-movement keys and delete again, the previous deletion is lost.

- Selected blocks directly deleted and replaced by typing new text on the keyboard. As mentioned in Chapter 9, a simple way of replacing a selected block of words with new words or letters is simply to type in the new text after selecting the part you want to replace. Undo will reverse this type of deletion.

- New text that you typed in. This can be undone (erased) back to the last time you issued a command.

- Character and paragraph formatting changes (if you select the Undo command immediately after making the change).

HOW TO USE UNDO

When you realize you've done something that you regret, select Edit ➪ Undo. Unlike in real life, it usually works in Write.

Remember that the Undo command can only recall the last action, though. If you decide you have made a mistake, either while entering or deleting, you must undo the damage before using any other editing or formatting commands.

Another salient point: Not all commands can be undone. For example, Undo will not return a section of text to its original location once it has been moved. After you've moved a block of text, you'd have to reverse the procedure step by step if you decide it was better off where it was. That's just one example. There are too many others to list. If you'd like to undo an action and you're not sure if you can, just select Edit ➪ Undo. If it does the wrong thing, such as undoing something you did an hour ago, then you know that you're last action couldn't be undone. Select Undo again and you'll be returned to the state you were in just before the Undo. Then fix the problem manually.

SEARCHING FOR AND REPLACING TEXT

Write offers Find and Change commands to look for specific letters, words, or series of words in your text. Once the word processor finds the text, you can have it automatically replace that text with other text if you wish. Though Write calls its commands for this Find and Change, this type of operation is more typically referred to as *search and replace*.

You can also use searching to get to a particular place in your document quickly. If you put unique markers (for example, ##1, aaa) in your text, you can search for them to move from one part of a document to another specific point. (Another way to do this is to use the Search ➪ Go To Page command, if you know the page you want to get to. But it doesn't take you to a specific location or a given page, only to the top of the page, and it requires that you update the pagination, as explained later in this chapter.)

Using Find and Change together, you can replace abbreviated words with the full word after you're done typing. For example, in preparing the manuscript for this book, we replaced *W* with *Windows* and *wp* with *word processor*. This eliminated lots of repetitive typing.

HOW TO FIND
A SPECIFIC WORD OR TEXT STRING

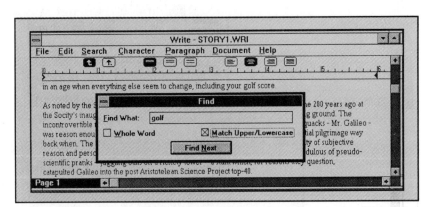

TIP The dialog box is actually a window and can be moved around the screen. You may want to adjust the size and position of your document window so that the Find window doesn't overlap it. Otherwise, if you are doing lots of searching, it will occasionally obscure the found word and you'll have to move the Find window to see it. The window stays on the screen ready for searching until you close it by clicking on its Control box.

Here's how to use Find to locate a specific word or group of words.

1. Choose Search ⇨ Find. The dialog box you see in Figure 10.10 will appear.

2. Type the text you're searching for and press ↵ or click on Find Next.

3. The cursor moves to the next instance of that text.

4. To find out if there are any other occurrences of the text, click Find Next again, or just press ↵. Write will try to find the text again. Write always remembers the last word you searched for so you can repeat the action

Figure 10.10: The Find dialog box. Type the word you want to find and set the options. As set, this will search for the word *golf*.

more easily. It also scrolls the document for you so you can see the text if and when it's found.

When there are no occurrences of the text you're searching for and the entire document has been searched, a dialog box will appear, saying:

Search complete.

Just press ↵ or click on OK.

If no occurrences of the word are found at all, a dialog box will appear, saying:

Search text not found.

SPEED TIP You can repeat a find without having the Find dialog box on the screen. After closing the box, you can use the Search ⇨ Repeat Last Find command or simply press F3.

Just press ↵ or click on OK.

There are two other options when searching: whole-word matching and case matching. Sometimes you'll want to search for a word that could also be embedded in other words. For example the word *pot* would be found in the word *potato.* If you don't want the search to stop at *potato,* set the Match Whole Word check box on before doing the search.

If you set the Match Upper/Lowercase check box on, the search will find only text that exactly matches the case of the text you type in the Find What area. For example, if you had typed in the word *Golf,* it would not find *golf.*

The search command always starts at the current cursor location and searches to the end of the document. Then it wraps around to the beginning and continues until it again reaches the cursor.

HOW TO REPLACE SPECIFIC WORDS

To replace a text string with another text string you use the Change dialog box. As an example, let's assume you want to replace the word *golf* with *tennis.*

1. Choose Search ⇨ Change. A slightly larger dialog box appears. There is an additional text area in the dialog box called Change To. This is where you type in the text you want the found text changed to.

2. Set the Whole Word or Match Upper/Lowercase check boxes on if you need them to aid in the search.

3. Now click on Find Next, Change then Find, Change, or Change All, or Change Selection. Here's what each does:

BUTTON	EFFECT
Find Next	Finds the next occurrence of the word, but doesn't change anything.
Change, Then Find	Changes the next or currently highlighted occurrence of the word and then moves on to find and highlight the next occurrence. This happens very quickly.
Change	Changes the currently highlighted occurrence of the word, and doesn't move. You can see the change and adjust things if you need to.
Change All	Automatically finds and changes all occurrences of the word. You don't get to see what's happenning.
Change Selection	Causes an automatic search and replace within the selected text area. (This option is only available if you have an area of text selected.)

4. Depending on which option you chose, you may want to continue the process by clicking again on a button.

5. Close the window when you're through by clicking on its Control box.

TIPS FOR USING SEARCH AND REPLACE

The search and replace commands have a number of other options that you may want to use from time to time. When searching, you can use a wildcard character to broaden the range possible matching words that Write will find. Say you wanted to find all words that started with *t*, had four letters, and ended in *l*. For the search word, then, you would type in *t??l*. The question marks are wildcards that will match with any letter. Thus, both *tool* and *teal* would be found. Or you could search for all five-letter words, say, by using *?????* as the search criteria.

Here are some other special characters that Write recognizes with the search and replace commands:

TYPE THIS	TO FIND OR REPLACE
^w	White space. White space is any combination of spaces, tabs, nonbreaking spaces, new lines, paragraph marks, and hard page breaks. This cannot be used as a Replace item.
^d	A page break (described later in this chapter).
^p	A paragraph mark, the invisible mark used to separate paragraphs.
^-	An optional hyphen (described later in this chapter).
^?	A question mark
^^	A caret
?	Any character

To enter one of the special characters in the search or replace string, type Shift-6 to get the caret (^).

COPYING BETWEEN TWO DOCUMENTS

As discussed in the last chapter, you may often need to copy portions of text between two documents. Many professionals use word processors because they enable them to use "boiler-plate text" to piece together new documents from existing ones. This is particularly useful for constructing legal documents or contracts that regularly include standard clauses or paragraphs. A more domestic example is creating a series of somewhat similar letters to a number of friends.

Since Windows lets you have multiple programs running at once, you have a fair amount of flexibility here. Though Write doesn't let you open more than one document at a time, Windows *will* let you run more than one session of Write. So you can run Write for each document you want to open. (The number of simultaneous sessions of Write you can have open at one time depends on the mode you're running in, the amount of RAM you have, and the size of the documents. Each copy of Write itself takes up 33K of RAM.)

Once your documents are open, you can select text from one, copy or cut it, and then open another window, position the cursor and paste it in. Adjust the windows so that you can see enough of each document to easily select and insert text. Figure 10.11 shows an example of two Write documents open simultaneously.

Of course you can use the multiple-Write windows for simply writing or viewing more than one document at a time, too. For example, you may be working on several news stories, several letters, or several chapters of a book. Just iconize the documents you're not actively working on but want to have close at hand.

Here are the general steps for opening two Write documents and transferring material between them:

1. Run Write and open the first document (or just leave the window as is if you're creating a new document).

2. Adjust the window so it takes up the top half of the screen.

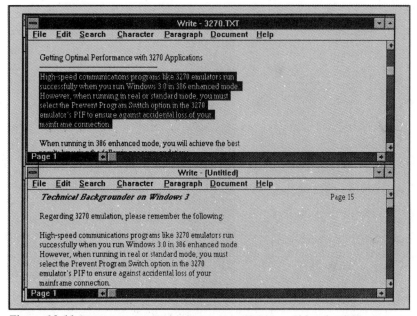

Figure 10.11: You can run multiple copies of Write and load a different document into each window. This lets you easily transfer material between them or switch between writing tasks.

3. Switch to the Program Manager and run Write again.

4. Open the file from which you're going to be cutting or copying.

5. Adjust the position of this window to fit the lower half of the screen.

6. Minimize the Program Manager and any other active programs to get them out of the way. Close programs you're not using, to free up more memory. This should leave nothing but two Write documents on the screen.

7. Cut, copy, and paste to your heart's content, switching between windows. The Clipboard will temporarily store whatever you copy or cut so you can switch between the documents, exchanging the information.

USING OPTIONAL HYPHENS

Write does not handle hyphenation automatically. As a result, the words on some lines in a justified paragraph will have large spaces between them. This is Write doing its best to keep the left and right margins flush. Sometimes it has to push a large word to the next line and add space along the remaining words on the line. As a reasonable cure for such problems, you can insert what are called *optional hyphens* into your text. These are invisible codes that tell Write where to break a given word, and usually suffice to fix the most obviously "loose" lines. Figure 10.12 shows two examples of a justified paragraph, the second one with rebroken optional hyphens.

Here are the steps for entering optional hyphens into a word that you want Write to hyphenate.

NOTE Write will always break a word at a real hyphen, such as in *helter-skelter.* However, you need to enter an optional hyphen in a regular word because the optional hyphen will only appear when Write needs it to break the word across two lines. Otherwise it will be invisible.

1. When you see a loose line, try hyphenating the first word on the next line. Position the insertion point at the optimal hyphenation point.

2. Press Ctrl-Shift-hyphen (the hyphen key is above the P on most keyboards). The word should split, with the first section being pulled up to the previous line. If nothing happens, the first part of the word would not fit on the

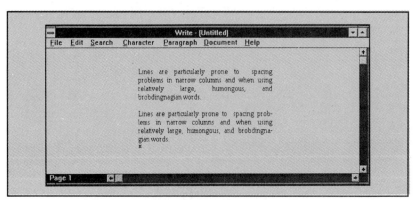

Figure 10.12: Inserting optional hyphens will show Write where to break a long word so it can better justify a line. Here you see the same line before and after hyphenating the words *brobdingnagian* and *problems.*

previous line. Try inserting another optional hyphen after the first syllable.

PAGINATION, PAGE BREAKS, AND PAGE SIZE

The word *pagination* refers to the numbering of pages. If we were still printing on continuous, long rolls of paper as the Egyptians did with their papyrus scrolls, pagination could be dispensed with. Current tradition requires breaking text into separate pages, so Write lets you preview the pages on your document as best it can. This way you can see just where the page breaks occur, and thus where your text will be divided into pages when printed.

As you scroll through a long document, Write shows page breaks as a double arrow (>>) in the left margin of the screen. Also, the status line indicates what page the cursor is on.

Like any good word processor, Write automatically minds the page breaks for you. Write even prevents against widow and orphan lines: short, single lines that might otherwise be left hanging alone at the beginning or end of a page.

AUTOMATIC PAGINATION

As you edit your text, Write doesn't bother to repaginate for you. Repagination only occurs when you select File ⇨ Repaginate. You'll have do this before printing, or the page numbers may be wrong. To repaginate the document:

1. Choose File ⇨ Repaginate. The dialog box shown below will appear:

2. Click on OK, or if you want to confirm each page break and possibly make adjustments up or down, click on the Confirm Page Breaks box and then click on OK.

The document will be correctly paginated, and the page-break markers will be repositioned within the document. If you chose to confirm the page breaks, you'll see the dialog box shown in Figure 10.13, with a highlight on the line which will be the first line of the next page. You can always move the break up, which would shorten the page. You can't always move it down, though, because the printed page is only so long and Write knows this. Clicking on Down will result in a beep if there's no more room left on the page. You'll then have to move the break up or leave it as it was.

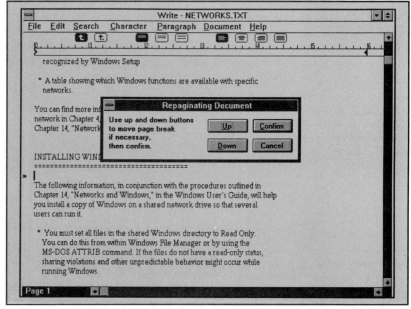

Figure 10.13: When you've chosen to confirm the page breaks, you'll see this dialog box. Use the buttons to move or confirm the break.

ADDING MANUAL PAGE BREAKS

You can break a page and start a new page at any point. For example, you might want to create a title page with just a few words on it, or break before a table that would otherwise get cut in half. You could enter lots of blank paragraphs to move down to the second page, but that's a hassle, and it will be unreliable if you ever edit the text above the paragraph marks again, because you might change the number of lines and shift the break. Instead, you can insert manual page breaks at specific locations in the text.

❐ When you get to the position where you want to break to the next page, press Ctrl-↵. A dotted line will appear across the screen, as shown in Figure 10.14.

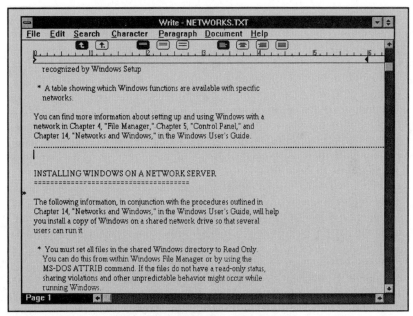

Figure 10.14: Enter a manual page break by typing Ctrl-↵. The dotted line appears to indicate the break.

HEADERS AND FOOTERS

Once you've successfully entered and edited a document, you may want to fine-tune it prior to printing. One of the changes you'll probably want to make is the addition of headers and footers that will print on each page.

A header is a line of text that appears at the top of every printed page, such as a page number, or chapter title. Footers, which print at the bottom of the page, typically contain similar text. Write lets you include headers, footers, or both in each document.

Headers and footers can include text you enter on the Header and Footer windows, and/or the page number for each page. You can also opt to start the header or footer on the second rather than the first, in case you want a title page for the document.

To add a header or footer:

1. Choose Header or Footer from the Document menu.

2. A new window appears. The footer screen is show in Figure 10.15. (It looks like a new document but it isn't.)

3. Type in the header or footer as you want it to print. If you want the page number to appear as part of the text, click on Insert Page # in the dialog box. The word *(page)* will be inserted in the text. This is the code that Write

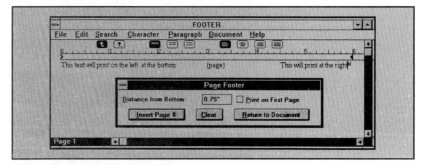

Figure 10.15: The footer screen with a sample footer. Type in any text you want in the footer and format it to meet your needs. Then set the options from the dialog box shown.

uses to print the page number.

Don't forget that since headers and footers can include anything that normal text can, you can change the alignment, font, and size, too. For page numbers, you will typically use center or right alignment. If you want some text on the left margin, some in the middle and some on the right, use tabs and spaces to position text across the screen. Clicking on Clear erases everything, letting you start from scratch.

4. Click on Return to Document when you are satisfied with the header or footer. It will not appear on your screen. Headers and footers only appear when printed, so you might want to test out your settings by printing a few pages.

TIP You can create multiple-line headers or footers. Write will compensate for the multiple lines by decreasing the amount of text it prints on each page of the document.

ADDING GRAPHICS TO YOUR WRITE DOCUMENT

Although it's sort of a bare bones word processor, Write does allow you to insert graphics into your documents. You can get the picture or graphic from other Windows applications such as Paintbrush. Once you've inserted them in the document, you can then cut, copy or paste them. You can also change a graphic's size or move it around. With this feature you can do such things as adding your company logo to every letter you print, putting your picture on your letterhead, or putting a map on a party announcement. Figure 10.16 shows examples of graphics inserted into Write documents.

Of course you'll have to create the graphics in another program since Write doesn't let you create or edit graphics. For a photo, have the photograph digitized with a scanner and then loaded into a Windows program that reads files created by the digitizer. Then copy the picture onto the Clipboard and paste it into Write.

In Write, graphics created with color drawing programs are converted to black and white, and all graphics are displayed in

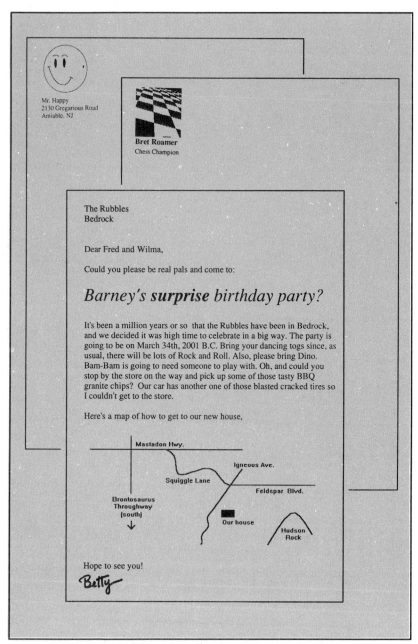

Figure 10.16: Examples of graphics in Write documents. Graphics are imported from the Clipboard, and then can be moved and sized.

a screen resolution comparable to what your printer is capable of. Sometimes the image may seem a bit distorted on screen due to your monitor's *aspect ratio* (ratio of height to width display), but it should print out okay.

IMPORTING A GRAPHIC FROM THE CLIPBOARD

To import a graphic into your document, follow these steps:

1. Get the picture on the Clipboard by copying it from the source application, such as Paintbrush. As long as it can be cut or copied, you can paste it into Write.

2. Open the Write document or activate its window.

3. Position the insertion point on the line where you want the picture to start, and select Paste.

The graphic will be dropped into the document at the left margin. Figure 10.17 shows an example. Now you can move it horizontally or resize it with the commands explained in the next section.

POSITIONING THE GRAPHIC

Once the graphic is pasted in, you can move it around with the following techniques:

1. Place the insertion point on the graphic. It will become highlighted.

2. Choose Edit ➪ Move Picture.

3. Use the arrow keys or mouse to move it to a new location. The cursor changes shape and a dotted box will indicate the graphic's potential new position as you move the cursor around. You can only move left or right, not up and down.

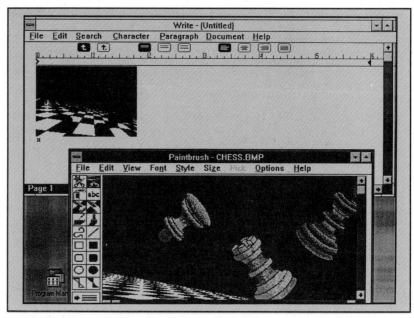

Figure 10.17: The flying chess board picture *chess.bmp* copied from Paint into a Write document

NOTE To move a graphic up or down, you have to cut it, reposition the insertion point, and then paste it again on a new line.

Click or press ↵ when the position is correct. The hourglass "please wait" cursor will appear for a minute while Write thinks about things, and then the graphic will move.

SIZING THE GRAPHIC

You can resize a graphic too. Here's how:

1. Select the graphic by clicking on it or placing the insertion point on it

2. Select Edit ⇨ Size Picture. The cursor changes shape. Stretch or shrink the frame of the picture just as you would a window. Notice that you can distort the picture if you want to, by making it long and skinny or short and fat.

TIP As you size the picture, its size is reported in the status line of the document (in the lower-left corner). It is recommended that you keep the x and y values the same and to keep them in whole numbers rather than fractions if you want to avoid distortion when the picture is printed.

3. Pressing Esc will return the picture to its previous size if you do this before you press ↵. Undo will return it to its previous state after it's been resized.

MANAGING YOUR WRITE FILES

As you may have noticed when opening and saving Write files, there are some options that pertain to file formats, conversion, and so on. Normally you'll just open and save Write *.wri* files using the defaults in the dialog boxes. The defaults open only files with *.wri* extension, and upon saving, store them in the proprietary format that Write expects. However, since not all text files are alike (different programs use different codes to store formatting information), this gives rise to the need for dealing with other text file formats.

OPENING DOCUMENTS STORED IN OTHER FORMATS

When you open a file that doesn't have a *.wri* extension, Write asks if you want the file to be converted. You should have no problem opening many types of files created by Windows programs without converting. This is because many Windows programs use ANSI standard text files, which Write also needs.

However, there are times when you'll want to convert the file, or at least try to. For example, when you load a Microsoft Word file, you'll have to convert it. You should have no trouble here. If you load another type of file, and it doesn't look right on the screen, try opening it again and doing a conversion the second time. If it still doesn't look right, chances are you can't use it in Write without modifying it.

Typical conversion problems have to do with the line endings and the loss of paragraph and character formatting. You'll almost certainly lose the formatting when you load a file from a major word-processing program not made by Microsoft. That's just the way the cookie crumbles in the business world. Microsoft wants to lock you in. If you want to load a file from another program, the best idea is to convert the file to Word format through some utility. You can also try copying to the Clipboard and then into the Write document. This may work at least for the text. The formatting will be lost, though.

Opening straight ASCII files (such as the kind made by PC-Write) doesn't work correctly because Write will treat each line as a separate paragraph. This is because ASCII files have a "carriage return/line feed" pair at the end of each line, by definition. Your text will look okay at first, but paragraphs won't format in more than one line at a time. There is a way around the problem, though, using the Change command. It's a three step conversion process.

1. First you execute a search and replace. Search for all real paragraph separations by looking for ^P^P (this assumes there is a blank line between paragraphs and thus two paragraph end marks in a row) and replace these with some unique character string such as %%. (Note that to find a paragraph mark you have to set Match Lower/Uppercase to off.)

2. Now search for all the paragraph marks (^P) and replace them with nothing. (Don't type anything in the Change To box of the Change dialog box.) This kills all the paragraph marks that are screwing up the formatting.

3. Finally, search for the unique markers (%% in this example) and replace them with a paragraph mark (^P). This puts a paragraph mark at the end of each paragraph—where they belong as far as Write is concerned.

I've tried this with PC-Write files, and it works fine. The other thing to know about foreign file formats is that Write works with files in RAM. Thus, the size of the files you can work with is limited by the amount of free RAM in your system. If you're having space-limitation problems, close some applications, get more memory, or use another program to edit the file.

DIFFERENT WAYS TO SAVE YOUR DOCUMENT

When you save a file in Write you have the usual file list and directory list to choose from. You also have three other boxes to deal with, as shown below:

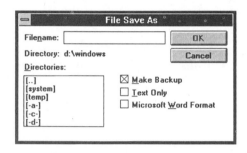

Here is a description of the options:

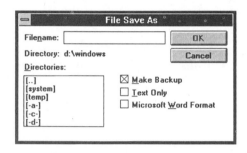 *TIP* If you set both Microsoft Word and Text Only on, you'll save the file as an "unformatted Microsoft Word" file. This can be read by Word, but will have no formatting information in it.

OPTION BUTTON	EFFECT
Make Backup	When you set this on, Write makes a back-up copy of the file each time you save. The backup file is given the extension *.bkp*. If you save the file in Word format, the back-up file is given the extension *.bak*. The first part of the file name is left unaltered.
Text Only	This option causes the file to be saved without the character and paragraph formatting. It is stored as a Windows ANSI text file. This file could be opened by a text editor such as PC-Write, Wordstar, or Side-Kick as a plain text file.
Microsoft Word Format	This stores the file in a format readable by Microsoft Word. However, graphics in your Write file will be lost.

PRINTING YOUR DOCUMENT

When you are about ready to print, don't forget to save your file first just in case the computer or the printer goes berserk in the process and you lose your file. The rest you already know from previous chapters. Just choose File ⇨ Print. You'll be presented with a dialog box asking you about the following options:

OPTION	MEANING
Copies	The number of copies of each page to be printed.
Pages	If you want to print all the pages, click on All. If you want to print specific pages only, type in the page numbers you want to print. Make sure to repaginate first, so you know the correct page numbers!
Draft Quality	This prints a bare-bones copy of the document with nothing but the text. Pictures are printed as empty boxes, and there is no text formatting.

Turn on the printer, make sure it has paper and is on line, and press ⏎ or click on OK.

CHAPTER
ELEVEN

11

Using Terminal for Telecommunications

To send a text file, 362

> choose Settings ⇨ Text Transfers. Set the desired options. Choose Transfers ⇨ Send Text File. Select the file or its name. Choose line-feed options if you want. Click OK and the file will be sent.

To send a binary file, 365

> choose Settings ⇨ Binary Transfers. Set the desired error checking protocol. Tell the other computer to receive a file. Choose Transfers ⇨ Send Binary File. Select the file or type in the name. Click OK and the file will be sent.

To receive a binary file, 367

> choose Settings ⇨ Binary Transfers. Set the desired error checking protocol. Tell the other computer to send the file. Choose Transfers ⇨ Receive Binary File. Type in the file name. Click OK and you will receive the file.

To print text as it's coming in, 373

> select Settings ⇨ Printer Echo. (Turn off printing by selecting the command again.)

To exit your communications session, 374

> log off the service or other computer. Choose Phone ⇨ Hang-up. Save the settings if you haven't already. Close Terminal by double clicking its Control Box.

CHAPTER 11

The Terminal program supplied with Windows lets you and your PC make contact with other computers to exchange or retrieve information. With Terminal and the right hookups, you can share data with other computers, whether they are in your own house, around the block, or on the other side of the world.

Information shared this way would typically consist of electronic mail, instant stock quotes, or complete files (such as word-processing or spreadsheet documents). Many people use communications programs to connect to their company's computer so that they can work from home—sometimes called *telecommuting*.

There are many types of information available for use with PCs and communications programs. Nowadays, many clubs and organizations have their own dial-up *Bulletin Board Systems* (BBSs) where members can leave messages and read notices of interest. Numerous BBSs also provide a wide variety of public-domain software and shareware that anyone with a computer, a modem, and a communications program can have just for the taking. With your PC, a modem, and Terminal, you can start to take advantage of the conveniences of computer communications.

ABOUT THIS CHAPTER

The information in this chapter is necessarily somewhat general. Since a communications program such as Terminal can be used to connect to an almost endless variety of information services and computers, it's impossible to cover all the specific situations. What's more, each service typically has its own way of logging on, transmitting and receiving files, and so on, which adds another complication. So, instead of demonstrating exact procedures, I'll discuss all the aspects of the Terminal program and explain the general steps you'll have to understand in order to use it effectively.

SETTING UP YOUR COMMUNICATIONS SYSTEM

TIP The Terminal program supplied with Windows 3 can use the setup (*.trm*) files from version 2 of Windows Terminal. If you have created files containing setup information for your most frequently used communications sessions, you'll be able to load them in the new Terminal program with the Open command on the File menu.

In most cases, you'll be using Terminal to communicate with outside dial-up services such as CompuServe, Dow Jones News/Retrieval, the Source, or MCI Mail, or to call up a friend's or colleague's computer to exchange files. The other computer can even be of a different type, such as a Macintosh. This type of communication from a distance (as opposed to communication between computers in the same room) uses telephone lines and modems, which must be connected to the computers.

The word *modem* stands for "modulator/demodulator." The modem provides the electrical connection between your computer and the phone line by converting digital information from your computer into an analog signal. On the other end of the line, the receiving modem does just the reverse. (See Figure 11.1.)

HARDWARE REQUIREMENTS

Though you can run Terminal to experiment with it, you can't use it over the phone without having a modem. To connect a modem, you'll need an unused COM port and external modem/cable combination, or an unused COM port, along with a modem card installed inside your computer. (If you don't have a free COM port, Terminal will warn you when you start it up, though it will still run.)

In either case, the general installation procedures are similar. You install the modem, plug your telephone line into it, and run a communications program (in this case, Terminal).

The main distinguishing factor among modems is the speed at which they can transfer data over the phone lines. As of this writing, the most popular modems transmit data at 1200 or 2400 baud. The word *baud* refers to the number of bits of data transferred in one second. The larger the number, the faster the transmission.

Since we can't cover all the ins and outs of modem purchasing here, we'll leave the purchase and installation details to you. However, my advice is to purchase a modem that uses Hayes-compatible commands. Hayes compatibility lets you take advantage of some useful features of Terminal (and most other communications programs) such as the ability to dial the phone for you automatically, redial busy numbers, and so on. If you don't have a Hayes-compatible modem, you can still use Terminal, since two other popular modem types—the MultiTech and TrailBlazer—are also supported. If you don't have any of

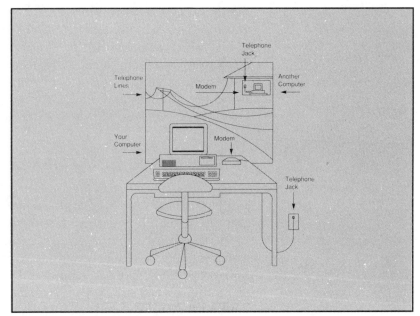

Figure 11.1: A telecommunications setup

these, there's a dialog box into which you can type in the particular commands used by your modem. You'll just have to do a little research first unless you know the commands already.

Make sure you have installed your modem properly, following instructions in the modem's manual, before continuing. Incorrect modem installation (most often caused by improper switch settings) is a frequent cause of communications problems.

BEGINNING A COMMUNICATIONS SESSION

You begin a session by double clicking on the Terminal icon in the Accessories group. A Terminal window appears. The status line at the bottom of the screen is blank because you aren't currently connected to another computer for communications.

Once you have the window open, you have to set up various parameters before you can begin communicating with the other computer. Actually, Terminal has built in defaults for these settings, which may, by chance, suffice for your session. However, success is not guaranteed since there are so many variables. Usually you'll need to set some parameters and modify others at least a little. You should go through the following five sections carefully to establish that the settings are correct for your communications session. While doing so, keep in mind that the settings on both ends of the communications link must be identical. Once you have the settings correct, you can save them to a *.trm* file so that next time you can just load the file and be guaranteed success without having to resort to your memory.

The five groups of parameters you need to check and possibly alter are shown below.

SETTING	PURPOSE
Phone Number	Used for setting the telephone number you want to dial.

Communications	Used for setting the speed and format for data sent between the two connected computers.
Terminal Emulation	Lets you choose between three types of terminals that the Terminal program can cause your screen and keyboard to simulate. Both the remote computer and your software must be set to the same terminal type to communicate correctly.
Terminal Preferences	Used for determining how data will be displayed on your screen and how Carriage Returns and Line Feeds will be processed. The screen font for text display, cursor shape, number of text columns per screen, and several other parameters may need adjusting here too.
Modem Commands	Used for telling Terminal what kind of modem you have. If your modem is not listed, you can enter the commands that Terminal should use to control your modem.

HOW TO MAKE THE PHONE NUMBER SETTINGS

If you have a Hayes-type modem, Terminal can dial the phone number of the remote computer for you. But to have your modem do this, you have to fill in the Phone Number settings as follows:

1. Choose Options Settings ➪ Phone Numbers and you'll see the Phone Number dialog box.

2. Type in the phone number you want your modem to dial. You can type in the number in any of the following forms:

```
(415)-555-1111
415-555-1111
4155551111
555-1111 (if you are calling a local number)
```

The dashes and parentheses won't affect the dialing.

Using Alternative Long Distance Services

If you're using an alternative long distance service such as Sprint, MCI, or others, and you don't have direct access to the carrier by simply dialing, you can enter all the digits necessary into the box (up to a maximum of 100 digits). You can also insert commas into the phone number to tell your modem to pause before moving ahead to the next digit. On Hayes–compatible modems, each comma results in a two-second pause. At least one comma is usually necessary for alternative services, since it can take several seconds for the second dial tone to come on after the initial connection to the service.

Here's an example showing the number you'd use to dial long distance via an alternative service to MCI Mail in Oakland, California, from a company phone requiring a 9 to get an outside line. Assume the relevant numbers are as follows:

```
To get an outside line:   9
Your long distance access number:   555-1311
Your private access code:   8273645
The number you're calling:   415-555-1111
```

Then the number you'd type into the Phone Number field would be

```
9,555-1311,,8273645,415-555-1111
```

Notice the placement and number of commas. You may have to change the number of commas (particularly of the double set) based on how many rings it takes for your long distance service to answer and then come on with the second dial tone. Hayes-type modems do not acknowledge when the phone on the other end of the line has been answered, so you compensate for for this with the commas.

There are three other sections in the Phone Number dialog box. You should set them according to your needs. Here are the meanings of each. Chances are good that the default settings will work fine.

SETTING	*MEANING*
Timeout if not connected in 30 Seconds	Timeout means "give up" here. This setting tells Terminal how long you want it to wait after dialing the phone number of the other computer before hanging up. Normally Terminal tries to connect to the other modem for 30 seconds, after which it hangs up. You may have to increase the time setting if you find that Terminal is hanging up too soon. If you're using a long distance service that takes a few seconds to click in, or the modem on the other end takes several rings to answer, add ten seconds to the timeout value and try again.
Redial After Timing Out	Do you want Terminal to try dialing again after "timing out" and hanging up? Turn this check box on if you do. Since timing out can result from the the other computer's phone line being busy, setting this button on gives you a better chance of getting through. It's like having the computer act like a telephone's automatic redial button.
Signal When Connected	When this is set on, your computer will beep if a connection is made. This is particularly useful when you might not be paying attention to the computer while

waiting for a connection, or if you've iconized the Terminal application and can't see its window.

SETTING THE TERMINAL EMULATION

Before PCs were invented, people used computer *terminals* to communicate with one another and with mainframe computers. Terminals are essentially nothing but a screen and keyboard with which data can be entered and displayed. They have no internal computing power or disk storage as does your PC. Since more than one manufacturer made such terminals, certain standards had to be established regarding how data was displayed on the terminal screens and how their keyboards worked.

These standards continue today, and apply to communications setups using PCs as well as to terminals. As the name implies, Terminal, among other things makes your PC act like an old-style terminal, but with the added brains and storage capabilities of a computer. Some of these added brains allow your PC to be a chameleon—*emulating* more than one type of terminal with a change of options in a dialog box.

In telecommunication, there first has to be an agreement between the two computer systems about what kind of terminal is at each end. So, before beginning a communications session, you have to figure out what the other computer expects, and then try to meet the requirements. This is called setting your *terminal emulation.* To set or check the terminal emulation,

1. Choose Settings ➪ Terminal Emulation. The small dialog box you see below appears.

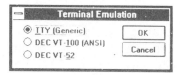

The VT-100 ANSI (the default setting) should work for most purposes. If you find your screen acting unpredictably or displaying bizarre letters, try the TTY setting.

NOTE If you need to know the exact codes Terminal sends to the other computer when you use each of the emulations, there's a very detailed list in Appendix C of the Microsoft Windows User's Guide.

OPTION	EFFECT
TTY (Generic)	This terminal type has the highest level of compatibility of the three. However, it is the least sophisticated. If you do not know which terminal emulation to use, try this. It makes your PC emulate what's known as a "dumb" terminal, meaning that the only formatting codes it uses in communication to the remote computer are carriage return, backspace and tab characters.
DEC VT-100 (ANSI)	Emulates a standard ANSI terminal. Use this for communicating with mainframes as though using a DEC VT100, VT220, or VT240 terminal or compatible. Also, Many IBM PC-based bulletin board services use ANSI, too.
VT52	Emulates the DEC VT52 terminal. Use this for information services such as Compu-Serve and The Source, BBSs, electronic mail services, and so on.

2. Click on OK.

SETTING THE TERMINAL PREFERENCES

You should at least check the next group of settings before making a connection to another computer. Normally, you won't have to change the terminal settings, but occasionally you will. To see or alter the terminal settings, choose Settings ⇨ Terminal Preferences. The Terminal Preferences dialog box appears, as shown in Figure 11.2.

There are six groups of settings in this box. The next six sections discuss them.

Terminal Modes

This box has three check boxes that also affect how information will appear on your screen.

OPTION	EFFECT
Line Wrap	Causes incoming text that is longer than the width of your screen to wrap to the next line. Normally, line wrap is set on.
Local Echo	"Echoes" what you type on your keyboard to your screen, so you can see what you're typing. It may sound strange, but in some communications sessions you may find you can't see what you're typing, because the remote computer may not be programmed to echo your transmission back to your

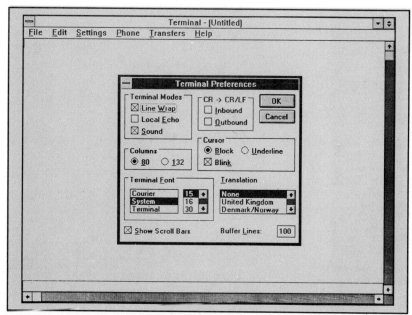

Figure 11.2: From this dialog box you make fine adjustments to the terminal emulation. Most of these are cosmetic refinements for your convenience.

screen. Normally this will not be a problem, but if you find you are typing "in the dark," simply set Local Echo on. With two PCs running Terminal, both should have Local Echo on. On the other hand, if you see double characters on the screen (such as HHEELLLLOO!!), turn Local Echo off.

Sound   Sometimes the remote computer will send your computer the code that causes a beep sound. You may want to disable this if you find it annoying. Setting this check box off disables the beep.

CR → CR / LF

The second section, CR → CR/LF, is included to deal with some remote (sometimes called host) computers' habit of not moving the cursor down a line and moving back to the left side of the screen after sending the previous line of text. If all the incoming data appears on a single line that gets continually rewritten, or the cursor moves to the right margin and seems to get stuck, try setting the Inbound option on. For most sessions, however, leaving both boxes off will work fine.

OPTION	*EFFECT*
Inbound	Adds a line feed (moves down a line) to the end of incoming lines.
Outbound	Adds a line feed to the end of outgoing lines.

Columns

This setting can change the number of characters accepted before Terminal wraps the data to the next line. Instead of showing only 80 columns of characters across the screen (including spaces), the 132 setting results in the appearance of scroll bars on the Terminal window. You'll have to scroll to the right to see columns in excess of 80.

If the sending computer doesn't know you can receive 132 columns per line, however, it may continue to send carriage returns and line feeds after 80 columns. In this case, you wouldn't see any change by selecting this option. However, many BBSs and information services have on-line commands for telling their system how many columns your screen can handle.

Cursor

Nothing more than a cosmetic alteration, the cursor setting modifies the look of the text cursor on the screen.

SETTING	EFFECT
Block	The cursor appears as a large block, the height of a capital letter
Line	The cursor takes the shape of the familiar underline you see in DOS and in most DOS applications.
Blink	This is normally on, but turning it off stops the blinking (a welcome relief!).

Terminal Font

Another cosmetic option, this one determines which font and type size Terminal will use to display both incoming and outgoing characters. This is actually a thoughtful feature, giving tired eyes a break when you're doing lots of telecommunications. If you increase the font size beyond a size that will allow a complete line of text to fit in the window, scroll bars will allow you to scroll horizontally to see it. However, it's rather a nuisance to do this, and it's better to stick with a smaller size, such as 12 to 14 point.

Translation

When you send a text file to or type interactively with a computer in another country, codes are interpreted somewhat differently from how they are in the U.S. To eliminate this problem, Terminal has a translation capability that converts the codes according to the International Standards Organization (ISO) 7-bit codes. If you're communicating with a computer in another country, select *that* country from the list. (*Your* country should already be set from the Control Panel's International icon.)

Show Scroll Bars

This is normally on, but you can turn it off. Having them on lets you scroll to see information that is off the screen—a very useful feature. With many communications programs, information that scrolls off the top of screen is "lost"; that is, you can't view it again. In Terminal, however, text you type or receive while in interactive communications sessions is stored in a *buffer,* which brings us to the next and final setting in the box.

Buffer lines

Normally this setting is 100 lines, but it can range from 25 to 400. With a setting of 100, Terminal will store the last 100 lines that scrolled off the top of the window. The lines go in the temporary buffer, and if the scroll bars are on, you can scroll back up to see them. Note that you will have to scroll back down before you can see what you're typing.

SETTING THE COMMUNICATIONS PARAMETERS

Once you've made the phone, emulation, and preference settings, you should next check the Communications parameters. Choosing Settings ⇨ Communications brings up the dialog box shown in Figure 11.3.

Let's look at the eight option boxes one by one.

NOTE If you plan to use the defaults, of course, you can just skip over this entire dialog box altogether. Chances are it will work as is, since the defaults were designed to work with most services.

Baud Rate

As discussed before, baud rate determines the speed at which data is transferred between your PC and computer at the other end of the line. You'll need to set the baud rate to match that of your modem and that of the remote computer's modem. In other words, all parts of the communications link must be set for the same speed.

Some modems can automatically sense the baud rate and adjust themselves accordingly. Others cannot do this and must be set with switches. You should consult your modem's instruction manual regarding this. If baud rates are mismatched, you will fail to get a connection, or you may see weird characters or punctuation marks on your screen instead of normal text.

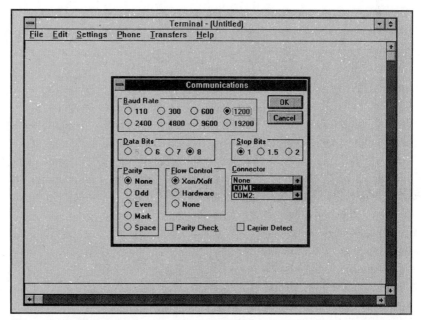

Figure 11.3: The Communications dialog box. From here you set the parameters that directly affect how the computers on each end of the communications link transfer data. All settings except for the COM port and Carrier Detect must be identical for both computers.

NOTE If you are connecting two computers directly to each other (without using modems), you might want to refer to a book on the subject, such as *The RS-232 Solution* by Joe Campbell (SYBEX).

Most communication via modem (as opposed to direct connection to another local computer, as explained later in this chapter) takes place at 300, 1200, or 2400 baud. It usually makes sense to use as fast a speed as possible to miimize the connect time over the phone. However, poor phone connections, not infrequent with long distance calls, can require dropping your speed down a notch (from, say, 2400 to 1200) to avoid loss of data. Also, most information services, such as CompuServe, charge twice as much for 2400 baud connect time than for 1200 baud.

Data Bits

The Data Bits setting refers to the number of bits (the smallest division of computer information) you want to send out in each packet of data. For example, each letter is typically stored in your computer as eight bits. (Eight bits is called a *byte.*) Suffice it to say that this setting is almost always going to be 8, and must be 8 if you are intending to transfer binary files between computers. Binary files include all programs and any documents that consist of more than plain ASCII characters. Thus, formatted word-processing documents, spreadsheets and graphics documents are binary files. The other popular standard is 7 bits. The 5- and 6-bit options are rarely used. If you are specifically told that the other system uses a setting other than 8 bits, change this setting.

Stop Bits

Stop bits are used by the computers on both ends to indicate the end of one character and the beginning of the next. You can probably leave this setting as is. Change this setting if you are specifically told that the other system uses 2 or 1.5 stop bits.

Parity

Parity is a means by which the communications software can check if an error has occurred in the transmission of each byte of data. Parity can only be used if you have set the Data Bits parameter to 7. Otherwise parity should be left at None. If you are specifically told that the other system uses parity checking, find out what kind, and change this setting.

Flow Control

In the process of receiving and sending data, the computers on each end of the line often have to attend to other tasks as well, such as storing information on disk. Sometimes these tasks can distract the receiving computer from handling its incoming data. As was mentioned in Chapter 6 (in the discussion of printer connections), *handshaking* is used to prevent data from falling through the cracks during these processes. Handshaking provides a way for the two computers to agree when to stop and start the sending process so that other contingencies can be handled.

Most often, at least when using modems, the Xon/Xoff *convention* (or *protocol*) will be employed. When the receiving computer wants the sending computer to pause, it transmits an Xoff (a Ctrl-S) signal. When ready to receive data again, it sends an Xon (Ctrl-Q) signal. This is the default setting, and will work for most dial-up information services.

When connecting computers to each other directly via a cable (without a modem), you may want to use the Hardware setting. To use this option, you must make sure you have a special kind of cable.

If you know that the other computer uses no handshaking, select None from the dialog box. Regardless of which handshaking setup you are using, remember that both computers must use the same type.

Connector

The last section of the Communications dialog box lets you tell Terminal which *port* your modem is connected to. Most PCs have two serial communications ports, called COM1 and COM2, though more fully expanded systems may have COM3 and COM4 as well. The default is for Terminal to use COM1 as the port. Your COM1 port may be tied up for use with a printer or other device, though, in which case your modem should be connected or set up for another port such as COM2, and this setting in the dialog box should match it.

Parity Check

NOTE When sending files rather than communicating interactively, errors such as these can be automatically detected and usually corrected if you use an error-checking scheme. This is explained in the section "Sending Binary Files," later in this chapter.

When this is set on, you will see every byte, even if a parity error was detected. In other words, you might see the wrong character, as in

Welcome to Do-Dad Enterprises On-line Database:
Please enter your $qssword

If Parity Check is set off (the default) you'll see a question mark in place of any byte (character) in which an error was detected. Seeing the question mark is more useful than seeing the byte for most purposes, as it will clue you in to the fact that the character was lost and that you will have to fill in the gaps. For example, if you see this when working interactively with another computer:

Welcome to Do-Dad Enterprises On-line Database:
Please enter your ??ssword

NOTE Remember that all of these options, except Connector and Carrier Detect, have to be identical on each end (in each computer) before successful communications can begin. If you are in doubt about how to set one of them, there's a simple solution. Just find out what the settings are for the computer at the other end of the line and set yours accordingly. If you can't find out what those settings are, try the default settings that show up when you open a new document. If those don't work, then start systematically altering the settings one at a time.

you can assume some information was lost, and that the correct word is *password*. This setting has no effect if the party is set to None.

Carrier Detect

Normally the modem determines if the modem on the other line is actually connected and ready to send and receive data. It knows this by detecting the presence of a carrier, which is a high pitched tone. If the carrier is detected, the modem relays this to your computer, and Terminal alerts you to this fact. Only then can you begin your communications session. If for some reason the modem isn't detecting the carrier (and Terminal isn't acting as if you're on-line), try setting this check box on. Then Terminal will use its own method of detecting the carrier.

SETTING THE MODEM PARAMETERS

The next and final step before beginning your session is to set the modem parameters.

1. Choose Settings ⇨ Modem Commands. The box you see in Figure 11.4 will appear.

2. You probably won't have to modify anything in this box except the type of modem you have. Select the type of modem you have or one that's compatible with it. Check your modem's manual for compatibility information.

If you don't have a modem that's listed in the Modem Defaults, (or one that's compatible), choose None. If the modem accepts software commands, you should then type in the commands in the appropriate boxes in the Commands section of the dialog box. Some commands have two parts—a prefix and suffix. The prefix generally tells the modem the class of command is it going to receive, or requests attention from the modem. The suffix then supplies the specifics of the command. Check your modem's manual for the commands it uses.

If you don't type in the commands, you can still use the modem. You'll just have to control the modem manually (if it

TIP The Prefix section of the Dial row in the dialog box sends a command to your modem before dialing a phone number. Terminal will send whatever command you enter here prior to dialing the number. For example, you may want to tell your modem how many rings to try before giving up trying to connect with a remote computer. Or if you don't have a touchtone service you can tell the modem to use pulse dialing instead. Or you can set up the modem to answer an incoming call. As an example, to dial with pulses from a Hayes modem, change the ATDT to ATDP.

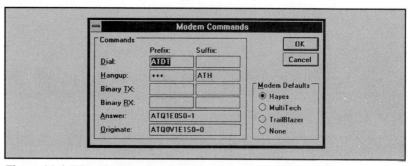

Figure 11.4: The Modem Commands dialog box. From here you select the modem type you have or fill in the commands your modem expects. Check the modem's manual for compatibility with one of the Default types. Then you won't have to bother with the boxes.

has switches for that purpose) or type in the commands at the keyboard while connected to the modem.

SAVING YOUR SETTINGS

With some practice you'll see that only a few of the settings need alteration for each new type of communications session. What's more, once you have the details of a particular hookup ironed out, you can save your settings on disk for future use. Your settings are saved as a file with a *.trm* extension.

To save your settings:

1. Choose File ⇨ Save. The familiar Save As dialog box will appear.

2. Give your file a name, preferably a name that will help you remember which information service or computer the settings are for.

MAKING A CONNECTION

When your settings are correct, the next step in starting a communications session is to make the connection to the remote computer.

❒ To initiate the connection, choose Phone ⇨ Dial. A dialog box will appear, telling you that the number is being dialed, and counting down the seconds from the Timeout value you set earlier.

The phone number being dialed (along with the commands telling the modem how to dial it) shows up in the work area of the screen, like this:

ATDT5401114

If your modem has a speaker in it, you may also hear the number as it is being dialed. When the phone on the other end is picked up, you may hear some high pitched tones indicating that the modems are "talking" to each other.

If connection is successful, you may see the word

CONNECT

on the screen. From then on, everything you type on the key-board will be sent to the other computer. If you have the Func-tion key indicators showing (choose Settings ⇨ Show Function Keys), the time indicator will change to show elapsed time, in-forming you of the amount of time your computer has been connected to the remote machine.

If the connection is not successful, after about 15 seconds you will probably see the words

NO CARRIER

just under the phone number. This means the modem gave up trying to make a connection. Typical reasons for failure at this point are

- The other phone was busy.

- The other phone/modem didn't answer.

- The modems are set at different baud rates so they didn't recognize each other.

If the phone number you dialed is busy, your modem may report the word BUSY to the screen, and you may hear the busy signal on the modem's speaker. Usually the modem will hang up and wait for a message from the computer to try again. To dial again, choose Phone ⇨ Dial again.

If you want to stop a dialing that is in progress, click on Cancel in the Dialing box.

SENDING AND RECEIVING DATA

Assuming the connection proceeds without difficulty, you can begin to transfer data between computers. What you do now depends entirely on what the other computer expects from you. If you are calling an information service, BBS, or a mainframe computer, you will typically have to *sign on* to the remote system by typing your name and possibly a password.

If you are calling a friend's computer or connecting locally, you can probably just begin typing as I will describe here. In any case, once the initial connection is made, there are several ways that you can begin to transfer data between the two computers. The next several sections describe these techniques and how to use them.

HOW TO SEND AND RECEIVE IN INTERACTIVE MODE

The simplest way to transfer data is directly from your keyboard. As mentioned earlier, once you're connected to the other computer, everything you type is automatically sent out to it. Conversely, characters typed at the other computer will be sent to your computer, showing up on your screen. Sending and receiving data this way is called working in *interactive* or *terminal* mode. Communication sessions often begin in terminal mode, with each person typing to the other's screen.

NOTE   As each new line of text is received, or typed in by you, it will scroll upward in the Terminal window. Once it reaches the top of the window, it disappears from view, though the information is retained in the buffer. To recall the information, use the vertical scroll bar. Then scroll back down to continue interacting with the other computer.

Terminal mode is often used, too, when connecting to many of the information services and electronic mail services that are interactive in nature. With these, you type certain commands to the host computer and it responds by sending you some data. As information comes over the line to your computer, it will appear on the screen, as shown in Figure 11.5.

Capturing Text

Obviously, there will be times when you'll want to somehow save this incoming data while you're in Terminal mode, so you can work with it later. You can *capture* incoming text at any time during a communications session with the Receive Text File command on the Transfer menu and save it in a disk file for later reading, printing, or editing.

Here is the basic procedure for capturing text:

1. Choose Transfers ➪ Receive Text File.

2. A standard file dialog box appears, asking you to name the file you want the captured text stored in. Select the directory and type in the name, but don't press ↵ yet.

3. There are several options you might want to choose from before saving the file:

OPTION	*EFFECT*
Append File	Adds the incoming text to the end of the preexisting file you choose from the file box. This is useful for archiving a series of electronic mail conversations with a particular person, for example,

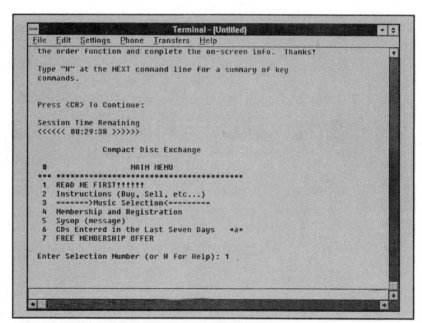

Figure 11.5: A typical interactive session. Notice that text from both sender and receiver appear on the screen.

or compiling information about a particular topic. Using this method, you can keep capturing data, even from session to session, into the same file.

Save Controls   Saves control characters (formatting codes above ASCII 128) that might be in the file.

Table Format   Converts two or more consecutive spaces into tabs. This is a great convenience if you're receiving lists of information that you later want to format and print. With spaces converted to tabs, you can adjust the tab alignment and spacing later in your word processor. You can also use proportionally spaced fonts and still have the columns line up.

4. Click on OK. The file will be opened and the status line at the bottom of the window will appear, showing the number of bytes (characters—including spaces, carriage returns, and line feeds) that have been "captured," and the file they are being saved in (see Figure 11.6).

5. Continue with your session. Whatever you type will be captured too, along with the incoming text. When you want to stop capturing text, click on Stop in the status line. The status line message will disappear, and the text will be stored on the disk.

Capturing Selected Portions of Text

During text capturing there may be sections of text you don't want to save interspersed with portions you do. A case in point would be reading menu choices or sign-on messages from BBSs,

MCI Mail, or CompuServe. You can turn text capture on and off at will to accommodate this situation. Here's how to do it (assuming you've already chosen Transfer ➭ Receive Text File, there will be a Pause button in the status line and text capturing will be active):

1. Click on Pause in the status line when it looks as though a section of unwanted text is coming across the screen. This pauses the capturing, even though your session continues on screen as though nothing happened. The button changes to read Resume instead of Pause.

2. When you want to start capturing again, click on Resume. All subsequent text will be added to the file.

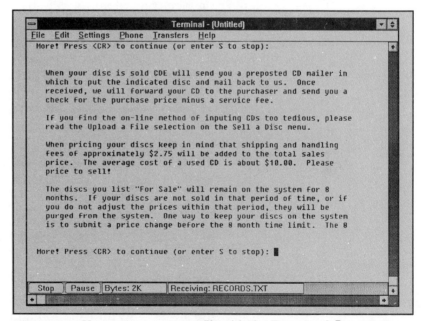

Figure 11.6: You capture text to a file with the Transfer ➭ Receive Text File comand. The status line changes to the file name and the number of bytes received. Stop or pause the capturing with the buttons on the left.

TIP You can view a file in Terminal without having to open it in Notepad, Write, or another program. Choose Transfers ➭ View Text File and enter the file name. Use the Pause button to control the scrolling.

SENDING AND RECEIVING FILES

Obviously just sending text to another computer by typing it in from your keyboard isn't very efficient. Terminal gives you an alternative to this approach by letting you send documents already prepared by a word processor or other program. This is a much more efficient method of data transfer.

There are two ways to do it. One method uses error correction to insure that the other computer receives your file without any loss of data. The other technique does not use error correction, but it is compatible with a wider variety of host computers.

Sending Text Files

The Send Text File command on the Transfers menu is the method without error correction. Use this command to send letters via electronic mail services, BBSs, and information services. By composing your messages first with a word processor or text editor, you can minimize the connection time (and resultant cost).

Note, however, that you can use the Send Text File command only with ASCII files (plain text files without control codes in them), so make sure the file you want to send was created, or at least saved, as an ASCII file from whatever program you created it in. You cannot send programs (files with the extensions *.exe* or *.com*) with this command. Captured text files are ASCII files, as are all Notepad files and Write files saved in Text Only format. Typically, electronic mail services such as MCI Mail receive files in this format.

Before sending a text file you might want to check the settings in the Text Transfers dialog box. To do so,

1. Choose Settings ➪ Text Transfers. A dialog box will appear. It has three settings of importance. You can have Terminal send information a line at a time, a character at a time, or using the Standard Flow Control. Standard Flow Control is the control setting you made in the Communications box. It's probably the way you want to

send text files, and it's probably Xon/Xoff, which is the most popular standard. You should choose Line if the system you're sending to wants to receive text a line at a time, send back an acknowledgement, and then request the next line. Sending text a character at a time is very rarely used, and is extremely slow besides.

2. If you created the text in a word processor, the lines of text in the file may have a length that suits your needs but not that of the person receiving the file. You can predetermine the line length for the receiving party if you like. Turn on the Word Wrap check box and set the line length you desire.

Now to actually send a text file, follow these steps.

1. Make a connection to the other computer.

2. Choose Transfer ⇨ Send Text File.

3. A dialog box will appear (see Figure 11.7). Enter the file name or select it from the file box.

4. Consider the two option boxes. If you want to add a line feed to the end of each line of text you send, check the Append LF option. If you want to strip out the line feeds from the end of each line you send, check Strip LF. (See "Setting the Terminal Preferences" earlier in this chapter

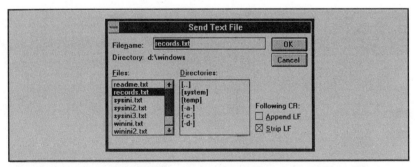

Figure 11.7: To send a text file, choose Transfers ⇨ Send Text File. Select or enter the file name, set the check boxes, and click on OK.

for a discussion of line feeds.) Then click OK. You might have to talk with the person running the other computer to determine whether they want line feeds added or excluded. Or you could try sending a few small files and vary the selection to see which one works best.

5. The status line will come on at the bottom of the window, and the text will scroll up the screen as the file is sent so that you can monitor the progress of the transfer. The status line also has a document bar in it that graphically displays the amount of the file that has been sent and the amount remaining, as shown in Figure 11.8.

6. You can pause, resume and stop the transmission by clicking on the buttons in the status line or choosing the identical commands in the Transfers menu. When Terminal reaches the end of the file, the status line disappears.

If you notice that letters are missing at the beginning of each new line of text on your screen, you will have to stop the transfer and change the Flow Control setting in the Settings ⇨ Text Transfers dialog box. Choose Line at a Time, and enter a value greater than the default of $1/10$ of a second as the Delay Between Lines setting. For example, enter a 2 in place of the 1, for a $2/10$ of a second delay. The Delay Between Lines setting controls how

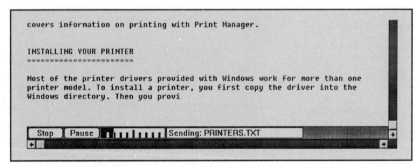

Figure 11.8: When you send a file, the status line will appear, reporting the file being sent and the progress of the transmission. It also lets you stop, pause, or resume the transmission.

long Terminal will pause at the end of each line before beginning the transmission of the next line.

Sending Binary Files

> *NOTE* A binary file will arrive just as you sent it, with no modifications (for example, no adding or stripping of line feeds). All types of files, including program files can be sent and received as binary files. Formatted text as well as program files *must* be transmitted as binary files, or information will be lost. If you want to send such files to another person through an electronic mail service that doesn't accept binary files, such as MCI Mail, you you will have to use a utility program that converts binary files into a special type of encoded 7-bit file before sending it. The receiving party will then have to reconvert the file on their end with the same utility program.

It's not uncommon for data to be lost or corrupted during the transmission process over telephone lines, particularly when long distances are involved. As we all know, long distance lines often suffer from noise, static, or even other people's conversations accidentally being crossed with ours. Usually we just put up with the noise, asking the other party to repeat their last sentence, or one of the parties redials the call.

Computers are less tolerant of such maladies. Noise on the line between two computers can cause a plethora of erratic data alterations during a file transfer. In response to this, computer scientists have devised numerous error detection and error correction schemes to determine whether errors have occurred in transmission, and various methods to correct them. Terminal uses two of these schemes with its Receive Binary File and Send Binary File commands from the Transfers menu.

The first one, the XModem protocol, is an error correction scheme devised by Ward Christensen and given to the public in 1977 for use on microcomputers, which were just then becoming available. XModem is now widely used and supported by many communications programs as well as some information services, such as CompuServe. The other one, Kermit, is functionally similar.

Error detection and correction schemes divide a file into a series of small sections, called blocks. The blocks are then sent sequentially, and each one is accompanied by a mathematically calculated code based on the contents of the block. After getting the block, the receiving computer looks to see if its contents match this calculated code. If it does, the sending computer is advised to send the next block. If there is a discrepancy, the receiving computer asks the sending computer to retransmit the block until it's received properly. This process continues until the entire file is transmitted error free.

The XModem protocol has two modes—CRC (Cyclical Redundancy Check) and checksum. Some receiving systems may have one but not the other. Terminal, when set to transfer binary files with the XModem CRC setting, tries CRC first, and then if the other system isn't responding, it switches to checksum mode.

Obviously, the system on the other end has to be using the same error detection scheme or the computers won't be able to communicate about the success or failure of the transmission. In fact, the transfer will not even begin. Nothing will happen. Between Kermit and Xmodem, you should be able to send binary files to most other systems, since most communications programs support one or the other, or both.

In addition to catching errors in transmission, these protocols allow you to transmit all types of files, including programs, spreadsheets, and graphics. It doesn't matter what's in the file.

To send a binary file, follow these steps.

1. Make sure you're on line (connected).

2. Choose Settings ⇨ Binary Transfers.

3. From the dialog box, choose the error detection protocol you want to use (the one the receiving system uses).

4. Make sure the receiving computer is ready to receive an XModem or Kermit file. How you do this depends on the computer system, BBS, or information service to which you are connected. If you are sending a file to another PC, you may want to type a message in Terminal mode telling the operator to do what is necessary to prepare for receiving the file.

5. Choose Transfers ⇨ Send Binary. A file dialog box will ask for the name and type of the file. Type in the path and file name or use the file and directory boxes to locate the file, and then click OK or press ↵. This will begin the file transfer.

The progress of the transfer will be reported in a status line. You won't see the file on the screen (if it's not all text it would look like garbage anyway).

If errors are detected, they will be reported in the status bar next to Retries. If more than 10 consecutive errors are detected during transmission, Terminal will abort the sending process.

You can't pause a binary transfer, but you can stop it in midstream by clicking on Stop or choosing Stop from the Transfers menu.

Receiving Binary Files

You'll want to use the Receive Binary File command to receive files from other PCs, BBSs, or information services that support the XModem or Kermit protocol. This will ensure that they are received without error. Receiving a binary file is essentially the reverse of the sending process.

1. Choose Settings ⇨ Binary Transfers and select Xmodem or Kermit, depending on the protocol that the other computer uses to send binary files.

2. In interactive mode, tell the sending computer to send the file. How you do this varies depending on the computer and program(s) involved. With some systems, you control the sending from your computer. In other cases a person at the other end will issue the command. BBSs typically will say something like:

   Ready to receive Y/N?

   or

   Press ⏎ to start download

3. Choose Transfers ⇨ Receive Binary File. The file dialog box appears because you are telling Terminal to save the incoming data as a file. Enter the file name (and path if not the current path) or choose it from the directory and file boxes. Do this quickly, since the other computer is already trying to send the file. It will wait, but usually not too long.

5. Click on OK or press ↵, and the transmission should begin. A dialog box will appear, indicating the number of bytes received, the name of the file being transmitted, and a Stop button in case you want to bail out. You won't see the file on the screen.

If errors are detected during the transmission, they'll be reported next to the word Retries. If more than 10 consecutive errors are detected during transmission, Terminal will abort the receiving process.

Since Terminal doesn't know the size of the file being sent to it, there isn't a little gauge indicating how long the whole transmission's going to take. Occasionally, you may run out of disk space while receiving a file. This is a real hassle, particularly if you've spent half an hour receiving most of a large file only to get an error message from Terminal saying there isn't enough room on your disk for the rest of it. Terminal will abort the receiving process if there isn't enough room, so *make sure* the disk you choose to store the file on has enough free space on it before you begin the transfer. If you forget to do this, you'll have to change disks or drives and start the process again.

USING THE FUNCTION KEYS TO CUT DOWN ON TYPING

Terminal has a feature that helps cut down on typing repetitive commands. This is a blessing when you're working on-line with systems that require that you type in the same information each time you log on or interact with them. You can assign up to 32 different commands to your keyboard's function keys (four for each key from F1 to F8). When you press the key, the command is sent as though you typed it. It's just like a *macro* or the automatic key substitution that programs like SmartKey, ProKey, and some word processors have built in. However, since the basic function keys are used for other purposes (such as getting Help), you have to press Ctrl-Alt while pressing function keys to get these results. There are two steps to using the keys: assigning the commands and executing them.

ASSIGNING THE FUNCTION KEY COMMANDS

To assign a command to a key:

1. Choose Settings ➪ Function Keys. This will pop up a dialog box, as shown in Figure 11.9. Each key from F1 to F8 has two slots to type into. The Key Name is the name that will show up on the bottom of the screen when you elect to show the function-key settings. The Command is what pressing the key will enter as if typed from the keyboard. If you don't name a key, it won't show up on the bottom of the screen.

2. Enter the names and commands you want for each key.

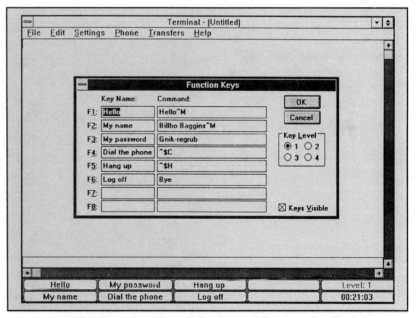

Figure 11.9: The Function Keys dialog box, with examples. Each key can have a name that shows on the screen.

3. If you want more than eight commands, click on Level 2 and enter more names and commands. Use Levels 3 and 4 if you want to. All told, you can enter as many as 32 key definitions.

4. Set the Keys Visible check box on if you want the keys to automatically display at the bottom of the window when you open the *.trm* file next time. This setting is saved with the file. (Normally keys are hidden until you choose Settings ➪ Show Function Keys.) Don't forget to save your settings with the File ➪ Save command.

Entering Complex Commands

You'll typically assign your name and password to function keys so you won't have to type them each time you log onto an information service. However, you may want to assign more than just text to function keys. You can also assign control-key commands, some menu commands, and the ⏎ key. Here's the list of special codes you can use to assign such actions to keys. These can be strung together and interspersed with normal text. Enter the caret (^) with the shifted 6 key above the letter T on the keyboard.

CONTROL CODE	EFFECT
^A –^Z	Sends Ctrl-A through Ctrl-Z.
^$D<*n*>	Causes Terminal to delay for *n* seconds before continuing.
^$B	Causes Terminal to transmit an 117-milli-second Break code. (Some computers stop a process in midstream when they receive the Break code.)
^$C	Has the same effect as choosing Phone ➪ Dial.
^$H	Has the same effect as choosing Phone ➪ Hangup.
^$L1 –^$L4	Changes to key level 1 through 4.

Here's an example of a complex command for one function key:

^$C^$D03^M$D03FJONES^M^$D03password^M

If you break it down, you'll see that it dials the number stored in the Settings ⇨ Phone dialog box, waits 3 seconds, enters a ↵, types in the user's name, *FJONES*, waits three seconds again, enters the password, and enters another ↵. This is a typical sign-on procedures for many services, such as MCI Mail. (You can increase the waiting periods if your commands seem to be issued too soon.)

USING THE FUNCTION KEYS

When you want to use the function keys:

1. If the keys aren't displayed already, bring them up on-screen by choosing Settings ⇨ Show Function Keys.

2. To switch to another level of commands, click on the Level button. The level will be switched, and the command names will change. (If there's only one level of settings, the button will be grayed).

3. Click on the button representing the command or words you want transmitted to the other computer.

As an alternative to clicking on the key, you can press Ctrl-Alt and a function key on the keyboard. (F1 through F4 correspond to the buttons on the top line of the display. F5 through F8 correspond to those on the bottom line.)

If you want to hide the buttons again, choose Settings ⇨ Hide Function Keys.

MANIPULATING TEXT FROM THE DOCUMENT WINDOW

You can manipulate the text in the document window in various ways while in a Terminal session. You can

- Copy it to the Clipboard.
- Transmit selected text or the Clipboard's contents to the other computer as though you were typing it.
- Print incoming or selected text.
- Clear all the text in the window.

COPYING TEXT TO THE CLIPBOARD

Any text you can see on screen can be copied to the Clipboard. Once there it can be pasted into other applications or sent to the other system.

1. Select text with the mouse, just as in any other program, such as Write or Notepad. (Refer to Chapter 9 for exact instructions on selecting text.) To copy the entire document (all the text that's in the buffer) choose Edit ⇨ Select All.

2. Choose Edit ⇨ Copy. The text is now on the Clipboard.

TRANSMITTING TEXT

Sometimes you'll want to send text from a different application to the other computer. If the document is in another window, this is very easy. You don't have to create and send a new file. Just follow these steps:

1. Copy the text to the Clipboard. It can be text from a Terminal window, or any other application window, such as Word, Excel, Write, Ami, PageMaker, etc.

2. Switch back to the Terminal window and choose Edit ⇨ Paste. The contents of the Clipboard will be sent to the other computer, unchanged. If the other computer is using Windows, the user could then select the information, copy it to the Clipboard, and paste it into another document.

Note that only text can be transferred in this way. If a graphic is on the Clipboard, you cannot Paste it.

You can also transmit selected text from the Terminal window without having to copy it to the Clipboard. This is a quick way to repeat a command you've typed in once already.

1. Select the text.

2. Choose Edit ⇨ Send.

PRINTING INCOMING TEXT

If you want to print text as it comes onto your screen from the remote computer, follow these steps:

1. Set up your printer and put it on-line. Select the correct printer from File ⇨ Printer Setup.

2. Choose Settings ⇨ Printer Echo. A checkmark will appear next to the menu selection. All received text will be printed. (If Local Echo is set on from the Terminal Preferences dialog box, everything you type will be printed too.)

3. To stop printing, choose Settings ⇨ Printer Echo again to turn it off.

PRINTING SELECTED TEXT

You can't print selected text directly from Terminal. However, here are two ways you can print what's come over the line:

❒ Select the text you want to print, and copy it onto the Clipboard. Then open Write, Notepad, or another word processor and paste the text into the document, edit it, and print it as usual.

❏ Save the incoming text as a file, as explained in the earlier section "Capturing Text." Exit Terminal, and then open the text file in a word processor and print it.

RUNNING MULTIPLE COMMUNICATIONS SESSIONS

There probably aren't too many times that you'd want to run multiple communication sessions, but it is possible to have two communications sessions connected at the same time. To do this, run Terminal a second time and open a new communications document while you still have the first one open. Set the parameters and connect as usual. You must *not* use the same communications port as you're using for the first session. From the Communications dialog box you'll have to select the unused COM channel (1 or 2) as the port for the second session. Of course, you'll need another modem (or cable in the case of direct connection) connected to the second port, as well. By using the Pause command wisely and jumping between windows, you could juggle the two communications sessions.

ENDING A COMMUNICATIONS SESSION

Once you've finished your work (or play) during a session, you should end it by following some simple rules.

1. If you want to save the settings you've made, choose File ⇨ Save and name the file.

2. If you are logged onto an information service, electronic mail, or BBS, follow the system's instructions for

signing off. This may be important to free up a connection for other users, or so that the service will cease billing you for connect time.

3. Choose Phone ⇨ Hangup.

4. Close Terminal by double clicking its Control Box.

TROUBLESHOOTING

Despite great strides in the field of communications, mostly due to conveniences spurred by the personal computer market, communications is still a bit of a black art. Chances are that you'll run into some problem or another while transferring files, sending mail, or whatever it is you end up doing with Terminal. The fault will not necessarily lie with Terminal, but much more likely will be the result of improper wiring, faulty modems, noisy telephone lines, incorrect log-on procedures, or incompatible software on the other end of the line.

Here's a small list of tips and possible cures in the event of trouble.

COMMUNICATION DOESN'T EVEN BEGIN

- Check to see that the modem is on.

- If you're using an external modem, make sure it is connected to the correct serial port.

- Check to make sure you selected the correct port from the Settings ⇨ Communications dialog box.

- If you're using an internal-type modem, did you select the correct port assignment (COM1 or COM2)? Make sure there are no conflicts with other equipment, such as printer ports, a serial mouse, or others. Only one device can be assigned to a port. You may have to switch to COM2 if COM1 is being used by another device.

- Test the link between your computer and modem this way: If you are using a Hayes modem, choose Connect ⇨ Connect. Type **AT** (uppercase) and press ↵. The modem should respond with **OK** on your screen. If it doesn't, there may be something wrong with the wiring, the modem, or the port selection.

- If you and the person on the other end of the line see garbage on the screen, such as

    !!!12#())))@(#^&**(&@#%^,

when you type in terminal mode, most likely you are transmitting at different baud rates. Hang up, call the other person, agree on a baud rate, and try again. (Also check the number of data bits and stop bits.)

TIP If your Hayes modem (external type) answers the phone even when you don't want it to, open the modem and set switch 5 to the down position. This disables automatic answering.

YOU CAN'T LOG ONTO AN INFORMATION SERVICE OR BBS

- Try pressing ↵ or Ctrl-C upon seeing a prompt from the host computer.

- Did you type the log-on, password, and so on exactly as they are supposed to be typed? Uppercase and lowercase letters are often distinguished by remote systems.

YOU HAVE DIFFICULTY TRANSFERRING A FILE

- If you're using XModem, you will have to start both computers (sending and receiving) at roughly the same time; otherwise they will time out. XModem programs will completely abort the transmission process after a time out. Terminal only waits about 1 minute before aborting an XModem sending or receiving attempt, after which you will have to begin the process again.

    If you're using Send Text or Capture Text and characters at the beginning of each line are lost in the process, increase the end-of-line delay of the sending computer. If the sending computer is the PC running Terminal, you do this from the Transfer ⇨ Send Text dialog box.

- If you need to perform many file transfers between a Macintosh and your PC, you may want to consider other alternatives, such as hardware/software products devised specifically for that purpose. TOPS, an interoperating system local area network from Tops Corp. in Alameda, California is a good example. Also, some Macs can now directly read 3½-inch floppy disks from a PC.

YOUR COMMUNICATIONS SESSIONS ARE TERMINATED UNEXPECTEDLY

- If while running a communcations session you are abruptly cut off, the culprit may be "call waiting." You know you were cut off because the screen will probably say something like

    NO CARRIER

when the other party didn't really hang up on you. Call waiting allows you to be interrupted by a new incoming call when you're already talking to someone. However, modems don't like call waiting at all. (They're even less forgiving of it than some of my friends.) When the second call comes in, the modems' carrier tones are interrupted and they think the party's over, so they unceremoniously hang up the phone. The solution is either to use a line that doesn't have call waiting or to see if you can turn it off. In Berkeley, California for example, where I live, I can turn off call waiting by dialing *70, waiting for a second, and then dialing the number. Call waiting is then disabled until I hang up. If I'm concerned about being interrupted in a communications session, I'll tell the other person that I'll call *them*, so that I can turn off my call waiting first. (If they call me, I can't.) I also use the *70 command in front of any

phone numbers I enter into the Terminal phone settings, like this:

*70,415-555-1212

CHAPTER
TWELVE

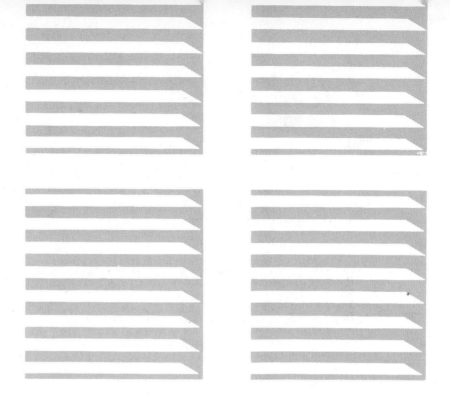

Using Paintbrush

Fast Track

CHAPTER 12

PAINTBRUSH IS THE LAST MAJOR APPLICATION
program supplied with the Windows package that I'll cover in
this book. (The remaining applications are discussed in Chapter 13.)

Paintbrush is a drawing program, to a number of other graphics
drawing programs on the market. The most popular of these
are PC-Paintbrush, MousePaint, and PC-Paint. All of these
programs, including Paintbrush resemble MacPaint for the
Macintosh, which became very popular as a basic, functional
drawing tool. Although Paintbrush, like Write, isn't a top-of-the-
line product in its class, the price is right, and it's not bad. In
fact, it has some unique features.

In the personal-computer world there are two basic classes of
graphics programs—bit-mapped and object-oriented. With bit-
map programs, you create a painting or drawing on the computer screen as if you were painting a picture on a canvas with
paint. Paint you apply to the canvas irreversibly covers up the
underlying surface.

Object-oriented programs create a drawing or graphic in a
manner more analagous to a collage or like those felt boards
used in grade school. Each item you place (lines, circles, text,
etc.) retains its identity as a separate object. These objects can
later be moved, sized, cut, copied, and otherwise altered
without affecting anything else in the picture.

Paintbrush is of the first variety. Rather than being defined by
objects, a Paintbrush bit-map drawing consists of a series of dots.

Your computer's screen is divided into very small dots (pixels or pels) that are controlled by the smallest division of computer information—bits. A bit map is a collection of bits of information that when assigned ("mapped") to dots on the screen (or on paper), create an image. This is similar to a sports scoreboard that can display the score, a message, or even a picture, by turning on and off specific lightbulbs in a grid.

In the simplest of bit maps, one bit controls one dot. Since in computers a bit is like a light switch and can either be on or off, each dot on the screen can either be on or off. So, a drawing is created by a matrix of dots that are on or off. When you create a graphic with a bit-map drawing program, what you are doing is determining which dots are on and which are off. If the program uses color (as Paintbrush does) or gray-scaling, additional bits are required to store the color information for each dot, but that's another story. Anyway, the basic theory remains the same. Though this may seem academic now, it will make more sense later when you learn about editing the bit map with the Zoom command.

Enough theory. With Paintbrush, you can

- Create signs
- Create computer art
- Create technical drawings
- Create illustrations for printed matter
- Create images for use in other Windows programs such as Cardfile
- Design invitations
- Enhance digitized images or photographs
- Draw maps
- Make wallpaper images for your Windows desktop

STARTING A NEW DOCUMENT

To bring up Paintbrush:

1. Open the Accessories group and double click on the Paintbrush icon.

2. The Paintbrush window appears. Maximize the window. Figure 12.1 shows the Paintbrush window and its component parts.

The work area is where you do your drawing. You use the tools selected from the Toolbox along with selections from the Palette and Linesize box to create your drawings.

NOTE The size of the drawing is determined by the amount of memory you have in your computer since while you're working on it, the entire picture is contained in RAM. If you have only a small amount of available memory, because other programs are open or you're simply short on RAM, the size of your drawing will be limited. You will be alerted if there is too little RAM to load a large picture.

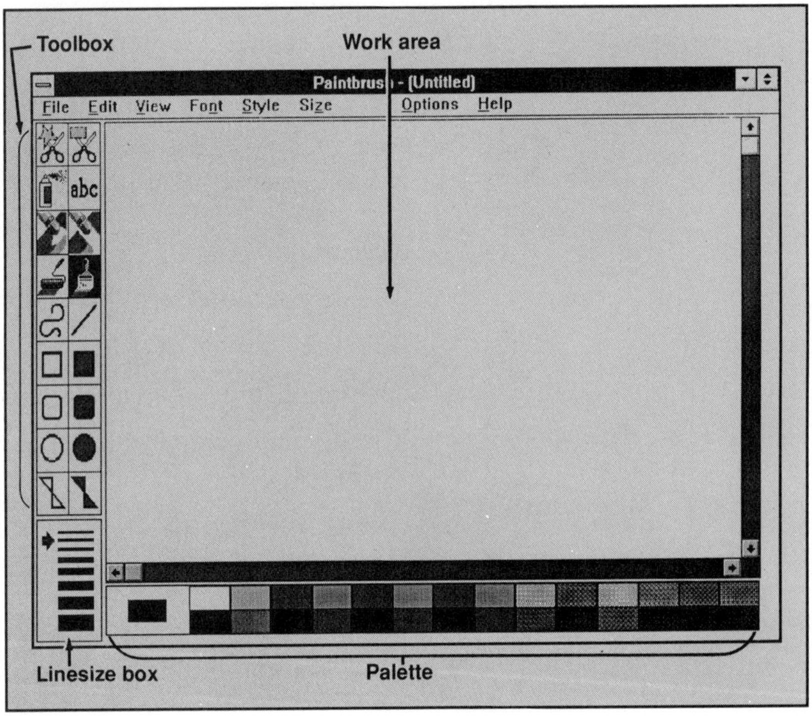

Figure 12.1: The Paintbrush screen

LOADING AN EXISTING DRAWING

To load an existing picture, do the following:

1. Choose File ➪ Open.

2. Select the file name from the file and directory boxes. Figure 12.2 shows the *chess.bmp* file loaded.

Now you can edit the file and save it under a new name, or copy a part of it to the Clipboard for use with other programs.

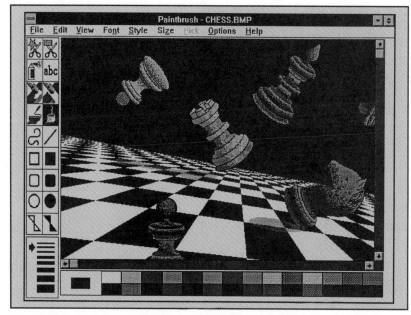

Figure 12.2: Opening a file loads it into the workspace

SEEING MORE OF THE DRAWING

Sometimes the entire drawing is larger than the work area. If it is not too much larger, you may be able to see and work with the entire picture at one time. In any case, you can increase the viewing area in several ways.

1. Choose View ⇨ Tools and Linesize. The Toolbox and Linesize box along the left margin disappear and are replaced by more of the picture. You still have the scroll bars and menu options though, and whatever tool you're working with (we'll discuss tools later in this chapter).

2. Choose View ⇨ Palette. The Palette disappears, with similar advantage.

3. Choose View ⇨ View Picture. This shows as much of the picture as will fit on the screen at one time, though not necessarily the entire picture. However, this is only for checking your work, and doesn't allow you to work on the drawing. Clicking anywhere on the screen or pressing any key returns you to the working screen.

3. To see the entire picture, even the space where you haven't drawn anything, choose View ⇨ Zoom Out. Paintbrush will shrink the image to fit within the work area. The size of the image displayed is based on the size you declare in the Image Attributes dialog box (as described in the next section). Though you can cut, copy, and paste in this zoomed-out mode, you can't draw anything new until you choose View ⇨ Zoom In.

SPEED TIP
Double clicking on the Pick tool (the one with the scissors and dotted box) has the same effect as choosing View ⇨ View Picture.

It's more likely that you'll want the Toolbox on and the Palette off if you need to see more of the drawing, since the tools are used more frequently. To return to the Toolbox and the Palette, just choose these commands again from the View menu, since they are toggles.

ALTERING THE SIZE OF THE DRAWING

The first thing you should determine when starting a new document is the size of the final drawing you're trying to create. When Paintbrush is run the first time on your system, it examines the video display you have and the amount of RAM in your computer. Based on these factors, it determines an appropriate drawing size. However, it's likely you're going to want to change this for some drawings. You set the drawing size on the Image Attributes dialog box reached from the Options menu.

1. Choose Options ⇨ Image Attributes. The dialog box you see below appears.

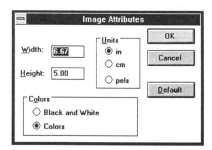

2. Enter the new width and height for your drawing, and click on OK.

You can change other options from this box, too, as follows.

SETTING	EFFECT
Units	Determines the units for entering the width and height. The default is inches, though you can choose centimeters or pels. Pels are virtually the same pixels, or bits. That is, each pel is equal to a dot on the screen.
Colors	Determines whether your picture is created in black and white or in color
Default	Resets the drawing size to the amount Paintbrush originally figured as optimum for your system, though not necessarily the size you want.

Once you make these settings, they are stored and used each time you run Paintbrush. The thing to remember is that the settings won't affect the drawing you're currently working on. You have to change the settings *before* you start drawing a picture, and then choose File ⇨ New.

If you make the settings too high (e.g., 200 inches by 200 inches), the next time you run Paintbrush, you may get a message saying there isn't enough memory in your system to edit a picture.

Here are some points to keep in mind when altering the image size:

- You can print the image in two resolutions—screen and printer. Printer resolution requires more memory than screen resolution.

- If you plan to print at printer resolution, you should enter the exact size in pixels of the final printed image.

- The dimensions you enter should be in proportion to those of the screen image of the drawing to avoid distortion of the image when printed.

SETTING THE BACKGROUND AND FOREGROUND COLORS OR PATTERNS

NOTE   The term *color* describes either a color or a colored pattern selected from the color Palette. If you are using a black and white screen, colors in the Palette may appear as shades of gray, or varying densities of dot patterns.

After setting the drawing size, the next step in creating a new picture or even modifying an existing one is to set the foreground and background colors selected from the Palette.

The foreground color is the color you want a new item to be. For example, when you draw an item such as a circle, you'll want to assign a specific color to it. It's like deciding which color of paint to put on the brush before painting a stroke.

The background color determines the overall color of the canvas, or backdrop for the picture. This is its primary function. It also has some effect on the drawing tools, determining the outline color of circles, squares, and enclosed polygons, and the color of text shading and outlining.

The current settings of the foreground and background colors is shown at the left side of the palette. The box in the middle shows the foreground color. The frame around it shows the background color. The default colors are black on white and always come up that way when you run Paintbrush.

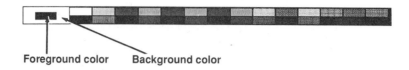

Foreground color   Background color

SETTING THE BACKROUND COLOR

To set the background color or pattern for the entire background of a new drawing:

1. Point to the color or pattern in the palette and click the *right* mouse button.

2. Choose File ➪ New. The new document will have the assigned background.

NOTE You can only determine the overall background color for a drawing once. If you want to change it later, you'll have to paint the new color on top of the old one with one of the tools.

To change the assigned background color after starting a new drawing, just use step 1. This will not change the background color of the drawing itself, but it will affect the tools as explained above.

SETTING THE FOREGROUND COLOR

Set the foreground color as follows:

1. Point to the color or pattern you want.

2. Click the *left* mouse button. Now, whatever you draw with the tools will appear in this color until you change it.

Typically, you'll change the foreground color very frequently if you're creating a drawing to be viewed on-screen. If you didn't, everything would have the same color, which is pretty boring. If you're drawing a picture to be printed on a black-and-white printer (which is likely, since color printers are relatively expensive and scarce at this point), you won't have much latitude in this regard. Paintbrush does try to render colors in shades of gray, though it doesn't do this as well as some other programs do. You may want to experiment a bit with your printer to determine what happens when you try to print colors. If the results aren't satisfactory, stick with the default foreground and background colors of black on white.

SETTING THE LINE, BORDER, AND BRUSH WIDTH

Probably the next thing you'll want to set is the line width for the drawing tools. The line width determines how thin or fat lines are. This includes lines around boxes and circles, curvy lines, and so on. To change it,

❒ Click on the width you want in the Linesize box. This becomes the default until you choose a new size.

Note that if you don't specify a background color as different from the drawing's background, the lines around items you draw won't show up because they'll be the same color as the background. If this happens, change the background color and draw again.

USING THE TOOLS

Once the preliminaries are out of the way, you can begin playing. Unlike with the other programs supplied with Windows, using Paintbrush is largely a matter of trial and error, just as if someone gave you a brush and some paint and said "go to it." All you really need to know is the basics of each tool, a few tricks with menu options, and then how to save the file and print it. The rest is up to you and your imagination.

In this section I'll explain each of the tools and suggest some tips and tricks for them. You might want to sit at your computer and work with each of the tools as you read, changing colors (if you have color), and line widths along the way. Start by creating a new file so you don't ruin one of the supplied ones. (Choose File ⇨ New.) Then begin experimenting. Pretty soon you'll have a good high-tech mess on your screen, at which point you can just choose File ⇨ New to clear it and be ready for more experimentation. (When asked about saving the thing you created, click No unless you really like it.)

Figure 12.3 shows the tools icons and their names. To choose a tool, you simply click on its icon in the Toolbox. The tool is then activated (and highlighted), and the cursor changes shape when you move back into the work area. The tool stays selected until you choose another one, zoom out, or use the Paste From command. The following sections will describe each of the tools, referring to the names in the figure.

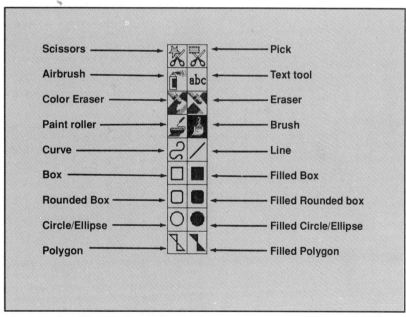

Figure 12.3: The Paintbrush Toolbox

ABOUT PASTING DOWN

One thing you should know before moving on has to do with "pasting down" items that you draw. A nice feature of Paintbrush is that items that you add to the drawing don't immediately stick to the surface and become a irreversible part of it until you switch to another tool, use a scroll bar, open another application, or resize the window. Once you do any of these things, the new addition to the drawing gets pasted down, and what was behind it can't be reclaimed.

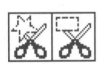 **TIP** To erase any work you've done since the last time you pasted down, choose Edit ⇨ Undo.

On the other hand, until you take any of the actions that paste down the new material, you can erase or modify what you've done with the Undo command or the Backspace key. You can make a major mistake and still not mess up your picture. Try experimenting with these options as you work with the tools.

❐ To selectively erase some of the work you've done since the last time things were pasted down, press Backspace. The cursor will change to a box with an arrow in it. (You can adjust the size of the box by choosing a different line size.) The box is a selective eraser that erases only the unpasted material (lines, circles, airbrushing, etc.) but leaves what's behind it intact.

THE CUTOUT TOOLS

There are two tools for selecting portions of a drawing. In Paintbrush, a selection of the drawing that you cut or copy is called a *cutout*. Thus, the tools are called cutout tools. To differentiate them, the left one is called the Scissors tool, and the right one the Pick tool (why *Pick*, I don't know).

To use the Scissors:

1. Select the tool.

2. Move to the spot where you want to start cutting. Draw a line completely around the object or area you want to cut out or alter. If you make a mistake, press the right mouse button and make the selection again.

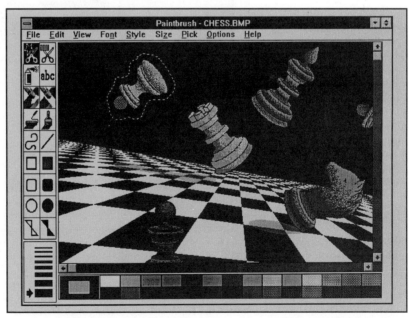

NOTE The Scissors tool lets you do a free-form selection of a portion of the screen, as if using a pair of scissors, by drawing a line around the portion of the picture you want to cut or copy. It's useful because it lets you select a very specific area that can conform to the shape of an object. If you plan to paste objects together in close proximity to each other, use this tool rather than the Pick tool to do the cutting. It will help to insure that the edges of pasted items don't overlap each other.

3. You can move the object by dragging it with the mouse, cut or copy it, or perform other manipulations on it from the Pick menu (which are all explained in the sections "Using the Pick Menu Commands" and "The Goodies," later in this chapter), such as inverting its colors or rotating it. The cutout area will be marked by a dotted line, as shown in Figure 12.4.

The only difference between the Pick tool and the Scissors is that the Pick tool selects a rectangular area. It's faster to use, since you just drag the mouse to define a boxed area. You can easily select the entire drawing if you need to.

1. Select the Pick tool.

2. Move to the upper-left corner of the boxed area you want to select. Click and hold the left mouse button.

3. Drag the mouse down and to the right. Release the button.

Figure 12.4: You select a non-uniform cutout area with the Scissors tool. A dotted line indicates the cutout.

A dotted line indicates the area of cutout. Once again, you can cut, copy, or drag the cutout, or use the commands on the Pick menu.

Figure 12.5 shows the results of copying and dragging.

If you hold the shift key while dragging any cutout, the original cutout will be left in place. This is similar to copying and pasting, but easier. If you press the right mouse button when dragging, the image will be copied opaquely. That is, the background and image in the cutout will overlay and obscure what's behind it. If you drag using the left button, the image will be copied transparently (any background color and image behind the selection will show through), assuming that the background of the cutout and the current selected background color are the same. By selecting an area, then shift-dragging,

Figure 12.5: Once a cutout is defined, you can manipulate it in a variety of ways. Here you see chess pieces from the chess.bmp file copied and placed across the drawing.

releasing the button, and shift-dragging again and again, you can create a repeated pattern of the same image.

THE AIRBRUSH

Here's a tool that's a legal outlet for repressed graffiti artists. The Airbrush works like a can of spray paint. It uses the selected foreground color, and as long as you hold the mouse button down, it sprays away. Think of the mouse button as the button on the top of the spray can.

1. Click on the color or pattern you want the Airbrush to spray.

2. Click on the line width that you want the spray to have.

3. Position the cursor in the work area and press the left mouse button. Move the mouse around and spray the color onto the work area. Note that the speed of movement affects the density of the spray, just as it does with a real spray can. Moving the mouse quickly results in a finer mist. Letting it sit still or moving very slowly plasters the paint on solid.

TIP Remember, you can make selective corrections to new items by hitting Backspace and moving the eraser square over your new material. This is particularly useful for touching up after the Airbrush.

Figure 12.6 shows an example of some airbrushed writing.

THE ERASER

As its icon suggests, the Eraser works like the eraser on a pencil—only you don't have to rub. Just passing it across an area erases whatever it touches, leaving nothing but the background color. Use the Eraser when you want to obliterate something that's already pasted down, or when you want to touch up some stray dots or lines.

1. Select the Eraser tool. The cursor will change to a hollow box when moved into the work area.

Figure 12.6: The Airbrush works like a spray can. Just point and spray.

TIP Selecting a non-matching background color and then using the Eraser with the line width set to maximum is a fast way of drawing really fat swaths of any color. Just keep changing the background color and then erasing another section of the screen. The lines of color are wider than those available with the Brush or the Airbrush.

2. Set the background color to the same color as the area you're erasing in. If you don't then, the object you erase will disappear, but it will be replaced by another background color.

3. Set the line width to determine the width of the Eraser. For fine work, use the thinnest setting.

4. Drag the mouse over the material you want to erase. Hold the Shift key down while moving the mouse if you want to constrict the mouse pointer's movement to just vertical or horizontal.

Figure 12.7 shows an erasure. The white boxes were created with the largest line-width setting and single clicks of the Eraser. The paper.bmp file was loaded into a new document with the

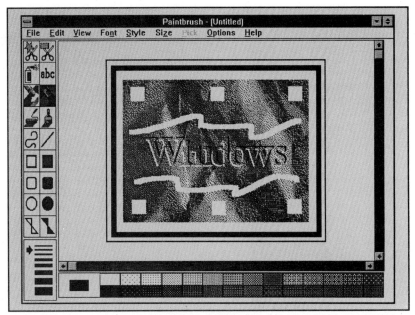

Figure 12.7: Use the Eraser tool to remove any part of the drawing. The current background color will show through.

Edit ⇨ Paste From command and then repositioned in the center of the work area. (The Edit ⇨ Paste From command loads a bit-map file from the disk into the Clipboard.)

THE COLOR ERASER

The Color Eraser is an interesting gadget. It lets you erase a specific color rather than everything it touches. It can also replace a specific color with another color.

1. Select the Color Eraser tool (it's the eraser on the left). The cursor changes to a box with a plus sign in it when moved into the work area.

2. Choose the color you want to erase by clicking in the Palette with the left button.

3. Choose the color you want to replace the erased color with by clicking in the Palette with the right button. (What you're really doing here is assigning the background color.)

4. Set the line width to adjust the size of the eraser.

5. Press the mouse button and move the eraser over the area to be erased. If you have set the backgound color to match the preexisting background, the effect of erasing will be to neutralize the color. If you have set it to another color, the effect will be that of replacing the existing color with a new color. This is a great feature that makes changing the color scheme of a drawing really easy.

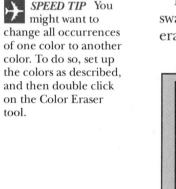

SPEED TIP You might want to change all occurrences of one color to another color. To do so, set up the colors as described, and then double click on the Color Eraser tool.

Figure 12.8 shows an effect resulting from replacing two swaths of color at the top and bottom of the drawing. The color eraser was set to the largest line width.

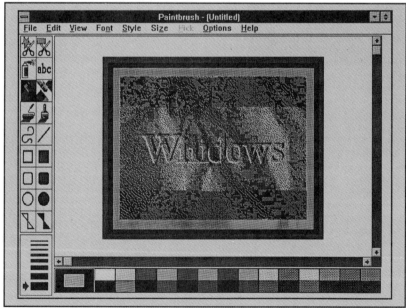

Figure 12.8: Use the Color Eraser to remove a specific color or to replace that color with a new one

BRUSH

The Brush tool works like a paint brush, pen, or marker. Use this tool to create freehand drawings.

1. Choose the Brush icon.

2. Select the color and width.

3. Press the left button and start drawing. Hold the button down as long as you want to continue the line. Release the button when you want to stop drawing the line. Repeat the process to draw another line.

SPEED TIP You can open the Brush Shapes box quickly by double clicking on the Brush icon.

If you hold the Shift key while using the brush, only horizontal or vertical lines will result. You can change the brush shape if you want for special effects. Choose Options ⇨ Brush Shapes. The following dialog box will appear.

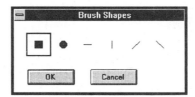

4. Choose the shape you want and click on OK. All subsequent drawing will use the shape.

Figure 12.9 shows a simple brush drawing.

LINE

Use the Line tool to draw straight lines.

1. Select the tool.

2. Select the color and width.

Figure 12.9: A freehand drawing made with the brush

 Use the Shift key to constrain the line to vertical, 45 degree, or horizontal.

TIP To help you align things such as lines, choose View ⇨ Cursor Position. The column and row of the current position will then be displayed in the upper-right corner of the window. The units of measurement are determined by the Image Attributes dialog box.

3. Move into the work area. The cursor becomes a cross hair. Press and hold the left button, and move the mouse. A straight line will appear between the beginning (anchor) point and the end point. You can move the end point around until you are satisfied with its location, even in a circle around the anchor point.

4. Release the button when you want to stop drawing the line.

Figure 12.10 shows an example of a drawing made up of lines only.

CURVE

The Curve is a strange tool. It works like the line initially, but then allows you two chances to "pull" the line you've drawn—

Figure 12.10: You can create drawings such as this with only the line tool and the Shift key. (You could, however, shorten the task with the Box tool.)

SPEED TIP If you want to quickly erase a line and start over without having to use Undo, Backspace, or the Eraser, *don't* release the left button. Keep it down and press the right button too. This will erase only the line you are drawing. (Remember, Undo erases everything not pasted down.) This applies to the Curve, Box, Filled Box, Rounded Box, Filled Rounded Box, Circle/Ellipse, Filled Circle/Elipse, Polygon, and Filled Polygon tools too.

once from one location, and then once from another—to make a curved line. The result might be something of a semicircle, or it might be more like an "S" shape.

1. Choose the Curve tool, and then use the same techniques as for drawing a line.

2. Once the line is drawn, release the mouse button. Then move the cursor to one side of the line, hold down the left button, and drag the cursor away from or towards the line. As you do so, the line will stretch like a rubber band. Release the button when the bend is correct.

3. If you don't want to add another bend to the line, click on the endpoint (not the anchor point end).

4. If you want to add another bend, move near another position on the line, such as on the other side of it, and drag the cursor again. The line will again stretch like a rubber band. When you are satisfied with the final line shape, release the mouse button. The color and width will then be added to the line.

Figure 12.11 shows the process of drawing a curve.

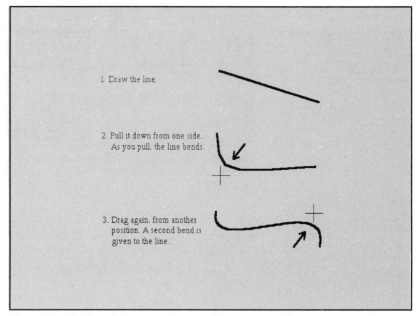

Figure 12.11: The three steps in creating a curved line

BOX AND FILLED BOX

The Box tool draws boxes and rectangles. The boxes are hollow, and the box's border appears in the foreground color.

1. Select the tool.

2. Set the color and line width.

TIP To constrain ellipses to be perfect circles, hold down the Shift key as you draw. This applies to filled circles as well as to hollow ones.

3. Click where you want one corner of the box to start. This sets the anchor. Then drag the cross hair down and to one side. As you do, a flexible frame will appear.

4. Release the mouse button when the size is correct. (You can erase the box you've just drawn by pressing the left and right mouse buttons.)

The filled box works the same way. However, the filled box uses the foreground color for its insides, and the background color for its border. Set both colors before drawing. If you want a solid box of a single color, set the foreground and background to the same color.

ROUNDED BOX AND FILLED ROUNDED BOX

These two tools are identical in operation to the Box and Filled Box. The only difference lies in their appearance—their corners are rounded instead of having sharp 90 degree angles.

CIRCLE/ELLIPSE AND FILLED CIRCLE/ELLIPSE

These two tools again work in much the same way as the Box, only they create circles and ellipses (ovals). Use the same basic drawing technique. The rules regarding the fill and border colors of boxes apply to ellipses too. Figure 12.12 shows a healthy population of bubble-like objects created with the Filled Circle/Ellipse tool and the Shift key.

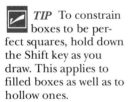

TIP To constrain boxes to be perfect squares, hold down the Shift key as you draw. This applies to filled boxes as well as to hollow ones.

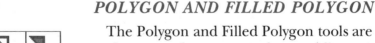

POLYGON AND FILLED POLYGON

The Polygon and Filled Polygon tools are similar to the Line tool, except that you can keep adding more and more endpoints. Paintbrush then connects them all. With these tools, you can create an endless variety of polygonal shapes, and they come in handy for quickly creating irregularly shaped objects. You could draw them by hand with the brush, but it's usually

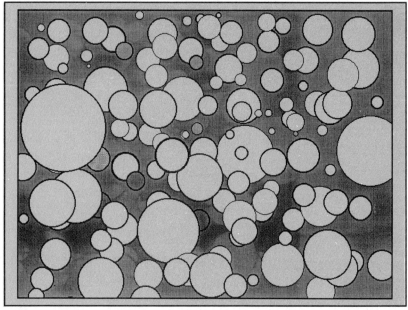

Figure 12.12: Perfect circles are created with the Shift key and the Circle/Ellipse or Filled Circle/Ellipse tools

easier with the polygons. The filled polygon is even more fun because of the way it fills.

1. Select the tool.

2. Select the color and line width.

3. Click where you want the first anchor point to be. (Hold the button down.)

4. Now move to the point you want a straight line drawn to and release. A line will appear, sort of "connecting the dots." This defines the first side of the polygon.

5. Move to the next point and click again. Another line will be drawn. Continue this until you have drawn all the lines in your polygon. When you want to stop the drawing, double click. (The last and first points will be connected by Paintbrush if you don't line them up.)

TIP To constrain the lines of the polygon to be vertical, 45 degrees, or horizontal only, hold down the Shift key as you draw.

TIP If you want to see the lines as you are drawing them (as opposed to when you click), modify the technique a bit by clicking and holding as if drawing a normal line. When you reach the desired endpoint for the first line, release the button. Then, keeping the mouse still, click and hold again while drawing the next line.

Note that a polygon's sides can cross each other, as in the tool's icon. The polygons don't have to be symmetrically shaped the way hexagons or octagons are. You can haphazardly click all over the screen and, until you double click, Paintbrush will keep connecting the dots.

The filled polygon is created the same way. Only in this case, Paintbrush will fill the inside of the polygon with the foreground color. (The background color, just as with filled circles and boxes, determines the border color.)

You can create a cubist artistic effect with this tool because of the way Paintbrush calculates an "enclosed" area. It starts at the top of the screen and begins filling areas. If your polygon has lots of enclosed areas from multiple lines overlapping, Paintbrush alternates the fills. Thus, adjacent enclosed areas will not all be filled. Using the tool with the cutout tools and the Inverse command can lead to some rather interesting geometrical designs. (Inverting is covered in the section "The Goodies.")

Figure 12.13 shows an example of what can be done with the tool.

PAINT ROLLER

I've put off discussing the Paint Roller since using it requires understanding the other tools a bit. The roller will fill in any enclosed area with the foreground color, unless the area has already been filled with one of the colors that has a grainy texture (any of the last 12 colors on the right side of the color palette). An enclosed area can be defined by any lines or curves in the drawing area. So, three separate lines set up to form a triangle constitute an enclosed space just as much as a box's border does. Since the entire drawing area is also considered an enclosed space, you can use the roller to change the background of the drawing. Letters you create with the Text tool (discussed next) can be filled too.

1. Select the tool
2. Choose the foreground color for the fill.

Figure 12.13: A geometric design created with the Filled Polygon tool

3. Point the roller's sharp edge at the item to be filled, and click. The enclosed area will be filled with the foreground color.

Note that the color flows to fill the entire enclosed area. If there is a leak in what you thought was an enclosed area, the "paint" will seep through the crack, so to speak, and fill everything until it is stopped by a complete boundary. You may accidentally fill the entire work area. If this happens, just choose Undo.

THE TEXT TOOL

The text tool lets you put characters on your creations. This is convenient when designing flyers, invitations, maps, instuctions, and the like. The fonts and sizes of text you can use are determined by the printer you have installed.

1. Choose the text tool (the abc).

2. Choose the style of type from the Style menu. Note that Normal turns off all the other options. Bold, Italic, and Underline can all be on at one time. Only one of Outline or Shadow can be on at a time.

3. Choose the color for the text. Shadows and Outlines use the background color, while the text itself will appear in the foreground color.

4. Pick the type size you want to use. Grayed sizes are not available. Sizes with an asterisk will look smoother on your screen than sizes without an asterisk. However, they will all print with the same resolution, so don't worry if some sizes of text look "jagged" on the screen.

5. Place the cursor where you want to start typing and click. This places the insertion point. There isn't any word wrapping but you can use the ↵ key. You can erase mistakes with the Backspace key until you paste the text down. You can also change the style, size, font, and color of text until you paste the text down. (See "About Pasting Down" earlier in this chapter.) After text is pasted down, you'll have to use the Eraser or the cutout tools to delete it.

Figure 12.14 shows some of the type styles available on my system. Yours may differ, depending on your printer.

THE GOODIES

So much for the tools. Now for the goodies. All the major goodies except for one are on the Pick menu. The Pick menu is dimmed until you select a cutout area. Once you do, you can open the menu and select commands from it. The following sections describe these commands.

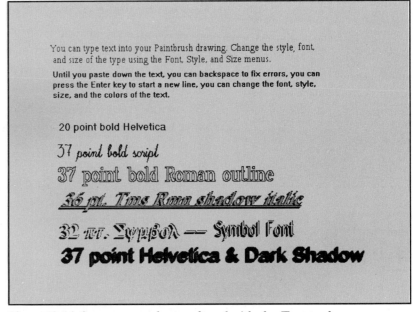

Figure 12.14: Some type styles produced with the Text tool

FLIP HORIZONTAL AND FLIP VERTICAL

Flip Horizontal and Flip Vertical are simple commands. They just flip the selected cutout around, just as if you took a color slide and turned it over, put it back in the projector, and looked at it again. Suddenly, the picture is reversed, either horizontally or vertically. You can use this command to create symmetrical drawings and patterns by defining a cutout of an existing shape, copying the cutout, pasting it into the same picture, flipping it, and repositioning it. This way, you don't have to draw the shape several times in different directions. Figure 12.15 shows an example.

To try the Flip Commands,

1. Select the cutout with one of the cutout tools.

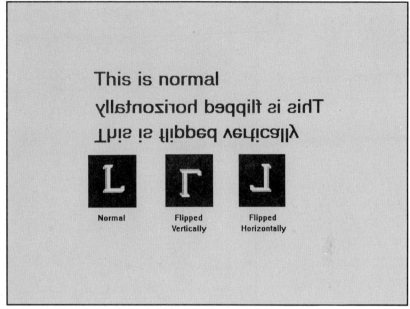

Figure 12.15: Cutouts flipped horizontally and vertically

2. Copy and paste the cutout if you want. When you paste, the pasted material is automatically selected as the cutout, so commands will affect it, not the original.

3. Choose Pick ⇨ Flip Horizontal or Pick ⇨ Flip Vertical. The selected cutout will be flipped appropriately.

INVERSE

Inverse reverses the color in the cutout. Thus, black will turn to white, and white will turn to black. If you're working in color, the colors will turn to their complements. Complementary colors are defined here as being the color on the opposite side of the RGB (Red, Green, Blue) color wheel. This is a really fun tool. Try selecting several slightly overlapping squares of a picture and inverting them in sequence. An example is shown in Figure 12.16.

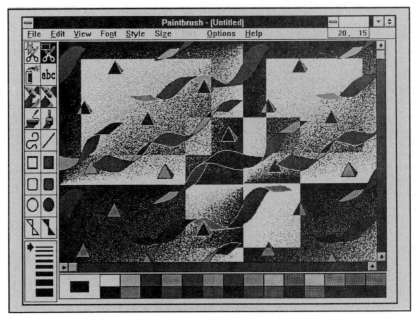

Figure 12.16: Inverting a section of a drawing by selecting the cutout area and then choosing Pick ⇨ Inverse

To try this,

1. Select the area to have its colors inverted.

2. Choose Pick ⇨ Inverse.

SHRINK AND GROW

Shrink and Grow is a command that lets you increase or decrease the size of a selected area. Suppose you drew a section of a diagram too small. Rather than erasing it and drawing it again, you could increase its size with this command. You can also use this command to repeat patterns or shapes with copy and paste in various sizes in the drawing.

TIP If the Pick ⇨ Clear setting is on, the original cutout will be erased when the newly sized copy is created. Otherwise, the original will be left as is.

TIP To maintain the exact proportions of the cutout, hold down Shift while selecting it. This selects it in a perfect square. Then hold down Shift while creating each new box.

To try this command:

1. Select the cutout area to be enlarged or shrunk.

2. Select Pick ⇨ Shrink and Grow.

3. With the cross-hair cursor, draw a box roughly approximating the size you want the cutout to appear. When you release the mouse button, the cutout appears in the box in its new size.

4. Repeat the last step as many times as you want, replicating the cutout in a variety of sizes. You can distort the image's proportions by drawing boxes that are substantially different in proportion from the original cutout. See Figure 12.17.

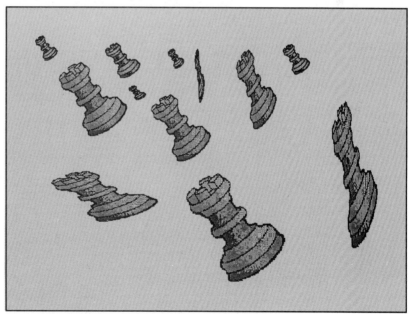

Figure 12.17: Stretched and shrunken bishops

TILT

The Tilt command lets you stretch a cutout on a slant:

1. Select a cutout area.

2. Choose Pick ⇨ Tilt.

3. Move the cursor to a new location and then click and hold down the mouse button. A box the exact size of the cutout area will appear. Keep the mouse button down and move the mouse left and right. The box will tilt, like a parallelogram, about the anchor point, which is its upper-left corner. Release the button when the box is tilted the way you want. You'll probably have to experiment a few times to get it to look the way you want it.

Figure 12.18 shows some examples of tilting.

TIP If the Pick ⇨ Clear setting is on, the original cutout will be erased when the newly tilted copy is created. Otherwise, the original will be left as is.

TIP If you position the cursor in close to the same location as the original anchor point of the cutout, the tilted version will overlay the original.

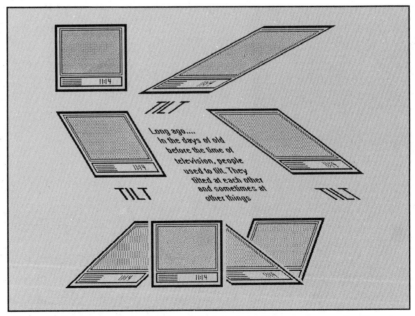

Figure 12.18: Examples of tilting. Notice that tilting can grossly distort an object and can also give text that "Star Wars" movie credit look.

SWEEPING

Sweeping a cutout is a neat trick that smears numerous copies of the cutout across the drawing area as you move the mouse. You can use this technique to suggest motion of an object, or to create interesting artistic effects.

To try it,

1. Select a cutout area.

2. Drag the cutout area while holding the Ctrl key down. Copies of the cutout are made as you drag the cursor around.

Figure 12.19 shows an example of sweeping.

TIP As with copying, you can do opaque or transparent sweeping. Transparent sweeping lets the images in the background show through the cutout you're sweeping. Opaque sweeping overlays them. Press the right mouse button when dragging to create opaque sweeping, or the left button for transparent. The background color of the cutout and the current background color have to be the same for transparent sweeping to work.

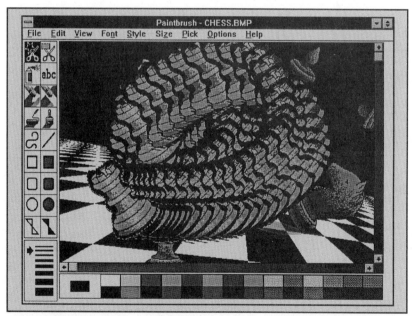

Figure 12.19: Sweeping a cutout makes numerous copies on a single sweep of the mouse

PIXEL EDITING

Pixel editing lets you blow up a portion of the drawing to do "microsurgery" on it. In this mode, the pixels in your drawing seem to become quite large, so that you can fine tune them. This is useful for smoothing out lines, creating highlights on objects, creating minute patterns, and so forth.

To edit the pixels of an image,

1. Choose View ⇨ Zoom-in. The cursor becomes a box on the screen. (If it doesn't, you were zoomed out. Choose Zoom-in again.)

2. Position the box over the area you want to fine tune, and click. The screen changes dramatically, showing a closeup of the section. The normally sized section you're working with is displayed in the upper-left corner of the work area, and will reflect any changes you make. The cursor becomes a pointer. Figure 12.20 shows an example.

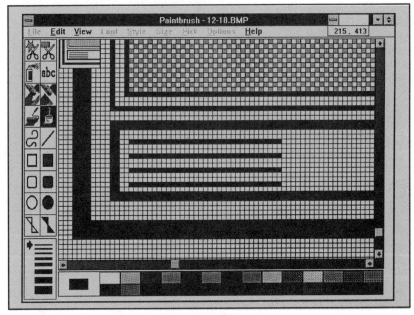

Figure 12.20: Zooming in to do pixel editing

3. Each time you click on a little box with the left button (which represents a pixel in normal size), the selected foreground color is assigned to it. Use the right button to assign the background color to the pixel. Basically, you just paint in the picture, dot by dot. Change the colors assigned to the mouse buttons whenever you want. You can use the Roller while pixel editing, too.

4. When you're happy with the state of things, choose View ⇨ Zoom Out.

EDITING THE COLORS

If you are working in color, you may want to create custom colors. If you are working in black and white, you may want to create a new pattern. To do either,

1. Select a color or pattern you want to fine tune (or even radically change, say, if you never use it).

2. Choose Options ⇨ Edit Colors.

✈ SPEED TIP
Double click on a color in the palette to open the Edit Colors dialog box for that color.

3. The dialog box you see below will appear. Move the sliders. As you do this, the resulting color or pattern is displayed in the box to the right of the sliders. If you are working in black and white, the sliders all move together, changing from lighter to darker patterns. You can't adjust them individually. When you are satisfied, click OK. Click Cancel to drop the changes or Reset to put the sliders back in their original positions to begin again. (Note that the changes you make do not affect any drawing you did with that color or pattern previously.)

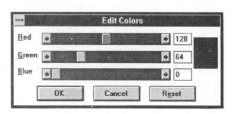

You can save the color settings for a drawing with the Options ⇨ Save Colors command. You can load a color-settings file with the Options ⇨ Get Colors command. The colors will be used until you reload Paintbrush or change them again in the same session. Paintbrush uses the default colors unless you load a specific color set.

SAVING YOUR WORK

As you work, you'll want to remember two things. The first is that you should paste something down whenever you don't want to lose it. The easiest way to do this is to select another tool, or even the same tool you're using. By pasting down work you're satisfied with, you won't accidentally lose it when you press Backspace or issue the Undo command.

Second, you should save your work to disk occasionally.

SAVING FILES

You can save files in a variety of formats. Normally, however, you can just let Paintbrush take care of the saving process.

When you open, edit, and then close a file, Paintbrush uses the same format it was created in. When you save a file for the first time, Paintbrush uses the Windows bit-map format, unless you stipulate otherwise by clicking on options. Here are the formats and their descriptions:

FILE TYPE	DESCRIPTION
PCX	Paintbrush format. This is a graphics file format that can be used by many graphics programs. Originated by Paintbrush.
Monochrome Bitmap	For non-color Paintbrush bit maps.
16-Color Bitmap	Use when you have 16 colors or fewer in your picture.

NOTE Microsoft suggests using the bit-mapped formats over other formats so that you can be assured of using the pictures with later versions of Windows. However, many more programs use PCX files than the proprietary Windows bit-mapped formats at this time. It's up to you. Decide which other programs you'll use the files with. Note that the more colors you save, the larger the files become, and the more disk and RAM space they'll need. Sixteen-color bitmap files are roughly eight times larger than PCX files of the same drawing. (Incidentally, you cannot save a file in Microsoft Paint format.)

256-Color Bitmap	Use when you have more than 16 and fewer than 257 colors in your picture.
24-bit Bitmap	Use when you have more than 256 colors in the picture. (This is highly unlikely.)

LOADING FILES

When you open a file, the default extension is *.bmp*. If you want to load a PCX file or MSP (Microsoft Paint) file, click on the appropriate button in the File Open dialog box. The file box will then show only files with the correct extension. Find the file using the boxes, or type in its name. If you are loading an MSP file, Paintbrush will ask if you want to convert it. *Once you convert it you won't be able to get it back to MSP format.*

If you want to scan in an printed image or photograph, use software and hardware that produces BMP, MSP, or PCX files. Unfortunately, Paintbrush doesn't read TIF files, so loading in a gray-scaled image is not possible. Incidentally, Paste From gives you more flexibility than Open, because you can determine the overall drawing size and reposition the pasted image. If you just open a drawing, it's likely to be stuck up in the upper-left corner.

PRINTING

Finally, you might want to print out your work! Here's how you do it:

1. Open the file.
2. Prepare the printer.
3. Choose File ⇨ Page Setup. Set up the margins and headers and footers (if you want them).
4. Choose File ⇨ Printer Setup and make sure the right printer is connected.

5. Choose File ⇨ Print. The Print dialog box will appear, as you see below:

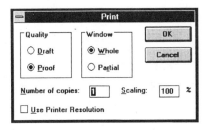

Make the settings using the following information:

SETTINGS	*EFFECT*
Quality	*Draft* prints in the fastest possible mode for your printer. *Proof* (the default) prints in the highest resolution.
Window	*Whole* prints the whole drawing. *Partial*, when selected, displays the whole drawing on the screen when you click on OK. From there you define a section to print by drawing a box.
Number of copies	Type in the number of copies you want printed.
Use Printer resolution	You can print in screen or printer resolution. If you use printer resolution, the picture will probably be more detailed, but it will take longer to print. You might also get some distortion in the printed output if you use printer resolution, since the height-to-width ratio may be different for the printer than for the screen, and Paintbrush doesn't compensate for this.
Scaling	If you want to increase the size of the picture, choose a percentage above 100. Percentages below 100 shrink the picture.

Large scaling changes can have unpredictable effects on some printers. Experimentation is the key to success, here, I'm afraid. Remember that the size of the picture is best determined in the first step of creating it—setting the image attributes. And don't forget that you can scale a drawing with the Shrink and Grow command. Just select the whole drawing and stretch or shrink it.

CHAPTER THIRTEEN

13

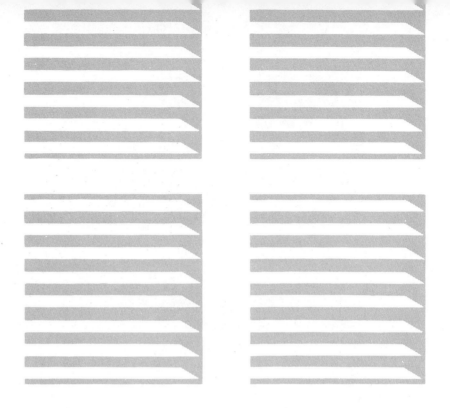

The Other Accessories

Fast Track

About the Notepad: 427

It's an ASCII text editor. Use it for creating and editing non-formatted text files, including system files such as *autoexec.bat* and *config.sys*. Files can be up to 50K. Double click on the Notepad icon in the Accesories group to run it.

To search for text in a Notepad file, 430

choose Search ⇨ Find. Type in the text you want to search for, and choose Foreward or Backward to determine the search direction.

About the Cardfile: 432

It lets you keep track of small scraps of information on cards. Each card has an index line and a section for your notes. To run the Cardfile, double click on the Cardfile icon in the Accessories group.

To add a Cardfile card, 434

press F7 or choose Card ⇨ Add. Type an identifying word or phrase into the index-line dialog box. Click on OK. Type the data into the information area of the card.

To search for a specific card (by index line), 435

choose Search ⇨ Go To or press F4. Type in two letters or more and click OK. Pressing Ctrl and a letter jumps to a card's index line that starts with that letter.

To search through the text on all the cards,   437

> choose Search ⇨ Find. Type in the search text and click on OK. Choose Search ⇨ Find Next to find the next card.

About the Calendar: 443

> It's a utility that keeps track of your appointments. Double click on Calendar in the Accessory group to run it. Type in your appointments next to the times. To change the time increments, choose Options ⇨ Day Settings. See the whole month by choosing View ⇨ Month. Click on the scroll buttons to move between days and months.

About the Recorder: 448

> It's a macro recording and playback utility. It can record all keyboard and mouse actions. Double click on the Recorder icon in the Accessories group to run it.

To record a macro,   449

> position the cursor where you want the macro to begin. Switch to the Recorder window. Choose Macro ⇨ Record. Fill in at least the macro name. Click on OK. Perform the actions you want to record. Click on the blinking Recorder icon or press Ctrl-Break to stop recording.

To play back a macro,   452

> press the assigned shortcut key, or double click on the macro's name in the Recorder window.

CHAPTER 13

THERE ARE A FEW WINDOWS ACCESSORIES THAT I haven't discussed yet. They're not terribly complicated programs, and you may already have figured out how to use them just through experimentation or by running them and reading their Help screens. They are the following:

PROGRAM	HELPS YOU
Notepad	Read and write short to medium length text files
Cardfile	Record and look up short bits of information, something like a Rolodex file or box of index cards.
Calendar	Keep track of appointments and organize your daily schedule.
Calculator	Perform standard arithmetic as well as scientific computations.
Recorder	Cut down on typing and mouse movements by memorizing your actions and automating them for you. It's also used for creating automatic demonstrations of Windows programs.

(Three other programs are discussed in subsequent chapters. The PIF Editor is discussed in Chapter 14. Swapfile and Sysedit are discussed in Chapter 15. The two supplied games—Solitaire and Reversi—are not discussed in this book. I'm sure you can figure them out. And we've already discussed the Clock.)

THE NOTEPAD

Think of the Notepad as a scaled down Write. It works similarly, but sports few frills. When you want to jot down some fairly lengthy notes, type up a quick memo with no fancy formatting, or read or print an existing text file (straight ASCII only), this is the tool for the job. It's a bit like the notepad in SideKick, if you've ever used that. It's handy and uses relatively little RAM (about 13K plus any file you open with it.) Since it's purely an ASCII editor, the files created have no special codes in them that would confuse other ASCII editors or programs that might need clean ASCII files. Thus, you can create or edit your *config.sys* or *autoexec.bat* files with Notepad.

If you just keep the Notepad open and on your desktop, you can then easily switch to it when you have something to jot down. If you only want to jot down a few notes about something, consider using the Cardfile instead.

The Notepad has the following limitations.

- It has no paragraph or character formatting capability. It will wrap lines of text to fit the size of the window, however, which is a nice feature.

- Files are limited to text only. WordStar, Word, Word for Windows, WordPerfect, and other non-ASCII files won't load into the Notepad properly.

- Files are limited in size to about 50K. This is fairly large, accomodating approximately 15 pages of solid single-spaced text, or 20 or so pages of regularly spaced material.

- It doesn't have any fancy pagination options, though it will print with headers and footers via the Page Setup dialog box.

RUNNING THE NOTEPAD

To run the Notepad, double click on the Notepad icon, as you might expect. It's in the Accessories group. If you try to load a file that is too large, Notepad will warn you with the message:

> File XXXX.XXX is too large for Notepad;
> use another editor to change the file.

If you try to load a file of the wrong format, it may load and look like garbage, or it may not load at all and you will see a message:

> XXXX.XXX is not a valid Notepad file;
> ensure the file is a text file.

ENTERING AND EDITING TEXT

You can enter and edit text in the Notepad as you would expect, with a few exceptions. To enter text, just start typing. The insertion point will move, just as it does in Write or in dialog boxes. However, as you reach the end of the window, the text will not wrap. The window will pan to the right, shifting the insertion point to about the middle of the window. This is a rather inconvenient way to enter your text, since you can't see much of what you just typed. Each paragraph will keep scrolling to the right. When you press ↵, the window will pan back to the far left again, ready for the next line of text. Figure 13.1 shows an example of text in this state.

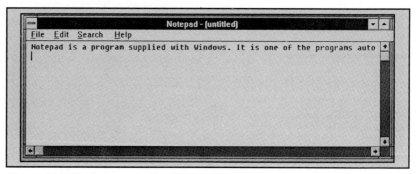

Figure 13.1: Each paragraph of text will normally stay on one long line unless unless Word Wrap is turned on

Choosing Edit ⇨ Word Wrap causes the text to wrap within the constrains of the window. This doesn't affect the text file itself however. That is, Notepad does not insert line feeds or carriage returns at the points where the lines wrap. If you resize the window, the text will rewrap to fit the available space. Figure 13.2 shows the same long line of text reformatted with Word Wrap turned on.

To edit your text, just move the cursor to the point you want to change. You can select, cut, copy, and paste text with the mouse, using the same techniques described in Chapter 9. To select all of the text in the file, choose Edit ⇨ Select All.

To move around in the text, you can use the scroll bars, of course. You can also use the following keys

KEY	MOVES INSERTION POINT TO
Home	Start of a line
End	End of the line
Ctrl-Home	Start of the file
Ctrl-End	End of the file

TIP Certain types of program files, such as batch and *config.sys* files are line oriented, and are better edited with Word Wrap off. This allows you to more clearly distinguish one line from the next in the case of long lines.

ENTERING THE DATE AND TIME INTO YOUR TEXT

A common use of a notepad-type program is to take notes pertaining to important phone conversations or meetings with

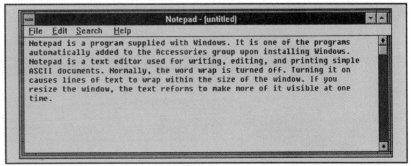

Figure 13.2: Text will wrap within a window if Word Wrap is turned on

clients or colleagues, or to type up memos. Typically, you'll want to incorporate the current date and time into your notes, to document developments as they happen. The Time/Date command on the Edit menu does this quickly.

To enter the date and time at the cursor:

1. Position the insertion point where you want the date and time inserted.

2. Press F5, or choose Edit ➪ Time/Date.

Another option is to automatically have the date and time added to the bottom of the file whenever you open it. This is useful for creating a time log of entries, when taking orders by phone, for example, or logging scientific observations of some type.

1. At the top of the file (first line, first column) add the letters **.log**.

2. When you open the file next, a blank line and the time and date should be added to the bottom of the file. The insertion point will be on the next line waiting for you to enter new text.

SEARCHING FOR TEXT

You can search for specific text in a Notepad file, but you can't replace it automatically. Follow these steps to search:

1. Choose Search ➪ Find. The dialog box shown below will appear:

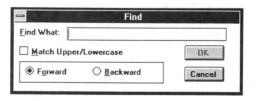

NOTE This feature doesn't yet work correctly in Windows 3.0. Only the date is printed. (The time does not appear.) Later releases of Windows may correct this bug.

TIP If you have several Notepad files that you use regularly, you might want to put them into a program group as Notepad icons. Then you can just click on them to run the Notepad and open the file. The easiest way to do this is to drag the Notepad *.txt* file from a File Manager window into the destination Program Manager group window. This technique works for all Windows and non-Windows documents that have associated program files (see Chapter 4 for a discussion of Associations).

2. Type in the text you want to search for.

3. Check the Match Upper/Lowercase box if you don't want the search to ignore capitalization.

4. Click on Backward if you want to search the portion of text above the current insertion point, otherwise the Notepad searches from the insertion point to the end of the file and stops. Unlike Write, the search does not wrap around to the top of the file and continue down to the insertion point.

5. If you want to search again for the same word, press F3 or choose Search ⇨ Find Next.

PRINTING A NOTEPAD FILE

To print a Notepad file, do the following:

1. Make sure the correct printer is currently selected.

NOTE These special header and footer codes can be used in the header and footer dialog boxes of many of the supplied accessory programs.

2. Alter the headers and footers and page margins from the File ⇨ Page Setup command. If you want to add some indents to the left and right sides of the page, increase the margin settings. The effects won't show up on the screen, but they will affect the printed page. As for the headers and footers, the defaults will print the file name at the top of the page and the page number at the bottom. Here are the other options you could enter:

CODE	EFFECT
&d	Includes the current date.
&p	Includes the page number.
&f	Includes the file's name.
&l	Makes the subsequent text left-aligned at the margin.
&r	Makes the subsequent text right-aligned at the margin.

&c   Makes the subsequent text center-aligned.

$t   Includes the time of the printing.

You can enter as many of these codes as you like.

THE CARDFILE

The Cardfile is one of my favorite accessory programs. I use it all the time to keep track of people's phone numbers, make notes about things I have to do, and store bits of information about pending projects. For example, I have a Cardfile file in which I've added tips and tricks about Windows to put into this book.

The Cardfile works like a desktop Rolodex file or box of index cards. Each card has a title line (called the index line) and room on it for up to 11 lines of text. The index line is used for identification, just so you can quickly see the topic of each card in the list when they are cascaded or listed on the screen. Cardfile automatically alphabetizes the cards according to the index line, so it's also used to keep them in order. Obviously this is perfect for keeping people's phone numbers and addresses in order, since you can add and delete cards and leave the re-alphabetizing to the Cardfile.

The number of cards you can have in a file depends on the amount of RAM in your computer, the number of other programs running, and the amount of information on the cards. If you have graphics on a card, it will take up more memory than a card containing just text.

RUNNING THE CARDFILE

To run the Cardfile, simply double click on the Cardfile icon. It's in the Accessories group. The program comes up with a new card file that has only one card in it, as shown in Figure 13.3.

1. For the first card, you have to use a command to enter the index-line information. (On subsequent cards, the dialog box opens automatically.) There are three ways

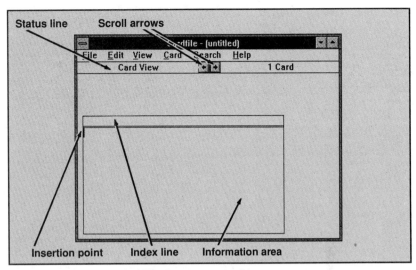

Figure 13.3: A new Cardfile document and its component parts

to open the index dialog box:

- Press F6.
- Double click on the index line of the card.
- Choose Edit ⇨ Index.

Once you do one of these, the index-line dialog box opens, as shown below:

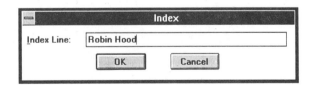

2. Type in something about the card's contents that will help you remember what it's about. Then click on OK. What you type will be displayed in the card's index line.

3. Now the insertion point drops to the information area, ready for you to enter the text for the card. As you type,

the text will wrap. When you reach the end of the card, you'll hear a beep, and you won't be able to type in any more characters. You can edit the text with Cut, Copy, Paste, Backspace, Delete, the arrow keys, and Undo. Double clicking a word selects it. Add blank lines by pressing ↵.

When you run out of room on a card, it can be frustrating. The first thing to do is try editing the information down. Be more concise or use abbreviations. If that won't do, add a new card with the same index line but with a number as a suffix, such as

Robin Hood 2

The Cardfile will keep them next to each other in the stack. Actually, you can use the same index line again and again for new cards, but then it's hard to tell the order of the series when you're looking up information later.

ADDING ANOTHER CARD

Adding a new card is simple:

1. Press F7, or choose Card ⇨ Add.

2. The Add dialog box appears. It's really the same one as the Index dialog box. Just type in the new index line for the card and click on OK. Your new card is added to the pile of cards and the stack is re-alphabetized.

3. Fill in the new card's text.

Continue filling in cards for each item of information. As you add new cards, they are cascaded, just like windows, only from right to left instead of from left to right. The number of cards is indicated at the side of the status line.

EDITING THE INDEX LINE

You may need to edit the index line of a card. To do so,

1. Move to the card.

2. Double click on its index line, press F6, or choose Edit ⇨ Index.

3. Enter or edit the index line. To edit, click somewhere in the line first or press one of the arrow keys. This de-selects the text so that it isn't all erased when you start typing.

VIEWING THE CARDS

Once you have a bunch of cards entered, it's easy to retrieve the information on them. You've probably already figured out at least one way, but there are several.

❐ The easiest way is to click on any part of the card. The list will quickly rotate: The stack stays in order, but the cards in front will move to the back and the selected card will scroll forward to the front.

❐ You can scroll through the list, card by card, until you get to the one you want. Press the PgDn or PgUp key, or click on the Scroll arrows at the top of the box. Press Ctrl-End to go to the last card or Ctrl-Home to go to the first.

❐ You can Press F4 or choose Search ⇨ Go To and type in at least two letters into the resulting dialog box. (Capitalization doesn't matter.)

❐ The keyboard shortcut is to press Ctrl and the first letter of the card you want. The first card beginning with that letter will pop to the front. This will at least get you close to the card you want, possibly bringing it into view. Then click on the card or scroll to it using the scroll arrows or PgDn key.

Switching to List View

There's another way to view the cards that you might find helpful. It's called the List view. As opposed to Card view, in which you see the stack of cards and the information on the front of the first card, list view displays only the index lines. The advantage is that you can see more index lines in this view than in Card view (Figure 13.4). Notice that the status line indicates you're in List view. Use the scroll bars and arrow keys to move through the list if there is more than a windowful.

Once the cards are displayed in a list, you can do two things with them:

- Edit the index line of any card line by first double clicking it.

- Read and edit the card's information by clicking on its index line and then choosing View ⇨ Card.

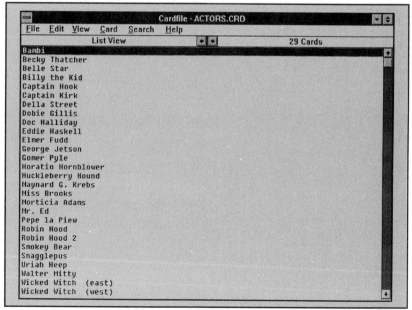

Figure 13.4: You can view cards with their index lines arranged in a list. Choose View ⇨ List to switch to this view.

SEARCHING FOR TEXT IN A STACK OF CARDS

One terrific feature of the Cardfile is that it can find a needle in a haystack. Once you have lots of notes on cards, it's likely that you'll forget where some little gem of information is located.

Suppose you're a casting director for movies and you'd like to look up someone in your list of actors who has a specific talent. If you had included a description of each actor's special talents on their cards, you could easily search for such information. For example, say you want to find out who can play the bongo drums. Here's how to perform the search.

1. Choose Search ⇨ Find. The Find dialog box will appear.

2. Type in **bongos** and press ↵ or click on OK. The Cardfile will display the next card containing any words matching the description, and will highlight the found text. In my case, it is Maynard's card, as shown in Figure 13.5.

3. If you want to repeat the search to see if there are other matches, choose Search ⇨ Find Next. If no other matches are found, the Cardfile will let you know about it in a dialog box.

Incidentally, searching starts from the current card to the end of the file, then jumps to the beginning of the file, and continues until the starting point is reached again.

MAKING COPIES OF CARDS

You can duplicate cards if you need to. This is useful in cases where several cards will have primarily the same information on them.

1. Make up the first card, and bring it to the front of the stack.

2. Choose Card ⇨ Duplicate. A duplicate card will be made and will appear at the front of the card stack.

3. Edit the card as necessary.

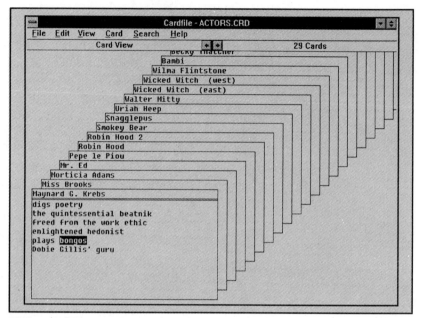

Figure 13.5: To search for a particular card based on text in its information area, choose Search ⇨ Find. The card jumps to the front with the
text highlighted.

DELETING A CARD

If you want to remove a card from a stack for some reason, do
the following:

1. Bring the card to the front of the stack through a search
    or any other method.

2. Choose Card ⇨ Delete. A dialog box will ask for confir-
    mation. Be careful with this command since deleted
    cards can't be restored.

COPYING, CUTTING,
AND PASTING TEXT AND GRAPHICS

You can copy and cut text between cards with the Clipboard.
You can also pull graphics from the Clipboard onto a card,
which is a pretty nifty feature for illustrating your cards.

To copy or cut text between cards, simply select the text in question, then choose the Cut or Copy commands from the Edit menu. Then move to the card to be pasted to, position the cursor and and choose Edit ⇨ Paste.

Pasting graphics from another program onto a card can be very useful. For example, a Police department might want to make up a card file with scanned photographs of every person in a most wanted list. Each card could contain the photo and relevant information on the person. Or, as an educational aid for children, you could make up a "flashcard" stack by drawing pictures of items whose names you are teaching. The items' names could be shown below the pictures, or you could put the names on the following cards, thereby requiring a press of the PgDn key to see the answer.

In any case, you have to make up the graphic in another program, cut or copy it to the clipboard, and then switch to Cardfile.

Then, to copy graphics onto a card, use these steps:

1. Move the destination card to the front of the stack.

2. Choose Edit ⇨ Picture. This puts Cardfile in Picture mode, in which you can work with graphics.

3. Choose Edit ⇨ Paste. The Clipboard's contents will be placed into the card's upper-left corner.

4. Drag the picture to the desired location. If the picture is too big to fit on the card, only a portion will show. To adjust the part of the picture that will show, use the arrow keys on the keyboard.

5. When the graphic is adjusted to your satisfaction, choose Edit ⇨ Text. This pastes down the graphic and returns to Text mode.

If you later want to move the graphic or cut it from the card, just get into Picture mode again, and drag the picture or choose Edit ⇨ Cut.

A card can only have one graphic on it, so if you try to add a second picture, the first one will be replaced. Pictures can only be displayed and printed in black and white. Color pictures are converted to black and white before they are added to the card, unfortunately, and a fair amount of detail is lost in the conversion process. Results will be best if you start with a black and white image. The resolution of the graphics on your cards (and in all Windows programs) is determined by the resolution of your screen. If you need to incorporate more detailed pictures into your cards, consider using a higher resolution screen that supports Windows 3.0.

Undoing Changes to a Card

If you have second thoughts about changes you've made to a card, you can back out and undo them with the Restore command. However, this is only possible if you do it before bringing another card to the front of the stack.

To restore a card,

❏   Choose Edit ⇨ Restore.

The card will be returned to its previous state, prior to any edits that were made since it was brought to the front of the stack.

DIALING THE PHONE FROM A CARD

If you have a phone number on a card and a Hayes compatible modem hooked up, you can have the Cardfile dial the number for you. If you do lots of phone calling, this may be a boon, unless you're already using a program such as Prodex or Hotline which manage phone numbers and calls for you. This is a sort of bare-bones approach, but it will certainly suffice. Once the call is made, you can take notes on the card, too. Here are the steps required.

1. Make sure your modem is on and hooked up.

2. Move to the card you want to dial from. It should have a phone number on it. The number can have an area

TIP The Cardfile looks for the first number of four digits or more on the card, and assumes that's what you want to dial. If you have more than one number on the card, such as an address, or two phone numbers, such as a work number and home number, Cardfile can get confused and might not know what number to dial. It might even try to dial the persons's street address if the number is entered above the phone number on the card. As a general rule, put phone numbers above addresses.

code in it, too. Acceptable number formats are the same as those for the Terminal program. Please refer to Chapter 11 for the particulars on that. Card file dials the first number on a card. If you have additional phone numbers on the card, select the one you want to dial before choosing Autodial.

3. Choose Card ⇨ Autodial. The following dialog box will appear (with a different phone number, of course):

```
┌─────────────────────────────────────────┐
│ ▬             Autodial                   │
│ N̲umber: │555-1212│      ┌──────────┐      │
│                        │    OK    │      │
│ Pre̲fix: │9,      │      ┌──────────┐      │
│                        │  Cancel  │      │
│ ☒ U̲se Prefix           ┌──────────┐      │
│                        │ S̲etup >> │      │
└─────────────────────────────────────────┘
```

4. If you need a prefix such as 9 for an outside line, enter it and click on Use Prefix. (The prefix will precede the phone number itself when Cardfile dials for you.) Leave the check box off if you don't need the prefix dialed. You can also type in an area code in the prefix section, or commas, if you need them. Each comma tells the modem to wait two seconds before sending the next part of the number. You may have to add a comma after a prefix if your phone system requires a second or two to switch to an outside line and dial tone. Typically you would use

    9,

as a prefix (assuming 9 is the outside line access number)

5. Click on OK. The phone number will be dialed, and a dialog box will tell you to pick up the phone to talk.

6. Pick up the phone, and then click on OK in that box. This tells the modem to hang up so that you and the modem aren't on the line simultaneously.

If dialing doesn't work, you might want to check the modem setup. Try to dial again, and then choose Setup from the Autodial box. Set the COM port, baud rate and dialing type (pulse or tone) to match your modem's switches and type of phone service.

MERGING CARD FILES

Sometimes I wind up with a few card files that aren't really that different in overall concept and should probably be joined together. As a typical example, I recently found I had an Odds & Ends file, a Misc file, and a General file. These all contained really general information, so I decided to join them into one card file. That way I wouldn't have to remember which one to use each time I wanted to record or retrieve some general piece of information. Cardfile lets you join files together.

1. Open one of the files that you want to combine.

2. Choose File ⇨ Merge

3. The File Merge dialog box comes up. Choose the file you want to merge with the currently open file, and click on OK. Repeat this process for each file you want to merge. As you merge files, the new cards will be added and alphabetized.

4. Either save the file as it now stands, or if you want to keep the original file as it was, use File ⇨ Save As to save the file under a new name.

PRINTING YOUR CARDS

TIP Just as with the Notepad, you can add a Cardfile document icon for a particular file to a group. Then you can just click on the icon to open a particular card file.

Occasionally you may want to print you cards. Here's how.

1. Set up the printer as usual.

2. Switch to Card view if you're not already in it.

3. To print the current card, choose File ⇨ Print. To print all the cards choose File ⇨ Print All.

The cards are printed four cards to an 8½ by 11 inch page in portrait layout. In landscape layout, two cards are printed per page.

THE CALENDAR

The Calendar program is an electronic version of a paper calendar. You can keep track of your time, schedule appointments, and so forth, just as you would on a calendar or electronic pocket scheduler. The Calendar also has an alarm function that will alert you to upcoming appointments if you wish. This program had an internal "perpetual" calendar formula to calculate the layout of every month for any year between 1980 and 2099.

STARTING THE CALENDAR

1. To start the Calendar, double click on its icon in the Accessories group. A blank calendar will appear, as shown in Figure 13.6. On your system, the current day will be shown (if it isn't, correct the system's date from the Control Panel).

2. This is the Day view, one of two calendar views. The other one shows the whole month. Double click on the status line, press F9, or choose View ⇨ Month to switch to the Month view. Figure 13.7 shows an example.

MOVING AROUND IN THE CALENDAR

It's simple to move from month to month and day to day. In Day view, click the right and left scroll buttons. Each click moves one day forward or backward. The scroll bars move through the day's appointment times.

In Month view, the scroll buttons move from one month to the next. Double clicking on a day's square in the month view quickly brings up that day's apointment list (the Day view).

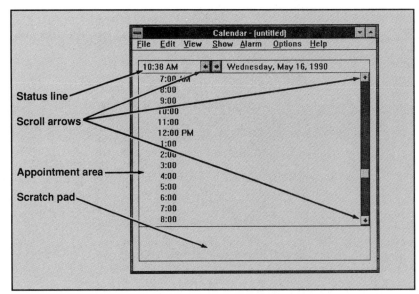

Figure 13.6: A blank, new calendar. This is the Day view.

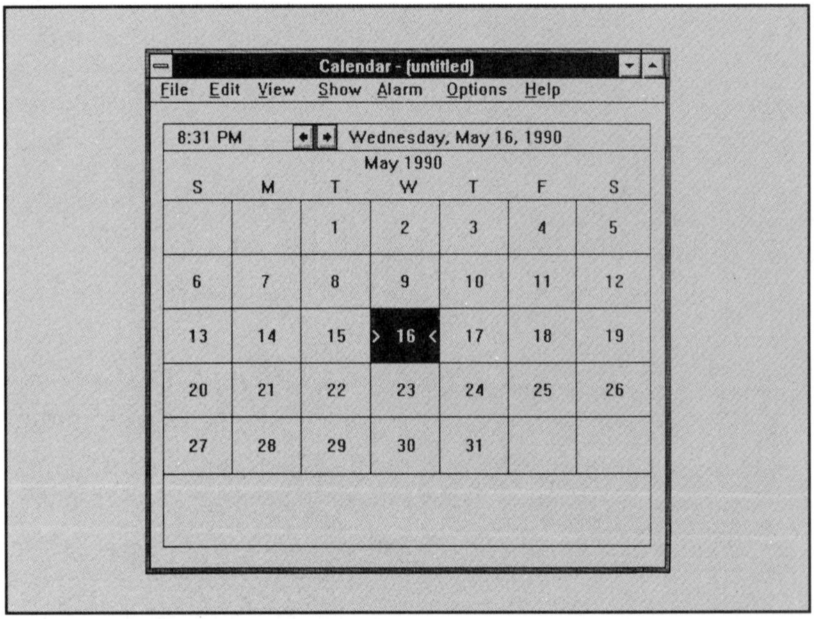

Figure 13.7: The Month view. The currrent date is marked with angle brackets: > 16 <.

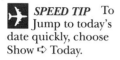 *SPEED TIP* To Jump to today's date quickly, choose Show ⇨ Today.

To get to a specific date directly, choose Show ⇨ Date or press F4. Then type in the date. Use the form 3/6/91 or 3-6-91. Leading zeros aren't necessary.

ENTERING APPOINTMENTS

As a default, a new calendar will have time increments set to the hour. You may want to use the half hour or quarter hour intervals. Choose Options ⇨ Day Settings to alter this according to your needs. The resulting box also lets you change the time you want each day's appointment list to begin. The default starting time is 7:00 AM. Type in the new starting time and click OK.

To actually enter appointments,

1. Click to the right of the time and begin typing. You can enter up to 80 characters.

2. To add an appointment at a time that doesn't fall exactly on one of the listed times, choose Options ⇨ Special Time. Type in the new time and click Insert. You can later delete the special time with the same box.

Adding Notes in the Scratch Pad

Each day has room in it for general notes. You have room for three lines of text at the bottom of the window (you may have to enlarge the window to see it), in what's called the Scratch Pad.

SETTING THE ALARM

You can set an alarm as a reminder for as many times in the day as you like. To set an alarm for a specific time:

1. Position the cursor on the alarm time.

2. Press F5, or choose Alarm ⇨ Set. A small bell will appear to the left of the alarm time.

3. When that date and time arrive, you will be alerted by a beep. If the Calendar window is active, a dialog box will

also appear. If it's inactive, its title bar will flash (though you might not see it). If it's iconized, the icon will flash.

4. To acknowledge the alarm and turn it off, open the Calendar window and click OK in the dialog box that reports the apointment.

You can turn off the beeper for all alarm settings or set your alarms to all ring a specific number of minutes early by Choosing Alarm ⇨ Controls and setting the options in the dialog box.

PRINTING YOUR APPOINTMENTS

To print your appointments, do the following:

1. Set up the printer.

2. Choose File ⇨ Page Setup to set the margins, headers and footers, if you want to alter them from the defaults. You can use the special headers and footers codes listed in the Notepad section of this chapter.

3. Choose File ⇨ Print. A dialog box will appear, asking you for the dates you want to print. The current day, as selected in the month or day view will be typed into the dialog box for you. If you only want that day, just press ↵ or click OK.

CAUTION Unless the Calendar is running, alarms will be inactive. Nothing will happen at all. Remember to run Calendar upon booting up your computer in the morning, or else you may miss your appointments!

THE CALCULATOR

The Calculator is modest in appearance, but it's quite a sophisticated accessory. It's a pop-up tool that you can use to perform simple or complex calculations. There are really two calculators in one—a Standard Calculator and a more complex Scientific Calculator for use by statisticians, engineers, computer programmers, and business professionals.

To run the Calculator, click on its icon, as you would expect. A reasonable facsimile of a hand-held calculator will appear on your screen, as shown in Figure 13.8.

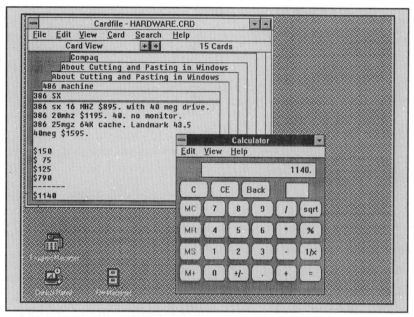

Figure 13.8: The Standard Calculator

If your Calculator looks larger, it's the Scientific one. Choose View ⇨ Standard to switch back to the basic calculator. The program always remembers which type was used last, and comes up in that mode.

To perform a typical calculation, follow these steps:

1. Clear the calculator's display by pressing Esc or clicking on the C button.

2. Enter the first value in the calculation by clicking on the numbers or using the keyboard. (If you set the keypad's Num Lock on, you can use it to enter the numbers, and the four mathematical operators. This is easier than using the number keys across the top of the keyboard.) You can use the Backspace key to fix mistakes, click C to clear the calculator and start again, or CE to clear the present entry.

3. After entering the first number, click on the mathematical operator you want to use. (The asterisk represents multiplication, SQRT calculates the square root, and 1/x calculates the reciprocal. The others are self-evident.)

4. Enter any additional numbers followed by the desired operators.

5. Press ↵ or click on the calculator's = button. The answer appears in the display. (You can use the Enter key on the numeric keypad, if you want.)

You can also use the memory keys just as on a standard calculator. MS stores the displayed number in memory, MR recalls the memory value to the display for use in calculations, M+ adds the current display value to the existing memory value, and MC clears out the memory, resetting it to zero.

Among the myriad options you have while using the calculator is a useful feature that cuts down on typing and typos when you're entering numbers into reports or memos. Just use the Calculator for your computations, and then, when the result you want is in the display, choose Edit ⇨ Copy (or press Ctrl-Ins). The figure will be copied to the Clipboard. Then switch back to your document, position the cursor where you want the result, and paste it in.

THE MACRO RECORDER

The last tool to be covered is the Recorder. The Recorder falls into the category of programs known in the computer world as macro editors. Macro editors help automate your work and cut down on the keystrokes you have to enter. They do this by "memorizing" a series of words or letters you type and then playing them back at a predetermined time, or whenever you press specific keys.

For example, I've used a macro program to type the word Windows throughout this book. All I type is Alt-W, and the macro program does the rest. If you're a seasoned PC or Mac user, you've probably used a macro program such as Tempo,

SuperKey, SmartKey or others. Some of the more popular macro programs will also respond to a program's prompts, entering information automatically, but not before the application is ready for it. This allows for unattended automation of such things as telecommunications sessions in which files are uploaded or downloaded during the night when phone costs are lower.

The Windows Recorder does all this with the exception of running unattended at a predetermined time. However it has one feature that makes it particularly useful with Windows applications. It can record mouse movements. Thus, with Recorder, you can simulate a person using a Windows program, complete with key-presses, mouse movments, dragging, clicking, and so forth. This is particularly useful for unattended demonstrations of Windows applications, though it obviously has everyday utility for anyone using Windows.

For example, you could:

- Cut down on typing of recurring phrases within a word-processing document

- Quickly repeat complex calculations or a series of commands while using a spreadsheet

- Amaze your friends when you computer automatically draws a picture with Paintbrush.

To record a sequence of actions,

1. Position the widows so that the application you want to automate and the Recorder window are both visible. My suggestion is to shrink the Recorder window to a small strip at the bottom of the screen.

2. Place the application's cursor (such as its text cursor) in the position from where you want to start recording. If it doesn't have a cursor other than the mouse pointer, skip this step.

3. Switch to Recorder's window and choose Macro ➪ Record. The dialog box shown in Figure 13.9 will appear. The default settings will be fine for most macro work. However, when you have lots of windows on the screen, macros can get a little hairy, and might not work as planned. If this happens, you should try adjusting some of the settings, as explained in the section "Other Options" below.

4. In the Record Macro Name area, type in a name for the macro. You can use up to 40 characters. Make it descriptive so you can later remember what it's for.

5. Enter the Shortcut Key that you will later want to use to trigger the macro. This is optional but recommended. You can start a macro with the mouse, but a key is much faster. If you want to use Ctrl-A, check the Ctrl box and type A in the text box. Choose common keys other than

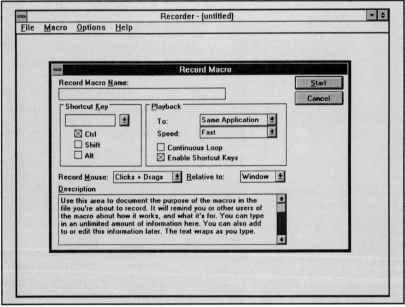

Figure 13.9: Check and/or change the macro options from this dialog box before beginning the recording process

letters and numbers from the drop-down list box. Avoid using Alt, since Alt-key combinations are used for Windows menu selections.

6. Click on Start. The Recorder window automatically becomes iconized, and the icon blinks as long as you are recording. Now go ahead and type in your text, or make whatever mouse movements or menu selections you want to record, though it's best to keep mouse movements to a minimum, since they often screw up later when you play them back.

7. When you are through recording, click on the icon. If you can't see it because it's covered up by a window, press Ctrl-Break. A dialog box will appear, asking what you want to do now.

8. The Save Macro option will be selected, so just click on OK. The macro will then be saved. (If you want to resume the recording to add more actions to the macro, or cancel the recording, click the appropriate option button and then click on OK.)

Repeat the above steps to add each new macro to a file. For example, you might want shortcut keys for all the repetitive phrases you use while typing (this is the most common application). Just keep opening the Recorder window, choosing Macro ⇨ Record, and following the above steps. Each time you open the Recorder window, you will see additional macro names and their associated shortcut keys listed. This is a quick way of reminding yourself what shortcuts you have recorded. Figure 13.10 shows an example of macros I have created to cut down my typing.

SAVING AND LOADING MACRO FILES

Macros, once created, can be saved in a file. You can have files of macros for different applications, and load them whenever you wish. You can only have one set of macros open and functional at a time, though, or they might conflict. To save your macros, choose File ⇨ Save or File ⇨ Save As. The extension *.rec* is added to the name you choose.

You load Recorder files as you might expect: Run the Recorder, choose File ⇨ Open, and choose the name. As a quicker alternative to running a macro you use a lot, add a macro document icon to a Program Manager group. (Drag the *.rec* file from a File Manager window into the destination Program Manager group window.) Then you can just double click on it to run the Recorder and open the file.

TO USE A MACRO

SPEED TIP You don't have to save a macro file before using it. If you don't want to use a macro again, don't bother saving the file. This will spare you time, bother, and disk space.

Once you have created a macro, you can use, or *trigger*, it in three ways.

❏ Open the Recorder window and double click the macro you want to run.

❏ Highlight the macro you want to run and choose Macro ⇨ Run.

❏ Press the shortcut key from any location.

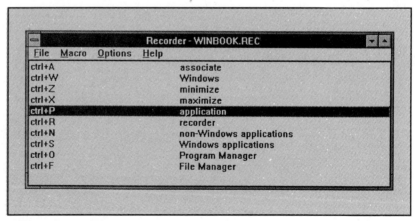

Figure 13.10: Macros you create are listed in the Recorder window. These are all Ctrl-key combinations that type recurring phrases or words in this book.

When you do any of the above, the window belonging to the application in which the macro was created is activated, and the macro is played in it. You don't have to worry about activating the window. Recorder does that for you.

If you run the macro while working in an application window other than that in which you created the macro, recorder will activate the correct window, deselecting the one you're working in. Using my example, if I press Ctrl-W while in a Notepad document, the word *Windows* will not be typed into it. Rather, the Write document currently open will be automatically activated, and *Windows* will be typed at the cursor location. This is because I created the macro while in Write.

If you try to run a macro when the application it is for is iconized, you'll hear a funny-sounding beep. If you try to run it when the application isn't even open, you'll get a rather ominous error-message dialog box that says

Recorder Playback Aborted!

and has three lines of information in it about the source of the error. The first line will say that the playback window wasn't open. So make sure you have the application running and its window open before running the macro.

To stop the execution of a macro press Esc.

OTHER OPTIONS

As you probably noticed in the Record Macro dialog box, there are lots of options that can affect how macros are recorded and played back.

Playing Back Macros in Other Applications

First off, if you want a macro to work with any application, you can change the Playback To setting in the Record Macro dialog box either when you make the macro or afterward. To change it afterward, select the macro by clicking on its line. Then choose Macro ➪ Properties. The Macro Properties dialog box will appear (this is almost the same box used for recording). Open the *To* drop-down list and select Any Application. Then click OK. Now the macro will work on any application.

The macro may not always work correctly in another application, of course, since the keystrokes or mouse movements may be inappropriate for some programs, but you'll have to judge that by experimentation.

Keeping the Macro Window Open When Playing Back a Macro

Normally the recorder's window is minimized when a macro runs. You can keep it open if you choose Options ⇨ Minimize on Use, to turn off the check mark.

Recording Every Mouse Movement or No Mouse Movements

Normally, only mouse clicks and drags are recorded. This is because other motions are probably irrelevant and take up space in a macro. However, some programs may make use of mouse movement on the screen even when the buttons aren't clicked. To record these types of movements, open the Record Mouse drop-down list in the Record Macro dialog box and choose Everything.

NOTE If you are recording "everything," you should end recording with Ctrl-Break. Otherwise, even the mouse movement to the Recorder icon will be recorded.

If you want the Recorder to ignore all mouse movements (this saves space in the macro file), choose Ignore Mouse from this list. Use this setting when you don't know what kind of computer the macro is going to be played on. If it has a different type of screen (e.g. CGA instead of VGA), the mouse motions won't work anyway, so it's better to avoid them.

Recording Relative to Window or Screen

The Relative To setting in the Record Macro dialog box determines whether the mouse activity is tracked relative to the position of the window's edge or the screen's edge. Even if you expect to be changing the size and location of the playback window, recording relative to the window works fine. The Recorder compensates for these adjustments during playback. This is the default setting.

If you are working with applications that run full-screen, however, and are having trouble getting a macro to line up its activities in the window, try recording relative to the screen. Unfortunately, this is a parameter that can't be changed after-the-fact. You have to decide when you record the macro. Once again, experimentation is the key.

Preventing Macros within Macros

Normally, you can have a macro run another macro. That is, you can create a macro that presses a shortcut key that's assigned to another macro. With this technique you can combine predefined macros in a vast variety of ways. Each macro can contain up to five levels of *nested* macros (including the first).

You can disable the use of nested macros while recording. You might need to do this when an application uses key sequences that would otherwise run other macros. To do this, turn off the Enable Shortcut Keys check box in the Record Macro dialog box.

Running a Macro in a Continuous Loop

For demos or instructional macros, you may want to have a macro run nonstop. This way, people passing a booth at a trade show or in a store, or learning a program will always see the demo in motion. Set the Continuous Loop check box on for this type of operation. You can do this before recording the macro or from the Macro Properties dialog box afterward.

You may also want to slow down the speed of the playback to more closely simulate the real operation of a program. Do this by setting the Playback Speed in the Record or Properties dialog box to Recorded Speed.

Deleting Macros

You can delete a macro from a file by highlighting it and choosing Macro ⇨ Delete. You'll then be asked to confirm the deletion.

TIP The Recorder always returns to the original defaults when you record a new macro. To change the defaults so that you don't have to modify the settings in the Record Macro dialog box each time, choose Options ⇨ Preferences. Make the changes there and click OK. The new defaults will take effect with the next macro recorded.

Merging Macro Files

As explained above, you can save your macro files to disk and load them again later. Keep in mind that the reason for having a series of macros in one file is so that they can be loaded together, all available for use at one time, usually with a specific application.

Now, just as you can merge Cardfile files, you can also merge your macro files. Say you have delveloped two sets of macros that you'd like to have available for a single application, such as Excel. By merging these two files, you'll be able to load and use both sets of macros at the same time.

To merge two files, open the first one and choose File ⇨ Merge. Then choose the second file and click on OK. If you want to keep the original file unsullied, use File ⇨ Save As to save the new merged file under a different name.

GENERAL RECORDER TIPS

The Recorder is a useful tool but it's a bit finicky. With so many variables, such as screen resolution, window sizing and placements, and different applications, that's not suprising. You'll no doubt have to rely on some trial and error to debug your macros after they're created. Unfortunately, there is no editing feature that lets you examine a macro's operation step by step. Still, when an error is encountered, it's reported in a dialog box. With some experience, you'll be able to catch the drift of the error messages and possibly avoid them next time.

While recording and running macros, keep these points in mind:

- Only use the Recorder with Windows applications.

- Close unused windows on the screen when recording. (They may complicate matters if left open).

- Avoid overuse of the mouse. It tends to cause problems. For example, choose menu commands with the keyboard whenever possible.

- Avoid moving a window on the screen as part of a macro. The next time the macro moves the window, the macro may bomb out, saying the pointer is outside the screen boundaries.

- Recording and playing macros with computers set up for different countries (on the Control Panel's International setting) can cause keyboard incompatibility problems, such as typing the wrong letters or commands when the macro is run.

- Make sure other settings in the application won't prevent the macro from operating correctly. Such things as incorrect margin settings in Write, foreground and background color selections in Paint, or files set to Read Only may interfere with proper macro execution. Become familiar with the application that you're designing the macro for in order to preclude such conflicts.

- If you find that the Recorder is not sophisticated enough for your needs, consider one of the programs from other sources, such as Tempo, from Affinity Microsystems, 1050 Walnut St., Suite 425, Boulder, CO, 80302. Their phone number is 303-442-4840.

PART
THREE

3

Advanced Topics

Part III of this book consists of two chapters that deal with more esoteric aspects of Windows operations. Chapter 14 addresses the fine-tuning of your non-Windows applications to run under Windows, covering such topics as memory management, multitasking operations, and techniques for running batch files and memory-resident programs. Chapter 15 explains a variety of approaches for increasing the speed and improving other performance factors of your Windows setup.

If you are not having trouble using Windows with your applications, you might choose only to skim these two chapters so that you know generally what your options are and where to look for them should you need help later.

If you *are* having problems with your non-Windows applications, such as memory shortages, first refer to Appendix B, which lists specific problems and their solutions. Then look through Chapters 14 and 15.

CHAPTER
FOURTEEN

14

Fine-Tuning
Your Non-Windows
Applications with PIFs

About PIFs:

A PIF, or Program Information File, is an optional, auxiliary file that controls how Windows will run a specific, non-Windows application. PIF's contain settings that pertain to memory usage, multitasking options, video modes, keyboard shortcut keys, foreground and background processing, and full-screen or windowing operations. When there isn't a PIF for a non-Windows program, Windows uses its own defaults.

About the PIF Editor:

The PIF Editor is an accessory program that you use to create PIFs. You use the PIF Editor only when you want to fine-tune a non-Windows program or when it doesn't run correctly. Some non-Windows applications come with PIFs. Many do not.

To run the PIF Editor,

Open the Accessories group and double-click the PIF Editor icon. The window you see will be determined by the mode you are running in. Standard and Real modes have one dialog box, while 386 Enhanced mode has another type. You can change the mode for which you are assigning the PIF settings by opening the Mode menu and choosing the mode you want. Since PIF files store settings for each mode, you can declare settings for Real/Standard mode and 386 Enhanced mode separately. The settings used when you run the program will be determined by the mode Windows is running in at the time.

To alter the settings in a new PIF,   468

make sure you have opened the dialog box for the correct mode. Fill in the settings you want to alter. The Program Filename is required. Others are optional. Refer to the explanations in this chapter or use the Help system if you don't understand the meaning of a setting. Then save the PIF with the File ⇨ Save command. Save the file with the same first name as the application but *.pif* as the extension.

To edit an existing PIF,   469

use the File ⇨ Open command to load the PIF. Make the changes you desire and save the file. To make several PIFs for a program, each of which has different settings, save them under different names. To activate each PIF, run the application from the PIF instead of the application's executable file.

To use pop-up programs, such as SideKick, in Windows,   488

run the program from within Windows, as you would any non-Windows application. If the hot-key for the program conflicts with Windows, create a PIF for the pop-up program that reserves the shortcut keys for it.

To load installable device drivers or memory-resident drivers,   489

add their command lines to the *config.sys* or *autoexec.bat* file just as you normally would. If only a particular non-Windows application needs the memory-resident driver, create a batch file that loads it and then runs the program. Run the batch file as you would any non-Windows application. The application and memory-resident driver will be removed from memory when you quit the program.

CHAPTER 14

THIS CHAPTER COVERS NON-WINDOWS APPLICATIONS of various types. The first section examines the PIF Editor and explains how and when to use it. The next section explains the procedures you'll have to use to make memory-resident and pop-up programs work properly within Windows, along with a few other tips about running non-Windows programs. There's also a section describing the 386 Enhanced settings you can make from the Control Panel, as referred to in Chapter 5.

If you are having specific problems running non-Windows programs, you should read this and the next chapter as well as Appendix B.

THE PIF EDITOR

Windows is a sophisticated graphical operating environment that attempts to make the best of a bad situation. The bad situation is that there are many more non-Windows applications than Windows applications written to run on the PC. This is a very different situation than with the Mac, which, initially came to market with a pretty well designed graphical user interface (GUI) along with "Apple evangelists," as they were called, waiting in the wings to help software developers write Mac programs that would comply with the user interface's rules. The result? Almost all Mac programs run fine on any Mac, assuming you have the right version of the operating system and enough memory. This includes what are called DAs (desk accessories) that are memory resident—similar to PC pop-up programs such as SideKick.

Windows, on the other hand, has to be much more ingenious in managing your computer's hardware resources and scoping out what type of programs it's running. This is primarily due to the discrepancies between Windows and non-Windows applications.

Windows applications are designed to peacefully coexist while running simultaneously in the same computer. Windows manages the distribution of your system's resources such as RAM space and CPU time so that well-written applications will rarely clobber each other or tie up more memory than is needed. When you switch between windows, RAM is reallocated to give the current application as much memory as possible in order to maximize the number of programs and documents that can be open at once. Windows sometimes uses hard-disk space as a temporary buffer (a form of virtual memory) in this process. All this happens rather seamlessly (though sometimes slowly), without much fuss, and behind the scenes.

Non-Windows applications, on the other hand, were designed to run one at a time, and are usually memory hogs. They often need at least 640K of RAM, and some may require expanded or extended memory to perform well. When you switch between non-Windows applications, memory is not re-allocated. This leaves potentially large amounts of memory tied up even when a program isn't actively in use, with little or no remaining room for additional programs. Running a non-Windows program with several other programs (particularly *other* non-Windows programs) is conceptually like bringing a bunch of ill-mannered guests to a formal dinner.

The moral of all this is simply that Windows has a lot of housekeeping to do in order to keep non-Windows applications happy. In essence, what Windows is doing when running non-Windows applications is giving each of them a simulated PC to work in. The applications don't really "know" that other applications are running, and they expect to have direct access to all the computer's resources such as RAM, printer, communications ports, screen, and so on. In most cases, Windows 3 does pretty well at faking out the application without your help, using various default settings and its own memory-management strategies. (This was not the case with earlier versions, which regularly ran out of memory.) However, even Windows 3 isn't omniscient, and you may occasionally experience the ungracious locking up of a program, or messages about the "system integrity" having been corrupted.

In dealing with such problems, the more you know about how Windows manages vital resources for your non-Windows programs, the better you can make them run. This is because Windows lets you fine-tune your applications by storing relevant settings in what are called PIFs (Program Information Files). PIFs, or PIF files, help Windows successfully run non-Windows programs. The correct PIF settings help an application to take advantage of Windows' considerable conveniences, hopefully saving you from unnecessary aggravation when your program crashes, runs too slowly, or exhibits some other annoying anomaly. Eventually, problems such as these will diminish as more and more programs are written with Windows in mind. However, in the meantime, you may have to do a little work yourself with the PIF Editor, which is a Windows accessory program for making and editing your own PIF files.

NOTE Chapter 15 covers the nuances of RAM management. PIFs and RAM management are interdependent. You should also read the on-line documents *readme.txt*, *winini.txt*, *sysini.txt*, and *networks.txt* for additional notes and tips about specific programs and hardware.

ABOUT PIFS

First off, PIFs are only used with non-Windows applications. Windows applications already know what to do with Windows. PIFs are short files stored on disk, usually in the same directory as the application or in the Windows directory. They contain settings Windows will use when running a particular application. These settings affect many aspects of the application's operation, such as, but not limited to:

- The file name and directory
- The directory that becomes active once an application starts
- Conventional memory usage
- Expanded or extended memory usage

- Multitasking priority levels
- Video adaptor modes
- The use of keyboard shortcut keys
- Foreground and background processing
- Full-screen or windowed operation

PIFs generally have the same first name as the application, but have *.pif* as the extension. Thus, the PIF for WordStar (ws.exe) would be ws.pif.

When you run a non-Windows application from Windows (using any technique), Windows first searches through your files in hopes of finding a PIF for it.

If a PIF is found, Windows uses the settings contained in it to run your application. (If you chose to have Setup install applications for you when you installed Windows, it may have created some PIFs for you. Therefore, you might have some PIFs on your hard disk that you didn't even know about.) If no PIF is found, Windows uses default settings. Microsoft claims these will work with most applications. However, there are notable exceptions to this, particularly among programs that expect or prefer to use expanded memory. But more about that and the other settings included in PIFs in a moment.

USING PIFS SUPPLIED WITH PROGRAMS

Some programs come supplied PIFs. When you want to use such a program in Windows, you should copy its PIF to the appropriate directory and drive. The PIF might be identified in the program's manual as designed for IBM's TopView rather than for Windows, but that doesn't matter. It will work with Windows. The install program for the application might copy the PIF over to your hard disk or it might not. Consult the supplied manual for this.

Use the File Manager to copy the PIF from the floppy disk onto the directory in which the program is located if the install program doesn't do this for you. For example, if ws.exe is in the

---

NOTE Only directories listed in the search path as set up by your *autoexec.bat* file are examined for PIFs.

TIP You can run a program directly from its PIF. Just double click on it's name in a File Manager window, add it to a group as a program icon and double click that, or type its full name into the File ⇨ Run dialog box. (This is the same technique as for running any program.) Running directly from a PIF is useful when the PIF isn't in the current search path, or when you have more than one PIF for an application, each with its own settings.

c:\ws directory, put the PIF there, too. Then add the PIF to a Program Manager group as you would any other program. When you double click on the icon to start the program, the PIF will then be found and used.

USING THE PIF EDITOR

Okay, now for the PIF Editor itself. You'll find it in the Accessories group. It is simple to use once you understand how it works. Essentially it presents you with a dialog box from which you choose or enter settings. Then you save the settings as a PIF.

Every PIF can have two complete groups of settings—one for Real and Standard modes, and one for 386 Enhanced mode. The different settings are required since Windows manages system resources differently in the two modes. The 386-Enhanced-mode settings additionally include those needed for advanced options such as multitasking and expanded memory use. When creating a new PIF for an application, you can choose which mode you want to make the settings for. Then, when you run the application, Windows uses the settings that go with the mode you're currently running Windows in.

To bring up the PIF Editor,

1. Open the Accessories Group and and double click the PIF Editor icon. A new PIF is opened. If you are in Real or Standard mode, you will see the box displayed in Figure 14.1. If you are in 386 Enhanced mode, you will see a different dialog box, as we will discuss in the section "The 386 Enhanced Mode Settings." The new PIF has the default settings already filled in, so if you were curious, you can see the settings Windows uses for applications that don't have PIFs.

2. The options you'll see displayed are the ones for the mode you're now running in. If you want to change the options for another mode, you can do that by opening the Mode menu and choosing it. You'll be alerted to the fact

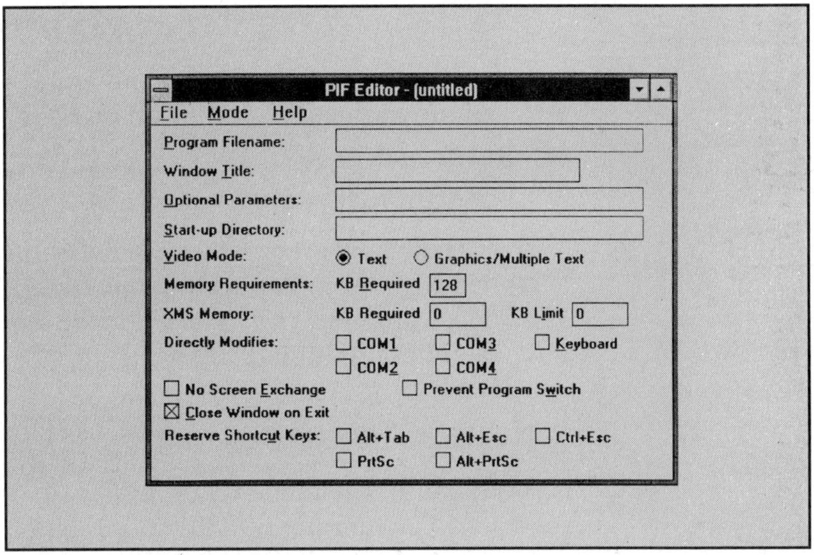

Figure 14.1: The PIF Editor as it appears for making Real- or Standard-mode settings

that you're trying to alter settings for the wrong mode. Just click on OK.

3. When the correct PIF options are displayed, go ahead and make the changes to the default settings as you deem fit, either from your knowledge of the needs of the particular application, or from information in the application's manual. (The meaning of all the options for each mode are described on the following pages.)

4. Save the PIF as you would any other file (with File ➪ Save or File ➪ Save As). It should have the same first name as the application it works with and should be stored in the Windows directory or in the application's directory. This way it is sure to be found when you run the application. You edit a PIF by reloading it into the PIF Editor with the File ➪ Open command.

SPEED TIP If you're creating a series of PIFs for the same or similar applications, create and save the first one. Then use it as a starting point for modifying and saving the subsequent files. Just open the saved PIF, modify it slightly, and save it under the new name. This way you don't have to start from the default settings each time.

THE REAL AND STANDARD MODE SETTINGS

In this section, I'll explain each of the Real and Standard mode settings. The 386 Enhanced settings are covered next.

Program Filename

Type in the name of the application that the PIF goes with. Include the complete path name of the file and its extension, too. For example, *c:\wp\wp.exe.* The file can be a *.com, .exe,* or *.bat* file. You have to fill in this box or the PIF won't work.

Window Title (Optional)

This is the name that will show up in the title bar for the window (if running in 386 mode) and under the program's icon. Make it descriptive if you like, such as Joe's Lotus 1-2-3. If you leave this blank, the PIF will still work. Windows will use the program's name instead.

Optional Parameters

In this space, you type any parameters you want to pass to the program as it starts up. For example, you might want to tell a program to start up in a specific mode, or to load a particular file when it comes up. Whatever information you type in here will be added to the program's line as if you entered it on the DOS command line. For example, say you wanted the PIF to run its application and open the file *letter.doc* You'd enter

    letter.doc

on this line. Windows takes care of inserting one space between the command name and the parameter. Some parameters require a slash (/) before them. If you normally use a slash when typing your command at the DOS prompt, make sure to enter it here, too. Paremeters can be up to 62 characters long. If you enter nothing but a question mark in the box, you'll be prompted for parameters when you run the PIF. This is handy when you want your application to immediately open a file of your choice each time you run it.

Start-Up Directory

After the application has started, which drive and directory do you want to be the default? Often you'll enter the directory which contains the application. This is the safest approach since your application may need to use support files, such as spelling dictionaries or overlays, that are stored in that directory. Having a different directory on this line may leave your application unable to find its files unless the program uses the DOS search path when looking for them (and the search path includes the directory that holds the necessary support files). If it *will* use the search path, then you can use the start-up directory setting to have Windows switch to the directory with the data files you want to have access to. If it *won't* use the search path, it still may be okay to specify a different start-up directory as long as the program doesn't need access to support files. (Many programs don't). If all else fails, and the program does use support files, and it doesn't use the search path to find them, then you have to either put all your data files for that program in the same directory as the program itself, or you have to use the program's own commands for switching directories after it starts up.

Video Mode

There are two video modes that an application can use. One shows only text, the other shows text and graphics. The setting you make here tells Windows how much memory to set aside for storage of a program's screen when you switch to another program. By saving the program's screen in memory, it can restore it quickly when you switch back to it.

Text   Choose this option for programs that you know only use text characters on the screen. dBASE, CrossTalk, WordStar 4, and XTREE are just a few examples of text-only programs. Even though there may be lines or boxes on a program's screen, it may still be "character-based," using only the accepted IBM text characters (which include lines and boxes, smiley faces, and so on). This setting uses less system memory to store the screen image, and so is preferable to the graphics setting, since memory used to store the screen diminishes the memory available for the application. But don't use this setting if you think your program might use graphics mode. Some applications, such as Microsoft Word in graphics mode, use graphics to display what looks like text.

Graphics/Multiple Text   Choose this setting for programs that use the screen's graphics mode, or that use more than one page of the video controller's memory to store more than a page of text at a time. If you're unsure of the setting you should use, this is the better bet. It will prevent you from getting locked into an application's window with no escape but to terminate the program.

Memory Requirements

In this text box, type in the minimum number of kilobytes the program needs in order to run (refer to its manual). When you run the application, Windows will then compare this amount with what's available to determine if the program will run. If extra memory is available, Windows will give it to the application, so don't worry about that. You might have to do some experimentation to figure out the amount of memory really needed for the application, since manuals are often inaccurate on the topic and typically include the amount of memory needed for DOS, device drivers, and buffers in their estimates.

XMS Memory

XMS memory is extended memory that conforms with the Lotus-Intel-Microsoft-AST standard. Not many applications use this standard, so it's not a big deal. You can probably leave these two settings alone (set at 0) for most applications, unless you're using Lotus 1-2-3 version 3.0, which does use extended memory, or you know that your program expects some.

KB Required Enter the amount of XMS required for your program to run at all. If more is available, Windows will allot it, but if less is available, you'll get a message saying the program won't run because of an XMS memory shortage. Leave this setting at 0 if your program doesn't require or use extended memory. When applications use extended memory, your system will slow down.

KB Limit Enter the maximum amount that should be allotted to the application. Keep this number as low as possible, since Windows needs as much extended memory as it can get to run efficiently. If you enter –1 in this box, all available extended memory will be given to the application, but it may slow Windows to a crawl.

Directly Modifies

Some programs directly control the hardware in your computer, while others use the operating system to do this. Using the operating system to control such things as the keyboard or screen usually guarantees higher compatibility with other programs and machines, but sacrifices potential speed improvements. Some software makers write their programs to control certain parts of the machinery directly. In other cases, there is no choice but to do so. Regardless of the reason, Windows needs to know whether your application expects to monopolize the COM ports or the keyboard, so that it doesn't allow other programs access to them, which would cause problems.

COM1, COM2, COM3, COM4 If your program uses one of these ports, turn on the check box for the port. Communications programs typically use COM1 or COM2. The other two are rarely used.

Keyboard Some programs directly control the keyboard, rather than going through the BIOS and operating system.

Check this box if your application does this. When programs take over the keyboard in this way, you can't control Windows with the normal Ctrl- and Alt-key combinations. As a result, you can't switch between windows, or copy parts of the screen onto the Clipboard. Therefore, you won't be returned to Windows until you exit the program. However, Windows will take this as a sign that it can give your application memory that it would otherwise use to store the screen display for switching purposes, since it assumes you won't be needing it.

No Screen Exchange

Setting this on prevents you from copying portions of the screen (or all of it) to the Clipboard with the PrtScr and Alt-Prt-Scr keys. If you don't expect to be making copies of your application's screen, set this option on since this will give your application some additional memory.

Prevent Program Switch

Setting this on prevents you from switching out of the non-Windows application until you exit the program. This also gives the application more memory since Windows assumes you won't need RAM to store the screen's contents during switching.

Close Window on Exit

If you want the program's window to disappear and dump you back into Windows when you exit the program, set this box on. Otherwise, the remains of the application stay on the screen when you quit, and nothing happens. You will then have to press any key to return to Windows. In most cases you'll want this box set on.

Reserve Shortcut Keys

These options let you specify which Windows Alt- and Ctrl-key combinations your application needs to use. Specifying these prevents a conflict between your application and Windows when you press the keys. When a box is checked, Windows relinquishes use of the key (and it's normal functioning with Windows) and allows your application to use it. Check one or more of these boxes only when your application needs the key combination(s).

THE 386 ENHANCED MODE SETTINGS

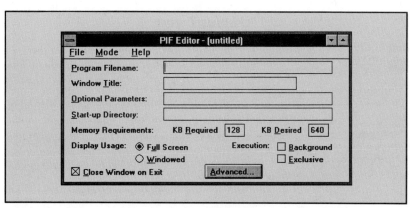 *NOTE* Also see the last section in this chapter, "Making 386 Enhanced Settings from the Control Panel," for information about device contention and background and foreground prioritizing.

In 386 Enhanced mode the PIF Editor comes up with a slightly different dialog window, as shown in Figure 14.2.

These are the basic settings. You can get to additional settings by clicking on Advanced, but I'll cover that after explaining all the basic settings. (Program Filename, Window Title, Start-up Directory, and Close Window on Exit all have the same meanings and explanations as for Standard and Real mode settings.)

Optional Parameters

The description of these settings is the same as for Standard and Real mode, but parameters are stored separately for each of the two modes. Because of this, you can have one parameter for Standard and Real modes and another for 386 Enhanced mode. Which parameter is used will depend on which mode Windows

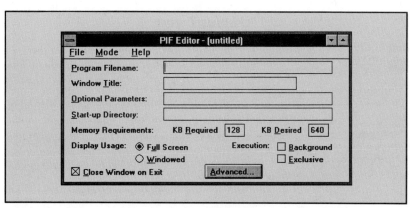

Figure 14.2: The default settings for 386 Enhanced-mode PIFs

is running in at the time you run the application. You might find saving two sets of parameters useful with programs that you want to behave differently in 386 Enhanced mode. For example, some programs let you dictate in the command line what kind and amount of extended or expanded memory they can use. Since only in 386 Enhanced mode can an application use expanded memory, you would want to use a different parameter for that mode than in Standard or Real mode, where only extended memory is available.

Memory Requirements

This controls the amount of conventional memory given to the application.

KB Required   See the same section under Standard and Real mode for an explanation of the KB Required box. Setting this to –1 gives the application as much conventional memory as is available.

KB Desired   This sets the ceiling for the amount of conventional memory the application can have. 640K is the maximum. If you want other applications to have some memory, set this amount lower than that. A setting of –1 allocates as much as possible, up to 640K.

Display Usage

386 Enhanced Mode lets you run a non-Windows application either full-screen or in a window. This setting determines which of those two ways your application will initially come up. Of course, as explained earlier in this book, you can toggle between these two views with Alt-↵. Note that in full screen display, the mouse is surrendered to the application. When the application is running in a window, Windows takes over the mouse. Then it can only be used for Windows operations. When running in a window, the application also uses more memory.

Execution

This section determines whether the application will run when it's not in the foreground. It also determines whether other programs will be allowed to run in the background.

Background   When checked, this box tells Windows to keep running the application even when it's inactive or iconized, and you're using another program. Otherwise, the application stops running until you activate the window again. Set this on when you want a program to keep working (such as a database doing a sort or a spreadsheet calculating) while you go back to work on something else. Theoretically, a communications program could also be assigned to continue working in the background sending or receiving data, though you should experiment with it just to see whether any received data is lost. Your computer may not be able to keep up with the incoming data while servicing other programs that you are running.

Exclusive   When checked, this box tells Windows not to work on other programs while this application is active, even if the other program's are set to work in the background. This gives the program more of CPU time, and more memory. For maximum memory advantage, also run the program full-screen.

ADVANCED 386 SETTINGS

If you need to get into the real nitty-gritty with your applications in 386 Enhanced mode, Windows will certainly let you. When you click on Advanced in the 386 Enhanced PIF Editor dialog box, a bigger, more intimidating dialog box with 29 more settings comes up, as shown in Figure 14.3. (And we were told Windows made everything easy!)

Well, you'll typically only have to deal with the second section because it covers expanded and extended memory usage.

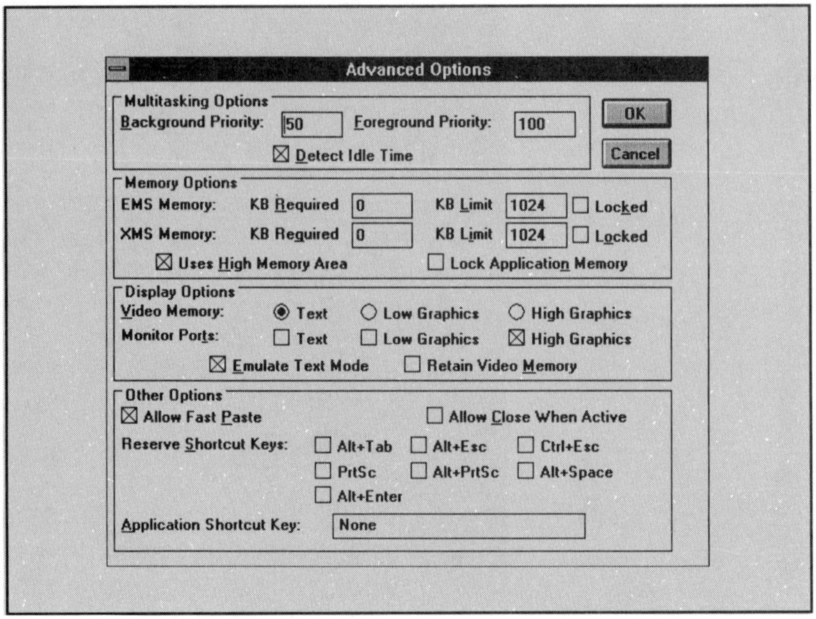

Figure 14.3: Advanced PIF Editor settings for 386 Enhanced mode

Multitasking Options

This section determines the allocation of CPU time to the application under three different circumstances.

Background Priority   The number you type here determines the relative amount of CPU time the application gets when running in the background. This number doesn't have any affect unless the application's background operation is enabled, as described earlier. The number can range from 0 to 10,000, and the default is 50. Since all applications are normally set to a background priority of 50, they all get equal amounts of CPU time when in the background. If they were all set to 10,000, they would still get equal amounts of time, since the setting is a relative figure. If you want one program to have more CPU time when in the background, increase its number. Remember that the program in the foreground (the active application program) also takes CPU time.

Foreground Priority   This determines how much CPU time the application gets when it's active (in the foreground), relative to other applications' settings. The default is 100. Normally you'll want to set this number higher than the background setting, so the application works faster when the window is active and slower when inactive or iconized. There might be instances when you would want this number to be relatively low compared to other programs, though. For example, some programs, such as simple word processors, need only a little CPU time to keep working fairly smoothly. If you want to give more CPU time to your background programs, try lowering the settings (both foreground and background) for the foreground program.

Detect Idle Time   When this option is set on, Windows will stop giving CPU time to an application when it senses that the application isn't doing anything new. Applications often sit around waiting for you to type something on the keyboard. So, instead of continually checking to see if you've typed something, the CPU can do more productive things like working on background applications. This option is set on by default and should probably be left that way.

Memory Options

Now for the dreaded memory options. This is where things can get a little sticky. Make sure you understand how your application works vis-à-vis memory. Does it use expanded or extended memory? What are its minimum requirements and maximum limits? How much do you really need for the work you do? My advice is to answer these questions *before* you start tinkering with the memory settings. If you are sketchy about distinctions between EMS and XMS, you might want to refer to Chapter 15 as well as to the discussion below.

EMS Memory   EMS is *expanded* memory. Not to be confused with *extended* memory, this is another form of memory above the normal 640K DOS limit. Some programs, (Ventura for example) can use expanded memory to greatly improve their performace. One of the big advantages of running Windows in 386 Enhanced mode is that it gives your applications access to expanded memory. Though Windows requires that you set up any memory above 640K in your computer as extended memory, and uses it as such, it can simulate expanded memory for programs that need it. It does this on the fly, by loading an expanded memory manager and giving up some of its system memory normally used for Windows applications.

There are two settings for EMS memory. These work just like the settings for conventional and XMS memory. The KB Required setting tells Windows how much has to be available before even trying to run the application. If it isn't available, you'll see a message telling you to free up some memory and then try running the application again. Set this to zero (0) to indicate that none is required for the application to run, even though it might benefit from having some.

The KB Limit setting prevents the application from taking all the available EMS (which it will do unless told otherwise). If you want some EMS left for other applications, enter a number in here that is less than the total EMS but more than the Required amount. A zero (0) entered here prevents Windows from assigning any EMS to the program.

The Locked option, when on, will prevent Windows from swapping your application's EMS data to hard disk when other applications need it, or to simulate more EMS than is physically there using virtual memory management. Locking the EMS cuts down on the EMS available, but increases overall performance of the application since disk swapping takes time.

XMS Memory   Same as in Real and Standard Mode. The locking option has the same effect as described immediately above, but affects XMS memory instead.

Uses High Memory Area   When checked, this box tells Windows that the application can use the first 64K of extended memory (just above the 1 megabyte boundary). This area is called the High Memory Area or HMA, and lots of programs use it as a way of avoiding RAM shortages. For example, many memory resident utilities, BIOS "shadowing" programs, and network drivers use this area. If your application expects to use this area, set the check box on.

When you boot up Windows, if no other program is using the HMA, Windows will let other programs use it. If it's already in use, say, for a network driver, when you boot up Windows, Windows notes this and won't let any programs use the HMA even if their PIFs are set to use it.

Also, Windows is smart enough to prevent contention between multiple programs that use HMA. So, you can have more than one program using HMA at a time in Windows, whereas under DOS this is impossible. Windows does this by swapping the 64K of HMA in and out as you switch between programs.

If you don't know whether your program uses the HMA, leave this box checked. If you want to prevent the program from using HMA, turn the setting off.

Lock Application Memory   This is similar to the lock options for EMS and XMS memory, but it applies to conventional memory only. It prevents Windows from swapping out your application's memory to hard disk when you switch to another application, as long as your application is running. Checking this could speed up the application, but it will probably reduce the efficiency of Windows in general, since it may make Windows do more swapping of other applications than it would normally have to.

Display Options

This section of the Advanced PIF options affects the way Windows controls your screen and the memory it uses to store the screen image when switching between windows.

Video Memory   This determines how much memory your application initially needs for the screen when you run it. Text mode uses about 16K, Low Graphics use 32K, and High Graphics use 128K. Windows can adjust the amount later as you switch modes, calling on available memory for storing the screen image, should you switch away from the application. However, if you choose a mode that's too low for your screen's and application's needs, your screen can get weird or go blank when you switch to the application. But using too high a mode uses up more memory. As a rule of thumb, CGA screens only use Text and Low Graphics. VGA and EGA screens use only High Graphics. If in doubt, experiment by running the PIF with different settings and see what happens. If you've chosen too low a setting, your application's window will be partially or totally missing. If you want to ensure that there's always enough memory available for the application's screen, choose High Graphics and turn on the Retain Video Memory option. Retain Video Memory prevents windows from releasing memory to other applications when that memory is not being used as temporary storage for your display.

Monitor Ports   If your application directly writes to the display adaptor's (the card in your PC) hardware, you might have to use one or more of these options. Windows assumes applications use acceptable means (DOS and the BIOS) to write to the screen. Some programs don't, however. (An example is Microsoft Flight Simulator which writes directly to the screen.) Use these options to tell Windows to "monitor," or watch, what your application is doing to your display card, so that the screen reappears correctly when you switch away from the program and return to it. Note that these settings are irrelevant to IBM VGA and some other adaptors. Most application require the High Graphics setting, so it's the default. Few require monitoring in Text and Low Graphics modes.

Emulate Text Mode   If you see garbage characters on the screen when your application is running, if the cursor is in the wrong location, or if the application won't run at all, try turning this setting off. Normally it is on and speeds up text display.

Retain Video Memory   See "Video Memory," above.

Other Options

This section contains some odds and ends about such sundries as shortcut keys and pasting information into your application.

Allow Fast Paste   Normally this option is on. If you have trouble pasting information into your application from the Clipboard, quit the application, modify its PIF by turning this off, and try again. The pasting will be slower, but it might work.

Reserve Shortcut Keys   Same as in Real and Standard mode.

Allow Close When Active   When checked, this box lets you exit Windows or close the application's window without actually terminating the application itself. This is a risky option, because you would lose data if you didn't manually close the files you were working on with the application. Only use this option if you know the application uses MS-DOS file handles to flag which files are open. Windows will ensure that they are closed when it closes the application. If you're in doubt, don't use this option!

Application Shortcut Key   The key combination you enter here will, when pressed, cause your application to jump to the foreground. Whenever the application is running, the shortcut key will work. Otherwise, it's deactivated. This is a great feature that means you don't have to use the Task List, or click on the application's window, or press Alt-Esc to get to an application.

By giving each one a special shortcut key, you can switch between them quite easily. To enter the shortcut key, click on the text area for the key, and then press the key combination you want to assign to the application. It has to include the Alt or Ctrl key, or both. You can use function keys in the combination. Three keys are okay, too, such as Shift-Ctrl-F8, or Alt-Ctrl-Z. Don't set a shortcut key to be a combination that other programs might use, such as Alt-F (which many Windows applications use to open their File menu), since the shortcut keys are exclusively assigned to the application the PIF is for. Also, you can't use Esc, ↵, Tab, the spacebar, PrtScr, or Backspace. Choose OK after entering the key. To erase a shortcut key, click on the text area, then press Shift-Backspace.

CHANGING SETTINGS WHILE A PROGRAM IS RUNNING

You can change some PIF settings while a program is running in 386 Enhanced mode. (Other modes don't allow this.) There are four changes you can make. You can:

- Change the display from full-screen to windowed or vice-versa

- Change the foreground and background priorities

- Change the multitasking options to turn on or off background processing and/or make the program the exclusive task

- Terminate the non-Windows program (in case it bombed or you somehow lost control of it)

To change the settings:

❑ Open the Control menu for the application's window and choose Settings. The dialog box such as the one shown in Figure 14.4 will appear. The application's name will be in the window's title bar. In this case, it's WordStar Professional, since that's the program that was running in the window.

The settings are identical to the ones in the PIF dialog boxes, with the exception of the Terminate option. Use the Terminate button as the last resort when a non-Windows application bombs (crashes, hangs, unexpectedly terminates, or whatever you like to call it) in Windows. This might result from a bug in the application, a bug in Windows, or simply a bad relationship between the two. With so many variables, it's hard to know the cause of a crash. As you experiment with PIFs, you're likely to come up with a few crashes, so get used to this option. The good news is that instead of rebooting your computer, which could have adverse affects on the programs you're running, Windows lets you close the bombed application, save any other open files, close applications, exit Windows, and *then* reboot your computer. Do reboot, so that DOS and everything else is reloaded. Don't just rerun Windows, since DOS or the device drivers might have been corrupted when you terminated the application program!

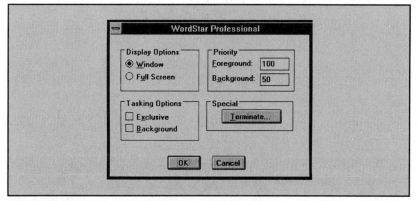

Figure 14.4: You can change a few PIF settings for a running application from this box. You open it by choosing Settings from the application's Control menu.

PIFS FOR BATCH FILES

Though it might sound strange at first, you can create a PIF for a batch file rather than just for applications per se. Using a PIF for a batch file lets you set the various PIF parameters for it. When the batch file is run from its PIF, all the settings come into play, and they will affect all the programs in the batch file. (A batch file is a group of commands that executes DOS in sequence for you, without your having to type them in.) A typical batch file might switch directories, load a memory-resident program, and then run an application. For example, I have a batch file for running Ventura called *v.bat* that looks like this:

```
cd\wyse
nscreen graphics
vpprof
```

I have to load the *nscreen* program for my screen to work with Ventura. If I don't load it, Ventura bombs. Therefore, I can't start Ventura the usual way with *vpprof* (which, incidentally, is also a batch file). What do I do? Well, I could run *nscreen* first, and then run Ventura, but that's a pain, since it means going through the motions of running two programs instead of one. Or, I could just run my batch file from Ventura too, as I would any other program. But here's the catch. When executing a batch file, Windows doesn't look for the PIF file that goes with each application in the list. It only looks for the PIF file with the *batch file's* name. Thus, when I run *v.bat*, it looks for *v.pif.* Even if *vpprof.pif* exists and has all the necessary PIF settings in it, they won't go into effect! This is really dumb on Window's part. Ventura needs special PIF settings since it uses expanded memory, so I had to create a PIF file called *v.pif* with all the same settings I'd normally use for Ventura.

The moral is this: If you use batch files to run applications that need PIFs, make sure you have a PIF for the batch file, too. Put the same settings in the batch file's PIF that you'd put in the applications' PIFs.

If the batch file runs multiple applications that normally use different PIF settings, try to concoct a PIF containing settings that will accommodate the needs of all the programs. In other words, make it as generous as possible in assigning memory, screen modes, and so on.

If the applications require radically different settings, such as lots of expanded memory for one, and lots of extended memory for the other, you're out of luck. This is just a limitation of Windows that you will have to live with. You'll have to run the applications separately, or perhaps use a utility such as a fancy macro program that can run applications sequentially from within Windows.

ALTERING THE DEFAULT PIF SETTINGS

As mentioned earlier, each time you run a program that doesn't have a PIF, Windows uses default settings for the application. (To see what the defaults are, open a new PIF file and examine it.) If you want to change the default settings, you can. This might be useful if you want all the programs without PIFs to run a particular way, such as full-screen, with exclusive attention of the CPU, etc.

NOTE These settings don't affect the default settings you see in a new PIF.

To do this, just create a PIF called *_default.pif.* (Note that the first character in the name is the underline character.) Leave the Window Title box empty, but type any valid program name in the Program Filename box. (*c:\command.com* is a good choice). Windows will ignore the program name when it uses the PIF as a default, but the PIF Editor needs a file name or it won't save the file. When you run any program that doesn't have a PIF, these *_default.pif* settings will go into effect.

USING MEMORY-RESIDENT PROGRAMS

Many DOS utilities and small programs are *memory-resident* programs. When loaded under DOS, they take up some memory space and stay in place in your system RAM until manually unloaded or until you reboot your computer. This is unlike normal applications, which relinquish memory when they are closed. Sometimes memory-resident programs are called TSRs, for *terminate and stay resident.* Pop-up programs such as SideKick or screen capture programs like HotShot are examples of TSRs.

Device drivers that control hardware such as a mouse, tape backup units, CD-ROM players or network cards are also memory-resident programs. Commands in the *config.sys* file typically load this type of program into your system's RAM when you boot up your computer. Device drivers are necessary for using certain hardware add-ons to your system, but you do not usually interact with them directly.

In any case, there are some rules you should know about the use of such programs with Windows. These are described below.

USING POP-UP PROGRAMS

To load a pop-up program, run it from within Windows, not outside of Windows. Run it the same way you run any other non-Windows application. Once the program is loaded, Windows will confirm that it is in memory. To use the program, just press the keys that usually bring up the program (such as Ctrl-Alt for SideKick). If the pop-up program uses keys that would conflict with keys used by Windows or Windows programs, make a PIF for the pop-up program and reserve its pop-up key with the Reserve Shortcut Keys option.

USING DEVICE DRIVERS

If all the programs you intend to run need a certain device driver, just add it to the *config.sys* or *autoexec.bat* program. This is how manufacturers usually tell you to install their drivers.

If only a particular non-Windows application needs the driver, then create a batch file with the utility in it (it has to be an *.exe* or *.com* file, though—not a *.sys* file) followed by the related program. The Ventura batch file I explained earlier is a good example of this. It loads a screen driver, and then Ventura:

```
nscreen graphics
vpprof
```

If you're running in 386 Enhanced mode, you can install a driver that affects only Windows applications. Just add the driver name to the *winstart.bat* file, as explained in Chapter 15. Then only Windows applications will have access to the driver.

MAKING 386 ENHANCED SETTINGS FROM THE CONTROL PANEL

As mentioned in Chapter 5, if you are running in 386 Enhanced mode, you'll have an additional icon in your control panel. This icon is labeled 386 Enhanced and looks like a computer chip. When clicked on, it brings up the dialog box shown in Figure 14.5

Unlike PIF settings or those you make from a running application, the settings you make from this dialog box affect all running programs. This includes both Windows and non-Windows programs. The settings will stay in effect until you change them.

THE DEVICE CONTENTION SETTINGS

The first section of the dialog box, Device Contention, controls the way Windows handles situations in which simultaneously running applications try to gain access to the same port.

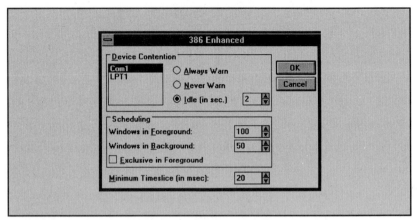

Figure 14.5: The 386 Enhanced settings dialog box reachable from the Control Panel.

For example, suppose you printed a spreadsheet from a Windows program such as Excel, and then switched to a non-Windows program and tried to print from that too. If both programs expected to print to the same port, there would be a data collision, resulting in a garbled mess in your printout. When two applications expect unimpeded access to the same port, you have what's called a "hardware contention" problem.

If you're only running Windows programs, you can forget about this section, since Windows arbitrates such problems automatically. As I explained in Chapter 7, the Print Manager handles all Windows application printing chores, preventing contention by virtue of print queueing. Hardware contention problems only occur between Windows and non-Windows applications, or between two or more non-Windows programs.

You can avoid printer-port contention yourself quite easily. Just remember not to print from a non-Windows program when another application is printing to the same printer on the same port. That's the easiest rule of thumb. If you have several printers (such as network printers) connected to different ports, you can print one job to each port without trouble. Just be diligent in remembering what you've sent where, and wait until the print job for a port is over before sending it another.

To help prevent data collisions on a port, Windows provides the dialog box settings. To use the settings, select the port in question, and click on one of the three options. Here's what each one does:

SETTING	DESCRIPTION
Always Warn	If one program is already using the port, and another one tries to, Windows will warn you in a dialog box. You will then have the option of selecting which program should have access to the port. In most cases, you should use this setting.
Never Warn	You will not be warned about device contention problems. Multiple programs will be allowed access to the same port. Results may be undesirable, however, with the typical example being garbage printouts, or printouts containing information from two or more documents—a sort of unintentional merging of documents. If you know that no two programs will ever try to gain access to the port at the same time, or you want to ensure that Windows won't tie up your operations by displaying a warning dialog box, use this setting.
Idle	The time you type in here determines how much time should pass between applications' use to prevent Windows from displaying the warning message. The range is 0 to 999 (milliseconds).
	As explained above, if the Always Warn option is set on, Windows will alert you if two programs try to access the same port at *exactly* the same time. However,

programs don't always use a port continuously, which could lead to a false reading. If there is a temporary lull in activity on a port or device, Windows could allow another program to use it when the first program isn't really through with it. For example, you might be using the COM1 port with a communications program. If you were distracted momentarily, perhaps to go answer the door, it's likely that no data would be flowing across the COM1 port due to your temporary inactivity at the keyboard. Windows could then assume you were finished using the port. Another program might then seize the port, ruining your communications session even if the Always Warn option were set on. To prevent this, you'd want to increase the idle time.

FOREGROUND AND BACKGROUND CPU SCHEDULING

The second section determines how CPU time is split between Windows and non-Windows programs during multitasking. To comprehend the settings, it's important to understand that Windows applications are always multitasked, even in Real and Standard modes. You cannot control the time-slicing or CPU allocation for those applications. Windows shares the CPU time equally among them. What we're dealing with here are settings that determine the amount of CPU time Windows programs will *give up* to non-Windows programs running in 386 Enhanced mode. In Real and Standard mode, this is not an issue, since a non-Windows program, when active, takes over all the CPU time. In 386 Enhanced mode, however, CPU time can be shared between non-Windows and Windows programs.

All the Windows programs are treated as one program, all receiving the same amount of time. Here are the descriptions of each setting (you may want to refer to the Multitasking Options description earlier in this chapter for more detailed descriptions of these settings):

SETTING	DESCRIPTION
Windows in Foreground	This determines the amount of CPU time allotted to all Windows applications when one Windows application is running in the foregound (active). As long as one Windows application is active, then they will all get CPU time determined by this setting. The important issue is the ratio between this setting and the sum of the Foreground settings for all other non-Windows programs that are running. (Their *backgound priority* PIF settings as described earlier in this chapter determine this ratio). If your Windows applications slow down considerably when non-Windows programs are running in the background, you might try increasing this number. (You could also try decreasing the non-Windows applications' background priority, or setting their background-execution options off.
Windows in Background	This determines the relative amount of CPU time that all Windows programs collectively receive when running in the background—that is, when a non-Windows program is the active window.
Exclusive in Foreground	When set on, this option prevents all non-Windows applications from running whenever *any* Windows application is in the foreground.

| Minimum Timeslice | This determines the minimum amount of time allotted to any application before Windows redirects the CPU to the next application. Normally this is set to 20 milliseconds. Thus, up to fifty applications could be serviced every second. (Keep in mind, however, that all running Windows applications taken together are treated as a single application.) Increasing this number will improve the overall efficiency of your programs. This is because the switching process in and of itself requires CPU time. So, reducing the number of times the CPU switches between application per second leaves more CPU time for your applications. However, Windows appears to run more smoothly when the switching rate is faster (timeslice is smaller). If you want to increase the smoothness of Windows, decrease this number. If you want to marginally increase the efficiency of your programs, increase the number. If you don't know what to do, leave it alone, since the default of 20 is a reasonable compromise arrived at through experimentation by the engineers at Microsoft. |

CHAPTER
FIFTEEN

15

Supercharging Your System for Windows

Fast Track

CHAPTER **15**

TO RUN WINDOWS AT ITS BEST ON YOUR COMPUTER
system, you can't rely on the Setup program alone. Setup does
an excellent job of configuring things, but you'll need to get
your hands dirty and customize your system yourself for optimum Windows performance.

Windows supercharging has two main goals: increasing speed
and boosting memory capacity. Obviously, you want your programs and Windows itself to run as fast as possible, so you don't
have to wait unnecessarily while you work or when you switch
from program to program. You also want to be sure you have
enough memory to run all the programs you use at the same
time, with enough left over for all the data your programs keep
in memory.

The easiest way to achieve both goals is to upgrade your computer hardware with a faster processor, more memory, a bigger
hard disk, and a faster graphics adapter. We'll talk about some
of the things you should consider when choosing new hardware
for a high-performance Windows system a little later in the
chapter.

Almost as important in optimizing Windows is the art of
"tweaking" various system software settings to make best use
of the hardware you have available. That's the main focus of this
chapter. Even if you have a state-of-the-art computer loaded with
memory, you'll want to squeeze every ounce of performance
out of your expensive investment through minor adjustments.

WHAT DETERMINES WINDOWS' PERFORMANCE

Before you can begin a supercharging program, you'll need to understand the major factors that affect the performance of Windows. The most important of these are your computer's— its memory, its hard disk, its graphics adapter, and its microprocessor. Microsoft refers to the first two items, memory and disk space, as your *system resources,* but the capabilities of your graphics adapter and microprocessor also have a telling impact on performance. Together, these four components determine which programs you can run, how many of them you can run at the same time, and how fast they run.

YOUR COMPUTER'S MICROPROCESSOR

Windows runs on any computer compatible with the IBM line of personal computers, whether the microprocessor is an 8088, 8086, 80286, 80386, or 80486. However, the type of microprocessor in your system and the rate at which it's set to run have a major impact on Windows' speed and capabilities.

If money were no object, you'd get yourself a new Windows machine with an 80486 processor running at the fastest possible rate (25 megahertz or better, in the case of an 80486). Most people, though, can't afford to junk their present computers, slow as they may be. A compromise that works well for many owners of 8088, 8086, and 80286 computers is to keep the old machine and upgrade the microprocessor.

For as little as $250 to $500, you can drop an add-in board containing an 80286 or 80386 chip into almost any 8088 or 8086 system. While your upgraded computer might not be quite as fast as a whole new machine, the performance boost will be dramatic. If you have an 80286 system, you can upgrade it by installing an 80386-based add-in board.

Remember that speed isn't the only reason to upgrade your microprocessor. On an 8088 or 8086 machine, you can only run Windows in Real mode; upgrading to an 80286 will let you run in

Standard mode as well. If you move up to a 80386 processor, you can run in 386 Enhanced mode too.

Unless you have a 80486 computer, another way to boost performance in some situations is to add a math coprocessor to your system board (an 80486 has its own built-in math coprocessor). A math coprocessor is a special-purpose calculating chip that handles mathematical computations far faster than the regular microprocessor. Depending on the type of computer you have, the right math coprocessor for you machine may be the 8087, 80287, or 80387.

Although Windows itself doesn't take advantage of a math coprocessor, many Windows and non-Windows programs do. Examples include Excel (a spreadsheet program), Arts&Letters Editor (a sophisticated graphic design program), Pixie (a business charting package), and even Publisher's Type Foundry (which lets you design your own fonts). All will run much faster if your system has a math coprocessor on board.

UNDERSTANDING MEMORY

Your computer's memory (RAM) serves as the temporary work space for everything you do with your system. To run any program—or Windows itself for that matter—your computer must first load the program into memory from disk. In turn, your programs need memory to store the information they're actively working with.

The amount and type of memory you have directly affect Windows' performance in several ways. Obviously, the size of the programs you can run and how many you can run at the same time depend on how much memory you have. In just the same way, the amount of memory determines how much data your programs can work with at a time; in practical terms, that can mean that the size of your spreadsheets or the complexity of your graphics will be limited by how much memory you've installed.

The memory available in your system doesn't necessarily put an absolute limit on the number of programs you can run or the size of their files. Many programs are designed to work with as much of a file as will fit in memory at a time. When this kind of program finishes working on part of say, a spreadsheet or graphic, it stores that section of the file on disk, and then loads the next section into memory. As we'll see, Windows itself can use a similar technique to run more programs and store more data than will fit into memory. But even though this method lets you work around memory limitations, the amount of memory you have still has an impact on your system's performance. The more memory in your system, the less time will be wasted on the relatively slow process of transferring data back and forth between memory and your hard disk.

The Types of Memory

IBM-compatible computers can be equipped with three types of memory: conventional, extended, and expanded.

Conventional memory is the fundamental type of memory found on all computers that run MS-DOS, no matter what microprocessor is installed. Conventional memory provides a maximum of 640K of usable memory, and you'll need the full 640K as a bare minimum to run Windows. DOS itself occupies some conventional memory, along with any device drivers or memory resident (pop-up) utilities you install. Windows then takes whatever remains.

Most 80286, 80386, and 80486 computers come with at least 1 megabyte of memory. Ordinarily, everything beyond the first 640K of conventional memory in these systems is *extended memory*. So, if you have an 80286, 386, or 486 system equipped with 1 megabyte of memory total, it has 640K of conventional memory and 384K of extended memory (a megabyte is equal to 1024K).

Extended memory works almost as quickly as conventional memory, so it's the ideal kind to use. However, there was a hitch before Windows 3.0. Extended memory is designed for the advanced memory-accessing capabilities introduced with the 80286 microprocessor. Unfortunately, MS-DOS was developed before the 80286 chip was. For this reason, DOS simply won't allow programs to take advantage of extended memory, even when you run them on an 80286 or 80386 computer. Since Windows is based on MS-DOS, that posed a problem. (In contrast, Microsoft's other operating system, OS/2, was designed specifically for the 80286 processor and uses extended memory fully.)

The problem was solved when several software developers came up with a way to let specially designed MS-DOS programs use extended memory. These techniques are called "DOS extenders." True to form, Windows 3.0 has a cutting-edge DOS extender built right in, and can make full use of extended memory. (The exception is in Real mode, in which Windows utilitizes extended memory only for temporary storage of some low-priority data). Programs developed specifically for Windows 3.0 can take advantage of Windows' DOS extender as well. The practical upshot is simple: give Windows as much extended memory as you can.

Optimal functioning of extended memory requires an extended-memory manager. This special software sees to it that Windows and all your programs coexist peaceably in the available extended memory. Windows comes with an extended memory manager called himem.sys, which was probably installed for you when you set up Windows if your system has extended memory.

In contrast to extended memory, *expanded memory* can be installed on any computer that runs Windows, including systems with an 8088 or 8086 microprocessor. Expanded memory works by creating a small "window" in conventional memory through which the microprocessor can access large amounts of memory it would normally be unable to address. (The window is usually 64K wide.) In order to make this trickery work, you must install a piece of software called an expanded-memory manager. The expanded-memory manager serves as the go-between for a program and the memory it needs, supplying additional memory through the window as the program asks for it.

Before the DOS extenders came along, expanded memory was the only place to turn for programs needing more memory for larger files. Lotus 1-2-3, the all-time best-selling spreadsheet, is just one of many DOS programs that utilize expanded memory. Some Windows applications also use expanded memory.

But expanded memory is slower than extended memory. The reason is simple: the expanded-memory window is too small. As you work with programs or data stored in different parts of expanded memory, the expanded-memory manager has to keep shifting the window to "view" different areas of memory, and this slows things down. For this reason, Windows itself uses expanded memory only in Real mode.

If you're not running Windows in Real mode, where does this leave you with programs such as 1-2-3 that are designed to tap expanded memory? To make expanded memory available to these programs in Standard mode on a 386 machine, you must install the expanded-memory manager that comes with Windows (called EMM386). The problem is that this program only runs on 386 machines. If you have a 386 machine, chances are that you wouldn't bother running in Standard mode. So it's kind of silly that Microsoft supplies an expanded memory manager that won't run on a 286 machine. Anyway, if you have a 286 machine and are running programs that need expanded memory, you'll have to use the expanded-memory manager supplied with your memory board. Then, any programs that use expanded memory will find it. If you can configure some of that memory as extended memory, consider doing so, since Windows will use it for its own housekeeping, with overall speed improvements being the dividend. Table 15.1 lays out the memory and memory management considerations for each mode and CPU type.

In 386 Enhanced mode you don't need the expanded-memory manager—Windows exploits the virtual memory capabilities of the 386 and 486 microprocessors to simulate expanded memory for non-Windows programs that need expanded memory. (Setting a program's PIF to request the use of this expanded-memory manager is explained in Chapter 14.)

One further detail: expanded memory comes in two flavors, an earlier version 3.2 and the current version 4.0. In Real mode, Windows needs the 4.0 variety for its own use, although

Table 15.1: Memory Requirements and Considerations for Each CPU Type and Windows Mode

CPU	MODE		
	Real	Standard	386 Enhanced
8086 8088	640K Conventional memory required. EMS can be used. Install your own EMS driver at boot-up. Both Windows and non-Windows programs designed for EMS will utilize it. XMS cannot be used since the 8088/8086 can't address more than 640K of RAM.	Not possible.	Not possible.
80286	640K Conventional memory required. EMS can be used. Install your own EMS driver at boot-up. Both Windows and non-Windows programs designed for EMS will utilize it. If XMS is present, and *himem.sys* is loaded, Windows will use it for its own purposes even though running in Real mode. This will improve performance. Your applications may be able to access the extended memory too, if they are compatible with the *himem.sys* driver supplied with Windows 3.0.	640K conventional memory and 256K XMS required. If EMS is required by your applications, install your own EMS driver at boot-up. If your applications do not use EMS, configure all extra RAM as XMS, and make sure *himem.sys* loads at boot time. Windows and Windows applications will use the XMS. Your non-Windows applications may be able to access the XMS too, if they are compatible with the *himem.sys* driver supplied with Windows 3.0. The amount of XMS available depends on how much EMS was requested by your EMS driver when it loaded. Whatever is left can be used as XMS.	Not possible.
80386 80486	640K Conventional memory required. If EMS is required by your application, you must use Windows-supplied *emm386.sys* or Windows 3.0-compatible expanded memory driver. If *himem.sys* is loaded and you have extended memory, it will be used, as explained above (286 in Real mode). The amount of XMS available depends on how much EMS was requested by your EMS driver when it loaded. Whatever is left can be used as XMS.	640K conventional memory and 256K XMS required. If EMS is required by your application, you must load the Windows-supplied *emm386.sys* or a Windows 3.0-compatible expanded memory driver at boot time. If applications need extended memory see note directly above (286 in Standard mode) about XMS and *himem.sys*.	640K conventional memory and 1024 extended memory required. Windows will automatically allocate EMS and XMS as needed to Windows applications. In the case of non-Windows applications, Windows will automatically allocate as much as 1024K of XMS or EMS in an attempt to accommodate the needs of the program. If your application needs more than 1024K of XMS or EMS, configure a PIF requesting it (as discussed in Chapter 14).

NOTE: XMS means Extended Memory; EMS means Expanded Memory.

Windows programs can store data in version 3.2 expanded memory.

Buying More Memory

Windows craves memory—the more memory you have, the better your system will run. So my basic advice is simple: buy as much memory as you can afford.

What kind of memory should you buy? The answer depends on the kind of computer you have. If you have an 8088 or 8086 system and you know you're not going to upgrade it to a more powerful microprocessor, buy an expanded memory board. Remember, this type of computer can only run in Real mode, and the only type of extra memory Real mode can use is expanded. Read the fine print when buying the board—the only type of expanded memory worth having is the kind that complies with version 4.0 of the expanded-memory specification version. You might still find the older kind of expanded memory boards on the dealer's shelf.

If you have an 80286, 80386, or 80486 computer, you'll probably want to buy extended memory. Generally, you can do this by plugging more memory chips into your main system board rather than buying costly add-in memory boards. This method also gives you the most direct connection between your microprocessor and the memory, ensuring the fastest operation possible. Since some programs store data in expanded memory, you may want to boost the expanded memory in your system as well. With rare exceptions, if you have an 80286 computer, you'll have to buy an add-in expanded memory board for this purpose. Just be sure the board you choose lets you configure the extra memory as either expanded or extended memory, or both for maximum flexibility, as your needs change. 80386 and 80486 machines can convert extended memory into expanded memory, so there's no need for an extra board.

No matter which type of computer you have, you'll want to make sure that the speed of the memory you buy is matched to the speed of your microprocessor. If the memory is too slow, it may not work reliably, or your microprocessor will waste time twiddling its thumbs waiting for the memory to ready itself. But don't buy memory that's faster than the computer can take advantage of. After a certain point, faster memory doesn't do anything to speed up your system—in this case, the microprocessor (or motherboard circuitry) becomes the bottleneck—and the memory costs too much. Memory speed is specified in nanoseconds (a nanosecond is one billionth of a second). Seventy-nanosecond (70 ns) memory is very fast, and relatively high in expense. If you have an older machine, such as an 8086 or 8088 running at 4.77 MHz, fast memory such as this won't be worth the expense. Even if you have a 12MHz AT or clone, you'll probably be fine with chips slower than that, such as 150 or 100 ns. To be certain, take a look at the computer's manual. There may be some indication of the minimum speed of RAM chips you add. If there is, buy that speed, and don't bother buying faster chips unless you intend to later put them into a faster machine.

THE IMPORTANCE OF HARD-DISK SPACE

You probably think of your hard disk as the place where you store your programs and files when you're not using them and where they stay when your computer is turned off. And that's certainly one of the disk's major functions.

But your hard disk also has another important role with Windows: as a temporary parking place for programs that Windows is running and for program data. As a result, the amount of free space on your hard disk—that is, the amount of space still available after all your programs and files are accounted for—can have a direct bearing on the performance of Windows.

The way Windows uses free disk space depends on which Windows mode you're running. In 386 enhanced mode, Windows can perform some really sophisticated tricks with your hard disk. In particular, Windows uses the extra room on your disk as virtual memory for your system when you run out of the real thing. It does this by *swapping* information stored in memory to a temporary storage file on the disk, thus freeing up memory for use by another program. Your programs don't know that the swapping has occurred—when a program needs to work with a portion of memory that has been swapped to the hard disk, Windows reloads that information automatically after first swapping out whatever had been occupying its place in memory.

Obviously, the more free space you have on your hard disk, the larger the swap file Windows can store, and the more virtual memory your system can have. If you know how much memory your system has, you can quickly see for yourself how much more Windows has added with the smoke-and-mirrors swapping technique. (You can check the free memory space by choosing Help ⇨ About Program Manager from the Program Manager.)

In the Real and Standard modes, Windows isn't quite as clever, but free disk space still has a big impact on how quickly you use up available memory if you're running non-Windows programs. In these modes, Windows creates a swap file for every non-Windows program you run. Every time you switch away from a non-Windows program, Windows conserves memory by parking some or all of the program in its swap file. Again, the more free disk space available, the more swap files you can have, and the more non-Windows programs you can run.

In all three modes, Windows programs often use temporary files stored on your hard disk to hold program sections or data that don't fit in memory or information currently in use. Some programs won't run if they can't create a temporary file because you've used up all the space on your hard disk.

HOW GRAPHICS ADAPTERS AFFECT PERFORMANCE

Even if you run Windows on a computer equipped with the fastest microprocessor around, and even if you equip your machine with plenty of memory and a big, fast hard disk, there will still be a noticeable time lag every time you change anything on a Windows screen. That's because of the graphical nature of the Windows environment.

Unlike the standard DOS text mode, Windows itself must redraw each and every dot on any part of the screen that changes. When you scroll a picture in a graphics program, Windows is responsbile for updating the thousands of tiny dots that make up the new view of the picture you eventually see. Even the text you see on a Windows screen must be generated one dot at a time.

If your system is equipped with an ordinary graphics adapter such as an EGA or VGA board, the main microprocessor is directly in charge of drawing all those dots. But the central processor wasn't designed for this job, and besides, it has better things to do.

To dramatically speed up your system, you can add a graphics board equipped with a microprocessor of its own that's designed specifically for graphics display functions. In fact, this may be the best way to spend your money if you're after the biggest peformance boost for your dollar. Boards with coprocessors may cost as much as $1,000, but they can cut the time it takes to display a screen by a factor of 4 or better in some cases.

SUPERCHARGING YOUR SYSTEM WITH SOFTWARE TECHNIQUES

Windows' performance depends almost as much on proper software setup as it does on your computer's hardware components. Fortunately, Windows does most of the work for you when you install it onto your hard disk. The Setup program analyzes your system in detail, making decisions about what configuration settings to use based on factors such as your computer's microprocessor, the amount of memory you have, and how much space is available on your hard disk. Still, the choices Setup makes for you may not be ideal for the software you plan to run. To ensure top-flight performance, you'll need to manually check the settings for each element of your system.

SUPERCHARGING YOUR CONFIG.SYS AND AUTOEXEC.BAT FILES

Two files are critical to optimizing your system for Windows. The first is *config.sys*, a unique file containing special instructions executed each time you start your computer. It's used to install device drivers, small programs that control the way your system interacts with various hardware components. For example, device drivers are often necessary for managing memory, CD-ROM players, and special graphics displays, among many other parts of your system. Other entries in the config.sys file control a variety of important system settings, such as the number of disk files that can be open at any one time.

Unlike config.sys, *autoexec.bat* is an ordinary DOS batch file. Like all batch files, it can execute a series of standard DOS commands in turn. However, autoexec.bat does have one special characteristic: your system automatically runs it each time you start the computer, immediately after carrying out the instructions in the config.sys file.

When you install Windows for the first time, the Setup program will automatically add or change a number of commands in both the config.sys and autoexec.bat files as needed by Windows. But Setup leaves many of the commands that are already present alone, and it doesn't always add all the commands that you may need. As a result, you'll generally have to edit these files yourself for optimum Windows performance.

EDITING YOUR CONFIG.SYS AND AUTOEXEC.BAT FILES

In this section, I'll outline the basic steps you should take to edit your config.sys and autoexec.bat files for top performance with Windows. In the sections that follow, you'll get detailed advice on what to add, what to change, and what to take out when you edit these two files.

Before you make any changes in your existing config.sys and autoexec.bat files, save copies of the files as backups. If you make a mistake while editing or if you want to switch back to your previous setup (see "Using Windows and DOS on the Same Computer" later in the chapter), you'll have the old files at hand. The Windows manual tells you to make a whole new system floppy disk but that's an unnecessary inconvenience.

To make the backup copies, just use the DOS *COPY* command to copy the files to another directory on your hard disk or to a backup floppy disk.

The easiest way to edit the files is to use the Sysedit program that comes with Windows. You can also use a word processor or text editor that can save files in standard ASCII format (also known as the DOS text format) without the formatting codes usually added to most word processor files.

If Sysedit hasn't been included in your Windows applications group, you can add it with the New command on the Program Manager's File menu, or by running Windows Setup from the Main group and using the Options ⇨ Set Up Applications command. Sysedit should be located on the drive that contains Windows. Alternatively, you can start it with the Run command on the File menu or from the File Manager (move to the *system* subdirectory in your Windows directory, then double-click on the program name *sysedit.exe*). You could also choose the Run command from the File menu in the Program Manager. In the dialog box that appears, type in

```
sysedit ↵
```

When Sysedit runs, you'll see a series of cascading Windows, one of which will be labeled config.sys, another autoexec.bat. To edit one of these files, click on its window to bring it to the top. After you've made the recommended changes, exit Sysedit, saving the files as you go. Then exit Windows.

Your changes won't take effect until you restart your computer. Do so by pressing Ctrl-Alt-Del (all three keys simultaneously). The computer will run the edited config.sys and autoexec.bat files. If you've made any errors in editing the files, note the messages you receive from DOS as the system starts. Then go back and edit the files again to correct the mistakes. If you make any really serious errors, you can start over by copying the original versions of the files from the directory or disk where you stored them in step 1 above.

I'll go over the changes you should make to your config.sys file on the next several pages. You'll find tips on editing your autoexec.bat file in the section that follows.

REMOVING UNNECESSARY COMMANDS FROM CONFIG.SYS

The first step in editing your config.sys file for Windows is to strip it of any commands Windows doesn't need. These commands consume memory and nine times out of ten they don't benefit Windows in any way. In fact, they may even be a serious drag on Windows' performance.

After you've opened config.sys, scroll through the file to locate any lines used to install device drivers Windows can do without. The preferred way to eliminate the installation of an unneeded device driver is simply to insert the statement REM at the beginning of the line for that driver.

For example, Windows has a built-in mouse driver, so unless you'll be using your mouse outside of Windows you don't need the standard mouse driver in your config.sys file. So if you have a line that reads *DEVICE=MOUSE.SYS*, change it to *REM DEVICE=MOUSE.SYS.*

Similarly, since Windows works best with extended rather than expanded memory, you may not need your expanded-memory manager any more (if you have a 386 machine and run in 386 Enhanced mode). If so, add the REM statement to the beginning of the line in config.sys that starts your expanded-memory manager.

ADDING WINDOWS COMMANDS TO CONFIG.SYS

Once you've taken out the unnecessary and unwanted lines from config.sys, it's time to add the commands that Windows needs. The specific lines you should add depend on the type of

CAUTION If you're running any subvariety of MS-DOS version 3, a REM statement in your config.sys file will result in the on-screen error message "Unrecognized command in config.sys" whenever your computer starts up. Don't panic—the message is harmless, and nothing untoward has happened. Unfortunately, though, you'll see the same message if you mistyped a config.sys command. You'll just have to count the number of times the message appears to be sure it's the same as the number of REM statements in the file. If the error messages bother you, you can shut them off by deleting all the lines with REM statements after you've verified that the config.sys file is working right. MS-DOS versions 4.0 and above recognizes REM statements properly.

computer you have, so you'll find separate sections on each of the major classes of IBM-compatible computers here.

The optimal entries in your config.sys file also depend on how much memory is installed, the kinds of programs you'll be running, and on other details about your system. I'll discuss the various config.sys options in brief in the sections on each type of computer below. Many of these options are covered in greater depth in later sections as well.

To add new commands to your config.sys file, just type them in as you would any other text. If a statement is similar to one that's already present in the file, just edit the existing statement to match the version recommended for Windows.

SETTING UP 80386 AND 80486 COMPUTERS

With enough memory, 80386 and 80486 computers can run Windows in all three modes: Real, Standard, and 386 Enhanced. Each time you start Windows, it figures out how much memory your system has and selects the best mode accordingly (you can override Windows' choice if you wish, as explained in Chapter 2).

Windows can run in 386 Enhanced mode only if you have at least 2 megabytes of total system memory (640K of conventional memory, the rest extended). You need 640K of conventional memory and at least 256K of extended memory to run in Standard mode. If your system has only the 640K of conventional memory, you're stuck with Real mode—but I strongly recommend that you add more memory.

If you have a memory board in your system that can be configured either as extended or expanded memory, set it up as extended memory according to the manufacturer's instructions.

To configure your computer, edit your config.sys file so that it contains the lines described below, where appropriate. (In each case the proposed line appears first, followed by its description.)

```
FILES=30
```

This FILES statement tells DOS how many files can be open at once and sets aside the necessary memory.

```
BUFFERS=10
```

The **BUFFERS** statement tells DOS how many disk buffers to create and sets aside the necessary memory. Assuming you're using SMARTDrive, you should set up 10 buffers as shown here. If you're not using SMARTDrive, you should define no more than 20 buffers. You'll find details on when to use SMARTDrive and how to set it up later in the chapter.

```
device=c:\himem.sys
```

This line loads the himem.sys extended-memory manager. You can substitute any compatible extended-memory manager that you prefer.

The following commands are recommended for most systems:

```
device=\windows\smartdrv.sys [size of cache]
```

This line loads the SMARTDrive disk cache, which dramatically improves Windows' speed when it must read information from your hard disk.

```
stacks=0,0
```

This STACKS statement is necessary if your system is running MS-DOS version 3.3 or later. You can omit it if your system is running MS-DOS 3.1 or 3.2.

These commands are required on some systems only:

```
device=[name of expanded-memory manager file]
```

This line loads the expanded-memory manager for an add-in memory board. You should use this line only if the memory board can't be reconfigured as extended memory.

```
device=\windows\emm386.sys
```

This line activates Windows' emulation expanded-memory manager, which converts extended memory in 80386 and 80486 computers into expanded memory. Use this line only if you're running Windows in Standard mode, and then only if you will be using programs that require expanded memory. An emulation expanded-memory manager is not necessary when you run 386 Enhanced mode.

device=c:\windows\ramdrive.sys *[size of RAM disk in kilobytes]*

This line activates the Windows RAM disk, RAMDrive, which emulates a disk drive in memory. Although a RAM disk can be useful for speeding up programs that store temporary files, your system will usually run faster overall if you let the SMARTDrive disk cache have the memory.

device=c:\windows\ega.sys

Add this line if you have an EGA monitor and you're using Windows to run non-Windows programs in Real or Standard mode. In other words, you don't need this line if you're not running non-Windows programs or if you're working in 386 Enhanced mode.

device=*[name of display driver]*

If you're running Windows with a special display such as a large screen monitor, you may need to add a line that activates the driver for the display to your config.sys file. Consult the manufacturer's instructions for details.

SETTING UP AN 80286 COMPUTER

80286 computers can run in either of two Windows modes, Real or Standard. Windows automatically starts up in Standard mode as long as you have a minimum of 1 megabyte of memory installed in your system. This 1 megabyte must consist of 640K of conventional memory and at least 256K of extended— expanded memory doesn't count toward the 1 megabyte total needed for standard mode.

Note, though, that Windows can't use extended memory to simulate expanded memory in Standard mode or Real mode. For this reason, your system must also have enough expanded memory as required by the programs you plan to run. On most 80286 computers, the only way to provide expanded memory is by installing an expanded-memory board.

If you do have a memory board in your system that can be configured either as extended or expanded memory, divide the available memory between the two types as the needs of your software dictates. Use the manufacturer's instructions to set aside only as much expanded memory as your programs require, and configure as much as possible as extended memory.

If you have your system has only the 640K of conventional memory, you're stuck with Real mode—but I strongly recommend that you add more memory.

Edit your config.sys file as follows:

```
FILES=30
```

This FILES statement tells DOS how many files can be open at once, and sets aside the necessary memory.

```
BUFFERS=10
```

The BUFFERS statement tells DOS how many disk buffers to create and sets aside the necessary memory. Assuming you're using SMARTDrive, you should set up 10 buffers as shown here. If you're not using SMARTDrive, you should define no more than 20 buffers. You'll find details on when to use SMARTDrive and how to set it up later in this chapter.

```
device=c:\himem.sys
```

This line loads the himem.sys extended-memory manager supplied with Windows. Since most other extended-memory managers are not compatible with Windows 3.0 (at the time of this printing), you should use the supplied driver rather than your own.

These commands are recommended for most systems:

device=\windows\smartdrv.sys *[size of cache]*

This line loads the SMARTDrive disk cache, which dramatically improves Windows' speed when it must read information from your hard disk.

stacks=0,0

This STACKS statement is necessary if your system is running MS-DOS version 3.3 or later. You can omit it if your system is running MS-DOS 3.1 or 3.2.

These commands are required on some systems only:

device=*[name of expanded-memory manager file]*

This line loads the expanded-memory manager for an add-in memory board. You should use this line only if you've configured the memory board for expanded memory. If you've set up the board so that all of its memory is extended, you don't need this line.

device=c:\windows\ramdrive.sys *[size of RAM disk in kilobytes]*

This line activates the Windows RAM disk, RAMDrive, which emulates a disk drive in memory. Although a RAM disk can be useful for speeding up programs that store temporary files, your system will usually run faster overall if you let the SMARTDrive disk cache have the memory.

device=c:\windows\ega.sys

Add this line if you have an EGA monitor and you're using Windows to run non-Windows programs in Real or Standard mode. In other words, you don't need this line if you're not running non-Windows programs.

```
device=[name of display driver]
```

If you're running Windows with a special display such as a large-screen monitor, you may need to add a line that activates the driver for the display to your config.sys file. Consult the manufacturer's instructions for details.

SETTING UP 8088 AND 8086 COMPUTERS

On 8088 and 8086 computers, you can only use Windows' Real mode. Frankly, Windows performs lethargically on these machines no matter how you set up your system. If you're intent on running Windows anyway, the best you can do is to buy and install the largest-capacity expanded-memory board you can find. At a minimum, you need the full 640K of conventional memory.

To configure your system, edit your config.sys file so that it contains these lines:

```
FILES=30
```

This FILES statement tells DOS how many files can be open at once, and sets aside the necessary memory.

```
BUFFERS=10
```

The BUFFERS statement tells DOS how many disk buffers to create and sets aside the necessary memory. Assuming you're using SMARTDrive, you should set up 10 buffers as shown here. If you're not using SMARTDrive, you should define no more than 20 buffers. You'll find details on when to use SMARTDrive and how to set it up later in the chapter.

These commands are recommended for most systems:

```
device=\windows\smartdrv.sys [size of cache]
```

This line loads the SMARTDrive disk cache, which dramatically improves Windows' speed when it must read information from your hard disk. SMARTDrive runs in expanded memory on 8088 and 8086 systems, so your system must have an expanded-memory board.

```
stacks=0,0
```

This STACKS statement is necessary if your system is running MS-DOS version 3.3 or later. You can omit it if your system is running MS-DOS 3.1 or 3.2.

These commands are required on some systems only:

```
device=[name of expanded-memory manager file]
```

This line loads the expanded-memory manager for your add-in expanded-memory board. Of course, if you don't have an expanded-memory board, you don't need this line.

```
device=c:\windows\ramdrive.sys [size of RAM disk in kilobytes]
```

This line activates the Windows RAM disk, RAMDrive, which emulates a disk drive in memory. Although a RAM disk can be useful for speeding up programs that store temporary files, your system will usually run faster overall if you let the SMARTDrive disk cache have the memory.

```
device=c:\windows\ega.sys
```

Add this line if you have an EGA monitor and you're using Windows to run non-Windows programs in Real mode. In other words, you don't need this line if you're not running non-Windows programs.

```
device=[name of display driver]
```

If you're running Windows with a special display such as a large-screen monitor, you may need to add a line that activates the driver for the display to your config.sys file. Consult the manufacturer's instructions for details.

OTHER CHANGES TO MAKE IN YOUR CONFIG.SYS FILE

No matter what type of computer you have, you may want to make one or two additional changes to existing commands in your config.sys file in the interest of saving memory. Your config.sys file may not include these commands, but if it does, here are the possibilities:

- You can change the disk-drive letter name following the LASTDRIVE command to a letter earlier in the alphabet. LASTDRIVE is used to specify the last valid disk drive letter name accessible to your computer. Working in alphabetical order, the LASTDRIVE command reserves a small amount of memory for each drive up to and including the one you name in the command. The downside of making this change is that you may not be able to access disk drives designated by letters later in the alphabet.

- You can reduce the size of the MS-DOS "environment" space by editing the SHELL command. You'll have less room for environment variables, but you'll save a little more memory (see your MS-DOS manual for more information about the SHELL and LASTDRIVE commands).

ALTERING YOUR AUTOEXEC.BAT FILE

When you've finished with config.sys it's time to tackle your autoexec.bat file. Don't worry, this part is a lot simpler. Switch to the autoexec.bat file window in Sysedit, and edit it as follows:

1. Be sure that your Windows directory has been added to the PATH statement in your autoexec.bat file. Setup should have done this automatically if you let it, but you should double-check. The PATH statement should look something like this:

    ```
    PATH=C:\WINDOWS
    ```

or

```
PATH=C:\;C:\DOS;C:\WINDOWS
```

If not, edit the path statement appropriately.

2. Remove all the commands that start memory-resident programs (except ones that you want available to all programs you run in Windows). They just hog good memory. If you want to use them some of the time, see "Using Windows and DOS on the Same Computer" at the end of this chapter, and "Using Memory-Resident Programs" in Chapter 14.

3. Designate a directory where your programs should store their temporary files. When a program wants to read or write a temporary file, it uses the directory designated by the TEMP environment variable. If you decide to park temporary files in the *park* directory on your hard disk, type in the line

```
set temp=c:\park
```

If you have plenty of spare memory, you may want to set up a RAM disk for your temporary files—RAM disks are much faster than hard disks. In this case, you have to create the temporary files directory, and then designate it. If your RAM disk is drive D and your temporary directory will be *park*, you should add the following two lines to your *autoexec.bat* file:

```
mkdir d:\park
set temp=d:\park
```

4. Leave undisturbed commands that set basic system functions, such as PROMPT, DATE, and TIME. Likewise, don't change any commands that have to do with your computer's functioning in a network.

> ⊙ *CAUTION*
> Always designate a subdirectory as your temporary directory, never the root directory. Since MS-DOS limits the number of files that can occupy a root directory, it's a remote possibility that you could run into that limit.

SUPERCHARGING YOUR HARD DISK

No matter how big and fast your hard disk is, Windows will make you wish it was bigger and faster still. In this section, you'll learn tips for freeing up space on your hard disk and for making it run as fast as it possibly can.

DELETING FILES YOU DON'T NEED

On a big hard disk, it's easy to build up a huge collection of files you just don't need anymore. There are multiple backup versions of letters and reports long outdated, electronic junk mail you read but forgot to delete, demo copies of programs you decided not to buy, *readme* files ad nauseam, and miscellaneous magnetic flotsam and jetsam of all types. Before you know it, you're down to a megabyte or two of free space on that 80 megabyte hard disk you thought would never fill up, and that's not enough for Windows to operate at its best.

Get rid of the useless files! Make it a point to occasionally sift through all the data files dated a month ago or earlier. Copy the ones you think you're going to need again to a floppy disk, and then delete the whole lot of them.

Windows itself installs many files you may not need on your hard disk. Delete all those pretty Windows wallpaper patterns you're not using—if you really want to switch wallpaper later on, you can save the files on a floppy first. To free up really big chunks of disk space, you might even consider deleting some of the Windows programs you use only occasionally. For example, you can free up about 472K by deleting the Windows programs Paintbrush (pbrush.exe and pbrush.hlp) and Write (write.exe and write.hlp).

Deleting Temporary Files

Temporary files are supposed to occupy space on your hard disk only while the program that created them is running, but they have a way of getting left behind. This almost always happens when the program or Windows itself comes to a halt without the proper exit procedures, usually when you lose power or your system hangs up for whatever reason.

Leftover temporary files never get used again, yet they're often very large and a few can easily consume several megabytes of disk space with their worthless data. You can delete them without fear. You'll find them in the directory you've specified with the SET TEMP command in your autoexec.bat file, as outlined in "Editing Your Autoexec.bat File" above. Their names begin with ~ and end in the extension *.tmp*. To delete these files, exit Windows, switch to the temporary file diretory, and enter the DOS command **del ~*.tmp** ⏎.

Another class of temporary files are the swap files used by your programs and Windows itself. With one exception, you should also delete any swap files left over after you've exited Windows. If you run in 386 Enhanced mode you have the option of setting up a "permanent" swap file, and you don't want to delete this file. Program swap files start with *~woa*, and they're normally stored in the same directory as Windows itself (but you can change this, as detailed in the section "Optimizing Windows Swap Files," below). The temporary swap file for 386 Enhanced mode is called win386.swp and is stored in the Windows directory; you can delete it as well without ill effect. Just don't touch the permanent swap files, called 386spart.par and spart.par.

To give yourself a clean slate automatically, you can include a line or two in your autoexec.bat file to do the job for you each time you start your computer. Let's assume you've specified the TEMP directory on drive C as the storage site for your temporary files. In this case, to have DOS automatically delete all your temporary and swap files for you, add these lines to the autoexec.bat file:

```
del c:\temp\~*.tmp
```

for all modes,

```
del c:\windows\~woa*.*
```

> ⊙ *CAUTION* Delete temporary files and swap files only from DOS when you're not running Windows or any other programs. If Windows or one or more programs is running, some of the files will probably be in active use.

for Real or Standard mode, and

    del c:\temp\win386.swp

for 386 Enhanced mode.

Some non-Windows applications use temporary files but may not store them in the temporary directory specified with the SET command. In this case, add a line deleting the appropriate files.

RUNNING CHKDSK

Once in a while, chunks of information lose their moorings and wind up on your disk taking up space, but not as part of a real file. The errant data usually come from files that a program was using when it shut down abnormally because of a power failure or system error, although sometimes DOS just seems to garble a file accidentally. In either case, you can use the DOS program CHKDSK to turn the lost information into files again. You can review the contents of these files to make sure they're not vital and then delete them.

CAUTION Run CHKDSK /F only after exiting Windows completely, never from within Windows.

To use CHKDSK to find and recover lost information, exit Windows, switch to your DOS directory, and type CHKDSK /F ↵ at the DOS prompt. If the program finds any lost data it will ask you whether to convert the data to files. At this point, if you know that the data is inconsequential, type **N** to have CHKDSK delete it immediately. If you want a chance to review the data before you delete it, type **Y** instead. In response, CHKDSK will save the data into one or more files named file0001.chk, file0002.chk, and so on. You can then view these files and extract information from them with an editor.

DEFRAGMENTING YOUR HARD DISK

Once you've freed up as much space as you can on your hard disk, you're ready to speed up the disk by *defragmenting* the files that remain. In normal operation, DOS often stores files in separate places on your hard disk. Fragmented files take longer to read than do files that are stored in one long stretch because the disk head has to jump around from place to place on the disk.

The solution is a disk defragmenting or compacting utility that collects all the fragments of files and copies them to continuous sections of the disk. Good defragmenting utilities are smart enough to move all the files in each directory to one area of the disk and to put the files you use most often closest to the disk head for fastest possible access. They can also protect your files should a power failure or other glitch occur during the defragmentation process.

ADJUSTING YOUR HARD-DISK INTERLEAVE

Another way to speed up your hard disk is to make sure that its *interleave* is set at the optimum value for your system. Interleave refers to the numerical ordering of the disk's sectors, the sections of the disk into which data on hard disks are organized. Disk-drive controllers read one sector of data at a time. Since some controllers read data more slowly than the disk spins, the sectors on many hard disks must be laid down out of numeric order. An interleave of 2:1 means that the controller skips over every other sector. If the disk is set to a 3:1 interleave, the controller skips over two sectors at a time. If your hard disk controller is fast enough, the most efficient interleave would be 1:1, so that the sectors fall in true numeric order—in other words, no interleave at all.

On many computers, the interleave setting is higher than it needs to be. That is, your controller can actually read data faster than the interleave setting permits it to. With a good hard disk utility, you can test your system to determine the optimum interleave value and then reorder the sectors to match, without disturbing the data on your disk. This can often speed up the disk by 50% or more. If you don't already have a utility of this type, I recommend SpinRite II or OpTune.

USING SMARTDRIVE

SMARTDrive, the Windows disk-caching utility, is one of the key elements in any Windows speedup program. Fine-tuning SMARTDrive for your system is essential for top Windows performance.

SMARTDrive's job is to boost the apparent speed of your hard disk. No matter how fast your hard disk is, it can't compare with the blazing performance of your system memory. Of course, you need a hard disk, since you can't store all the programs and files on your hard disk in memory at once. But SMARTDrive provides a way to make hard-disk data available at the speed of memory much of the time.

What SMARTDrive does is make a copy of the information your system reads from the hard disk in a reserved area of extended or expanded memory called a cache. The next time your system wants to read from the disk, SMARTDrive checks the cache to see if the requested information is there. If it is, there's no need to use the hard disk again—SMARTDrive turns the information over to the system immediately at the speed of memory. If not, as the system reads the new information from the hard disk, SMARTDrive adds it to the data already in the cache if there's room, or replaces the existing cache data with the new information. Over time, SMARTDrive adjusts the contents of the cache so that it contains the disk information you're accessing most frequently.

For safety, SMARTDrive doesn't intervene at all when your system is writing information on the hard disk. That way, you don't have to worry about losing data in the event of a system crash. On the other hand, this means that SMARTDrive does nothing to speed up writing to the disk.

FINE-TUNING SMARTDRIVE

The best SMARTDrive setup depends on your system and the way you work. Fortunately, the Windows Setup program is smart enough to install SMARTDrive in such a way that it will work very well on almost any system. If you want to squeeze out a few extra percentage points of performance, you can experiment with changing the SMARTDrive setup until you find the optimum settings. The other reason you may want to change the SMARTDrive setup is if you add extra memory to your computer after you've installed Windows.

It's pretty obvious that the bigger the cache, the more disk information SMARTDrive can park there, and the more often Windows' performance will benefit. On the other hand, the memory you reserve for SMARTDrive will be unavailable for use and reduces the number of programs you can run and the maximum size of their files.

Actually, though, SMARTDrive has some flexibility here. The great thing about SMARTDrive compared to other disk-caching utilities is that it can adjust the size of the cache as Windows' own memory needs change, within limits you set. When you install SMARTDrive by adding the command line to your config.sys file, you specify how big you prefer the cache to be at an optimum, but you also specify a minimum cache size that SMARTDrive will reserve no matter what Windows demands.

The minimum useful cache size for SMARTDrive is 256K. Anything less and you won't notice much performance improvement—essentially, you'll be wasting the cache memory, and the memory SMARTDrive itself consumes. If you don't have 256K left over when you're running Windows and your programs, you shouldn't install SMARTDrive at all. Otherwise, it's usually best to use the 256K value as the minimum setting for SMARTDrive. If you have tremendous amounts of spare memory, however, you can set a larger minimum cache size.

Ideally, to determine the optimal cache size, you would calculate how much memory you need for Windows and your standard set of programs, subtract that from the total available memory, and assign the rest to the cache. Unfortunately, there's no easy way to make that calculation, and it's easier just to start with a rough guess and then experiment until you find the cache size that works best for you. A good rule of thumb, however, is to use a cache no larger than 1024K unless you have gobs of memory. Although every extra chunk of memory will boost

SMARTDrive's performance, you'll notice the biggest gains come when you increase the cache from 256K to 1024K. Beyond that point, adding more memory to the cache has much less of an effect.

INSTALLING SMARTDRIVE

You install SMARTDrive by adding a command line to your config.sys file, as outlined earlier in this chapter. If you allowed the Windows Setup program to modify your config.sys file for you, the file will already contain the line (assuming you had enough memory in your system for SMARTDrive to work when you installed Windows).

Your SMARTDrive command line in the CONFIG.SYS should look something like this:

```
device=c:\windows\smartdrv.sys 1024 256
```

Using Sysedit or a text editor, make the following modifications for your system:

1. Change the part of the line that reads *c:\windows* in the above example to identify the disk and directory where your copy of SMARTDrive is stored. Unless you moved the smartdrv.sys file after you installed Windows, it will be in the same directory where Windows resides.

2. The first of the two numbers at the end of the line refers to the maximum cache size in kilobytes (or the *normal* size, if you use Microsoft's lingo). This value determines the maximum cache size within Windows and determines the cache size when you're not running Windows. Change the number to the whatever you want the preferred cache size to be.

3. The second of the two numbers is the minimum cache size in kilobytes. This will almost always be 256, but you can change it to a higher value if you have lots of extra memory.

NOTE   The actual size of the cache depends on your hard disk. SMARTDrive rounds down the values you specify to a size in which an even multiple of disk tracks will fit.

4. If you're setting up the SMARTDrive cache in expanded memory, add the notation */a* at the end of the line. Expanded memory is slower, but you must use it if your system lacks extended memory.

So, to set up a SMARTDrive cache in extended memory that is a minimum of 512K and a preferred (maximum) size of 2 megabytes, your config.sys file should contain the line:

```
device=c:\windows\smartdrv.sys 2048 512
```

Use this line to set up thc same cache in expanded memory:

```
device=c:\windows\smartdrv.sys 2048 512 /a
```

OPTIMIZING WINDOWS SWAP FILES

In 386 Enhanced mode, Windows can give you more memory than actually exists in your computer by storing programs and parts of Windows itself not currently in use in a temporary swap file on your hard disk. You can control the way Windows configures its swap file for best results with your system.

In Real mode and Standard mode, Windows creates separate swap files for each non-Windows application you run. In this case, your swap file settings are less important, but can make some difference in performance and convenience.

No matter which mode you run in, you need plenty of free hard disk space to get the most out of your swap files. Keep your hard disk free of all unnecessary files using the techniques described earlier.

OPTIMIZING SWAP FILES IN 386 ENHANCED MODE

The important decision you must make about your swap files in 386 Enhanced mode is whether they should be temporary or permanent. The trade-offs are pretty straightforward. You'll get top performance with a permanent swap file, primarily because a permanent swap file occupies an unbroken stretch on your hard disk for quick access, but also because Windows doesn't need to create it afresh for each session. By reserving space for a permanent swap file, you also ensure that Windows never runs out of disk space for the swap file, so you can count on a given amount of system space for programs and data.

On the other hand, a permanent swap file cuts down the disk space that's free when Windows isn't running. If you use programs outside of Windows that need a place to store temporary files, they may not have enough room.

The alternative is to let Windows create a temporary swap file during each session. A temporary swap file doesn't need to reside in an unfragmented, contiguous section of your hard disk. Also, Windows deletes it automatically when you exit, freeing up disk space for other temporary uses. The downside to a temporary swap file is simply that it makes Windows run slowly.

To determine which type of swap file you're currently using, start the Windows Setup program by choosing its icon in the Main Group in Program Manager. You'll see a little window of information, at the bottom of which is listed the swap-file type.

Using a Permanent Swap File

Windows comes with a special program expressly for the purpose of setting up a permanent swap file. It's called Swapfile, of all things. Here's how to create a permanent swap file or modify an existing one:

1. Since a permanent swap file requires a contiguous block of your hard disk, you'll unnecessarily limit the size of the swap file if your other files are scattered in random fragments all across the disk. Correct this problem by optimizing the disk with a compacting utility, as described earlier, to create the largest possible contiguous stretch of free disk space.

⊙ *CAUTION* Just because the temporary swap file is deleted when you exit from Windows doesn't mean you need any less free disk space than you would for a permanent swap file. If you fill up your hard disk with other files, Windows won't have room to create the temporary swap file, and you won't have the extra memory capacity it would have provided.

2. Starting from the DOS prompt, run Windows in Real mode by entering **win /r** ↵.

3. Make sure that only the Program Manager is running (close any other programs that start automatically when you start Windows).

4. Run Swapfile by choosing the Run command from the File menu and entering **swapfile** ↵ (no path is needed) in the dialog box that pops up, and then click OK.

At this point, if a permanent swap file is already installed, you'll see a message to that effect, and you'll be asked how you want to proceed. We'll cover modifications to a permanent swap file in a moment.

If you don't already have a permanent swap file, Swapfile automatically searches your hard disk to see if one will fit and how big it can be. You'll see a dialog box displaying this information and recommending an optimal swap-file size. An example of this dialog box is shown in Figure 15.1. (The size Swapfile recommends will consume no more than half of the free disk space.) If you have more than one hard disk, you can have Swapfile survey the other disk or disks as well by choosing the Next Drive command on the dialog box.

Once you've chosen the disk where you want to install the swap file, you can accept Swapfile's recommended size or change it to suit yourself. Then choose Create to go ahead and create the permanent swap file. Exit from Windows. Now, when you run Windows in 386 Enhanced mode, it will automatically use the permanent swap file whenever free memory runs low.

Modifying a Permanent Swap File

If you want to change the size or location of your permanent swap file, or disable it entirely, run Swapfile as outlined above. Swapfile will tell you how big the current swap file is and which drive holds it. The dialog box shown in Figure 15.2 will give you three options: you can delete the current swap file and create a new one, just delete the current file, or cancel the whole process and leave things the way they are.

If you choose the first option to change the current swap file settings, Swapfile will delete the existing swap file and then present you with the same dialog box you saw when you first set up the swap file, described just above. Proceed as you would if you were setting up the swap file for the first time.

To delete the swap file entirely, just select the appropriate option on the dialog box. Swapfile deletes the permanent swap file and resets Windows so that it uses a temporary swap file instead.

Finally, if you decide instead that you want to leave your current permanent swap file intact, choose Cancel.

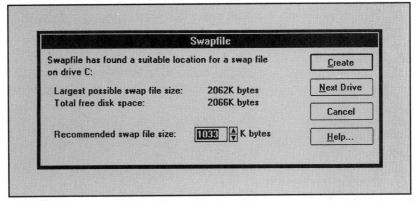

Figure 15.1: Running Swapfile brings up this dialog box, showing the available and recommended swap-file sizes

Using a Temporary Swap File

If you decide to go with a temporary swap file when you're running Windows in 386 Enhanced mode, Windows will take care of the whole process automatically. (The only exception is if you've been running with a permanent swap file and want to change back to a temporary one—in that case, use the instructions in "Modifying a Permanent Swap File" above.)

If you like, you can control the location of your temporary swap file and set a limit on its size. If you have more than one

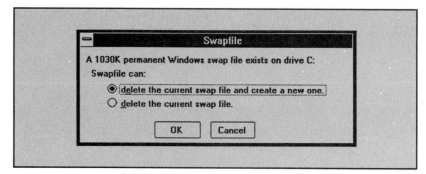

Figure 15.2: Running Swapfile when you already have a permanent
swap file brings up a slightly different dialog box, allowing you to
remove the file as well as modify it

hard disk, you should tell Windows to use the disk with the most
free space for its temporary swap file. If disk space is at a
premium, you may want to ensure that Windows doesn't use it
all up for storage of the temporary swap file.

To make either of these changes, you must modify settings in
your Windows system.ini file. Refer to the section below, "Using
Win.ini and System.ini."

USING (OR NOT USING) RAMDRIVE

Windows comes with a special utility program called
RAMDrive that can make a portion of your computer's memory
act just like a disk drive. In other words, you can copy files to and
from this *RAM disk* just as you would with your hard disk or a
floppy. Of course, there's one big difference between a RAM
disk and a regular magnetic disk: the contents of the RAM disk
disappear every time you turn off the computer.

The reason to create a RAM disk is to speed up disk operations. Since memory operates many times faster than a
mechanical disk drive, your programs can store and retrieve
data from a RAM disk in far less time than from even the fastest
hard disk. Besides the fact that you lose your RAM disk data
every time the power goes off, the only real drawback of a RAM

disk is the fact that it consumes memory that would be better used for other purposes.

If you had an infinite supply of memory, or at least enough for a RAM disk that could hold all the files on your hard disk, you would notice a tremendous speedup in all disk functions. But if your memory supply isn't that big, only the particular files you put in the RAM disk will benefit. Even if you create a fairly sizeable RAM disk—say several megabytes—you won't have room for all the disk files that Windows and your programs will need during a session. You'll only get the benefit of the RAM disk some of the time, but you'll have given up a lot of precious memory that could be used to run programs.

A better alternative is to let the SMARTDrive disk-caching utility shuttle disk information back and forth to temporary storage in a memory cache. On average, Windows' overall performance with a relatively small SMARTDrive cache (about one megabyte) will be about the same as with a RAM disk several times larger.

About the only time it makes sense to use RAMDrive is when you're running Windows on a networked computer that lacks its own disk drive. In this situation, the RAM disk would cut down on RAM available for Windows and the active applications.

If you decide to install RAMDrive, set it up by adding an appropriate line to your *config.sys* file. Use the techniques for editing your *config.sys* file described earlier to open the file. Then, following the lines that start *himem.sys* and your expanded-memory manager, if any, add a line that looks similar to this example:

```
device=c:\windows\ramdrive.sys 1024 /e
```

In your own *config.sys* file, replace *c:\windows* in the example with the disk-drive letter and directory where you stored the *ramdrive.sys* driver (unless you've moved the file, it will be in the same directory as Windows itself). Next, enter the size in kilobytes of the RAM disk you want next. The RAM disk created by the example would 1024K, or one megabyte.

CAUTION
RAMDrive version 3.0 doesn't work with Windows/386, a previous version of Windows.

You can configure RAMDrive to store the RAM disk in either extended or expanded memory. Add */e* at the end of the line for extended memory, as in the example. Add */a* instead for an expanded-memory RAM disk.

USING WINDOWS AND DOS ON THE SAME COMPUTER

Unless you use your computer exclusively for Windows, don't be surprised if you cause yourself new headaches by configuring your system for optimal Windows performance. The problem? Almost always, the system configuration that's ideal for ordinary DOS programs running without Windows is very different from the ideal Windows setup.

With Windows out of the picture, you'd probably like to run several memory-resident utilities before you start your main program, and you might want to install an expanded-memory manager or a driver that lets you switch from program to program at the press of a key. The trouble is that all these kinds of software conflict with Windows. When you load ordinary memory resident programs from DOS, they consume some of the precious 640K of conventional memory; Windows requires as much conventional memory as possible for top performance and may not even run at all if you load too many memory-resident programs. While Windows can use expanded memory when you run it in Real mode, Standard and 386 Enhanced modes don't get along too well with expanded-memory managers.

What you need is a way to switch between two different system configurations, one for Windows and one for DOS. Unfortunately, there's no easy method for doing this. If you've been running Windows and you want to switch to plain DOS, or vice versa, you have to change the system files (config.sys and autoexec.bat) and then restart your computer.

To make this cumbersome process as painless as possible, do it this way:

1. Edit your config.sys and autoexec.bat files so they contain the optimal configuration settings for Windows as outlined earlier in this chapter. When you're finished, save this pair of files on your hard disk as one *config.win* and *autoexec.win*.

2. Create a second pair of system files containing the ideal settings for your DOS programs. Save these files as *config.dos* and *autoexec.dos*.

3. Now create two short batch files, storing them in the root directory of the hard disk you boot your system from. Call the first batch file wingo.bat. It should contain these two lines:

```
copy c:\config.win c:\config.sys
copy c:\autoexec.win c:\autoexec.bat
```

Call the second batch file *dosgo.bat*, and put these lines in it:

```
copy c:\config.bat c:\config.sys
copy c:\autoexec.bat c:\autoexec.bat
```

4. If you've been using Windows and want to switch to DOS, exit Windows and type **dosgo** ↵ at the DOS prompt. Then restart your computer by pressing Ctrl-Alt-Del. To switch from DOS to the Windows configuration, enter **wingo** ↵ at the DOS prompt, and then restart the computer.

USING WIN.INI AND SYSTEM.INI

Windows stores important system settings in two files, *win.ini* and *system.ini*, located in your Windows directory. Windows reads the settings in these files each time it starts up, to determine how to configure itself. By altering these files, you can fine-tune your Windows setup in a number of useful ways.

TIP Don't bother
looking for infor-
mation on *win.ini* and
system.ini in the Win-
dows User's Guide—it's
not there. Instead, a
series of files in your
Windows directory ex-
plain how *win.ini* and
S*ystem.ini* work and
describe each of the in-
dividual settings in
detail. These files are
named *sysini.txt,
sysini2.txt, sysini3.txt,
winini.txt,* and
winini2.txt. You can
read them in Notepad;
print them out for refer-
ence if you like, but
make sure your printer
has plenty of paper.

The *win.ini* and *system.ini* files are standard text files. This means you can read them or change them with almost any word processor or text editor, including Notepad.

Both files are divided into sections of related settings. The code words for the sections and settings can be a bit cryptic, but they're readable, as in this excerpt from *win.ini:*

```
[windows] load=
run=cmdpost.exe
Beep=yes
Spooler=yes
NullPort=None
device=PostScript (Micrografx),MGXPS,LPT1:
BorderWidth=3
KeyboardSpeed=31
...
```

Each section in the *win.ini* and *system.ini* files starts with a section name in brackets. Individual settings are then listed in the format *keyname=value* where *keyname* is the settings name and value may be words or a number, depending on the setting.

The settings in *system.ini* relate mainly to the specific hardware components of your system. The file tells Windows which drivers to use for your display, mouse, network, and so on, and how to set up non-Windows applications, Standard mode, and 386 Enhanced mode.

The *win.ini* file, on the other hand, mainly controls various aspects of Windows operation according to your personal preferences. For example, *win.ini* settings in the excerpt above determine which programs start automatically when you start Windows, whether Windows beeps at you when you make a mistake, and so on. Individual Windows programs also store their own settings in *win.ini.* Corel Draw, a popular drawing program, uses *win.ini* to keep track of which fonts and file import utilities are installed, among other information.

The details of all the settings are explained in their respective on-line information files.

EDITING WIN.INI AND SYSTEM.INI

Because Windows maintains key settings in ordinary text files, you can easily check the files to ensure that the settings are correct and change them to your liking using any old text editor. But don't start changing things until you know what you're doing—it's fairly easy to accidentally alter or erase a key setting in a way that could foul up Windows' operation.

You can edit *win.ini* and *sys.ini* with any text editor that can read and save plain, unformatted ASCII text files. The easiest way though, is with the Sysedit program that comes with Windows.

When you start Sysedit, the program automatically opens *win.ini* and *system.ini* as well as *config.sys* and *autoexec.bat* files in four cascading windows. To edit one of these files, click on its window to bring it to the top of the stack, and then add, change, or delete text just as you would in Notepad.

When you've finished making changes, save the files and close Sysedit. The changes won't take effect until the next time you start Windows.

TIP You can change most of the settings in *win.ini* with the Control Panel. That's generally a better way to make the changes, since you're less likely to make errors.

CAUTION Always make a backup copy of *system.ini* or *win.ini* before you edit either file. That way, you can experiment freely and still restore all the original settings should something go wrong.

APPENDIX

A

Installing Windows

APPENDIX A

BEFORE YOU CAN USE WINDOWS, YOU'LL HAVE TO install it on your computer. Many programs are dificult to install but, fortunately, Windows is not one of them. The Setup program supplied with Windows pretty well automates the installation process. It installs the correct program files, printer and screen drivers, and printer and screen fonts. If a network is detected, it installs an appropriate network driver. Finally, it installs the supplied application programs and searches your hard disk for other Windows and non-Windows programs, setting them up in groups that you'll later use in the Program Manager. This appendix explains a few things to consider along the way, and some explicit steps you should follow.

Also, once you've performed the initial setup of Windows, it's possible you'll want to modify some aspect of it later. For example, you get a new video screen, mouse, or keyboard, or switch to a new type of network. The Setup program allows you to make such changes later and is covered in the second half of this appendix.

REQUIREMENTS

Before even beginning to install Windows, evaluate your system's components to ensure they meet the requirements of Windows:

Operating System	MS-DOS or PC-DOS version 3.1 or later.

Computer	An IBM compatible PC-XT, AT, PS/2, 80386 or 80486 computer that is IBM-compatible. You need at least an 80386 machine to run in 386 Enhanced mode. You need at least an 80286 machine to run in Standard mode. An 8086 or 8088 machine can only run in Real mode. (The modes are described at the beginning of Chapter 2.)
Memory	A minimum of 640K of RAM. However to work well, you should have at least 1 megabyte, and preferably more. The optimal amount you should have depends on the Windows *mode* you want to work in, and the number and size of the applications you intend to use. To work in 386 Enhanced mode, you need at least 640K of base RAM and 1024 of extended RAM. For Standard mode, you need at least 640K of base RAM and 256K of extended memory. For Real mode, you only need the 640K. Note that any memory over 640K should be set up as *extended* memory, not *expanded* memory, unless you plan to run only in Real mode. Standard and 386 Enhanced modes require extended memory. (Chapter 15 explains memory usage in detail.)
Disk Drives	You must have a hard disk, and it must have at least six megabytes of free space available. You need one floppy drive to install the program. As supplied, the Windows disks are in 1.2 megabyte (5¼-inch) or 720K (3½ inch) format. If your floppy drive only reads 360K disks, you'll have to request lower density disks from Microsoft. (There is a free order form for

	the 360K disk offer in every Windows package which explains the procedure.)
Screens	Windows supports many screens. Drivers are included for CGA, EGA, VGA, 8514/A, and Hercules adaptors, and a few permutations of these. To really see and use Windows well, you should have at least an EGA setup, and preferably a VGA. For other screens, you'll have to acquire a driver from the manufacturer.
Mouse	A mouse isn't required, but it's highly recommended. This book assumes you have a mouse. All the major mouse types are supported.
Printer	A printer is optional. Drivers for over 190 printers are included with Windows, so it's likely that your printer is among them.
Modem	A modem is also optional, but required if you want to use the Terminal program for communications or have the Cardfile dial phone numbers for you. A Hayes-compatible modem is recommended.

THE INITIAL SETUP

Assuming you've got the goods, you can proceed with the Windows installation. Just follow these steps to install Windows on your hard disk:

1. Depending on your Windows package, you'll either have 5¼-inch disks or 3½-inch disks. Pull out the first disk, labeled Disk 1, and put it in your floppy drive.

2. Log onto your floppy drive by typing

    A:↵

NOTE If you are installing Windows on a network server, you should refer to Chapter 14 of the *Microsoft Windows User's Guide* and follow the instructions there.

CAUTION Don't try to install Windows by copying files onto your hard disk with the COPY command. The files on your Windows disks are compacted so they can fit onto fewer disks. The Setup program expands the files during installation, and chooses which of the many hardware drivers to use. So you should only install Windows with the Setup command.

(use B if necessary).

3. Type

    setup ↵

The Setup program will start.

4. The first screen will come up, informing you about Setup, and giving you the options of exiting, continuing, or reading some helpful information about the installation process. Just press F1 if you want to read more about the Setup program, and then look at the bottom of the screen to see which keys to press.

5. When you decide to go ahead and run the installation, press ↵. Setup will want to know the drive and directory you want to install Windows into. The default setting of C:\Windows appears in a highlighted line on the screen. If you want, type in a new path and press ↵.

6. Press ↵. Setup will examine your system. If the target drive doesn't have enough free disk space (you must have 6.3 megabytes free), you will be alerted, and will have the option of using another drive or exiting the installation program. Do whatever you have to do to meet the space requirements. If you have to exit, you can run Setup again aftering freeing up space. Then continue from step 7.

7. Assuming you have enough space, Setup will examine your system to determine your hardware and operating-system configuration. A screen will appear displaying those assumptions and explaining how to change them if they're wrong. Figure A.1 shows such a screen.

8. If you want to alter any of the settings, use the arrow keys to highlight the item you want to change, and press ↵. A list of options will appear. Figure A.2 shows an example of a list of available screens. There may be more options than you can see in the box at one time. If so, you can use the up and down arrow keys to see the rest.

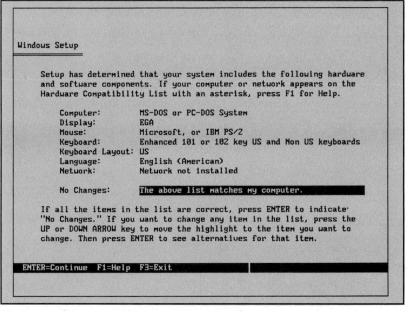

```
  Windows Setup

     Setup has determined that your system includes the following hardware
     and software components. If your computer or network appears on the
     Hardware Compatibility List with an asterisk, press F1 for Help.

          Computer:        MS-DOS or PC-DOS System
          Display:         EGA
          Mouse:           Microsoft, or IBM PS/2
          Keyboard:        Enhanced 101 or 102 key US and Non US keyboards
          Keyboard Layout: US
          Language:        English (American)
          Network:         Network not installed

          No Changes:      The above list matches my computer.

     If all the items in the list are correct, press ENTER to indicate
     "No Changes." If you want to change any item in the list, press the
     UP or DOWN ARROW key to move the highlight to the item you want to
     change. Then press ENTER to see alternatives for that item.


   ENTER=Continue  F1=Help  F3=Exit
```

Figure A.1: Setup examines your system and attempts to determine your hardware and operating-system configuration. You can change a setting by highlighting it and pressing ↵.

NOTE   If you are using a mono-chrome display with a VGA board, you should choose "VGA with Monochrome display" unless your mono-chrome screen can display gray-scales.

9. After ensuring that the system information is correct, press ↵ to continue with the installation. Windows will begin copying files to the hard disk. You will be prompted to insert disks as the installation progresses. Just follow the instructions you see on the screen. The copying and expanding can take a while, so have patience.

10. The screen will change to something more pretty as Windows begins to use your hardware. (If it doesn't, skip to the next section, "If Setup Crashes.") The mouse, if you have one, will become active. You will see a screen that gives you options to set up printers, set up applications that are on your hard disk, and read the on-line documentation that wasn't included in the Windows manual. These options all have little check boxes in

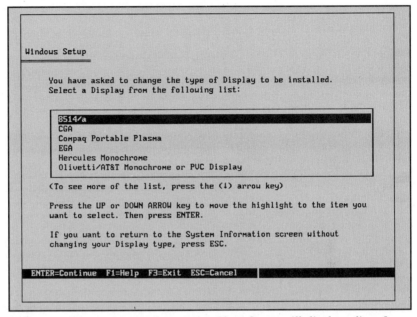

Figure A.2: If you want to change a setting, Setup will display a list of options in a box like this. Scroll through the box with the arrow keys to select a different option.

them, meaning they will be performed. Just follow the instructions on the screen. You can use your mouse to point at certain "buttons" on the screen to click on choices. Click on the button that says Continue, and the installation process will move ahead, prompting you for disks, and churning away on your floppy disk drive. A little gauge will indicate your progress for each disk. Finally, you will see the Windows applications added to your first two Program Manager windows.

11. You will now be asked if you want to have Setup modify your *config.sys* and *autoexec.bat* files for use with Windows. Setup is fairly intelligent at optimizing these files so that Windows runs well. If you're well-versed in Windows' operation, you might elect not to have the changes made for you or to review the changes first.

Otherwise, leave the setting as it is and click on Continue (or press ↵ , which has the same effect).

12. You will be notified that the files have been updated and old files saved under new names. Click on Continue or press ↵ again.

13. If you chose to install a printer, the printer section will now appear, asking you to choose a printer from the list. Follow the instructions on the screen. Position the mouse pointer on the little up or down arrows in the box of printer names and press and hold the right button to scroll through the listings until your printer type is displayed. Then release the button. Then click on the correct printer name. This highlights the name. Click on Install, and you will be prompted to insert a disk with the correct driver for your printer. (Refer to Chapter 6 for more details about installing printers.) Follow the instructions on screen to complete the installation of the printer.

14. If you opted to install your existing programs (Windows calls them "applications"), you will be presented with a box that asks where Setup should look for programs. Normally you'll want Setup to check all drives. If you want Setup to search a particular drive, position the pointer on the little down arrow next to the words All Drives, and click. A little list will appear giving you other options. Click on the option you want and then click on the OK button.

15. Setup searches your drives and concocts a list of programs it recognizes. (It tends to skip a lot of programs that it isn't specifically aware of.) To install all the programs into Program Manager group files for your convenience, click on the Add All button. Otherwise click on specific program names and add them one by one. The programs you list at the right are the ones Setup will prepare little icons for in Windows. Then you

can use the icons to run the programs. Chapters 3, 4, and 14 explain other ways to install programs if you decide not to do it during Setup.

16. If you chose to have Setup display the on-line files that have last minute information about Windows in them, the Notepad application will be run automatically, with the file *readme.txt* displayed. The little help box at the bottom of the screen will be obscured. Click on the help box to read it, and then click again anywhere inside the Notepad window to reactivate that window and continue reading the on-line information. The Setup program assumes a bit of expertise on your part at this point. If you don't know what's going on exactly, just move the pointer to the word File in the upper-left corner of the Notepad window and click. Select Exit from the menu that appears. This closes the Notepad file and finishes the Setup procedure. If you do know what's going on, continue reading the additional on-line information files about printers, the *win.ini* and *system.ini* files, and networks before choosing Exit from the File menu.

17. When you exit the Notepad, you'll see a box that will suggest that you reboot your computer. Click on the Reboot button rather than rerunning Windows or returning to DOS. This will ensure that the proper device drivers and config.sys settings are loaded to run Windows properly. (Make sure the A drive is empty or your computer won't boot up correctly.)

18. Then, to start up Windows, type

    win ↵

at the DOS prompt. If Windows starts, you can turn to Chapter 1 (or the Introduction, if you haven't read that yet) to begin learning about Windows. Otherwise, move on to the next section.

If you need to alter your Windows installation in the future, return to this appendix and read the section called "Altering Your Setup."

IF SETUP CRASHES

About halfway through the installation process, Setup switches over to running within the graphical user interface of Windows. To do this, it uses the screen and mouse settings you specified or, if you didn't change them, its own settings based on the hardware it detected in your system. If your hardware is too off-beat for Setup to recognize, or you chose the wrong settings, Setup might bomb out, presenting you with a blank screen and not progessing further. If your screen is blank, your hard or floppy disk isn't being accessed, and 30 seconds or so go by, then this is probably what has happened.

There are several steps you can now take. The first is explained below in the section "Running Setup from the DOS Prompt." Try that approach first, making sure that your hardware choices are correct. You might want to try a variation on your actual equipment. For example, if Setup is bombing when you select VGA, try VGA Monochrome, or if your screen can emulate EGA or CGA, try those settings, just to see if Setup will make it through and Windows will run. Then try to solve the incompatibility problem another way.

As a last resort, you can erase all the files in the directory that Setup created (typically \windows), and start Setup again with Disk 1. This is a drag, because of the time the installation takes, but it may be necessary. If you do this, start Setup this time with the command

    setup /i ↵

which tells Setup to ignore the system hardware and use its own defaults (which may or may not be correct, of course). Take extra measures to ensure that your hardware settings match your actual system this time. You'll have to set them all manually.

RUNNING SETUP FROM THE DOS PROMPT

Use this procedure if Windows didn't boot up the first time or if you need to install a driver supplied with your hardware.

If you or Windows were wrong about the actual hardware in your system, it's possible that nothing happened at the end of the Setup procedure, or your screen may have gone blank, your keyboard may have locked up, or some other evidence of a system crash may have become apparent. If so, all you can do is reboot and then run Setup from your DOS prompt. Luckily, it works from there just as well as from within Windows. Normally, you won't have to do this since Setup can usually guess correctly about your hardware installation, particularly the screen type. But I've met with apparent failure a time or two during installation when the wrong screen or mouse type was accidentally detected and installed. The good news is that you *don't* have to reinstall everything again. Setup is considerate enough to let you make modifications to the screen driver without copying and expanding all those files another time.

Note that you'll also have to use this technique of running Setup to install a driver not supplied with Windows or to update a driver for your hardware. You should be aware that Microsoft adds drivers to their own collection over time, and that they may have one if you can't get one from the manufacturer of your hardware. Make sure to follow any instructions that come with such a driver before following the steps below, or it may not work optimally (in other words, such things as screen fonts may be wrong).

1. If you're not at the DOS prompt, get there by exiting Windows. (Don't use the DOS prompt icon in Windows because it won't work.)

2. Type

   Setup ↵.

   Setup will start. If you get a "bad command or filename" message, switch to the Windows directory and try again.

3. A screen will appear listing the current hardware and software configuration. To change a setting, highlight it with the up and down arrow keys on your keyboard, and press ↵.

4. A list of choices for that setting will now appear. Highlight the correct one for your system, and press ↵. If you're installing a driver not supplied with Windows, but supplied from the manufacturer of the hardware, choose Other (it's at the bottom of the list).

5. You may be prompted to insert a disk that has the driver on it. You can specify the drive and directory where the driver is located, though the default is drive A. Insert the disk or specify the path if it's on the hard disk, and press ↵. Occasionally, a driver may have more than one disk, in which case you'll also be prompted to insert each one. In any case, the driver files and any associated files, such as screen fonts, will be copied to the hard disk.

6. The updated hardware list will be displayed. Press ↵ again, and you will be returned to the DOS prompt.

7. Type

   win ↵

   to start Windows.

ALTERING YOUR SETUP

The Setup program can be run again any time you want to modify the hardware setup or install new programs into your Program Manager groups.

CHANGING YOUR HARDWARE SETUP FROM WINDOWS

Typically you'll want to run Setup when you add a new type of screen, mouse, or network.

NOTE You add printer drivers to your system from the Control Panel within Windows. Refer to Chapter 6 for information on installing and removing printers.

You can run Setup two ways. If you've successfully installed Windows and it runs correctly, you can run Setup from Windows:

1. Double click the Setup icon in the Main group, and Setup will run. The Windows Setup window will then appear, listing your current screen, keyboard, mouse, network, and swap file. (Swap files are discussed in Chapter 15.)

2. You can make changes to these settings by opening the Options menu and choosing Change System Settings. All the current system settings are displayed in each of four lines of the Change Systems Settings dialog box.

3. Open the drop-down list for the setting(s) you want to change, select the appropriate choice(s), and then click on OK.

4. You may be prompted to insert a disk and indicate which drive it's in. This is because Setup may need a driver file that's on the disk.

5. Open the Options menu and choose Exit.

6. Now a dialog box will give you one or two choices, depending on the changes you made. You'll have the option of restarting Windows or Rebooting. If you have the option of rebooting, click on that button. Otherwise choose Restart Windows. Restarting windows or rebooting is necessary to ensure that the changes are applied.

Note that only the drivers supplied with Windows appear as options in the drop-down lists, so if you're trying to install a Windows 3 driver for a new screen, network, keyboard, or mouse that comes from the hardware manufacturer, you'll have to run Setup from the DOS prompt and follow the instructions in the previous section.

ADDING NEW APPLICATIONS WITH SETUP

After you have been using Windows for some time, you may acquire new programs that you want to incorporate into your Windows application groups. Though new programs can be added with a variety of techniques, as described in Chapter 3, you can use the Setup program to automate this task for you. Setup will add the new program's icon to the appropriate Program Manager group so you can run the program easily.

Here are the steps for adding a new program with Setup.

1. Install the application on your hard disk according to the manufacturer's instructions.

2. Run Setup (within Windows) by double clicking on the Windows Setup icon in the Main group.

3. From the Setup window, open the Options menu and choose Set Up Applications.

4. Choose the drive on which the application is installed by clicking on the small downward-pointing arrow next to the words *All Drives.* If you forgot which drive the application is installed on, just retain the default setting of All Drives.

5. Press ↵ or click on OK. Setup will search through the selected drive or drives for the application.

6. Setup then presents a list of programs it recognizes. To add your program, click on the application's name in the left box. Then click on Add. This moves the name to the right box. Don't do this for programs you've added previously (such as during the initial installation) or you will have duplicate program icons in your Program Manager groups.

7. Click on OK. Setup will add the appropriate icon to the Windows Applications or Non-Windows Applications

NOTE Only the most popular non-Windows applications are likely to be recognized by Setup. If your program doesn't appear in the list, Windows didn't recognize it, in which case you should use the techniques discussed in Chapters 3, 4, and 14 to install and run your program.

group in the Program Manager. Note that if you had changed the names of your Windows Applications or Non-Windows Applications group, or deleted the groups, Setup will re-create them.

APPENDIX

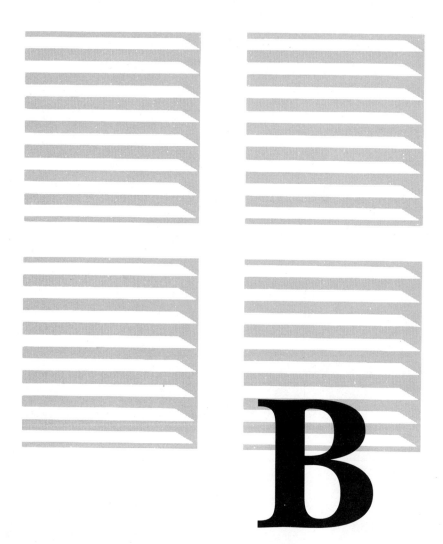

B

Troubleshooting

558

APPENDIX B

THIS APPENDIX IS DIVIDED INTO TWO SECTIONS. THE first section covers memory shortages and the second section covers other problems.

WHAT TO DO WHEN YOU RUN OUT OF MEMORY

It's not unlikely that you'll get an "insufficient memory to run application" message from Windows at some point. This usually happens immediately after you try to run a program. Windows checks to see if there is enough memory available for the program, and if there isn't, it aborts the process, and gives you an error message. When this happens, there are several simple things you can try before attempting to run the program again. If the simple things don't work, then you'll have to resort to more drastic means such as creating or modifying a PIF for the application.

Here are the simple solutions to try first.

- Close any applications you don't need open. You may only have to close one of them to get enough space for your application to run.

- If you have a wallpaper desktop background loaded, change the background to a pattern. A pattern of 50% Gray or None uses the least amount of memory.

- If you don't need what's on it, clear the Clipboard using the Clipboard utility (see Chapter 8). If you have something large on it, it could be taking up enough RAM to prevent your application from loading.

- Run non-Windows programs full-screen instead of windowed.

- Iconize any Windows programs that you want to keep open. Otherwise close them. They use less memory when iconized.

- Check your *config.sys* and *autoexec.bat* files for memory resident-programs that you don't need. Windows can only offer as much memory to programs as is initially available when Windows starts up. If you have lots of memory-resident software loaded when you boot up, they decrease what Windows has to work with, which affects all applications. Memory resident programs will adversly affect non-Windows applications more than Windows applications, but memory shortages have, at the least, a slowing effect on Windows' overall performance.

MORE ELABORATE TECHNIQUES FOR FREEING MEMORY

If none of the above techniques work, well, then you may have to get creative. There's probably a fix that will work, but it'll take some experimenting.

To be frank, even though the Microsoft Windows manual doesn't state this in so many words, if you're having lots of out-of-memory problems, you might just have to buy some more memory. Having a couple "megs" of extended memory really helps speed up Windows and eliminates most of those annoying messages. Before giving up and buying the memory card or chips, though, you might want to try creating or modifying the PIF(s) for the application(s) you're attempting to run. Here are the settings to consider altering, since they affect memory usage (see Chapter 14 for more information on these settings and on how to edit PIFs):

SETTING	*POSSIBLE ALTERATIONS*
Memory Requirements	Try decreasing the number in the Memory Required section of the application's PIF. (If it doesn't have a PIF, create one, as detailed in Chapter 14.) It's likely the application doesn't need as much memory as its manual states, anyway. Also, set the XMS or EMS (386 Enhanced mode only) memory requirements to zero (0) unless the program needs it.
Prevent Program Switch	By turning off the program switching ability, Windows relinquishes memory it would otherwise use to store the screen display when you switch out of the application. Try turning this option on.
Video Mode	Select the lowest video mode possible, which is text. Text mode uses the least amount of memory. If the application doesn't run with this setting, change it back. If the application uses text mode when it initially starts up, this technique should work to at least get the program running. However, if the application changes to a higher mode later to display some graphics, Windows might not let you switch out of the program until you close it, or until you return to text mode.
Tasking Options (386 only)	Set the application to exclusive tasking.
Retain Video Memory (386 only)	Clear this setting.

You might want to try making these changes one at a time rather than using the shotgun method. Save the PIF, making sure to close the PIF Editor, since it takes up memory too, and rerun the application. If, after making all the possible changes, you're still short on memory, change the PIF setting of other running non-Windows applications (if there are any). If you're not running any other applications at the same time as the one you're having trouble with, you've got a real problem. Check the amount of free memory via the Window ⇨ About Program Manager command. If it says you have tons of memory and the application still won't run, make sure you're assigning the right kind of memory. Maybe your application needs expanded or extended memory.

NOTE If all else fails, call the Microsoft technical support line. The number is (206) 454-2030.

OTHER TYPES OF PROBLEMS

This section discusses other types of problems you might encounter while running Windows. Some of the problems apply to Windows programs, others to non-Windows programs. Each problem is described briefly and followed by possible solutions.

Garbage characters appear on the screen when you're running Terminal or another communications program.

Try setting the COM port from the Control Panel's Ports window. The baud, stop bits, and parity may not match that of the modem. Check to see that no other applications are using the same port at the same time.

After you choose the Arrange Icons Command from the Program Manager the icons are still misaligned.

Close all the group windows. As long as a group window is open, the Arrange Icons command only arranges the program icons in the current group, not the group icons.

After you use the Tile command from the Task List, you can still see only some of the running programs. (Some are missing.)

Iconize the Program Manager. It is obscuring the programs that seem to be missing.

When trying to exit Windows, you're told that an application is still active.

The active program's icon will be highlighted, so you'll know what the offending program is. Open the program's window and quit that program. If you can't quit because the program is hung (crashed) try pressing Ctrl-C or Ctrl-Break. If that doesn't work, open the Task List by pressing Ctrl-Esc. Make sure the program's name is highlighted and then choose End Task. If the program's PIF has the Close When Active setting turned on, you'll then see a warning message. Go ahead and terminate the program. Then quit Windows. You should reboot after that. If the application's Close When Active setting isn't on, then you won't be allowed to quit the application this way. You'll have to reboot your computer by pressing Ctrl-Alt-Del, or pressing the reset switch on your computer, or turning the computer off and then on again. If you're running in 386 Enhanced-mode, you can terminate the program from the Control menu's Settings dialog box. You do not have to reboot.

You can't copy the screen onto the Clipboard.

The application's PIF may have the No Screen Exchange setting enabled. Edit the application's PIF to turn this setting off. Make sure the keys you're using to capture the screen aren't reserved for other applications that are running. Check their Reserve Shortcut Keys Setting or the current application's Application Shortcut Key Setting for a conflict.

You keep changing a PIF but the changes don't seem to take effect.

Put the PIF in the same directory as the program, or in the Windows directory. Give it the same first name as the application. Try running the program from its PIF instead of from the program itself. Ensure you're doing this by opening a File Manager window and actually clicking on the PIF's name.

After you finish a non-Windows program, the screen doesn't clear. You are not returned to Windows.

Edit the application's PIF and turn on the *Close Window on Exit* setting, or simply press a key, click the mouse, or if the application is in a window, double click the window's Control Box.

You can't switch out of a non-Windows application while it's running.

Check the application's PIF to see that the Prevent Program Switch option isn't set on. Check that the Reserve Video Memory setting is set on. Check that the shortcut keys used for switching aren't being reserved by the Reserve Shortcut Keys settings in the PIF. Make sure the correct video mode is selected in the PIF. Perhaps the program is using a high-resolution video mode that Windows doesn't support. This could be the case with programs that supply their own screen drivers, such as desktop publishing programs like Ventura. You'll have to exit the program before you can return to Windows. This is required because Windows knows that it can't restore the screen for you to switch back. Finally, some PIFs are designed to prevent your switching out of the application. If you make changes to the PIF that would allow switching, other problems might arise. If all else fails, call the program's manufacturer to get the PIF settings for Windows 3.0.

The application is displayed in a Window, but it suddenly isn't working at all. You can't interact with it.

Look at the title bar. If it says Select, Mark, or Scroll, it thinks you're trying to copy information to the Clipboard. This happens when you use the mouse in a non-Windows application that's displayed in a window. Press Esc to return to normal functioning. If that doesn't clear up the problem, switch the program back to full-screen mode. Some programs just can't run in a window, even in 386 Enhanced mode.

You press a key combination that the program should respond to and Windows does something else instead, such as switching programs.

Check the PIF for the application. Chances are good that you need to reserve shortcut keys for the application or clear them for use by Windows. Refer to Chapter 14 for a discussion of shortcut keys. If you're running Windows in 386 Enhanced mode and pressing a key combination constantly switches you back to a particular program, examine *that program's* PIF for the Application Shortcut Key Setting. It may be set to the combination you're trying to use in your other application. Clear the setting or close the application.

Your system is as slow as a snail when running an application.

If only a particular non-Windows application is slow, try setting its PIF to exclusive tasking or do this temporarily from the Control Menu's Settings dialog box (386 only). Also, look at the hard-disk light (or listen to it). Is the disk being used like mad every time you do the slightest thing? If so, your system is really short of memory. See the discussion above about memory. Also read Chapter 15 for other optimizing tips. Try turning off the Detect Idle Time setting in the application's PIF. If the application takes too much time doing internal operations when you're not typing, Windows might mistakenly suspend the application.

Windows crashes for no apparent reason.

Perhaps you're trying to run an older Windows program. Get an update or rerun Windows in Real mode and try again.

Perhaps your program is a bad copy of the original. Try another copy.

You may have some incompatible hardware, such as a screen or network. Check the hardware and software compatibility lists that came with Windows or call Microsoft.

Maybe your hard disk is messed up. Check it with a good hard-disk diagnostic program such as Disk Technician Advanced or SpinRite II.

Perhaps your copy of Windows somehow got bungled. Try reinstalling Windows from scratch. This is a last resort, mind you, since it's time consuming, and you run the risk of deleting some files you might need. If when you try to run the Setup program again, Windows says you don't have enough room on your disk, you'll have to erase all the files in your *windows* and *windows\system* directories. *Before you do this, back up any files you've created and stored there!!* In addition to any documents such as text and graphics files you might have saved, make a temporary directory and at least copy all the *.ini, .grp,* and *.pif* files to it. Then reinstall Windows. Then copy the files back into the Windows directory. (The *.grp* files store the information about your program groups. The *.ini* files store all the startup information such as the screen colors, as discussed in Chapter 15. The PIF files store information about non-Windows applications.)

APPENDIX

C

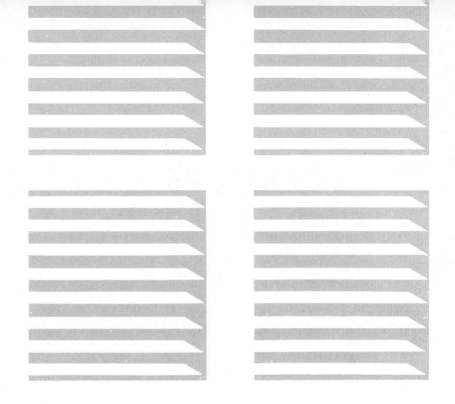

Using Windows on a
Network

APPENDIX C

ONE OF THE BIG IMPROVEMENTS TO WINDOWS IN version 3.0 is its support of local area networks. In earlier versions, sharing network devices while running Windows was problematic at best, and you had to make all your connections to printers and network servers prior to running Windows. Then, if you were lucky, Windows recognized the connections you had made. In addition, since Windows 2 used memory far less efficiently, you often wouldn't have much room for your application after DOS, the network shell, and Windows were all loaded into your computer.

With Windows 3, you'll usually have plenty of room to run applications after network connections are made, particularly on a 386 machine, due to Window's use of the 386's virtual memory capabilities. What's more, if you have one of the networks well supported by Windows 3, you'll have simple-to-use dialog boxes from which to choose a variety of network options. As a result, you can make changes to your network setup without exiting to DOS and typing in commands, as was required with Windows 2. Also, since the dialog boxes are easier to understand and control than are their text-based counterparts, Windows can actually render a network easier to use. You might consider Windows a friendly "front-end" to the network.

As of this writing, the networks supported by Windows are:

- Novell NetWare
- Banyan Vines
- 3Com 3+Open and 3+Share
- IBM PC LAN

- LAN Manager and MS-Net derivatives

If you have another brand of network, contact the manufacturer for Windows 3-compatibility information. They may have a network driver for you.

There are two basic ways that you can run Windows with a network:

- From a copy of Windows that you install on each user's machine
- From a copy of Windows that is installed on a network file server

Which approach you choose depends on your system needs, the number of users, the type of workstations on the network, and your approach to network security and backups. Some network administrators prefer to keep all programs and files on a central file server. This simplifies the process of backing up important files, and reduces the possibility of accidental data and program losses. As long as regular backups are made of the file server's hard disk, you're then pretty well insured against catastophic loss of data. Some network administrators even go so far as to use workstations that have no hard or floppy disks. It is then *assured* that all files are kept on the file server's hard disk.

Keep in mind, however, that running Windows over a network will slow the network somewhat. Windows does a lot of disk swapping (reading and writing data to and from the hard disk), and this may prove problematic in some setups. It could turn into a bottleneck, tying up your network, particularly if it's a relatively slow one. In cases where you may have many users on a network, or a significantly high amount of data traffic on the network for other reasons, you might want install Windows on the network users' hard disks instead of in a central location.

Unfortunately, considering the number of permutations of network topologies and the plethora of applications programs possible, making recommendations about where you should install your copy of Windows would be speculation on my part. This is one of those areas where you'll just have to experiment.

Try it both ways, for about a day each, and see which approach offers the greater advantages.

The instructions for installing Windows on a network server are rather complex, requiring you to expand the files first. You should refer to the *Microsoft Windows User's Guide*. The alternative is to install Windows on each workstation, running it on each one as described in this book. The only differences pertain to how you use the resources of the network, such as disk drives and printers.

The sections below explain special network procedures and possible problems you might encounter when using Windows on the network.

USING SETUP ON A COPY OF WINDOWS ON A NETWORK SERVER

If you or your network administrator has decided to put a single, shared copy of Windows on the network server, you would then use the Setup program to install it for your workstation, stipulating the configuration of your system. Setup then stores some of the Windows files (such as *win.ini* and *system.ini*) on your system's disk so that when you run Windows from your machine, the hardware and software settings you've chosen will be used. Another user may have different settings, which will be stored on that user's disk in similar fashion.

To set up your own copy of Windows from a network server,

NOTE If you're using a diskless workstation, specify a personal directory on the server's hard disk, but make sure that no one else is using that directory for Windows too, or your files will overwrite theirs.

1. Log onto the network server's hard disk and directory where Windows is installed.

2. At the DOS prompt, enter the command

    setup /n ↵

3. Setup will run similarly to the way it runs when it installs Windows on a local machine (see Appendix A). When asked which drive and directory you want to install on, specify a directory on the hard disk in your computer.

This way the files that customize Windows for your use will be stored in your machine.

SPECIAL CONSIDERATIONS WHEN RUNNING FROM A NETWORK

This section explains some aspects of Windows on a network that you should consider.

To run a shared version of Windows from a network workstation, you issue the *win* command from the DOS prompt (or from a batch file) just as you would for a local version of Windows. However, there's a difference in how Windows is actually found and loaded. The startup files that Setup stored in your local directory (or in a personal directory on the server in the case of a diskless workstation) direct your computer to load Windows from the server disk drive and directory rather than from your local drive. So far, this is all automatic. However, there are two important things to remember. Otherwise, Windows won't be found, and therefore won't run.

Make sure the network and your workstation's connection to it is up and running before you try to run Windows.

Make sure that your workstation is connected to the network drive that contains Windows, and that you have assigned that drive the same letter name it was assigned when you ran Setup. If it was drive E when you ran setup, it must be designated E when you run Windows. This is because Setup recorded the drive letter in the startup file during installation, and uses that each time it starts Windows.

Windows does not offer any special protection for files that are being shared by users on the network. The network operating system takes care of this. If you are storing your document files in directories that other users have access to, make sure the files are locked appropriately to prevent accidental modification by them. Confer with your network administrator (if there is one) or refer to the network software's manual.

BROWSING THROUGH AVAILABLE NETWORK DRIVES

Depending on the network, the Connect Net Drive dialog box may have an option for browsing through available drives. This lets you choose which drive you want before you actually connect to it. The resulting dialog box will differ depending on the brand of network.

DISCONNECTING FROM A NETWORK DRIVE

When you want to disconnect from a network drive, do the following:

1. Choose Disk ⇨ Disconnect Net Drive.
2. The Disconnect Net Drive dialog box will then appear. Select the drive you want to disconnect. Confirm the choice.
3. Click on OK. The drive will be disconnected.

Note that if you had connected to the drive prior to running Windows, you may not be able to disconnect in this way. Also note that some non-Windows applications let you connect and disconnect to and from network drives while in the application. If you use this technique to connect to a drive, you should disconnect from the drive before leaving the application.

PROBLEMS WITH NETWORK APPLICATIONS

This section discusses some problems you may have while using Windows on a network.

When installing your copy of Windows, the Setup program may at first seem to recognize that you are connected to a network, listing its correct name and version in the system configuration box and then when you continue with the installation, Windows may not actually connect to the network. If so, you will know that it hasn't, because the Control Panel will not show the Network icon, nor will other network options, such as connecting to a network drive from the File Manager be available. If you're having trouble getting a network to function with Windows, you may not have the latest version of some of the network's drivers. Read the *network.txt* for the latest information on Windows 3 compatibility for your type of network. You might be able to download the latest driver from an information service such as CompuServe, or get it from the manufacturer.

If you can't get a network driver that supports Windows 3, then making a few modifications to your setup may still allow Windows to run. If you're having trouble running in Standard mode on the network, try running Windows in Real mode by starting it with **win /r** ↵.

If you can't seem to get non-Windows applications to run over the network, try running Windows in a lower mode (386 Enhanced is the highest mode, Real mode is the lowest). Another possible solution is to avoid switching between applications. (Quit one application before switching to another.) Also, try setting the program's PIF for exclusive operation (you can do this in 386 Enhanced mode only).

If you can't seem to connect to a network drive or printer while in Windows, try exiting Windows and then connecting to the drive or printer from DOS or whatever network utilities you normally use for the purpose. Then rerun Windows.

USING NETWORK DRIVES

Assuming your network works with Windows 3, you'll have two options in the File Manager's Disk menu that were not described in Chapter 4. These are options that let you connect to and disconnect from drives on the network.

CONNECTING TO A NETWORK DRIVE

Network drives have their own style of icon, similar to the hard-disk icon. (They say NET on them.) Depending on whether you connected to a network drive before running Windows or not, your File Manager's Directory Tree window may or may not show any network drives when you first open it. If the drive you want access to is not showing, you can connect to it if you know its path name and its password. Follow these steps to connect to it.

1. Choose Disk ⇨ Connect Net Drive.

2. A dialog box will appear. It allows you to choose the letter name you want to assign to the drive. Normally this is the next available letter. Change it from the drop-down list if you want.

3. Type in the path of the drive in the Network Path text area.

4. Type in the password for the drive if it's required.

5. Click on Connect and the drive should be added to your Directory Tree Window.

Windows keeps a list of previous connections you have made, assuming the Add to Previous List check box was set on when you made those connections. Instead of having to type in the path name and password each time, you can make the connection once as a shortcut, and then use the Previous button in the dialog box to see a list of previous connections. Choose from the list the connection you want to make.

X

Selections from
The SYBEX Library

OPERATING SYSTEMS

The ABC's of DOS 4
Alan R. Miller
275pp. Ref. 583-2

This step-by-step introduction to using DOS 4 is written especially for beginners. Filled with simple examples, *The ABC's of DOS 4* covers the basics of hardware, software, disks, the system editor EDLIN, DOS commands, and more.

ABC's of MS-DOS
(Second Edition)
Alan R. Miller
233pp. Ref. 493-3

This handy guide to MS-DOS is all many PC users need to manage their computer files, organize floppy and hard disks, use EDLIN, and keep their computers organized. Additional information is given about utilities like Sidekick, and there is a DOS command and program summary. The second edition is fully updated for Version 3.3.

DOS Assembly Language
Programming
Alan R. Miller
365pp. 487-9

This book covers PC-DOS through 3.3, and gives clear explanations of how to assemble, link, and debug 8086, 8088, 80286, and 80386 programs.   The example assembly language routines are valuable for students and programmers alike.

DOS Instant Reference
SYBEX Prompter Series
Greg Harvey
Kay Yarborough Nelson
220pp. Ref. 477-1, 4 ¾" × 8"

A complete fingertip reference for fast, easy on-line help:command summaries, syntax, usage and error messages. Organized by function—system commands, file commands, disk management, directories, batch files, I/O, networking, programming, and more. Through Version 3.3.

DOS User's Desktop Companion
SYBEX Ready Reference Series
Judd Robbins
969pp. Ref. 505-0

This comprehensive reference covers DOS commands, batch files, memory enhancements, printing, communications and more information on optimizing each user's DOS environment. Written with step-by-step instructions and plenty of examples, this volume covers all versions through 3.3.

Encyclopedia DOS
Judd Robbins
1030pp. Ref. 699-5

A comprehensive reference and user's guide to all versions of DOS through 4.0. Offers complete information on every DOS command, with all possible switches and parameters -- plus examples of effective usage. An invaluable tool.

Essential OS/2
(Second Edition)
Judd Robbins

445pp. Ref. 609-X

Written by an OS/2 expert, this is the guide to the powerful new resources of the OS/2 operating system standard edition 1.1 with presentation manager. Robbins introduces the standard edition, and details multitasking under OS/2, and the range of commands for installing, starting up, configuring, and running applications. For Version 1.1 Standard Edition.

Essential PC-DOS
(Second Edition)
Myril Clement Shaw
Susan Soltis Shaw

332pp. Ref. 413-5

An authoritative guide to PC-DOS, including version 3.2. Designed to make experts out of beginners, it explores everything from disk management to batch file programming. Includes an 85-page command summary. Through Version 3.2.

Graphics Programming
Under Windows
Brian Myers
Chris Doner

646pp. Ref. 448-8

Straightforward discussion, abundant examples, and a concise reference guide to graphics commands make this book a must for Windows programmers. Topics range from how Windows works to programming for business, animation, CAD, and desktop publishing. For Version 2.

Hard Disk Instant Reference
SYBEX Prompter Series
Judd Robbins

256pp. Ref. 587-5, 4 ¾" × 8"

Compact yet comprehensive, this pocket-sized reference presents the essential information on DOS commands used in managing directories and files, and in optimizing disk configuration. Includes a survey of third-party utility capabilities. Through DOS 4.0.

The IBM PC-DOS Handbook
(Third Edition)
Richard Allen King

359pp. Ref. 512-3

A guide to the inner workings of PC-DOS 3.2, for intermediate to advanced users and programmers of the IBM PC series. Topics include disk, screen and port control, batch files, networks, compatibility, and more. Through Version 3.3.

Inside DOS: A Programmer's
Guide
Michael J. Young

490pp. Ref. 710-X

A collection of practical techniques (with source code listings) designed to help you take advantage of the rich resources intrinsic to MS-DOS machines. Designed for the experienced programmer with a basic understanding of C and 8086 assembly language, and DOS fundamentals.

Mastering DOS
(Second Edition)
Judd Robbins

722pp. Ref. 555-7

"The most useful DOS book." This seven-part, in-depth tutorial addresses the needs of users at all levels. Topics range from running applications, to managing files and directories, configuring the system, batch file programming, and techniques for system developers. Through Version 4.

MS-DOS Advanced
Programming
Michael J. Young

490pp. Ref. 578-6

Practical techniques for maximizing performance in MS-DOS software by making best use of system resources. Topics include functions, interrupts, devices, multitasking, memory residency and more, with examples in C and assembler. Through Version 3.3.

MS-DOS Handbook
(Third Edition)
Richard Allen King
362pp. Ref. 492-5

This classic has been fully expanded and revised to include the latest features of MS-DOS Version 3.3. Two reference books in one, this title has separate sections for programmer and user. Multi-DOS partitons, 3 ½-inch disk format, batch file call and return feature, and comprehensive coverage of MS-DOS commands are included. Through Version 3.3.

MS-DOS Power User's Guide,
Volume I
(Second Edition)
Jonathan Kamin
482pp. Ref. 473-9

A fully revised, expanded edition of our best-selling guide to high-performance DOS techniques and utilities—with details on Version 3.3. Configuration, I/O, directory structures, hard disks, RAM disks, batch file programming, the ANSI.SYS device driver, more. Through Version 3.3.

Programmers Guide to
the OS/2 Presentation Manager
Michael J. Young
683pp. Ref. 569-7

This is the definitive tutorial guide to writing programs for the OS/2 Presentation Manager. Young starts with basic architecture, and explores every important feature including scroll bars, keyboard and mouse interface, menus and accelerators, dialogue boxes, clipboards, multitasking, and much more.

Programmer's Guide to
Windows
(Second Edition)
David Durant
Geta Carlson
Paul Yao
704pp. Ref. 406-8

The first edition of this programmer's guide was hailed as a classic. This new edition covers Windows 2 and Windows/386 in depth. Special emphasis is given to over fifty new routines to the Windows interface, and to preparation for OS/2 Presentation Manager compatibility.

Understanding DOS 3.3
Judd Robbins
678pp. Ref. 648-0

This best selling, in-depth tutorial addresses the needs of users at all levels with many examples and hands-on exercises. Robbins discusses the fundamentals of DOS, then covers manipulating files and directories, using the DOS editor, printing, communicating, and finishes with a full section on batch files.

Understanding Hard Disk
Management on the PC
Jonathan Kamin
500pp. Ref. 561-1

This title is a key productivity tool for all hard disk users who want efficient, error-free file management and organization. Includes details on the best ways to conserve hard disk space when using several memory-guzzling programs. Through DOS 4.

Up & Running
with Your Hard Disk
Klaus M Rubsam
140pp. Ref. 666-9

A far-sighted, compact introduction to hard disk installation and basic DOS use. Perfect for PC users who want the practical essentials in the shortest possible time. In 20 basic steps, learn to choose your hard disk, work with accessories, back up data, use DOS utilities to save time, and more.

Up & Running with Windows
286/386
Gabriele Wentges
132pp. Ref. 691-X

This handy 20-step overview gives PC users all the essentials of using Windows -- whether for evaluating the software, or getting a fast start. Each self-contained lesson takes just 15 minutes to one hour to complete.

COMMUNICATIONS

Mastering Crosstalk XVI
(Second Edition)
Peter W. Gofton

225pp. Ref. 642-1

Introducing the communications program Crosstalk XVI for the IBM PC. As well as providing extensive examples of command and script files for programming Crosstalk, this book includes a detailed description of how to use the program's more advanced features, such as windows, talking to mini or mainframe, customizing the keyboard and answering calls and background mode.

Mastering PROCOMM PLUS
Bob Campbell

400pp. Ref. 657-X

Learn all about communications and information retrieval as you master and use PROCOMM PLUS. Topics include choosing and using a modem; automatic dialing; using on-line services (featuring CompuServe) and more. Through Version 1.1b; also covers PROCOMM, the "shareware" version.

Mastering Serial
Communications
Peter W. Gofton

289pp. Ref. 180-2

The software side of communications, with details on the IBM PC's serial programming, the XMODEM and Kermit protocols, non-ASCII data transfer, interrupt-level programming and more. Sample programs in C, assembly language and BASIC.

HARDWARE

From Chips to Systems: An
Introduction to Microcomputers
(Second Edition)
Rodnay Zaks
Alexander Wolfe

580pp. Ref. 377-5

The best-selling introduction to microcom-

puter hardware—now fully updated, revised, and illustrated. Such recent advances as 32-bit processors and RISC architecture are introduced and explained for the first time in a beginning text.

Microprocessor Interfacing
Techniques (Third Edition)
Austin Lesea
Rodnay Zaks

456pp. Ref. 029-6

This handbook is for engineers and hobbyists alike, covering every aspect of interfacing microprocessors with peripheral devices. Topics include assembling a CPU, basic I/O, analog circuitry, and bus standards.

The RS-232 Solution
(Second Edition)
Joe Campbell

193pp. Ref. 488-7

For anyone wanting to use their computer's serial port, this complete how-to guide is updated and expanded for trouble-free RS-232-C interfacing from scratch. Solution shows you how to connect a variety of computers, printers, and modems, and it includes details for IBM PC AT, PS/2, and Macintosh.

NETWORKS

The ABC's of Local Area
Networks
Michael Dortch

212pp. Ref. 664-2

This jargon-free introduction to LANs is fur current and prospective users who see general information, comparative options, a look at the future, and tips for effective LANs use today. With comparisons of Token-Ring, PC Network, Novell, and others.

The ABC's of Novell Netware
Jeff Woodward

282pp. Ref. 614-6

For users who are new to PC's or networks, this entry-level tutorial outlines each basic element and operation of Novell. The ABC's introduces computer hardware and software, DOS, network organization and security, and printing and communicating over the netware system.

Mastering Novell Netware
Cheryl C. Currid
Craig A. Gillett
500pp. Ref. 630-8
This book is a thorough guide for System Administrators to installing and operating a microcomputer network using Novell Netware. Mastering covers actually setting up a network from start to finish, design, administration, maintenance, and troubleshooting.

Networking with TOPS
Steven William Rimmer
350pp. Ref. 565-4
A hands on guide to the most popular user friendly network available. This book will walk a user through setting up the hardware and software of a variety of TOPS configurations, from simple two station networks through whole offices. It explains the realities of sharing files between PC compatibles and Macintoshes, of sharing printers and other peripherals and, most important, of the real world performance one can expect when the network is running.

UTILITIES

Mastering the Norton Utilities
Peter Dyson
373pp. Ref. 575-1
In-depth descriptions of each Norton utility make this book invaluable for beginning and experienced users alike. Each utility is described clearly with examples and the text is organized so that readers can put Norton to work right away. Version 4.5.

Mastering PC Tools Deluxe
Peter Dyson
400pp. Ref. 654-5
A complete hands-on guide to the timesaving—and "lifesaving"—utility programs in Version 5.5 of PC Tools Deluxe.

Contains concise tutorials and in-depth discussion of every aspect of using PC Tools—from high speed backups, to data recovery, to using Desktop applications.

Mastering SideKick Plus
Gene Weisskopf
394pp. Ref. 558-1
Employ all of Sidekick's powerful and expanded features with this hands-on guide to the popular utility. Features include comprehensive and detailed coverage of time management, note taking, outlining, auto dialing, DOS file management, math, and copy-and-paste functions.

Up & Running with Norton Utilities
Rainer Bartel
140pp. Ref. 659-6
Get up and running in the shortest possible time in just 20 lessons or "steps." Learn to restore disks and files, use UnErase, edit your floppy disks, retrieve lost data and more. Or use the book to evaluate the software before you purchase. Through Version 4.2.

Up & Running with PC Tools Deluxe 6
Thomas Holste
180pp. Ref.678-2
Learn to use this software program in just 20 basic steps. Readers get a quick, inexpensive introduction to using the Tools for disaster recovery, disk and file management, and more.

WORD PROCESSING

The ABC's of Microsoft Word (Third Edition)
Alan R. Neibauer
461pp. Ref. 604-9
This is for the novice WORD user who wants to begin producing documents in the shortest time possible. Each chapter has short, easy-to-follow lessons for both keyboard and mouse, including all the basic editing, formatting and printing functions. Version 5.0.

The ABC's of WordPerfect
Alan R. Neibauer
239pp. Ref. 425-9

This basic introduction to WordPefect consists of short, step-by-step lessons— for new users who want to get going fast. Topics range from simple editing and formatting, to merging, sorting, macros, and more. Includes version 4.2

Practical WordStar Uses
Julie Anne Arca
303pp. Ref. 107-1

A hands-on guide to WordStar and MailMerge applications, with solutions to comon problems and "recipes" for day-to-day tasks. Formatting, merge-printing and much more; plus a quick-reference command chart and notes on CP/M and PC-DOS. For Version 3.3.

Understanding Professional Write
Gerry Litton
400pp. Ref. 656-1

A complete guide to Professional Write that takes you from creating your first simple document, into a detailed description of all major aspects of the software. Special features place an emphasis on the use of different typestyles to create attractive documents as well as potential problems and suggestions on how to get around them.

Understanding WordStar 2000
David Kolodney
Thomas Blackadar
275pp. Ref. 554-9

This engaging, fast-paced series of tutorials covers everything from moving the cursor to print enhancements, format files, key glossaries, windows and MailMerge. With practical examples, and notes for former WordStar users.

Visual Guide to WordPerfect
Jeff Woodward
457pp. Ref. 591-3

This is a visual hands-on guide which is ideal for brand new users as the book shows each activity keystroke-by-keystroke. Clear illustrations of computer screen menus are included at every stage. Covers basic editing, formatting lines, paragraphs, and pages, using the block feature, footnotes, search and replace, and more. Through Version 5.

WordPerfect 5 Desktop Companion
SYBEX Ready Reference Series
Greg Harvey
Kay Yarborough Nelson
1006pp. Ref. 522-0

Desktop publishing features have been added to this compact encyclopedia. This title offers more detailed, cross-referenced entries on every software features including page formatting and layout, laser printing and word processing macros. New users of WordPerfect, and those new to Version 5 and desktop publishing will find this easy to use for on-the-job help.

WordPerfect Instant Reference
SYBEX Prompter Series
Greg Harvey
Kay Yarborough Nelson
254pp. Ref. 476-3, 4 ¾" × 8"

When you don't have time to go digging through the manuals, this fingertip guide offers clear, concise answers: command summaries, correct usage, and exact keystroke sequences for on-the-job tasks. Convenient organization reflects the structure of WordPerfect. Through Version 4.2.

WordPerfect 5 Instant Reference
SYBEX Prompter Series
Greg Harvey
Kay Yarborough Nelson
316pp. Ref. 535-2, 4 ¾" × 8"

This pocket-sized reference has all the program commands for the powerful WordPerfect 5 organized alphabetically for quick access. Each command entry has the exact key sequence, any reveal codes, a list of available options, and option-by-option discussions.

WordPerfect 5.1 Instant Reference
Greg Harvey
Kay Yarborough Nelson
252pp. Ref. 674-X

Instant access to all features and commands of WordPerfect 5.0 and 5.1, highlighting the newest software features. Complete, alphabetical entries provide exact key sequences, codes and options, and step-by-step instructions for many important tasks.

WordPerfect 5 Macro Handbook
Kay Yarborough Nelson
488pp. Ref. 483-6

Readers can create macros custom-tailored to their own needs with this excellent tutorial and reference. Nelson's expertise guides the WordPerfect 5 user through nested and chained macros, macro libraries, specialized macros, and much more.

WordPerfect 5.1 Tips and Tricks (Fourth Edition)
Alan R. Neibauer
675pp. Ref. 681-2

This new edition is a real timesaver. For on-the-job guidance and creative new uses, this title covers all versions of WordPerfect up to and including 5.1—streamlining documents, automating with macros, new print enhancements, and more.

WordStar Instant Reference SYBEX Prompter Series
David J. Clark
314pp. Ref. 543-3, 4 ¾" × 8"

This quick reference provides reminders on the use of the editing, formatting, mailmerge, and document processing commands available through WordStar 4 and 5. Operations are organized alphabetically for easy access. The text includes a survey of the menu system and instructions for installing and customizing WordStar.

The ABC's of WordPerfect 5
Alan R. Neibauer
283pp. Ref. 504-2

This introduction explains the basics of desktop publishing with WordPerfect 5: editing, layout, formatting, printing, sorting, merging, and more. Readers are shown how to use WordPerfect 5's new features to produce great-looking reports.

The ABC's of WordPerfect 5.1
Alan R. Neibauer
352pp. Ref. 672-3

Neibauer's delightful writing style makes this clear tutorial an especially effective learning tool. Learn all about 5.1's new drop-down menus and mouse capabilities that reduce the tedious memorization of function keys.

Advanced Techniques in Microsoft Word (Second Edition)
Alan R. Neibauer
462pp. Ref. 615-4

This highly acclaimed guide to WORD is an excellent tutorial for intermediate to advanced users. Topics include word processing fundamentals, desktop publishing with graphics, data management, and working in a multiuser environment. For Versions 4 and 5.

Advanced Techniques in MultiMate
Chris Gilbert
275pp. Ref. 412-7

A textbook on efficient use of MultiMate for business applications, in a series of self-contained lessons on such topics as multiple columns, high-speed merging, mailing-list printing and Key Procedures.

Advanced Techniques in WordPerfect 5
Kay Yarborough Nelson
586pp. Ref. 511-5

Now updated for Version 5, this invaluable guide to the advanced features of Word-Perfect provides step-by-step instructions and practical examples covering those specialized techniques which have most perplexed users—indexing, outlining, foreign-language typing, mathematical functions, and more.

The Complete Guide to MultiMate
Carol Holcomb Dreger

208pp. Ref. 229-9

This step-by-step tutorial is also an excellent reference guide to MultiMate features and uses. Topics include search/replace, library and merge functions, repagination, document defaults and more.

Encyclopedia WordPerfect 5.1
Greg Harvey
Kay Yarborough Nelson

1100pp. Ref. 676-6

This comprehensive, up-to-date Word-Perfect reference is a must for beginning and experienced users alike. With complete, easy-to-find information on every WordPerfect feature and command -- and it's organized by practical functions, with business users in mind.

Introduction to WordStar
Arthur Naiman

208pp. Ref. 134-9

This all time bestseller is an engaging first-time introduction to word processing as well as a complete guide to using WordStar—from basic editing to blocks, global searches, formatting, dot commands, SpellStar and MailMerge. Through Version 3.3.

Mastering DisplayWrite 4
Michael E. McCarthy

447pp. Ref. 510-7

Total training, reference and support for users at all levels—in plain, non-technical language. Novices will be up and running in an hour's time; everyone will gain complete word-processing and document-management skills.

Mastering Microsoft Word on the IBM PC (Fourth Edition)
Matthew Holtz

680pp. Ref. 597-2

This comprehensive, step-by-step guide details all the new desktop publishing developments in this versatile word processor, including details on editing, formatting, printing, and laser printing. Holtz uses sample business documents to demonstrate the use of different fonts, graphics, and complex documents. Includes Fast Track speed notes. For Versions 4 and 5.

Mastering MultiMate Advantage II
Charles Ackerman

407pp. Ref. 482-8

This comprehensive tutorial covers all the capabilities of MultiMate, and highlights the differences between MultiMate Advantage II and previous versions—in pathway support, sorting, math, DOS access, using dBASE III, and more. With many practical examples, and a chapter on the On-File database.

Mastering WordPerfect
Susan Baake Kelly

435pp. Ref. 332-5

Step-by-step training from startup to mastery, featuring practical uses (form letters, newsletters and more), plus advanced topics such as document security and macro creation, sorting and columnar math. Through Version 4.2.

Mastering WordPerfect 5
Susan Baake Kelly

709pp. Ref. 500-X

The revised and expanded version of this definitive guide is now on WordPerfect 5 and covers wordprocessing and basic desktop publishing. As more than 200,000 readers of the original edition can attest, no tutorial approaches it for clarity and depth of treatment. Sorting, line drawing, and laser printing included.

Mastering WordPerfect 5.1
Alan Simpson

1050pp. Ref. 670-7

The ultimate guide for the WordPerfect user. Alan Simpson, the "master communicator," puts you in charge of the latest features of 5.1: new dropdown menus and mouse capabilities, along with the desktop publishing, macro programming, and file conversion functions that have made WordPerfect the most popular word processing program on the market.

Mastering WordStar Release 5.5
Greg Harvey
David J. Clark
450pp. Ref. 491-7

This book is the ultimate reference book for the newest version of WordStar. Readers may use Mastering to look up any word processing function, including the new Version 5 and 5.5 features and enhancements, and find detailed instructions for fundamental to advanced operations.

Microsoft Word Instant Reference for the IBM PC
Matthew Holtz
266pp. Ref. 692-8

Turn here for fast, easy access to concise information on every command and feature of Microsoft Word version 5.0 -- for editing, formatting, merging, style sheets, macros, and more. With exact keystroke sequences, discussion of command options, and commonly-performed tasks.

DESKTOP PRESENTATION

Mastering Harvard Graphics
Glenn H. Larsen
318pp. Ref. 585-9

Here is a solid course in computer graphing and chart building with the popular software package. Readers can create the perfect presentation using text, pie, line, bar, map, and pert charts. Customizing and automating graphics is easy with these step-by-step instructions. For Version 2.1.

DESKTOP PUBLISHING

The ABC's of the New Print Shop
Vivian Dubrovin
340pp. Ref. 640-4

This beginner's guide stresses fun, practicality and original ideas. Hands-on tutorials show how to create greeting cards, invitations, signs, flyers, letterheads, banners, and calendars.

The ABC's of Ventura
Robert Cowart
Steve Cummings
390pp. Ref. 537-9

Created especially for new desktop publishers, this is an easy introduction to a complex program. Cowart provides details on using the mouse, the Ventura side bar, and page layout, with careful explanations of publishing terminology. The new Ventura menus are all carefully explained. For Version 2.

Mastering COREL DRAW!
Steve Rimmer
403pp. Ref. 685-5

This four-color tutorial and user's guide covers drawing and tracing, text and special effects, file interchange, and adding new fonts. With in-depth treatment of design principles. For version 1.1.

Mastering PageMaker on the IBM PC (Second Edition)
Antonia Stacy Jolles
384pp. Ref. 521-2

A guide to every aspect of desktop publishing with PageMaker: the vocabulary and basics of page design, layout, graphics and typography, plus instructions for creating finished typeset publications of all kinds.

Mastering Ventura
(Second Edition)
Matthew Holtz
613pp. Ref. 581-6

A complete, step-by-step guide to IBM PC desktop publishing with Xerox Ventura Publisher. Practical examples show how to use style sheets, format pages, cut and paste, enhance layouts, import material from other programs, and more. For Version 2.

Understanding PFS:
First Publisher
Gerry Litton
310pp. Ref. 616-2

This complete guide takes users from the basics all the way through the most complex features available. Discusses working with text and graphics, columns, clip art, and add-on software enhancements. Many page layout suggestions are introduced. Includes Fast Track speed notes.

Understanding PostScript
Programming
(Second Edition)
David A. Holzgang
472pp. Ref. 566-2

In-depth treatment of PostScript for programmers and advanced users working on custom desktop publishing tasks. Hands-on development of programs for font creation, integrating graphics, printer implementations and more.

Ventura Instant Reference
SYBEX Prompter Series
Matthew Holtz
320pp. Ref. 544-1, 4 ¾" × 8"

This compact volume offers easy access to the complex details of Ventura modes and options, commands, side-bars, file management, output device configuration, and control. Written for versions through Ventura 2, it also includes standard procedures for project and job control.

Ventura Power Tools
Rick Altman
318pp. Ref. 592-1

Renowned Ventura expert, Rick Altman, presents strategies and techniques for the most efficient use of Ventura Publisher 2. This includes a power disk with DOS utilities which is specially designed for optimizing Ventura use. Learn how to soup up Ventura, edit CHP files, avoid design tragedies, handle very large documents, and improve form.

Your HP LaserJet Handbook
Alan R. Neibauer
564pp. Ref. 618-9

Get the most from your printer with this step-by-step instruction book for using LaserJet text and graphics features such as cartridge and soft fonts, type selection, memory and processor enhancements, PCL programming, and PostScript solutions. This hands-on guide provides specific instructions for working with a variety of software.

SPREADSHEETS AND INTEGRATED SOFTWARE

1-2-3 for Scientists
and Engineers
William J. Orvis
341pp. Ref. 407-0

Fast, elegant solutions to common problems in science and engineering, using Lotus 1-2-3. Tables and plotting, curve fitting, statistics, derivatives, integrals and differentials, solving systems of equations, and more.

The ABC's of 1-2-3
(Second Edition)
Chris Gilbert
Laurie Williams
245pp. Ref. 355-4

Online Today recommends it as "an easy and comfortable way to get started with the program." An essential tutorial for novices, it will remain on your desk as a valuable source of ongoing reference and support. For Release 2.

SYBEX®

TO JOIN THE SYBEX MAILING LIST OR ORDER BOOKS
PLEASE COMPLETE THIS FORM

NAME _____ COMPANY _____

STREET _____ CITY _____

STATE _____ ZIP _____

☐ PLEASE MAIL ME MORE INFORMATION ABOUT **SYBEX** TITLES

ORDER FORM (There is no obligation to order)

PLEASE SEND ME THE FOLLOWING:

TITLE	QTY	PRICE
_____	_____	_____
_____	_____	_____
_____	_____	_____
_____	_____	_____

TOTAL BOOK ORDER   _____ $_____

CUSTOMER SIGNATURE _____

SHIPPING AND HANDLING PLEASE ADD $2.00 PER BOOK VIA UPS   _____

FOR OVERSEAS SURFACE ADD $5.25 PER BOOK PLUS $4.40 REGISTRATION FEE   _____

FOR OVERSEAS AIRMAIL ADD $18.25 PER BOOK PLUS $4.40 REGISTRATION FEE   _____

CALIFORNIA RESIDENTS PLEASE ADD APPLICABLE SALES TAX   _____

TOTAL AMOUNT PAYABLE   _____

☐ CHECK ENCLOSED   ☐ VISA
☐ MASTERCARD   ☐ AMERICAN EXPRESS

ACCOUNT NUMBER _____

EXPIR. DATE _____ DAYTIME PHONE _____

CHECK AREA OF COMPUTER INTEREST:

☐ BUSINESS SOFTWARE

☐ TECHNICAL PROGRAMMING

☐ OTHER: _____

THE FACTOR THAT WAS MOST IMPORTANT IN YOUR SELECTION:

☐ THE SYBEX NAME

☐ QUALITY

☐ PRICE

☐ EXTRA FEATURES

☐ COMPREHENSIVENESS

☐ CLEAR WRITING

☐ OTHER _____

OTHER COMPUTER TITLES YOU WOULD LIKE TO SEE IN PRINT:

_____

_____

OCCUPATION

☐ PROGRAMMER   ☐ TEACHER

☐ SENIOR EXECUTIVE   ☐ HOMEMAKER

☐ COMPUTER CONSULTANT   ☐ RETIRED

☐ SUPERVISOR   ☐ STUDENT

☐ MIDDLE MANAGEMENT   ☐ OTHER:

☐ ENGINEER/TECHNICAL   _____

☐ CLERICAL/SERVICE

☐ BUSINESS OWNER/SELF EMPLOYED

CHECK YOUR LEVEL OF COMPUTER USE

☐ NEW TO COMPUTERS

☐ INFREQUENT COMPUTER USER

☐ FREQUENT USER OF ONE SOFTWARE

   PACKAGE:

   NAME _____

☐ FREQUENT USER OF MANY SOFTWARE

   PACKAGES

☐ PROFESSIONAL PROGRAMMER

OTHER COMMENTS:

_____

_____

_____

_____

_____

_____

_____

PLEASE FOLD, SEAL, AND MAIL TO SYBEX

SYBEX, INC.
2021 CHALLENGER DR. #100
ALAMEDA, CALIFORNIA USA
              94501

SEAL

SYBEX Computer Books
are different.

Here is why . . .

At SYBEX, each book is designed with you in mind. Every manuscript is carefully selected and supervised by our editors, who are themselves computer experts. We publish the best authors, whose technical expertise is matched by an ability to write clearly and to communicate effectively. Programs are thoroughly tested for accuracy by our technical staff. Our computerized production department goes to great lengths to make sure that each book is well-designed.

In the pursuit of timeliness, SYBEX has achieved many publishing firsts. SYBEX was among the first to integrate personal computers used by authors and staff into the publishing process. SYBEX was the first to publish books on the CP/M operating system, microprocessor interfacing techniques, word processing, and many more topics.

Expertise in computers and dedication to the highest quality product have made SYBEX a world leader in computer book publishing. Translated into fourteen languages, SYBEX books have helped millions of people around the world to get the most from their computers. We hope we have helped you, too.

For a complete catalog of our publications:

SYBEX, Inc. 2021 Challenger Drive, #100, Alameda, CA 94501
Tel: (415) 523-8233/(800) 227-2346   Telex: 336311
Fax: (415) 523-2373

SHORTCUT KEYS FOR WINDOWS AND THE ACCESSORIES

CARDFILE

Edit
Undo .... Alt-Backspace
Cut .... Shift-Del
Copy .... Ctrl-Ins
Paste .... Shift-Ins
Index F6

Card
Add F7
Autodial F5

Search
Go To F4
Find Next F3

CALENDAR

Edit
Cut .... Shift-Del
Copy .... Ctrl-Ins
Paste .... Shift-Ins

View
Day F8
Month F9

Show
Previous .... Ctrl-PgUp
Next .... Ctrl-PgDn

Alarm
Set F5

Options
Mark F6
Special Time F7

CALCULATOR

Edit
Copy .... Ctrl-Ins
Paste .... Shift-Ins

CLIPBOARD

Edit
Delete .... Del

RECORDER
Stop Recording .... Ctrl-Break

GENERAL

OK
Accept settings in a dialog box,
open the Control menu for an
iconized application, choose the
highlighted command button in a
dialog box, or run a highlighted
program .... ↵

Cancel
Cancel a dialog box, close a
Control menu, or cancel
Select Mode .... Esc

DAYBOOK *

File
Open .... Ctrl-O
Save .... Ctrl-S
Exit .... Ctrl-X

Edit
Undo .... Alt-Backspace
Cut .... Shift-Del
Copy .... Ctrl-Ins
Paste .... Shift-Ins
Clear .... Del

Page (in Address mode)
Next .... Ctrl-→
Previous .... Ctrl-←
First .... Ctrl-↑
Last .... Ctrl-↓
New Page .... Ctrl-N

* Daybook is an application program from Asymetrix
that is included in your Windows 3.0 package. It is a
personal organizer that includes an integrated calendar, address book, and to-do list.